Control of the Laws in the Ancient Democracy at Athens

CULTURAL HISTORIES OF THE ANCIENT WORLD

James Ker and Emily Mackil, *Series Editors*

CONTROL OF THE LAWS IN THE ANCIENT DEMOCRACY AT ATHENS

Edwin Carawan

Johns Hopkins University Press
Baltimore

Printed in the United States of America on acid-free paper
2 4 6 8 9 7 5 3 1

Johns Hopkins University Press
2715 North Charles Street
Baltimore, Maryland 21218-4363
www.press.jhu.edu

Library of Congress Cataloging-in-Publication Data
Names: Carawan, Edwin, author.
Title: Control of the laws in the ancient democracy
at Athens / Edwin Carawan.
Description: Baltimore : Johns Hopkins University Press, 2020. |
Series: Cultural histories of the ancient world | Includes
bibliographical references and index.
Identifiers: LCCN 2020011674 | ISBN 9781421439495 (hardcover) |
ISBN 9781421439501 (ebook)
Subjects: LCSH: Constitutional history—Greece—Athens—To 146 B.C. |
Judicial process—Greece—Athens—History—To 1500. | Law, Greek—Political
aspects—Greece—Athens. | Judicial process (Greek law) | Athens (Greece)—
Politics and government.
Classification: LCC KL4361.32.A75 C37 2020 | DDC 347.38/5012—dc23
LC record available at https://lccn.loc.gov/2020011674

A catalog record for this book is available from the British Library.

To friends and colleagues at Missouri State University, especially those in the Department of Modern and Classical Languages and at Meyer Library in Acquisitions and Interlibrary Loan

ABBREVIATIONS AND CONVENTIONS

For ancient authors and their works, abbreviations follow the *Oxford Classical Dictionary*: https://oxfordre.com/classics/page/abbreviation-list.

Of particular note:

APF = J. K. Davies, *Athenian Propertied Families 600–300 BC* (1971).
BNJ = *Brill's New Jacoby* online, ed. Ian Worthington (2006–).
FGrH = Felix Jacoby, *Fragmente der griechischen Historiker* (1923–).
IG = *Inscriptiones Graecae* (1873–).
PA = J. Kirchner, *Prosopographia Attica* (1901–3).
RO = P. J. Rhodes and R. Osborne, *Greek Historical Inscriptions* (2003).
Tod = Marcus Tod, *Greek Historical Inscriptions* (1946–48).

Note also:
ARR = J. Lipsius, *Das attische Recht und Rechtsverfahren* (1905–15).
LAA = David Phillips, *The Law of Ancient Athens* (2013).

For the citation of journals and standard references in Classics and ancient history, the notes and bibliography use abbreviations from *L'année philologique*. These can be found online at https://guides.lib.berkeley.edu/c.php?g=381579&p=2585381.

Quotations from the texts of Aischines, Demosthenes, and their scholia (unless otherwise noted) are taken from the respective editions by Mervin Dilts (1983, 1992, 1997, 2002–09). The speeches are often cited by short title, naming the defendant (e.g., *Aristokrates* = *Against Aristokrates*).

Greek names are transliterated (not Latinized), except for those commonly found in English: e.g., Andokides, Ktesiphon, and Lykourgos; but Socrates, Pericles, Plato, and Plutarch. Key words transliterated from Greek and other languages are regularly italicized, except for these three cardinal terms, in the abstract singular: demos, nomos, and polis.

Control of the Laws in the Ancient Democracy at Athens

The People and the Law—Demos and Nomos

> The Athenian Democracy was such a tumultuous government as we can scarcely form a notion of in the present age of the world. The whole collective body of the people vote in every law, without any limitation of property, without any distinction of rank, without control from any magistracy or senate; and consequently without regard to order, justice, or prudence. The Athenians soon became sensible of the mischiefs attending this constitution: But being averse to checking themselves by any rule or restriction, they resolved, at least, to check their demagogues or counsellors . . . [For] they justly considered themselves as in a state of perpetual pupillage; where they had an authority, after they came to the use of reason, not only to retract and control whatever had been determined, but to punish any guardian for measures which they had embraced by his persuasion.
>
> —David Hume, "Of Some Remarkable Customs"

Sometime after the death of Pericles the Athenians developed a safeguard for their mercurial democracy that was to prove critical in the century to come: any decree of the people's assembly could be challenged as "unlawful," *paranomon,* and the court would then decide whether the bill would be law. As the democracy was twice dismantled and restored, as the empire was lost and a feeble successor rose up and then collapsed, as one champion after another laid claim to the leadership of the demos, this safeguard evolved. In the decade or so after 403 BC, a new process was devised for enacting "laws" in the strong sense (*nomoi,* permanent rules of general application), with a parallel mechanism for the court to control that process. In these Athenian remedies against legislation-gone-wrong, most scholars, for the past century or so, have come to see an awakening recognition that even the sovereign people are subject to some restraining principle. But, as Hume's description illustrates, that was not always the prevailing view.

Hume describes the Athenian regime as a perverse cycle of youthful recklessness and irascible maturity, as though the sovereign people made their laws like minor children on a whim, and then punished the tutors who minded them so poorly. Of course, he speaks with the presumptions of his era, with contempt for the very idea that any community could manage without rank and class distinctions. But there are two points in his perspective that are ironically apt, however at odds with more recent commentary: The Athenian mechanism for control of legislation was indeed designed to punish the authors of aberrant laws and decrees, not to acknowledge some law of laws superior to the people. Rather, that mechanism seems designed for the people themselves to reconsider their impetuous decision in a more sober setting; there was, after all, no recourse to a senate or supreme court.

Since the late nineteenth century, however, scholars of law and history have seized upon the Athenian experiment as a precursor to modern judicial review, often with little regard for the features that Hume treated with such disdain. In the last fifty years (or so) that conventional model has become ever more cumbersome, as we come to grips with problems in the evidence and the assumptions we bring to it. This book is an attempt to bring that work of the last half century into better focus, not without perspective from earlier critiques. It is written primarily for classicists and historians who want to understand the ancient democracy, but not without some reflection upon our own struggle with constitutionalism in the United States. For it was the glare of the American phenomenon that brought the Athenian parallel to light.

§1. The Modern Model and the Ancient Paradox

At the end of the nineteenth century James Bryce's monumental work *The American Commonwealth* found a receptive audience in the United States, and one of the most appealing sections was the treatment of the court as guardian of the constitution, which he compared favorably to "the European system."[1] It was that treatment that inspired a Yale professor of Greek, T. D. Goodell, to offer an assessment of the Athenian remedy against unlawful legislation as "a mark of [their] extraordinary political genius, that the Athenians so early contrived a similar bulwark of their constitutional democracy."[2] Goodell's appraisal was readily embraced by W. W. Goodwin and, with such backing, Goodell's approach was followed in the handbook on ancient Greek law that became standard in the mid-twentieth century: the Athenians' *graphē paranomōn* was readily regarded as "a parallel to a function of the Supreme Court of the United States."[3]

What Bryce articulated so well was a fundamental difference between the American model and the European regimes: in the parliamentary systems of Europe the legislature *is* the people or is indistinguishable from them; and those ministers for the people make laws without any constraint to conform to some prior, inviolable set of statutes; later law supersedes the older. In the American system, by contrast, the members of Congress are merely representatives, with delegated powers; the people themselves are (in principle) the original authors of the Constitution, and only the people can alter it through the amendment process. Of course, as an enactment of the people, the Constitution may now seem rather dubious; its making has been aptly described as "the framers' coup."[4] In the end, a better parallel between ancient Athens and the American experience may be found in the era before the "coup" (as we consider in section 3 of this introduction). But first let us follow the conventional analogy to its conclusion.

There is, of course, an institutional parallel: in the United States, when Congress has made a law at odds with the people's Constitution, the court may invalidate that aberrant legislation, just as Athenian courts could rescind their assembly's decrees. And in keeping with that role (at least in the US), the court assesses the later law by a largely legalistic method:[5] the judges set the older, more venerable text beside the more recent measures to see if the latter conform to the former. From this perspective, Goodell saw the Athenian suit against unlawful action as a bulwark that the sovereign people had set against their own recklessness:

> [T]he γραφὴ παρανόμων was the engine whereby any citizen might enforce upon the Demos, through a somewhat select body of citizens acting as a court, the restriction which the Demos had previously imposed upon itself. The doctrine that it was not the Demos . . . but the original proposer, who was responsible and reprehensible for the unconstitutional measure, was *a bit of legal fiction* that served an excellent purpose, making it easier for the people to retreat gracefully from an illegal position. ("Athenian Parallel," 1893, 69, emphasis added)

Goodell took note of the difference in the judges' qualifications, but he seems to have understood the operations of the two courts, ancient and modern, as essentially analogous, and he readily supposed that laws and decrees were judged by the same standard: Athenian *nomoi* were superior to their decrees (*psēphismata*) much as the US Constitution is superior to ordinary legislation, and new laws that came into conflict with the old were disposed of in the same way. For the *nomoi* that governed changes to the standing laws were considered fundamental and inviolable:

> The law regulating amendments to the constitution was held to belong so distinctly to the fundamental law, that the sovereign people itself could not violate it; any action taken in violation of it was *ipso facto* null and void. This was the ground on which the court made the decision. And if any other conflict was found between a newer and an older νόμος, instead of the later superseding the earlier, the rule was reversed; the later law was unconstitutional because the earlier was superior in authority. (72)

In other words, Athenian judicial review was rigorously positivistic: the judges measured the proposed legislation against laws that the demos had laid down, reckoning one text against another without much recourse to broader values or deeper principles.[6] And the ancient court resorted to that way of deciding the issue because they honored the older law as a binding restraint upon the people's own power.

This model of Athenian court control relies upon two tenacious connections. The first and perhaps most seductive is that standing law was a binding text and therefore judging laws and decrees was a simple matter of laying provisions side by side; any later intrusion that does not conform to the older law is rejected. That assumption seems reasonable enough where the court judges a decree by the laws (a *graphē paranomōn*). But then there is the further assumption that even laws in the strong sense, *nomoi*, were corrected in the same way, by the same standard, and through the same procedure. And it is that premise that leads to the conclusion that the sovereign people recognized a body of fundamental law, supposedly, enshrined in statute that they could not violate. That way of characterizing court control of the law has proved remarkably persistent in the scholarship for generations, even as the ancient evidence accumulated against it. But, in the end, the analogy between Athenian judicial review and the modern parallel that Goodell and Goodwin found so attractive now seems largely a figment of presumptions that prevailed in their time.

To be sure, the positivistic premise has some basis in ancient arguments where the prosecutor seizes upon conflict in the parallel texts. It was certainly essential to the process to post the old law and the new bill side by side for close comparison.[7] But the idea that this is the crux of the process, that the case should be decided upon that clash of texts, may be largely an accident of the evidence. For the dossier of surviving speeches is almost entirely made up of arguments for the prosecution; Demosthenes' defense speech for Ktesiphon, *On the Crown*, where contradictions in statute seem trivial, has been the singular exception.[8] It was that same Demosthenes who perfected the positivistic method that dominates the dossier, and what made some of those cases for the prosecution so notable was precisely the way issues of fairness and public interest seem secondary. The further assumption, that the people recognized some higher law embodied in the corpus of statutes, has also proven misleading at best. After all, as the accumulated evidence has shown, the Athenians readily made new law to replace the old. And the very notion that a new nomos was judged in the same way as a decree proved problematic from the very beginning of this exercise in exceptionalism.

When Goodell's essay was published, the London papyrus of the *Constitution of the Athenians* had only just appeared. This Aristotelian study summarizes the history and essential offices of the Athenian system of government (down to ca. 340–330 BC). Among the duties of the chief officers of the court, the *thesmothetai*, we find the remedy against introducing a law deemed "unfitting" (νόμον μὴ ἐπιτήδειον θεῖναι); it is listed alongside the suit against "unlawful action" (παρανόμων) and apparently distinct from it (*Ath. Pol.* 59.2). That was the clue that would lead, in time, to a serious reappraisal of what had seemed self-evident. For there prove to be two disparate procedures and somewhat differing assumptions for laws and decrees.

In recent years the old model of lawmaking and court review of laws under challenge has been radically recast, and the notion that the Athenians themselves saw their older body of statutes as something like fundamental law seems to me untenable. Their procedures for legislation changed significantly in the course of an eventful century, but the people's autocracy remained unchallenged. The Athenian model of lawmaking and constitutional control was indeed positivistic, bound by the rules that the sovereign demos laid down; but, in their understanding, the very fact that law resides in the text means that there is no law more potent than the people who made it. They could make of the law what they would, provided that some enterprising legislator was willing to take the risk.

This is not to say that they recognized no constraint upon the laws and decrees they made, only that we must look for it elsewhere, not in the realm of higher-order rules. This may seem, admittedly, a puzzling distinction, so it will be helpful here to explore a few comparisons.

The Athenians acknowledged nothing quite like the guarantees against arbitrary authority that proved fundamental to both Roman and Anglo-American law. In Athens there was no higher-order rule corresponding to that legacy of Magna Carta, the right to trial by a jury of one's peers; nor was there quite the equivalent of the Roman *ius provocationis*, the citizen's right of appeal to the people (represented in their *comitia*) against the sentence of their officers or, arguably, against the Senate itself.[9] To be sure, the Athenians certainly recognized and respected an old Solonian law that guaranteed the right of "appeal" (*ephesis*) from any judgment (above a modest fine) that officers might impose; likewise they guaranteed a man's right to jury trial on appeal from any sentence of the Council of Five Hundred (*Ath. Pol.* 45.1).[10] That is, a citizen condemned by an archon or by council might appeal to the "court of the people" (*heliaia*). That court of last resort was originally conceived as the whole body of the people convened to render judgment, and in this respect the Roman parallel (with appeal to the *comitia*) seems all the more tempting. But at Athens the defendant's predicament, the situation where he would need some safeguard against arbitrary power, was just the reverse. For a high-profile defendant was more likely to be victimized by decree of the demos itself than by overzealous officers on their own authority. For something over sixty years the assembly of the people regularly sentenced "traitors" and official wrongdoers by decree, without a court trial.[11] Those punitive acts were often challenged but, so far as we can see, there was no statute that specifically guaranteed a court trial in such cases, and none of the prosecutors who brought suit for unlawful acts (*paranomōn*) ever dared to suggest that citizen rights should prevail over the people's writ.[12] Even in the 350s, when impeachments were no longer decided by decree, in a decade when constitutional safeguards were closely reexamined, we are given no sign that the people's legislation was controlled by a set of rules beyond themselves.

Part of the misconception comes from taking the ancient pieties too literally. The Athenian orators sometimes regard their constitutional remedy as a fundamental feature of their inherited way of justice, suggesting that even Solon prosecuted such cases. Hedging their bets, historians in the early twentieth century saw this remedy as a product of the democratic revolution led by Pericles and Ephialtes (in the 460s), if not earlier. At either inception, it was a creature born like Athena, fully armed from the outset, to safeguard the body of law itself.

But then, in the same year when R. J. Bonner and Gertrude Smith's *Administration of Justice* embraced that model (1938), Ulrich Kahrstedt reduced it to a paradox. We know of no case that can be securely dated earlier than 415, more than forty-five years after Ephialtes. And, Kahrstedt argued, the function much acclaimed in the fourth century to protect the laws from aberrant decrees can only have arisen after 403, alongside the more rigorous procedure for making and maintaining the weightier *nomoi*—for it was only this development that made the laws different in kind and superior to the decrees of the people's assembly. The legalistic method that characterizes the fourth-century speeches, matching the new measure against standing law, could not have been standard until the archive provided ready access to the body of law, which only came about with the reconstruction of democracy, after 403/2 (or so Kahrstedt assumed). To retroject that method and its rationale back to the earliest cases is to suppose that *the safeguard was invented before the hierarchy of rules it was designed to protect.*[13] Kahrstedt's solution to that paradox was simply that *graphai paranomōn* in the era before 403 had a different function: not to safeguard higher law *per se*—there was no higher law than the people's decree—but to punish the officers and politicians who led the people into error.

Kahrstedt's reconstruction proves problematic on various points. The method of argumentation that Demosthenes perfected, finding higher principle within a litany of statutes, certainly has antecedents in the meager remains from the fifth century. And the archive that housed the laws, where one would gather evidence against unlawful measures, was probably more comprehensive and readily accessed earlier than Kahrstedt supposed.[14] So, in the era of the notorious trial of the Arginousai generals (406 BC), for instance, there was really no practical obstacle to the sort of text-based argument that Demosthenes and his contemporaries relied on—indeed, that case seems to explore the same path. But Kahrstedt's most contentious conclusion, that early *graphē paranomōn* was not introduced or regularly regarded as a bulwark against the people's infringement of the law, may prove to be more right than wrong.

Kahrstedt's insight has been largely lost in later work, even as a new understanding of the legislative process emerged to vindicate him somewhat. Perhaps most critical to this reappraisal is the recognition that, even in the fourth century, the demos seems to have unfettered power to make new nomos. In principle, they must resolve any contradictions that emerge in the process, but even that requirement seems to have been often disregarded. Even when the archive was well-ordered and open, there seems to be no clear sense that the people face any insuperable constraint that is spelled out in the written laws.

The Search for a Rule of Rules

And so, unconstrained by any preemptive statute, what constitutional principles, if any, would the Athenians acknowledge? In a seminal essay from the early 1960s, Ioannes Triantaphyllopoulos ranked the essentials as follows:

> The first rule of legislation is that new law not go against the ancestral constitution (*patrios politeia*). . . . What exactly is this ancestral constitution and what it consists of we are not able to say . . . [but] we can inductively isolate certain principles which comprise the core of [it]. Such a principle and indeed a

> fundamental one was *isonomia*, . . . equality before the law, which is even today the cornerstone of every democracy. From *isonomia* follows a further principle: that laws *ad hominem*—οἱ νόμοι ἐπ' ἀνδρί—were prohibited. Thus even in Rome, privileges [any exceptions or sanctions beyond the law] were prohibited according to the famous provision of the Twelve Tables (9,12) *"privilegia ne inroganto."*[15]

But that formulation may be a better description of Roman rules than Athenian. At Athens, equality before the law, *isonomia*, was rarely given much scope in the court speeches. In fact, "privilege" in the familiar sense, if not in the meaning of the Twelve Tables, was crucial to the Athenian political economy where civic benefactors were regularly rewarded with protections and exemptions from the duties that others in their class would face.

The speeches that survive point to a different sort of constraint upon the sovereign demos. The prevailing method for finding such barriers was tried and true, but it never seems to rely on fundamental law that can be taken for granted. Even with their best efforts, the constitutional litigators of the fourth-century BC could not venture beyond the well-worn path: they first needed to find the principle as revealed in various statutes and then apply that principle to the measure in question. Demosthenes and his contemporaries never advanced to the level of invoking fundamental rules, such as the right to "due process," as independent criteria that one might apply deductively to the case at hand. After all, there was no body of legal experts to recognize such superstatutory rules. Instead in each case, the prosecutor of an unlawful measure must construct his argument from the ground up, reasoning inductively from the particular wording and practical implications of relevant statutes (and some not so relevant). This was the puzzle that Hans Julius Wolff laid out so perspicuously in his study *"Normenkontrolle"*:

> [A]s surely as they could extricate themselves from bondage to the express wording, even so their conception of the *paranomon* remained fixed upon the idea of conflict with the particular provisions examined in isolation. Regardless of the fact that invariably the result was in each case the same and, moreover, always on similar grounds, they apparently knew no other method than to proceed from one statutory provision to another, in tiresome monotony, always describing how [each provision] stood in conflict with the indicted measure *ab initio* and without reference to the others. (1970, 66)

Largely in keeping with the constitutional model that emerged from the nineteenth century, Wolff seems determined to find some higher law in the accumulated corpus of statute but can only rationalize it as a constantly reinvented reality: "They had not yet reached the point where one could extract the principle that was recurrent in various provisions and recognized to be inherent in them all . . . as a *legal concept above and beyond the statutes* (als einen *überpositiven Rechtsgedanken*), a rationale superior to the particular laws and sufficient in itself to brand as *paranomon* the proposal that clashes with it" (66, the emphasis is his).

This is Wolff's paradox: the surviving arguments attest to an endless search for a set of rules that govern the others, a foundation that is, supposedly, fixed and self-evident but strangely resists any canonical formulation.

Procedures and Principles

The construction that Wolff put upon the ancient arguments has shaped much of the discussion for the last half century. To a large degree, much of this book is an essay in answer to his paradox. We shall have to reconsider both the workings of procedure and the rationale that seems implicit in it. Wolff made as much sense as anyone could of the evidence that was available to him, but we can now piece together more of the lawmaking process—ratification of *nomoi* by the special body of *nomothetai*—including legislation that was not yet published in 1970, and our perspective on *graphai paranomōn* may be somewhat improved with the publication of a substantial fragment from a defense speech by Hypereides.[16] From such findings, I think we must reassess the themes that Wolff and his contemporaries were inclined to dismiss as tendentious or beside the point. What struck them as misplaced emphases are likely to reveal something important to the ancient audience that may prove essential to their brand of constitutionalism. In sum, the accumulated evidence now suggests a rather different model of how the ancient procedures actually worked, and that mechanism will shed some light on the formative ideas.

As a first example, consider Demosthenes' speech against Leptines' law in 355/4. Demosthenes tells us that the accumulated body of *nomoi* had gotten so entangled in contradictions that the people have "for quite some time" elected special commissioners to sort it out—with no end in sight (Dem. 20.91–92). Wolff dismissed that testimony (and another that seems to confirm it) as "blustering and argumentative tirades [conjuring up] the complete breakdown of legislation and the hopeless degeneration of the assembly" (*"Normenkontrolle,"* 1970, 45). But it now seems more reasonable to suppose that, even if overblown a bit, this incidental comment by the young orator has much to tell us about the standards of lawmaking that he is trying to resurrect. For this confusion of statutes, which Demosthenes attests in the 350s, seems to be, indeed, the product of a rather perfunctory way of enacting *nomoi* so that in conception they seemed little better than decrees. Many of the jury may not have understood or much respected the difference between recent legislation and the older process. So just before this tirade, Demosthenes has tried to articulate perhaps the most formative principle governing the old way of lawmaking: the framers of the restored democracy saw that new nomos must be subject to a vetting like the one that confirms the officers who administer the *nomoi*; the people must decide twice, first in council and assembly and then, again, in court. That requirement for a "second decision" seems to be the one fixed idea in this otherwise frustrating search for rules that govern the rules.

This procedure for amending the body of *nomoi*, modeled on the confirmation of officers, Demosthenes calls a "scrutiny" (*dokimasia*), and Andokides attests to that terminology in the years soon after democracy was restored. That phrasing is usually ignored or dismissed as an artful play on words, but it seems to capture the formative analogy: *nomoi*, like the officers who enforce them, must be vetted and approved not once but twice; and, as in the officers' confirmation, the second decision rightly falls to a jury, a committee of citizens under oath. That order of business is not dictated by some institutional hierarchy or a need for special expertise; what is required is simply a body of the people in their critical mass. And that ideological frame shapes the argumentation. The essence of the process is not to reconstruct over and over again some higher-order principle that emanates from the statutes themselves, to find some law of laws that trumps the decisions of the people. Instead, Demosthenes and his contemporaries will argue that the court must decide by the very character of the demos, of which the laws are but a representation.

In this self-referential approach to legislation, the most perplexing problem facing the Athenians was, as Wolff described it, finding the boundaries: "If there were no scruples about venturing beyond the narrow sense of the wording, . . . it appears that, soon after first essay, prevailing opinions were fairly well defined on the question, at what point transgressions could qualify as breaching the bounds of *paranomon*. In the developed court practice of the 4th century [that boundary] lay there, where a measure violated general principles of legal-and-social order, anchored in positive law but not necessarily articulated as such" (*"Normenkontrolle,"* 1970, 46). Wolff seems to stumble upon this threshold from time to time,[17] most notably in the last paragraph of his fourth and crucial chapter: One sign that there simply was no "dogmatic authority" behind these prevailing arguments—no clearly recognized formulation of higher-order rules—is the regular recourse to "shallow grounds of utility," as though the principle (wherever one finds it) is not sufficient in itself. And most revealing is the simple fact the Athenians' positivistic arguments "typically betray the same backwardness of legal theory" (*theoretisch-juristische Ruckständigkeit*). For the latter Wolff cites Demosthenes' *Against Aristokrates* (two to three years after *Leptines*), with its tortured process of deducing what is in conflict (*gequälte Herleitung des Gegensatzes*) between the targeted decree and the law cited in section 37 of the speech. The latter provides humane protection to the condemned killer who abides by his exile, but under Aristokrates' measure, anyone who might kill the privileged character, Charidemos, could claim no such reprieve (arguably) and would be killed in violation of the venerable law.

> [Demosthenes] cannot find any more compelling basis than the predicament that would develop in the city [under Aristokrates' measure, as the Athenians] must either live alongside the "defiled" persons (specifically [the authors of the bill!] who would become indirectly responsible—αἴτιοι φόνου—by granting license to kill without trial); or, if they prosecute [the killer's killers] according to the general law, they put themselves in conflict with their own decree.[18]

The predicament may seem contrived but, it is only fair to say, these rules about how to handle a known or supposed killer were as crucial to the Athenian construction of their community as any. So perhaps these ceaseless failings of the Athenians to measure up to the standards that scholars have set for them should make us more wary of the very presumption that constitutionalism can only be found in the corpus of statute.

§2. The American Paradigm Revisited

The Athenians would not be the only pioneers of democracy to find their constitutional constraints in the inherited profile of the community itself. In this respect the Athenian *patrios politeia* is, again, reminiscent of the *mos maiorum* at Rome. But at Athens it is not always construed as a prescriptive pattern that the ancestors modeled for their descendants to follow. In fourth-century Athens the ways of their forebears were a constant reproach, as each succeeding generation fell further from that standard.[19] As though acknowledging that the heroic past cannot be revived, the Athenians insist upon a *politeia* that is not the ancestral ideal so much as the abiding polis. The court is the final arbiter of any conflict not because the founding fathers rule from the grave but precisely because the jury at hand is the truest constituency of the sovereign demos. And it is probably in this respect that the American paradigm most closely matches the ancient model.

At the Framing

In the American colonies before the framing of the Constitution, and in the states continuing into early years of the new republic, a jury of the people seemed to embody in itself the very rules that would trump any aberrant ordinance. As William Nelson showed, American juries of that era were finders of law as well as fact, and their verdicts were unabashedly based upon conventional values of the community. The body of the people, often guided by religious faith, was the ultimate decider of what the statute required. For instance, early American justice regularly dispensed with "special pleas," whereby a learned judge would exclude evidence that was immaterial; instead they favored "an absolute and general denial" of all charges, which put the whole package of allegations at issue before the jury. That jury was left to determine "not only the facts but also the legal consequences of the facts." Nor were they easily constrained to deliver "special verdicts" within narrow parameters that statute defined. As John Adams observed, juries were not "under any legal or moral Obligation to find a Special Verdict where they themselves are in no doubt of the Law," for the "general Rules of Law and common Regulations of Society . . . [were] well enough known to ordinary Jurors."[20]

There is, of course, an institutional difference reflected in the basic terms: in the Anglo-American development, the "court" is controlled by officers at the bench; the jury sits beside it, heeding the judge's instructions, or not. In Athenian justice the jury *is* the court. But as they were at Athens, so too at the birth of our union juries were considered "good judges of the common law of the land," competent to decide what the law requires from their own best understanding. For example, in a Connecticut case of 1788 to decide upon a black slave's suit for freedom, one juror was challenged for having the fixed opinion that "no negro, by the laws of this state, could be holden a slave." The state supreme court overruled the challenge on the grounds that having such a fixed opinion "upon a general principle of law" does not disqualify the juror in a case where that principle applies.[21]

Of course, American communities were divided by religious establishments and economic interests. The prevailing faith in each community was often determinative, as in that Connecticut case upholding a slave's suit for freedom. Those communities of conscience were reinforced by freedom of movement, as colonials who dissented from the values of one city or state would relocate to a more congenial setting. That regional reclusiveness shaped the Constitution itself through various bargains to secure control at the state level. But, for better or worse, it was that sovereignty of the people—or of each body of people in its sovereign state—that was the domineering spirit of the new republic:

> In discarding British rule and reconstituting their governments, Americans proclaimed that all law springs from popular will, at least insofar as elected representatives express popular will in legislation. If the people could remake their government, it followed that their lawmaking power must be "original, inherent, and unlimited by human authority." In short, the Revolution convinced many Americans that popular will was "the only rational source of power" and that there was "an original, underived and incommunicable authority and supremacy in the collective body of the people to whom all delegated power must submit and from whom there is no appeal."[22]

It was that source of authority, found in the will of the people, that led beyond positivism to deeper principles: what the Constitution embraced in particular wording points to broader obligations that neither Congress nor the executive branch can override. The text, after all, is a representation; it stands for something deeper and less articulate.

This glimpse of jury justice in early America is not meant to suggest that such righteous empowerment is always a good thing. But, on all counts, it is a better parallel for the constitutionalism that prevailed in ancient Athens. In particular, the Athenians would have readily embraced the early American commitment against any elite or superior body overturning the people's decisions. As one colonial wrote to another, granting any group of men the power to nullify acts of the people "would be more despotic than the Roman Decemvirate."[23] Likewise the Athenians saw that such power over the law was the downfall of the old democracy under the Thirty, and that specter loomed large in the constitution they rebuilt after 404 BC.

In the United States a divide between positivism and popular sovereignty was clearly drawn in the 1790s in a rift between Federalists and Republicans as the former struggled to build a stronger union while the latter defended the power of the people in each state. But even as the courts became the arbiters of any conflict in the rules, one could argue (as Nelson does) that John Marshall, the great Federalist justice, saw himself as a champion of "consensual values," which the sovereign people would embrace.

After the Framing

Marshall's opinion in *Marbury v. Madison* has become something of a mapping exercise for scholars to plot out how American constitutionalism began and thus to pronounce whether the current direction of the high court is on course. Where Nelson finds at least a glimmer of those community values that predominated in earlier jury justice, others would insist upon a more text-based positivism. Perhaps the most provocative rendering of *Marbury* in the latter vein, as rigorous recourse to the wording of prescriptive statute, is Robert Lowry Clinton's treatment from 1989: for Clinton the essence of *Marbury* is simply that the early Supreme Court disavowed any jurisdiction beyond what the Constitution expressly assigned to it.[24] Clinton's finding has been dismissed as "malarkey" or worse (in a study that seems at least as tendentious as his), but the way Clinton arrives at that conclusion is well worth the read as he documents judicial authority against repugnancy or outright contradictions in the legislated laws going back to the Roman jurisprudents.[25]

A milestone along the way is William Blackstone's Tenth Rule: laws or "acts of parliament that are impossible to be performed are of no validity; and if there arise out of them collaterally any absurd consequences, manifestly contradictory to common reason, they are, with regard to those collateral consequences, void." That rule was dear to the hearts of the framers,[26] and it seems to be, arguably, the essence of *Marbury*, for the Constitution (Article III, Section 2) plainly assigned to the Supreme Court only *appellate jurisdiction* in cases such as Marbury's and prescribed rather specifically those cases where the court would have original jurisdiction. Marbury's petition did not fit among the latter. Thus the Judiciary Act of 1789 that created Marbury's office could not be vindicated in this case because the Constitution gave the court no authority to enforce it in the first instance.

The further findings of Clinton's study may be less solid, but for our purposes it is the backstory that matters most. The practice of judicial review that Marshall inherited from Blackstone (and others) differs from the Athenian model in this respect: in the Anglo-American tradition the court focuses on the integrity of laws as a system of rules; on that principle, the Judiciary Act under which Marbury was appointed cannot be enforced by the Supreme Court because the Constitution gives jurisdiction in such cases only on appeal. Marshall never suggests that this distinction serves the greater good or the vital interests of the American people; that value may be implicit, but the express rationale focuses on repugnancy. The critical question at the dawn of the nineteenth century was whether the supreme arbiter of such conflict was the court or, as Jefferson himself insisted, each branch of government was to correct such contradictions by "coordinate review."[27]

The Athenians never seem to have arrived at that level of abstraction, where the body of laws is objectified and treated as an entity apart from the interests of the people. Their law of laws is not to be found in a realm of Ideas or a scheme for divided government. They never seem to argue over a balance of powers: this is not a system where the congress merely legislates and the court properly controls.[28] For them the close scrutiny of the relevant wording is all about the integrity of the *politeia* as it embodies the community of *politai*. They do not seem to regard the body of laws as an autonomous system of rules that can trump the arbitrary decision of the legislature. Their constitutional review is rather more focused on the balance of privilege and civic duty, and their deepest concern is the vested authority of groups or individuals, especially those who pose as champions of the people. One can argue that this political dimension is really what *Marbury* and subsequent decisions were all about,[29] but it is hard to read Marshall's opinion alongside any of the major speeches from the 350s BC and conclude that they were inspired by the same brand of positivism.

§3. The Athenian Evolution

The Athenian method was positivistic in the strong sense: law is what the sovereign has laid down.[30] But in their understanding, the sovereign people are not constrained by prescriptive text that they have framed in some defining moment, nor bound by any higher-order rules that trump the people's decision. Instead, it is because their authority is unconstrained that they must heed the commandment to "know thyself." They must reckon with the inviolable commitments they have made, the bargains that constitute their community, and the boundaries they have put upon themselves. In court this reckoning of self-knowledge translates into its own peculiar brand of positivism, as the prosecutor must base his case upon the clash between the defendant's legislation and standing laws that the people have made in their own image.

That is not to say that the standard is fixed and immutable. In the chapters ahead, we must reckon with significant changes in procedure and some shifts in thinking.

Between introduction and conclusion, this study is divided into three parts: The first part reconstructs the framework and original aims by which the court controlled the laws at Athens (chapters 1–3). The second part focuses on what we might call "the constitutional window," the set of speeches from the 350s BC that give us the fullest picture of procedure and working assumptions (chapters 4–7). And then, in the third part, we take up the last and most famous case in the dossier, the Crown Case, along with those that led up to it (chapters 8–9).

Chapter 1 begins with the Athenian model of constitutional review, sorting out the testimony on how *nomoi* were amended or repealed-and-replaced in the course of the fourth century. Then chapter 2 takes up the connected problem of personnel: Who were the lawmakers and judges who decided upon these cases of conflict in the corpus? From beginning to end, there is no hierarchical divide between the legislators who make the law and the judges who will ratify or rescind it; the speakers sometimes identify them as one cadre, sometimes rank one body over the other for its effectiveness. Chapter 3 concludes this first part with a reconsideration of the one case from the fifth century where we are given more than a glimpse of the argument, the impeachment of the Arginousai generals that was subject to an abortive challenge by *graphē paranomōn*. As Plato's Socrates famously recalled at his trial, not long after that legal challenge failed, the Athenians themselves recognized that their act in condemning the generals without trial was "against the law." Understandably, that Platonic perspective has guided historians of the law ever since. But it may be more true to the Athenian rationale to remember that the spokesman for the rule of law, who tried to block the impeachment decree, was himself threatened with prosecution for thwarting the will of the people.

The second part of this book focuses on a set of four speeches that appeared midcentury (355–51 BC), after decades of virtual silence in our sources. This constitutional window is largely the work of Demosthenes. Each text involves some post-eventum revision or expansion, sometimes adapting material from one of the other speeches in this series. So there is not much to be gained by following a strict chronological order; it seems rather more useful to follow the links between connected cases. Thus we begin at the end (chronologically) with the case that bears the strongest connection to the Arginousai decision: chapter 4 takes up the argument against Aristokrates (Dem. 23). Here the very principle of rule of law is subject to the most detailed analysis, for Aristokrates' decree would have suspended the protections of due process (arguably) against anyone accused of killing Charidemos. Chapters 5 and 6 deal with the campaign against a particular leader and his backers: the speech *Against Androtion*, for unlawful acts (*paranomōn*) as a member of council and the subsequent case against Timokrates who tried to introduce a law that would shield Androtion from a crippling fine. The earlier speech (*Androtion*) is a diatribe against the self-dealing politician. The later indictment (which may never have gone to trial) repeats substantial sections from the earlier speech and adapts that adversarial attack to a case against "unfitting legislation" (*nomon mē epitēdeion theinai*). Timokrates had bypassed the more rigorous process that was once required to repeal and replace standing laws and introduced his measure as a fast-track financial adjustment, without allowing for proper publicity and debate. Much the same constitutional concern is central to the earlier case of the same type, against Leptines' law (chapter 7). Here (or. 20) Demosthenes speaks for himself in his first high-profile public suit, and he seems to have resurrected old rules to fit the novel situation: Leptines' measure had been enacted into law but was blocked for over a year, and now the jury must decide whether to put it into action.

The Crown Case (the focus of chapters 8–9) perhaps needs no preview. In this instance the peculiar brand of constitutional argument that I find in the earlier speeches has been already recognized and well treated. Demosthenes speaks for the defense in an almost tragic mode: he has little to say on the legal issue, but he holds up a mirror to the Athenian people and convinces the jury that his leadership was true to their fateful character.[31] There are, however, procedural implications yet to resolve and, luckily, new evidence has shed some light on that inquiry. In Ktesiphon's case (which came to trial in 330), both of the surviving speeches indicate some measure of legislative intervention: the decree for trial has revived an old proposal to honor Demosthenes and, in the process, raised the stakes for the prosecutor. And it so happens that we now have a substantial fragment of a defense speech from a similar situation a few years earlier: Hypereides' *Against Diondas*. In that case, as well, the advocate of the decree remains liable, years after he made his proposal. And the text we have from Hypereides' defense, a few years before Ktesiphon's, indicates the same strategy: to turn the tables against those who would obstruct the people's will.

The conclusion proceeds from the Crown Case to a broader perspective on the Athenian model for constitutional review, a standard drawn from the demos itself.

PART I

LEGISLATIVE PROCEDURE AND COURT CONTROL

CHAPTER ONE

Making Law and Mending the Constitution

Blepyros: "What business was on the agenda, to draw such a throng at the crack of dawn?"

Chremes: "What else but the chairmen (*prytaneis*) decided to open debate on the city's salvation. . . . One fine pasty-faced youngster . . . jumped up to speak and proposed that we hand over the city to the women, and the crowd of shoemakers raised a ruckus, shouting that he was right. The men from the countryside booed and belched. . . . But they didn't have the numbers; the young fellow prevailed by sheer volume. He had a lot to say for the women and much to say against you . . . and this crowd of menfolk."

Blepyros: "So what was decided?"

Chremes: "To entrust the city to them (the women) . . . the only fix that hasn't been tried."

—Aristophanes, *Congresswomen* (393–458, much abridged)

A decade after democracy was restored Aristophanes conjured up this parody of reform-by-legislation: Imagine the women (otherwise excluded) disguised themselves as men and took over a session of the assembly to install a new regime with the women themselves in control of finance and executive offices. The comic premise—that a gang of outsiders might pack the *ekklēsia*—was prompted by recent innovation: in order to guarantee a quorum on time, payment for attending the assembly was introduced and then increased. At the date of this performance, a man would earn half a drachma—roughly half a day's wage—for brief attendance in the early morning. In Aristotle's era the stipend had to be raised to six obols for an ordinary meeting and nine for a principal, *kyria ekklēsia*.[1] The inflationary cycle had begun already in the 390s: pay for attendance was introduced by Agyrrhios at one obol, increased to two by a rival populist, and then raised to three obols by Agyrrhios himself.[2] At that point, evidently, the incentive worked all too well. And so we are to imagine that even the most unlikely second-class citizens might sneak in and take advantage of the motley crew who were drawn by such pay.

The women's regime is the last resort, "the only fix that hasn't been tried" yet, after twenty years of experimenting with constitutional reform. The comic premise, putting supreme authority in the hands of an unlikely group, probably pokes fun at the "law writers," the *anagrapheis* who reconstructed the laws when democracy was restored. It may also reflect disenchantment with the very idea of delegating authority—that the sovereign people can rely on a select committee to make decisions for them. But most striking of all is the picture of chaos in the assembly, which allowed the outsiders to take over. When major issues are decided by a highly motivated faction, who carry the vote simply because they are the first to show up, this is the democracy we get.[3]

Of course comedy is not the most straightforward evidence of what actually went on, but Aristophanes has taken pains to emphasize the officials and the formalities, and in some respects, his picture may be as revealing as much of the documentation that commentators and historians have seized upon. He gives no indication of any constitutional safeguard against seismic changes in the fundamental law. Instead it seems to be assumed that the *prytaneis* may call for "debate on the city's salvation," and the citizens who then convene have the authority to undo even ancient rules. That picture is at odds with what historians have concluded about Athenian legislation in the fourth century, but it may turn out to be closer to the truth.

From testimony of the orators, along with scholia and other ancient commentary, it has been generally supposed that "lawmaking" in the strict sense—enacting *nomoi* as opposed to *psēphismata*—was modeled on court trials. The "lawmakers" (*nomothetai*) were drawn from the cadre of citizen judges (*dikastai*): these were men of some maturity (in their thirtieth year of age or older), who had sworn to judge by the laws and were regularly empaneled to decide lawsuits. And, we are told, the lawmaking procedure was like a lawsuit, pitting the old statute against the new bill that would replace it. In this respect it is sometimes seen as a zero-sum process, in which no new law can be introduced without removing old laws that cover the same ground. Much of the evidence is at odds with that picture of legislation-by-trial, and some rather elaborate solutions were proposed in order to save it. Those constructions now seem overly inventive, and the model they built upon is certainly not the whole story. Much remains to be explained. Whoever the *nomothetai* were, at least by the mid-fourth century, laws were *often* enacted *without* any systematic control against contradictions or repugnancy.

Many a wrong turn has come from starting at the beginning with dubious documents and slim testimony then carrying over those implications to the later speeches. For our purposes it seems more promising to begin near the end, when the relevant laws are best attested: in the period 355 to 330 BC. Of course this retrograde approach cannot escape the difficulties inherent in the evidence: the speeches address an audience who heard (or read) documents in the case that are (mostly) lost to us. We are often left with no document to rely on or, indeed, one that does not match the description.[4] It seems the safest path to follow the orators' testimony first, with close attention to the issues in each case, and leave the inserted documents aside until we have an outline of the procedures they depict.

Thus we begin with the rather full commentary by Aischines and Demosthenes, confronting at the outset the way this evidence is skewed to the case; then we work our way back to the restoration era, when the basic structures were put in place but the testimony is slim. And only then should we turn to the dossier of documents that ancient editors have handed down to us.

§1. Aischines Poses the Problem

Roughly sixty years after *Congresswomen*, we find the most famous case in the dossier and perhaps the most problematic: Aischines' suit against Ktesiphon for a decree to honor Demosthenes with a ceremonial crown.[5] The issue may seem trivial, but the arguments go to the very crux of our problem: for Ktesiphon and Demosthenes would argue that, among the multiplicity of laws, there were some that made the decree viable, though others seem to bar it. Aischines argues to the contrary, that the process for resolving such contradictions is so rigorous that, surely, there can be no conflict or overlap in the laws such as the defense would claim; he describes this process as an annual "correction" to the corpus. And to put a respectable face upon that dubious certainty, Aischines emphasizes the burden upon the executive officers, the *thesmothetai*, as though they are personally responsible for making a thorough investigation of the corpus of laws each year. If we take him literally, we might suppose that these ordinary officials, chosen by lot among laymen with no special qualification, had become jurists poring over the vast archive. Under their magisterial oversight there could be no such confusion as Demosthenes and Ktesiphon rely upon to vindicate their self-congratulatory decree. "May you never sink to such chaos!" Aischines prays, and here he explains the safeguards:

> The lawgiver who established the democracy was not indifferent to such hazard; instead he expressly assigned [a duty] to the *thesmothetai*, each year in assembly to set the laws right (*diorthoun*) by precisely examining and considering if any

> law is inscribed in conflict with another or there is invalid law among the valid, or if more laws than one have been inscribed about any particular matter. And if they find any such thing, he orders them to write it up on planks (*sanides*) and post them before the eponymous heroes [monument]; the chairmen of council (*prytaneis*) are to schedule an assembly for *nomothetai*, and the chief presider is to put it to a vote in the assembly, to remove some laws and leave others in place, so that there be one and only one law on each matter. (3.38–39)

This picture of an annual correction appeals to our sense of order and, all too often, scholars have seized upon it. Aischines seems to be describing a procedure that is specifically designed to remove any repugnancy, where one statute wars against another; he puts the primary responsibility for finding those obstacles squarely on the shoulders of the *thesmothetai* (six of the chief officers). Then he describes a vote by show of hands in the assembly (*diacheirotonia*), managed by the presiders (*proedroi*), to resolve repugnancy by repealing any laws that conflict with the others. It seems to be a working model of constitutional integrity, but every feature of this scenario is problematic.

Twenty years earlier, in the 350s, Demosthenes describes a similar procedure to illustrate a principle very different from Aischines' correction. Demosthenes explains it as a "confirmation" or "scrutiny," like the regular confirmation of officers, to determine whether the standing laws can still do the job. In the speech *Against Timokrates* he speaks of an annual vote in the assembly, to determine "whether new law is to be introduced or the standing laws seem sufficient" (24.25). He gives a timetable beginning ten days into the new year but mentions no particular role for the *thesmothetai*. The orator himself puts considerable emphasis on the making of new law, not simply resolving conflict in the old; the inserted document (24.20–23) amplifies the disparity between the two accounts. Relying on the dubious document to flesh out Demosthenes' profile, scholars have often assumed that he is describing an altogether different creature from the one Aischines mentions. But the document does not really match Demosthenes' description (as we consider later in §5). Of course Demosthenes is skewing his explanation of the law to suit his case, just as Aischines did. So how much of Demosthenes' confirmation or the document beside it can be trusted?

One cautious approach is to discount that document altogether, and for the first part of this chapter we shall do essentially that: disregard the document as we consider the explanation in the speech. We turn back to the inserted documents in the concluding sections, after we have drafted an outline from the other clues, and then we can see how well the documents fit or not. First let us try to sort out the testimonies of Aischines and Demosthenes on their own. The discrepancies have convinced most commentators, since the early modern era, that the two refer to separate procedures. But that simple solution was not always convincing.

A Brief History of a Long Scholarly Debate

As early as 1635, Samuel Petit concluded that the two descriptions of constitutional review cannot be a match:[6] the correction (*diorthoun*) that Aischines describes was a process for abrogating old laws; Demosthenes' confirmation (*epicheirotonein*) was the first stage of a process for introducing new laws. And the timing is at odds:[7] Demosthenes schedules the confirmation early in the first prytany of the year, whereas Aischines' correction would have to come much later. After all, the *thesmothetai* could hardly be expected to have surveyed the vast body of law ten days after taking office, as Demosthenes' confirmation would require.

But then, from the eighteenth century to the early twentieth century, much of modern commentary proceeded on the assumption that Aischines' account must somehow be reconciled with the evidence in Demosthenes' speeches, both the orator's own testimony and whatever seemed reliable in the documents: the correction that Aischines describes and the confirmation or "vote of confidence" embraced by Demosthenes belong to the same legislative protocol. Thus the eminent Friedrich August Wolf took note of the confirmation document (Dem. 24.20–23) and acknowledged that it is likely to be a composite of provisions from several statutes, not without later intrusions; he concluded that Aischines' refers to the same vetting of the laws that Demosthenes finds in this statute.[8] Aischines describes a constitutional safeguard, requiring an annual correction of the corpus, which is consistent with what Demosthenes says in *Timokrates* (or. 24) as well as with the concocted document, if we acknowledge that "those fragments of laws" could hardly be expected to give a comprehensive account of the procedure. So Wolf, not without reservations, supposed that Aischines' more concise version referred to the same legislative protocol presented in *Timokrates*, but perhaps focused on preliminaries.

Petit's view, that the correction and the confirmation must be separate procedures, was defended, against Wolf, by Georg Friedrich Schömann in his early monograph *De comitiis Atheniensium*.[9] But then, nearly twenty years later, Schömann reversed himself and offered what seemed the obvious solution: the real work of vetting the corpus was done by the outgoing *thesmothetai* (in the previous year) and then introduced by their successors.[10]

Just a few years after Schömann's reversal, as though encouraged by it, Hermann Schelling proposed a more elaborate arrangement. In addition to legislation initiated by the *thesmothetai* and mandated by the people (as Aischines described), there was a parallel track for *new law introduced by concerned citizens on their own initiative.* And for each track there had to be another stage, to repeal laws in conflict with the new legislation. Schelling found the first distinction in the text of the law inserted at Dem. 24.23: he assumed a composite document (such as Wolf supposed), one that reprised older procedures alongside the new rules.[11]

Yet the special competence that Aischines assigns to the *thesmothetai* continued to puzzle the commentators. Richard Höffler (1877) argued, as Petit had (see notes 6 and 7), that the procedure Aischines describes (in 3.38–40) cannot be the same legislative law that Demosthenes describes in *Timokrates* and the document there (24.20–23) represents; for, again, the *thesmothetai* could not have reviewed the corpus so meticulously ten days after taking office. But where Schömann concluded that the real work of vetting the corpus was done by the outgoing *thesmothetai* and their findings were introduced by their successors, Höffler dismissed the idea on the grounds that officers were barred from handing on their caseload from one year to the next.[12] And Höffler seconded an objection from Anton Westermann's work on the documentary problem (1850): the two procedures, correction and confirmation (*diorthoun* and *epicheirotonein*) cannot be the same because the *thesmothetai* are supposed to preside at one and prosecute at the other—and no party can be judge in his own case.

The same preoccupation with the special jurisprudence that Aischines assigns to *thesmothetai* would carry over to Douglas MacDowell's seminal study "Law-Making at Athens" (*JHS* 95, 1975, 62–74), nearly a century after Höffler. Here we have to reconcile the terminology: MacDowell referred to the lawtext for what I call the confirmation (Dem. 24.20–23) as "the Review Law" and Aischines' correction as "the Inspection Law." In MacDowell's view, the latter was instituted some time after the long-running investigation that Demosthenes mentions elsewhere (20.91–92), but it served the same purpose, "for detecting and eliminating faults in the existing laws: the *thesmothetai* inspect the laws for faults, the *ekklesia* decides whether the faults uncovered are serious . . . and *nomothetai* decide which of the faulty provisions should be annulled." He explains, "the Review Law does not give to the *thesmothetai* the duty of inspecting the laws"; rather, "[it] is concerned with making new laws to replace existing laws." Conversely, the Inspection Law "seems to be for the purpose of deletion only" (71–72). If we take Aischines at his word—if we assume that his procedure is indeed devoted to resolving repugnancy, and the burden of discovering it falls to the *thesmothetai*—then MacDowell's solution seems eminently plausible.

It seems to me the basic disparity at the center of the debate from Petit to MacDowell is largely inspired by the emphasis that each prosecutor put upon the particular provisions that support his case. Demosthenes insists that Timokrates violated the timing and the strict protocol for introducing new laws that would alter the standing law, and those features are inevitably reflected in the document that a clever compositor has inserted in the speech (as we consider in §5). That protocol may have included procedures to repeal laws in conflict, but Demosthenes puts that later in his argument (24.33–34), and the compositor offers what seems to be a separate law. Aischines, on the other hand, emphasizes the repeal of laws in conflict because that simplification serves his case: the corpus can contain no discrepancy such as Demosthenes requires, because the laws are constantly subject to this process of correction. So the law that Aischines cited may have dealt with new legislation to amend or replace the old, but for him to comment upon those procedures would only distract from the point he wants to make. And for the same reason he emphasizes the research duties of the *thesmothetai*, as though they were exhaustive and infallible, rather than delve into a process that relied on "anyone willing."

But in fact, sixty years after *Congresswomen*, the idea that legislative control should be entrusted to some special bureaucracy seems no more agreeable to the Athenians than it was in Aristophanes' day. What Aischines seems to mean is that the *thesmothetai* were obligated to examine and introduce any challenge to a law that a concerned citizen might bring forward (if the officials found cause), and the assembly would then decide whether to act upon it. After all, none of the other sources give any indication that the *thesmothetai* were responsible for quite the burden that Aischines puts upon them. On the contrary, their role seems fairly consistent over time: they were not legal experts in their own right but servants of a system based on citizen initiative.

In the Aristotelian *Constitution of the Athenians* we are given a thorough account of the duties assigned to the *thesmothetai* (55–59, 63–64), but nowhere is there any suggestion that the officers have a duty to search through the body of law for contradictions. When would they find the time? The *thesmothetai* are especially responsible for administering the courts, organizing the allotment of jury panels, conducting preliminaries, and bringing to trial many of the high-profile cases that citizens undertake. The *thesmothetai* proper (the six "junior archons") have, indeed, special competence for cases involving wrongful legislation (59.2); that does not mean that they have to find the violations for themselves. Anyone willing to prosecute would bring his charge to those magistrates with a dossier of laws to support it, as Demosthenes' client did in the case against

Timokrates. That is where the *thesmothetai* have to do some research: it was their duty to see that the texts of law presented by the prosecutors were accurate and sufficient. These were the *paragegramménoi nomoi,* the laws listed in parallel, at the center of the dispute. It is that familiar task that seems to have prompted Aischines to describe the role of the *thesmothetai* as "precisely examining and considering whether any law is in conflict with another" (3.38).

Whatever the jury made of Aischines' argument (fewer than one in five voted for him), as far as we can see, the burden for finding repugnancy among the laws fell to concerned citizens on their own time and not to the officials scarcely ten days in office. There is no other reference to the delegated duty that Aischines seems to assign to *thesmothetai,* to survey the vast corpus and bring to light any defect, and so I think it is best to regard it as a figment of his argument. Aischines probably introduced an excerpt of the same law that Demosthenes had described in *Timokrates,* focusing on the initial stage of the proceedings; he had no reason to comment on the scheduling or other complications that Demosthenes emphasizes, or on the fact that the whole process relied on the initiative of concerned citizens. Their role in this correction would be familiar enough to the jury.

A Reductive Solution

On this reading, Aischines' correction and Demosthenes' confirmation are essentially the same process, though it is likely enough that some procedural adjustments were made in the twenty-odd years between one case and the other. The initial "vote of confidence" (*epicheirotonia*), to decide whether the standing laws are sound and sufficient or new law is needed, would come early in the first prytany, as Demosthenes reports. That scheduling would be opportune for amendments to recent legislation, enacted in the previous year, before it could be fully implemented. And it seems unlikely that there would be two such procedures at different times of the year, one strictly scheduled and another open-ended. Rather, at the very beginning of the year, anyone who intends to amend a standing law had to bring his proposal and supporting statutes to the *thesmothetai;* and then, to prepare that case in the first prytany, those officers would have their work cut out for them. For the *thesmothetai* would have to review the relevant body of law exhaustively to assure that the texts submitted were accurate and sufficient and to verify any other documents in the case. Then, in a council meeting prior to the first scheduled assembly, the *thesmothetai* would introduce the case against any laws in conflict, and the chairmen of the first tribe to preside in council would put that matter on the agenda for the first *kyria ekklēsia*. Thereafter, the *thesmothetai* would see to it that the texts of old law and new bills were in order, posted at the heroes monument for concerned citizens to study over the course of the next two meetings. And finally, drawing on that public scrutiny, the presiders in the third assembly would put the question to the people, to decide how they would proceed.

The *thesmothetai* also had the duty to prepare the case and preside at the trial of any lawsuit against unfitting law, as in the cases against Leptines' law and against Timokrates (Dem. 20 and 24). That overlap, between lawsuit and legislative reform, has added to the confusion, as we consider in the next chapter. By either procedure, the *thesmothetai* must investigate any claim of conflicting law that a concerned citizen or special advocate might present. In legislative correction (to recall Aeschines' description), they proceed in the assembly to identify any laws in conflict or any that are invalid or redundant, and if they find any such defective laws, they are to write them up on planks and post them at the monument of the eponymous heroes for full publicity. The *prytaneis* are then to schedule an assembly "for lawmakers," and there the presiders will put it to a vote of the people to remove the offending law(s), "so that there be one law and no more on each matter."

That description serves as an introduction to the reading of relevant laws, which should prove that Ktesiphon's decree is unlawful (none are preserved in the text). Thereafter Aischines insists that *if* there were two laws about proclamations for crowning a benefactor (as Demosthenes may claim), surely the *thesmothetai* would have discovered it, the presiders would have put the question to the assembly for *nomothetai* to decide, and one law or the other would have been repealed.

Here Aischines seems to say that the *nomothetai* who would make this decision were simply a special session of the assembly where the presiders would put the question to a vote of the demos.[13] On balance, there is no good reason to discount that reading, but let us be clear about the implications. Aischines is not describing the whole procedure for amending or replacing laws; he is only concerned with disparities in the existing corpus. If there is any law at odds with the others, then the assembly should have taken a vote on whether to retain it or replace it. So far as we can see, the assembly could not simply abrogate an old law; its options were to reject the challenge or authorize new legislation. Aischines is not interested in any new laws that might be made in the process. His focus is rather narrower, upon contradictions already on the books, and he has omitted any mention of the role that concerned citizens must play to resolve the conflict. Indeed, that simplification was probably presented with a delicious sense of irony: If there is such a contradiction as Demosthenes claims, someone should have fixed it. And if anyone bears the responsibility, that would be Demosthenes and his cronies who have zealously revived the old-fashioned rules. Be that as it may, of this we can be reasonably certain: there was more to the law than Aischines saw fit to tell us.

Aischines is referring to a procedure that should have been familiar to most members of the jury, if it was indeed a formality observed every year in the assembly. And yet he seems to explain it as though its implications were unfamiliar, as though it were a process that few had seen or understood in this way. In fact, the particular function that Aischines conjures up—a vote to resolve conflict between two standing laws simply by abrogating one or the other, without a replacement law to supersede them—was probably rare or hypothetical (as indicated in Dem. 3.10). Of course the known list of decisions by *nomothetai* is not long, and it is not surprising that we find no indication of any such process. But the one case that seems to call for a fairly straightforward decision between *two standing laws in conflict* was resolved in a lawsuit, not in legislative review; the case in *Leptines* (Dem. 20) pitted the restoration-era nomos assuring that "grants given by the demos shall be valid" against the recently enacted law revoking grants of exemption from certain "civic services" (as we consider in chapter 7). The odd turn of events in Leptines' case, with his law on the books for more than a year before it could be brought to trial, may be the exception that confirms the rule: ordinarily any defect in the old laws is resolved by new legislation, not by simply canceling one law or another. That is why Demosthenes has to insist that he and his colleagues have just such a replacement law in the works. Otherwise the silence is rather resounding. There was no procedure in the 350s that works quite as Aischines would suggest in 330, to decide between two standing laws that seem plainly in conflict. Rather, the ordinary recourse was for the concerned citizen to draft a new law resolving the conflict and, if it passes, the new law supersedes the old.

On this reading, there was no correction of the laws quite like what Aischines seems to describe: a straightforward vote in the assembly to decide between two conflicting laws already on the books, by a show of hands for one law or the other. After all, as we saw, the competence that Aischines assigns to the *thesmothetai*, to study the corpus and discover any repugnancy on their own, seems implausible, perhaps even ironic. And he assigns this correction procedure to the lawgiver that (re)established the democracy, though *proedroi* whom he pictures managing the assembly were probably not created until a decade or more after democracy was restored.[14] Instead there seems to be one *legislative* process for resolving conflict in the corpus, one that is represented in fairly credible and consistent terms by Demosthenes in the 350s. Alongside that legislative process, of course, there is a court procedure that can be invoked against new law that looms unfitting, and those overlapping remedies have caused much confusion.[15] But we can make better sense of their proper functions from Demosthenes' testimony.

§2. Demosthenes' Testimony in *Timokrates* and *Leptines*

Twenty years before Aischines' case against Ktesiphon, Demosthenes twice invokes a procedure that seems to serve the same function as Aischines' correction. But each case involves peculiar circumstances that put opponents of the law-in-conflict at a disadvantage.

Leptines' law had been challenged by a lawsuit within the year of its enactment, but the lead prosecutor died before the case came to trial and others abandoned the case; thus, more than a year after enactment, Leptines' measure had to be treated as a law of some standing, even though it had remained under challenge and never took effect. Now, in 355/4, the case was taken up by Demosthenes and his colleagues (led by the son of the original prosecutor), and they resorted to prosecuting Leptines' statute by a procedure that was designed to challenge laws *newly enacted*, not to remove standing law more than a year old. Demosthenes (as supporting speaker) has to explain that Leptines, when he brought forward his bill, did not proceed to challenge the older law that stood in its way, as he should have done under the old legislation law. And in that regard Demosthenes and his colleagues must anticipate the obvious objection, that *they* should proceed just as Leptines should have done: replace the old law with a new one. So they vow to do just that.

But in the midst of these complications, Demosthenes describes the proper sequence for introducing new nomos as an amendment or replacement to old law (Dem. 20.89): one is to write up or "indict" (γράφεσθαι) any of the standing laws that he thinks defective (μὴ καλῶς ἔχειν) and bring forward another that he would make law in its place, thus "undoing" that standing law (παρεισφέρειν δ' αὐτὸν ἄλλον, ὅν ἂν τιθῇ λύων ἐκεῖνον).[16] Then in justification for this old, supposedly Solonian lawmaking, Demosthenes says that the lawgiver modeled this scrutiny on the confirmation of officers: "the 'Solon,' the one that prescribed this method of lawmaking, thought it could not be right for the *thesmothetai* . . . to take office after being twice subject to scrutiny, in the council and (again) before you in court, but the laws themselves . . . after being enacted at random, take effect without first being scrutinized" (90). The best sense of Demosthenes' explanation is this: there has to be a vote to decide between the old law and the new, but then there must be a second stage to the scrutiny to confirm that decision of the council and the people, in court or some comparable tribunal; it is wrong to make law without one or the other.

A year (or so) after the case against Leptines' law, Demosthenes prepared a speech (or. 24) for the prosecution of a new law introduced by Timokrates, a law that allowed men indebted to the polis to post bond and avoid jail. This surety law had been recently enacted, in the first prytany of the year, indeed the very day after a confirmation or vote of confidence on the integrity of the corpus. That perverse timing makes the repugnancy all the more offensive, Demosthenes insists, because Timokrates did not bother to challenge the laws that would conflict with his bill. Instead, on the very day when the presiders called for a vote of confidence in the corpus, one of Timokrates' collaborators moved a decree to bring new laws before *nomothetai* the very next day.

Now compare the essential mechanism as described in *Timokrates* alongside the one in *Leptines*:

Leptines on the old legislation law:

> *The ancient law* (*palaios nomos*) . . . orders that lawmaking proceed by first writing it up [or "indicting" the target law], if anyone thinks that one of the laws in place is not right, he is to bring forward another measure in order to undo that [old law] as he enacts [the new], and you are to hear and choose the better.[17]

Timokrates on repeal and replacement:

> All these are laws *of long standing* . . . [the lawgiver] expressly prohibits anyone from introducing a law in conflict . . . nor is it allowed to undo any law, except before *nomothetai* . . . by *introducing another law in place of the one he would undo* . . . [thus] it is not allowed to introduce any law in conflict with the laws in place, unless one undoes the older standing law.[18]

In Timokrates' case, Demosthenes reminds the judges that a vote on the integrity of the laws was taken early in the first prytany, on the eleventh of Hekatombaion; if Timokrates had proceeded properly, he would have taken up that item on the agenda to challenge the standing laws in conflict with the measure that he would introduce. That contest of laws seems to be essentially the same mechanism described as the old legislation law (*palaios nomos*) in Leptines' case, but here we are told a little more about the process. If Timokrates *had* challenged the laws in conflict with his, he would then have followed the schedule for posting such laws for public discussion over the course of the next two meetings; then the assembly should decree for *nomothetai* to decide between the old law and the new bill. But, evidently, there had been no challenge to standing law, no period of public discussion, and instead a new legislative session was authorized immediately, by decree, for *nomothetai* to convene the following day. Their task was to consider measures that would affect financing for the Panathenaia (soon at hand). And it was in that session, the day after the vote to confirm the corpus, that Timokrates introduced his bill, though it seemed at odds with standing law and little to do with funding for the festival.

Notably, Demosthenes did not suggest that there was any problem with legislating in this expeditious way if there were no conflict. In the session of *nomothetai* the day after the confirmation, it would have been perfectly in order for Timokrates to introduce a bill for financing, if it were not at odds with standing law. Indeed, Timokrates' measure was probably presented as just such a quick fix against looming losses; it allowed wealthy guarantors to vouch for hefty penalties that were owed to the polis and might otherwise remain unpaid. Demosthenes insisted that this arrangement conflicted with long-standing laws about rights and remedies, but he could not deny that this sort of ad hoc procedure was regularly followed: *nomothetai* were convened on short notice to deal with adjustments that were not seen to contradict the standing laws on constitutional matters but simply to revise rules for funding or the like.

In the 350s even such ad hoc financing would have to be enacted by *nomothetai* because it amounted to a change affecting the legal formula for distribution of funds, the *merismós*.[19] The fragmentary record of fourth-century laws is abundantly clear in confirming that fact: by midcentury, any permanent change in the way revenue was collected or dispersed could not be properly enacted simply by decree of the demos in regular session of the assembly; it had to be enacted in a session of *nomothetai*, a body that was somehow distinct from the citizen assembly that approved the decree for those lawmakers to convene. It was not always so. Early in the fourth century, such funding measures were approved as decrees of the people; but by midcentury (at the latest), measures of any permanence had to be enacted by *nomothetai*. That change seems crucial to the evolving constitution: some laws could only be introduced (properly) through some version of constitutional review, what Aischines called (in 330) a correction to the laws and Demosthenes described (in the 350s) as a confirmation or scrutiny of the laws. That old protocol was less familiar precisely because the alternative "fast track" had proven prolific; by this path laws could be enacted whenever the citizen assembly decreed for *nomothetai* to convene. By the old legislation law, any changes affecting the *politeia*—the shared package of rights and remedies, offices, and obligations—had to be initiated in the annual review of the corpus, and that process had fallen into disuse.

That categorical division has been largely overlooked because the boundaries sometimes seem tenuous, and the timing is confusing. As we noticed, it so happened that the decree for an ad hoc legislative session, in which Timokrates would introduce his reprieve for state debtors, was passed the very day of the annual confirmation of the corpus. Demosthenes, of course, insists that Timokrates' bill should have been introduced through the more cumbersome process, because it conflicted with constitutional rules (undermining sentences of the court). But, be that as it may, he seems to accept the fact that, if it were not in conflict with old laws on rights and remedies, such ad hoc legislation was perfectly in order. Evidently there was no rule calling for such initiatives on the day when the laws were subject to a vote of confidence, but the timing may have been opportune for other reasons.[20]

Indeed, Demosthenes rants against politicians of a bygone era who somehow corrupted the legislative process and allowed for new laws to be introduced at random (he claims) and without constitutional constraint. As a result, he says, the body of law has fallen into hopeless confusion: a commission has been hard at work to sort out the contradictions, with no end in sight (20.91–92). This testimony led MacDowell ("Law-Making at Athens," 1975) to suppose that there was indeed some liberalization of the lawmaking process a generation earlier. Indeed, it would not be surprising to find that Demosthenes was demonizing a reform movement that had perfectly respectable aims.

Such was the change in lawmaking that I suggest emerged sometime in the decade or so before 375 (most probably). Before that time financial measures of almost all sorts, from trivial grants to major changes in coinage, were decided in the assembly by the people's decree. All such decrees were subject to the laws, of course—since 403, no decree can contravene a law—and the author of any such decree was subject to indictment for unlawful action (*graphē paranomōn*) if he infringed upon the laws. But there was no requirement that the decree must be integrated into the corpus by any such process as Aischines and Demosthenes describe for *nomoi*. Then, in the era that saw the rise of the Second Athenian League and reforms for citizen participation in the new hegemonic state, even minor financing measures (formerly decided by the people's decree) seemed to require a more rigorous process. And so it was proposed that any such measure that altered the city's ledger for the long term must be enacted by *nomothetai*, not simply decreed in the citizen assembly. What that requirement meant and what the advantages were we shall have to consider in the next chapter; for much depends on identifying the *nomothetai* themselves and understanding how they stood apart from the citizen assembly. Here at least we can see that the two-stage procedure, with decree of the assembly followed by decision of *nomothetai*, assured that the new legislation should be well considered, not sprung upon the lawmakers on the spur of the moment. And if, as seems plausible *prima facie*, the lawmakers called *nomothetai* were subject to important qualifications—in some way like the *dikastai* or chosen from the same cadre—then we can easily understand that this bicameral process conveyed greater legitimacy to measures that were once enacted arbitrarily at the people's will.

§3. The Old Legislation Law and the Fast Track

Thus far we have worked back from 330 to the 370s and, by this time, the lawmaking process (*nomothesia*) seems to have spun off a more expeditious alternative. Under old rules, the path to any amendment or revision to standing law begins in the annual review of the corpus, the confirmation of laws in the first prytany of the year. If the concerned citizen aimed to change a law affecting, say, the remedies against public debtors, he should persuade the assembly to open the door to amendments in that area, that is, to vote that the laws regarding the penalties and the magistrates in charge of them were not sufficient. Then in the course of the next three sessions of the assembly he would publicize and defend his alternative, and in the last of those meetings the people would decide whether to decree for *nomothetai* to make law of the bill or to reject it. That review requirement did not apply to routine measures for some particular expense or credit, such as the grant of a stipend or exemption for a public benefactor. Early in the century such measures were simply decreed by the demos, without recourse to *nomothetai*. But sometime in the decade 385–75 (probably), a new legislative procedure was introduced, to require those measures also to be approved by *nomothetai*, though not subject to the more burdensome confirmation. It is that development that accounts for the main disparity between Demosthenes' emphasis in *Timokrates* and the hard evidence of the inscriptions; the latter show that some matters of finance or administration could be decided by *nomothetai* at any time of year and apparently without need to alter or rescind earlier laws.

The most notable exception seems to prove the rule: Nikophon's Silver-Coinage Law of 375/4 (with new arrangements to monitor the currency) neither mentions nor implies any substantive change to earlier nomos (RO 25). Nikophon's measure did not create new offices for citizens to fill or otherwise affect the package of rights and remedies; it added to the cadre of public servants only by posting state-owned slaves as *dokimastai* (to test coins). It concluded with an order for systematic *removal of decrees* in conflict with the new law (53–56); and, as though to trump those old ad hoc decisions, this measure was introduced as a "decree" of the *nomothetai* (ἔδοξε τοῖς νομοθέταις). That is (as yet) an unparalleled formula, but it conveys the same concept as we find in later nomothetic decisions for financial adjustment: those measures are introduced with the formula, δεδόχθαι τοῖς νομοθέταις, "be it decided by the lawmakers."

And there is a note from the 350s to suggest that fast-track legislation went back twenty years or more. Thus Demosthenes commented on the fate of Agyrrhios himself (who introduced pay for attending the assembly) among other heroes of a bygone era (20.134–35): though jailed for unpaid debts or penalties at the height of his career, Agyrrhios did not have his backer Kallistratos pass *laws* to reprieve him—οὐκ ἐτίθει νόμους—as Timokrates did for Androtion. It was an ironic remark, not straightforward testimony, but Demosthenes seems to have assumed that fast-track legislation was available a generation earlier.

So let us suppose the two tracks diverged in the 370s or earlier: substantive changes in rights, remedies, offices, and obligations remained under rigorous review (in principle), while more routine decisions (especially for financing) were to be decided more promptly. The latter had been enacted by the people's decree but were now referred to *nomothetai*, presumably drawn from the same body that made laws in the more rigorous procedure. At the time, that adaptation was probably promoted as a constitutional control upon the people's decrees, but by 355/4 it had led to a confusion of *nomoi*, presumably because many lawgivers did as Timokrates would do and presented momentous amendments as ad hoc expedients.

In fact, in the year after the Silver-Coinage Law, we find that Agyrrhios himself, the same populist lawmaker with whom this chapter began, enacted his Grain-Tax measure under a more legalistic heading and statement of purpose (RO 26): "Law regarding the one-twelfth portion of the grain . . . so that there be grain for the people in common" (Νόμος περὶ τῆς δωδεκάτης τοῦ σίτου . . . ὅπως ἂν τῶι δήμωι σῖ[το]ς ἦι ἐν τῶι κοινῶι).[21] This statute governed the collection of an in-kind tax on grain (and other levies) from the island territories of Lemnos, Imbros, and Skyros. In some respects it seems kin to the Coinage Law of the year before; both involved new financial arrangements. But the one labeled "nomos" established a new public facility and probably nullified a number of old *nomoi* governing state contracts, whereas the Coinage Law canceled only decrees. After all, the Grain-Tax nomos created a new set of officers, ten overseers of the new arrangement, to be chosen in the same assembly where the generals were elected (presumably in the same way); these new officers were needed to manage the weighing and selling of grain under the new rules.[22] The Coinage Law made do with state-owned slaves. So, it seems reasonable to suppose, there was some difference in the way these two laws were passed.

In one respect the "fast track" was a continuation of the old way of lawmaking: law was what the people decided it was, and new decisions simply superseded the old. So one might suppose that the fast track came first, as a direct adaptation from the people's decree, and the more complicated confirmation process came afterward: initially decrees of the *nomothetai* were modeled on decrees of the demos, and the more cumbersome procedure was constructed thereafter. But just the reverse appears to be the case. The epigraphic evidence suggests that it was primarily legislation affecting the budget that was handled on the fast track in the later fourth century, while the testimony of the orators and the tradition that derives from them suggest that some sort of review process for constitutional laws (defining rights, remedies, and so on) goes back to the era when democracy was restored. So, most probably, the confirmation of the corpus came first, and then, a decade later, enterprising lawgivers reverted to a simpler process for changes in financing and operational arrangements that posed no obvious conflict with constitutional rules. And so this adaptation that Demosthenes would later describe as something like a coup was probably defended at its inception as a return to basics; it differed from the older way of lawmaking by decree only by requiring that *nomothetai* confirm what the demos decided.

On this reckoning, some version of the confirmation process was already in place when the fast-track procedure was introduced (in the decade before 375). The Silver-Coinage Law came of the latter. Conversely the Grain-Tax Law was probably a product of the older, more rigorous process: after a vote that relevant laws were insufficient, those laws governing state contracts were posted along with the bill for farming out the grain tax, for public notice and deliberation. When the new law was enacted, old measures arrayed against it were effectively amended by it or replaced.

By contrast, later decisions of *nomothetai* were introduced with the formula δεδόχθαι τοῖς νομοθέταις. So it was phrased, for example, in Kephisophon's measure of 337/6 for rebuilding the walls (*IG* ii^2 244). This formula is plausibly restored as early as Meidias'(?) amendment to the rules for First Fruits in 353/2, an enactment that built upon standing nomos and introduced no change in substantive law.[23] That statute contained a set of administrative instructions, to supplement a recent law of more consequence. The motion formula indicated a directive from one body to another,[24] rather like proposals for council to prepare a measure for the assembly's agenda when their decision seems a foregone conclusion.

Demosthenes' narrative in *Timokrates* shows that the fast-track procedure involved a decree of the assembly for *nomothetai* to convene as a separate body on another occasion (even if it was the very the next day). Thus, in fast-track legislation, the law was effectively approved in the assembly, in the form of a bill for *nomothetai* to confirm, in any month of the year; the measure seems to be regularly dated by the prytany in which the demos approved it. Thus Meidias brought forward his bill in the last prytany of the year, whereas products of the confirmation protocol were initiated in the first prytany and enacted promptly thereafter.

Of course, in all, we have little to go on. But to judge from the Coinage Law alongside the Grain-Tax Law, there were probably two nomothetic procedures operating within a year of each other in 375–73. Not surprisingly, the less rigorous process prevailed. In the 350s ratification on the fast track was the more familiar recourse, and the old confirmation protocol for making new law to replace the old had to be explained as though many among the jury might never have seen it in action. And as late as 336, the fast track seems to have been the default mechanism even for amendments with constitutional implications, as in Eukrates' law barring the Areiopagos from convening if democracy was overthrown.[25]

§4. Constitutional Review and the Restored Democracy

As for the origins of the older, more rigorous process, the evidence is as problematic as any we have wrestled with thus far, and it requires that we proceed along the same lines: first focus on the testimony of the orators themselves and reserve the secondary material, the scholia and inserted documents, for consideration hereafter.

We have seen that Demosthenes and Aischines each referred to a version of the review process that was relatively old, perhaps going back to the restoration era. To be sure, that feature of grudging agreement does not necessarily mean that they were reading from the same statute in the 350s and in 330, respectively. In fact, as we shall see, it seems likely that some amendment or addendum was made in the interim. But the core of the law may, indeed, go back to the decade or so after 403/2 to a set of rules that prescribed (1) a review of the corpus to determine if the standing laws were sufficient or some change was needed, followed by (2) an agenda for publicizing and debating those changes, and (3) a special legislative panel to decide upon those changes in the law, a body of *nomothetai* that was somehow distinguished from regular sessions of the citizen assembly. As we saw, Aischines ignored what was pointless for his argument, and Demosthenes was not altogether perspicuous about the distinctions he relied upon; but the testimony of both witnesses, twenty-some years apart, is at least consistent with this outline. Now let us turn to an earlier witness, Andokides making his defense in 400/399; for he also described an emerging process for review and adjustment of old laws that seems to embody or prefigure those three features.

Andokides, no less than the others, had a particular argument to make. He wanted to show that old laws and decrees, by which he would be liable for involvement in the sacrilege of 415, could no longer be enforced in 400; public remedies such as the warrant against him (by *endeixis*), though still valid under laws that remained on the books, were nonetheless time-limited or amended in some way, after a sequence of reconstructive measures (as I argue in more detail in Carawan, *Athenian Amnesty*, 2013, 186–202).

First, the body of constitutional rules was restored to its integrity through a process that Andokides described as a "scrutiny," implicitly analogous to the regular confirmation of officers. Andokides said that this body of statute was reviewed by law writers—*anagrapheis*, who were themselves sometimes called "*nomothetai*"—and confirmed by vote of the people or their proxies, but also subject to limitation: these laws apply henceforth only to the course of events beginning in the archonship of Eukleides, in 403/2 BC (1.80–82). Then Andokides proceeded to list a number of new constitutional rules (85–87), but he did not describe the procedure by which these *nomoi* were made. That is, presumably, because these new laws were enacted in a process that developed from the scrutiny he began with, the procedure for review of the corpus. Between the initial scrutiny of old laws and the litany of new constitutional rules, an ancient editor was so good (or officious) as to provide a version of the new legislative procedure, the document inserted in sections 83–84. That document is problematic—it is probably not the measure that Andokides called for the clerk to read—but it is likely to be based upon an historical account of these two connected reforms. And it is recognizably similar to the law for constitutional review that Demosthenes and Aischines would invoke generations later.

Demosthenes, again, described in *Timokrates* a regular review of the corpus, where one should properly challenge any old laws that required amendment, and he was probably referring to the same review process a year or so earlier in *Leptines*, when he described a process for enacting new law while "undoing" any old law that would conflict with it. That annual procedure for amending old laws and thus avoiding contradiction in the corpus is essentially the same mechanism that Aischines described in 330 (with some adjustments). The same principle seems to govern the process that Andokides described, which the dubious document was meant to illustrate: before new law could be introduced in any area affecting the *politeia*, the bill's proponent must identify some gap or defect in the standing laws that governed that area. That mechanism was not devised (apparently) for any partisan agenda but emerged from the ad hoc reforms of the early restoration.

First, as Andokides tells it, the Athenians set out to recover the basic laws of the old democracy from the mangled corpus that the oligarchic regime had left them. That process was entirely *re*constructive, with no notion of innovation. But then the law writers realized that certain changes would be needed in order to honor the Amnesty Agreement and establish democracy on that footing; it is this reframing of old laws that Andokides referred to as a "scrutiny." Most important (for Andokides), the old laws for prosecuting offenses against the polis were subject to a time limit (from 403/2) and capped with the rule that "no law that is not inscribed can be enforced." In compliance, for instance, the Periclean citizenship law had to be restated with its own limitation.[26]

And then, in addition to those adjustments to old law, there were important constitutional rules that were probably anticipated in the Amnesty Agreement, if not prescribed by it. Andokides introduced them simply as measures the people put in place "when we saw that disaster would befall many of the citizen body, some by the laws, others by decrees enacted earlier [than 403]" (86). Those reform laws were then read out, and thereafter Andokides listed them in summary: legal decisions and contract obligations (from before 404) remained valid, no decree could contravene a law, and laws targeting particular individuals are barred (88–89). Andokides did not explain the legislative process by which these laws were enacted, but the way he summarized the whole sequence suggests that this series built upon the scrutiny of old laws.

From this perspective, the early reforms proceeded as follows: First there was a process to restore old laws that the Thirty had removed or altered; this was accomplished through research and draft revisions by the law writers, debate upon on those revisions in council, and a vote of the people to confirm the council's decision. For instance (as *Ath. Pol.* 25.2 tells us) the Thirty had dismantled the old laws that took jurisdiction from the Areiopagos council and gave it to the citizen juries (especially regarding official accountings)—the people's jurisdiction was now restored. And in the law on wills, guaranteeing that a man may bequeath his property to whomever he chooses, the Thirty had removed the clause that allowed one to contest the will if the decedent was not of sound mind or was under undue influence—that path of litigation was now reopened. But then, beyond this restoration of old laws, there was the series of new fundamental laws, whose making Andokides did not explain.

§5. The Documentary Problem

As I have suggested, the documents in Demosthenes' account of the confirmation are likely to be an editor's reconstruction. And likewise, following Andokides' summary of legislative reform, the text inserted in the manuscript describes a procedure that does not quite match his description.

Andokides' Testimony and "Teisamenos' Decree"

The sequence of documents inserted in the major manuscript of Andokides has been the subject of much debate, and the problems are certainly not solved. It seems doubtful to conclude that the documents are either close copies from any text of record or utter "forgeries."[27] Of such documents, it seems rather more sensible to suppose, as Wolf (1789) did so long ago, that even the better examples are not transcript but patchwork. An enterprising editor has made the most of an historical account, one that quoted key provisions in commentary on the sequence of events or the orator's effectiveness in handling the issue. The editor who drew upon such material may have misjudged where the text ends and context continues, or he may have simply reconstructed what his source only summarized. The decree attributed to Teisamenos seems to be just such a concoction.[28]

> The people decreed, on the motion of Teisamenos, for the Athenians to govern themselves according to the ancestral rules, to apply the laws of Solon and his weights and measures, and to apply the *thesmoi* of Drakon, the same ones we applied in the earlier period.
>
> But whatever measures [lit. "as many as"] are needed in addition, these *nomothetai* chosen by the council shall write up on planks and set forth in front of the eponymous heroes [monument], for anyone willing to study; and they shall hand down [the laws that come of this process] to the officers within the month.
>
> The laws being handed down shall be subject to scrutiny first by the council and [then?] by the *nomothetai*—the five hundred, whom the demesmen have chosen—when they have sworn. And any private citizen who wishes shall have the right to approach the council and advise on any suggestion he may have, to the good of the laws.
>
> But whenever the laws are enacted, the council of the Areiopagos shall supervise the officers, as to how they apply the standing laws. And those of the laws being authorized, they shall write up on the wall where they were written up earlier, for anyone willing to study. (Andokides 1.83–84)

Consider the disparity between this procedure and the scrutiny of laws that Andokides described. Teisamenos' decree, as we have it, begins with a pious commitment to the Solonian rules, but its focus was the making of new laws, "measures [that] are needed in addition" to those standing laws. Hansen has argued that this procedure allowed for amendments to the Solonian laws recognized in the first section of this document. But, in my view, that provision to abide by Solon's laws, weights, and standards (νόμοις δὲ χρῆσθαι τοῖς Σόλωνος καὶ μέτροις καὶ σταθμοίς), as well as Drakon's *thesmoi,* is a statement of what must *not* change: it was a guarantee against devaluation and other strategies of redistribution, as well as a barrier against new avenues of criminal prosecution. The main provisions that follow, for "whatever measures are needed in addition" (ὁπόσων δ' ἂν προσδέῃ), describe the enactment of new rules without any suggestion that these are revisions, exceptions, or corrections to the old laws and standards.[29]

In other words, this is a not very apt description of the scrutiny that Andokides described, where the old law might now require no more than a time limit or similar qualification (82, 85). Teisamenos' decree (as we have it, 83–84) seems rather to describe the procedure for the new laws that Andokides would list thereafter (85–87): the new constitutional rules, such as "no decree shall contravene a law" and "no law shall be enacted against particular persons."

The inserted document is confusing because some provisions read as though they should apply to both sets of rules: we might expect both the old laws, as revived, and the new laws, added as needed, to be included in the set of "laws being handed down" to the officers who must enforce them. But where that handoff is first mentioned (83), it refers to the new laws in the making, and that is the natural sense in the second instance as well (*paradidomenoi nomoi* in §84). After all, it was only the new laws, which the officers would also have to enforce, that had to be vetted in this way. By contrast, the main body of law inherited from Drakon and Solon had not been altered by the oligarchs and was not now subject to revision—that was the point of the initial resumptive clause: to "apply the laws of Solon and . . . *thesmoi* of Drakon, the same ones we applied in the earlier period" (83). The officers would find them where they had always been consulted.[30]

Before they were given to the officers, the new laws were subject to scrutiny at two levels (at least): first by council and later by the five hundred *nomothetai* whom the demesmen chose. There was also a period for public comment so that any concerned citizen could have his say in council. And then, after enactment (ἐπειδὰν δὲ τεθῶσιν οἱ νόμοι), the new laws would be written up for public notice.[31] By contrast, the old Solonian laws, to judge from Andokides' explanation, were reauthorized expeditiously and needed no special publicity.

Thus the document describes a measure for drafting and enacting new laws, quite apart from the old laws that continued in force. The editor who found or cobbled together this document, from whatever source(s), was probably misled by the litany of laws that Andokides listed afterward, and perhaps this was the only relevant material he could find or reconstruct from accounts of this historic transition. It looks as though Teisamenos' was a later protocol that followed closely upon the scrutiny of old laws but took a different direction.

The first proceedings that Andokides recalled began with a committee of law writers chosen by the council to research and draft legislation to restore the corpus, and in serving that function they were called "*nomothetai.*" The slate of old laws was then (re)approved by vote of the council and the people. Teisamenos' procedure came thereafter, for framing new laws "needed in addition," and a new body was created to enact them. The vote to ratify the law (or not) fell to that jury of five hundred *nomothetai*, lawmakers in the strong sense. By contrast, in the restoration of Solonian statutes and the scrutiny that followed, apparently, the demos reauthorized the old laws directly, in the assembly, perhaps by one vote on each package that law writers had assembled and council approved.[32]

By this reading Teisamenos' decree probably represents the first steps toward later lawmaking; it was an innovation that Andokides could not yet appreciate. This is not to claim authenticity but rather that the outline makes sense (mostly) and was probably patched together from a reliable historical account (not without gaps and intrusions). Teisamenos' procedure was obviously not copied from descriptions of later proceedings; it seems instead to represent a transitional procedure from which the later protocol developed. Prefiguring the confirmation (as Demosthenes would describe it), Teisamenos set forth a similar purpose, made much the same demand for thorough publicity, and called up the special jury that would be required to finalize the process. That is, the aim of Teisamenos' procedure, to make laws "needed in addition," seems in line with later legislative review: it began where the standing laws were no longer sufficient. Both procedures arranged for a period of public comment with text posted at the heroes' monument, for concerned citizens to study and critique the new bill. And finally, Teisamenos seems to have introduced the body of lawmakers that would continue to ratify legislation in the later procedure.

But whereas Teisamenos called for a *one-time* process, to finish out the framework for the new democracy, the regime that Aischines and Demosthenes would describe, generations later, seems to require (at least in principle) an *annual* review of the laws. And that latter-day regime was not meant to expand the constitution but to preserve it: amending the basic law was presented as a zero-sum mechanism, to repeal and replace, as though the corpus of law was complete and one could not add a rule to the *politeia* without undoing what stood in its place. The two adjustments that Aischines and Demosthenes attested—review of the corpus every year (not just one-and-done) and replacement of any statutes that prove inadequate or contradictory—seem designed to fix a problem that Teisamenos did not anticipate: the accumulation of new laws, heaped in confusion upon Solon's foundation.

That problem emerged in the decade after democracy was reinvented. Harking back to that era, Demosthenes suggested that the new democracy began with an archconservative principle, but soon thereafter the trouble started. After all, an important set of new constitutional rules was introduced in the first few years, over and above the Solonian corpus (Andokides 1.85–88). And, so far as we can see, there was no check upon the making of new laws down to the time of Aristophanes' *Congresswomen,* ten years after the restoration. At that point it seems to be assumed that the assembly could create new officers, dismantle old institutions, and reroute funding for the general welfare without any oversight by a jury of *nomothetai.* During that decade, it seems to have been simply accepted that new lawmaking could proceed at any time when the people so decided (as in Teisamenos' decree); meanwhile the demos resumed its sovereign authority, *governing by decree* wherever the law would allow. Initially the only constraint upon this process was the inherited remedy against unlawful acts, the *graphē paranomōn.* We have no sign that constitutional change was yet restricted to a schedule in the first prytany. That regular review of the laws, with its zero-sum principle, may have followed within a few years of *Congresswomen,* in response to the same dysfunction that inspired the play.

Demosthenes' Confirmation and the Document to Illustrate It

Early in his argument against Timokrates, Demosthenes introduced a text of the old legislation law in order to establish the protocol that the defendant had not followed (24.20–23). This statute was probably not among the laws listed in the indictment (the *paragegrammenoi* that were crucial to the case and therefore likely to be preserved in some reliable form). But we may find viable evidence in it if we approach it with this modest assumption: it is not a close copy from any text of record but, probably, a version of relevant law roughly reconstructed from later tradition (as we consider in detail in chapter 6 §2, and chapter 7 §2). Like the insert for Teisamenos' decree, this document was probably the closest match the editor could make; it is not precisely the provision that the speaker would call for but a later adaptation reconstructed from the notices of historians or commentators.

The document begins with the scheduled date for the annual vote of confidence on the laws, the *epicheirotonia,* as it was called in the first provision and so titled in the manuscript tradition. That date, the eleventh of Hekatombaion, conforms to Demosthenes' narrative and could have been simply adopted from it. Then, to facilitate review of laws on the books, the corpus was divided into sections: the voting began with laws regarding the council, continued with "the common [laws]," and ended with the laws regarding "the nine archons and then the other officers." It is doubtful whether the corpus was organized in just this way, and it seems (to me) suspicious that Demosthenes did not mention that feature of the proceedings. Surely he would have seized upon one area or another to make his point that Timokrates should have initiated his bill by challenging the particular section of the code that needed fixing. But the orator may have failed to mention it simply because this arrangement, dividing the question by jurisdiction, was not yet part of the law when he invoked it.

At some point it may have proven useful to divide the question and, as Schöll argued long ago, the natural way to catalog most laws for ready consultation would be according to the officers who administered them, as the laws of the *archon basileus* were kept at his stoa, and the laws regarding powers and limitations of council were kept in the council building. So, whatever system was ultimately adopted for cataloging the laws in the archive, it is not unlikely that, at some point in the evolution of this annual process, the question was divided by broad categories: first regarding council, thereafter the nine archons, and then the other offices. That framework at least fits the model that Demosthenes insisted upon: the process for confirming or correcting the laws was inspired by the confirmation of the officers themselves.[33]

The second category, "the common [laws]" (δεύτερον δὲ τῶν κοινῶν), seems to depart from that model, and it has been suspect on that account. But the disparity is a sign that the editor seized on what he thought was reliable: if a forger were simply concocting a scheme from Demosthenes' comments, he had no reason to add this detail. And there is epigraphic evidence, after all, that rules regarding public or "common" assets (*ta koina*) were becoming an important category. So Agyrrhios, in preface to his Grain-Tax Law (lines 5–6), justified the new rules, "in order that there may be grain for the demos in the public domain," or in supply for the community (ἐν τῶι κοινῶι).[34] Perhaps the second question, regarding *ta koina*, dealt with the *nomoi* governing such resources and the officers who managed them, including the stewards created in Agyrrhios' Grain-Tax Law. It remains possible, of course, that this phrase was simply a figment of the compositor's ingenuity but, if so, we would expect to find something to inspire him in Demosthenes' remarks, where there is no such cue.

Demosthenes, in both *Leptines* and *Timokrates,* emphasized the protocol for publicizing the legislative agenda: the new law and the laws it would alter or amend were to be posted at the heroes' monument over the course of the next three meetings. That principle of publicity was vital, emphasized in both cases, and the offense against it was dramatic in Timokrates' case.[35] In the document, however, the order for posting the law(s) under consideration is represented in two versions tacked on near the end (Dem. 24.23): Schöll suggested that one was devised as an amendment or clarification to the other, but the two versions might easily be derived from accumulated scholia on Demosthenes' description.

By contrast the focus of the document was the confirmation itself: when some section of standing law failed in the vote of confidence (ἀποχειροτονηθῶσι), the *prytaneis* were to schedule the last of three successive meetings to decide the question, whether to submit the bill to *nomothetai* and thus to replace the old law with the new (21). The *proedroi,* those who happen to be presiding in that meeting, were required to address the practical arrangements for *nomothetai* (χρηματίζειν . . . περὶ τῶν νομοθετῶν), "how they shall be seated, and for the funding, from what source the *nomothetai* shall be paid" (καθ' ὅ τι καθεδοῦνται, καὶ περὶ τοῦ ἀργυρίου, ὁπόθεν τοὶς νομοθέταις ἔσται). At this point the text adds a clarification that the *nomothetai* were drawn from the ranks of those who had sworn the dikastic oath, and that detail may be superfluous, but it is not necessarily wrong.[36]

What follows does not correspond to anything Demosthenes said in the surviving speeches and it has been largely ignored in recent work, but it may be the most significant deviation. Here penalties are prescribed for officers who failed to follow the scheduling requirements. The terms can be made plausible but probably did not belong in the old legislation law that Demosthenes invoked.[37]

> But if the *prytaneis* do not schedule the assembly as prescribed, or the *proedroi* do not make the arrangements, each of the *prytaneis* shall owe 1000 drachmas, sacred to Athena, and let each of the *proedroi* owe 40 drachmas sacred to Athena. And let the information against them be [actionable] before the *thesmothetai,* just as when anyone holds office though in debt to the treasury; and the *thesmothetai* shall bring those indicted to court according to the law, or [if not] let them be barred from advancing to the Areiopagos for disrupting the correction of the laws. (22)

To appreciate the discrepancy, consider first of all when and why such recourse would be introduced. The main provisions for confirmation (in sections 20–21) seem designed to repair a system in disorder: (1) any new law that would alter the old must be introduced at a regular, scheduled event; and (2) that change in the corpus must be thoroughly publicized and debated over the course of three meetings, before *nomothetai* are convened. Presumably, prior to this regime things were done differently: changes had been introduced unexpectedly, at various times, without systematic deliberation and with untoward consequences. These problems that inspired the confirmation protocol would make it urgent business, not likely to be neglected. But the penalty clauses suggest that it had become a foregone formality.

At its inception, the framer of the legislation law probably did not prescribe particular penalties against the presiding officers because the new duties were not easily ignored. As members of council they were subject to accounting and could be made to answer for such failings. The part of the document that introduced specific penalties (22) was prompted by a subsequent problem, as the annual vote of confidence in the laws came to be disregarded in the course of that busy first prytany; at some point it was no longer considered necessary. Just so, in *Leptines* (355/4), Demosthenes has to explain the old legislation law as though it were arcane or largely forgotten, and he says that laws had proliferated and created such confusion that they were, even then, under continuing review by a special committee (91–92). A year or so thereafter, in *Timokrates,* he tells us that the confirmation vote was indeed called in that year, though apparently treated as a mere formality (28–29). In neither speech did he mention special penalties to emphasize the sanctity of that duty. But some toughening of the rules would make sense in the sequel, perhaps on the recommendation of that very committee for sorting out conflict in the corpus that Demosthenes mentioned.[38]

By this reading, the confirmation document (Dem. 24.20–23) was probably inspired by a later adaptation (sometime after 353), focusing on penalties and other remedies against disregarding the old protocol. After all, the only section of that dubious composition that does not correspond to anything in Demosthenes' testimony is this set of rules about the penalties for chairmen and presiders. From the sum of its features, it seems most likely the compositor of the document was working with material regarding an amendment to the old legislation law that he found in a speech or historical note that is otherwise lost to us; he recast that material to match Demosthenes' description, as he understood it. If so, that patchwork would explain the odd arrangement. Notably, the very last provision (in section 23), calling for advocates (*syndikoi*) to be chosen in the assembly to defend the standing laws, is mentioned in both speeches (20.146; 24.36) and probably figured prominently in the main clauses of the law; but in the document, this vital feature was tacked on at the very end with the note that these defenders of the old law were to be chosen on the first day of the process. That date, the eleventh of Hekatombaion, is mentioned in *Timokrates* (26) simply as the scheduled date for the confirmation vote, without mentioning defenders of the standing law. So it may have been simply the compositor's guess that this was the date when they would be chosen. Scholars have concluded as much: the election of these advocates might make better sense at the third meeting *if* their role was simply to defend the standing law against the new legislation *at a trial where the old law was defendant* (as in Leptines' peculiar case).[39] But if the original procedure was, indeed, radically conservative, it would serve that agenda more effectively for these *syndikoi* to be chosen at the beginning: whenever the people voted to consider new laws replacing the old, they would choose advocates to take up the debate from the outset.

The sequel falls in line with this reconstruction, for the next inserted document was probably not inspired by the original confirmation. Concluding section 32, the speaker describes the relevant text as "the law that expressly (διαρρήδην) bars anyone from introducing a law in conflict, and if anyone does so, orders him indicted." The insert then begins (33) with a restatement of the procedure for confirmation and ends with nothing more than a cross-reference to a *prior* statute that created the remedy against unfitting legislation, *graphē nomon mē epitēdeion theinai*: if anyone has followed the confirmation procedure (restated in the first clauses of the insert) yet introduces a measure "unfitting for the people or in conflict with any of the established laws, there shall be indictments against him in accordance with the law that stands, 'if anyone make law unfitting.'" The effect of some such clause in the amended confirmation rules will be explored in the next chapter in regard to the court's evolving role in the legislation process. Here suffice it to say, that formulation was not original to the law that created the confirmation.

§6. From This Chapter to the Next

Demosthenes was not aiming to deceive his audience when he conjured up the old legislation law in *Leptines*;[40] his argument simply had to be more complicated than scholars have understood. In an era when the annual vote to confirm the corpus was an obscure exercise, Demosthenes was trying to show that his case was at least true to the important principle behind that venerable formality. Whoever its author, it was enacted on the model of Teisamenos' decree or some such extension of the scrutiny of laws that Andokides' described. The original aim was not to undo contradictions (as Aischines suggested) but to augment or amend the law on the books. To that end, it was prescribed that the new bill be posted along with the standing laws that would conflict with it. Here the regular sense of λύειν τὸν νόμον applies: it is to "undo the law" or "break the law" in such a way as to make it powerless, by precedent or by introducing some new rule that overrides it—*lex posterior derogat priori.*

To be sure in lawsuits against unfitting law, "undoing the law" amounted to rescinding it outright, and in Leptines' case Demosthenes argued (for good reason) that the targeted statute really had to be repealed at once before the replacement law could actually be introduced. But as we shall see, that argument was dictated by the predicament peculiar to that case (detailed in chapter 7 §1). If we reconcile what Demosthenes tells us about the legislation law in the two speeches, little more than a year apart, it does not seem to require that old laws be formally canceled or voted down before anything to the contrary can be introduced; rather, the new law would naturally supersede the old.

The old legislative protocol was not designed for sorting out laws in conflict that somehow remained on the books but for recasting those with some gap or defect. That way of lawmaking fell into disuse as a more open-ended *nomothesia* prevailed: Demosthenes complained of the change, when that good, old-fashioned lawmaking was abandoned and (what I have called) the fast track took off (20.91). By this path legislative sessions could be convened by decree, at any time, to add practical expedients. These quick fixes were seen as corollaries or corrections to the standing laws, not as undoing them. Such were the adjustments to the "allocation" of funds, the *merismós*, as early as the mid 380s.[41] As business became more pressing, *nomothetai* were convened fairly often.[42] It was probably the abuse of that open procedure that soon led to the most notorious convictions for unfitting legislation (in 382/1), which Demosthenes recalled to the jury in *Timokrates* (138). In the 370s there seem still to be two viable avenues for legislation reflected in the Coinage Law and the Grain-Tax Law. But by the 350s Demosthenes' argument suggests that the older way of lawmaking was a largely forgotten formality.

At this point, that may be as far as we can go toward reconstructing the evolution of constitutional recourse from the evidence that bears directly upon that development. But there is another dimension to this set of problems: the role of citizens sworn to preserve the law, as judges and lawmakers. In the next chapter we focus on that adaptive character as the remedies developed to reinforce the legislation law and the juries were constituted to decide those cases.

CHAPTER TWO

Judges and Lawmakers

Take up the law that authorized the earlier lawmakers and read it. . . . You can see how well the "Solon" ordered legislation, first (in importance), that the bill come to you who have sworn.

—Demosthenes, *Against Leptines* (92–93)

In the 350s BC, as we noticed in the last chapter, Demosthenes identified the lawmakers of a bygone era with a body of "jurors," citizens bound by oath. In support of that testimony (or inspired by it) there is a persistent tradition in the manuscript documents, scholia, and other secondary sources that the *nomothetai* were indeed *dikastai,* chosen from the ranks of those who had sworn the judges' oath. But that identification is not nearly as straightforward as scholars have assumed. In Leptines' case, Demosthenes suggested that the very judges who decide the lawsuit serve as *nomothetai* to enact the replacement law that his colleague has proposed. But he also implied that the course of democracy has somehow departed from that ideal (20.92–93): those *nomothetai* who swore the oath were lawmakers who served formerly or once upon a time (οἱ πρότερον νομοθέται), which seems to be no longer so. Conversely, by speaking of lawmakers as "sworn," he may simply have been referring to the jury in a lawsuit against unfitting law, if that was once the first stage of a rigorous process to repeal and replace old law.[1]

In this chapter we take up these questions: Who were the lawmakers, who were the judges, and what were their respective roles in resolving conflict in the corpus of laws and decrees? If we are to understand how the Athenians constructed their constitutionalism, on their own assumptions, it is essential to sort out these overlapping duties. For it is clear that litigants could summon up constraints that went deeper than the particular statutes and insist that the jurors were bound by them; and, to our way of thinking, it may seem self-defeating to put that burden on the same persons who enacted the measure in the first place. How can those who control the law be the very legislators who made it? But the Athenians would probably have answered, "How could it be otherwise?" They had no separation of powers such as the American Framers adapted from Montesquieu. And yet there was a strong commitment to guard against lawmaking gone wrong.

The suit against aberrant decrees, "for unlawful acts" (παρανόμων), probably began as a remedy against overreaching politicians and may not have always required the sort of text-based study in repugnancy that we find in the well-documented cases.[2] As we consider in the next chapter, the constitutional principle seems to crystalize in the aftermath of the Arginousai generals' case. Up until that bitter recognition, it was not readily acknowledged that the sovereign people were bound by any deeper principle, let alone the particular wording of their past decisions.

The lawsuit against unfitting legislation (νόμον μὴ ἐπιτήδειον θεῖναι) was not introduced on the same assumptions; it was devised specifically as a remedy against new laws that created a conflict in the corpus. Its very description, as a remedy against "enacting" or introducing "law unfitting," along with the case history that we have (slim as it is), suggests as much: punishing the perpetrator was incidental; the important thing was to preserve the integrity of the body of laws.

Such cases, of both types, followed a well-trodden path: for any such momentous decision the proper venue was the court. But why should the trial jury take precedence over the citizen assembly, or for that matter, why should it stand apart from the *nomothetai* who made the law? In order to sort out the distinctions, let us begin with the judges and then consider the body of lawmakers that came after them.

§1. Who Were the *Dikastai*?

The jurors who served in court were distinguished by three qualifications: (a) maturity, by virtue of the requirement that *dikastai* must have reached their thirtieth year; (b) allotment, the randomized procedure for assigning jurors to their courts; and of course (c) their oath, the commitment that all jurors must swear to give judgment according to the laws, on the merits, and without prejudice.

Men of Certain Age

In the fifth century the courts seem as irascible and unrestrained as the assembly—or worse. In the recollections of historians and philosophers, the people's juries were in fact the gravest threat to the elite and deeply complicit in the downfall of the old democracy. The most damning depiction comes, again, from comedy. Thus the chorus of judges in *Wasps* (422 BC) proudly describe themselves as prickly characters:

> All considered, you will find our features and our way of life most resemble wasps: for, first, there is no creature quicker to anger when provoked, nor more ill-tempered, And, in other respects, we manage everything like wasps: Gathering in swarms, like wasps to the nest, some of us judge at the archon's court, some with the Eleven, others at the Odeion, crammed in . . . like larvae in their cells . . . [and] we are most resourceful, for we make our living by stinging everyone. (1102–21)

Their stinger (*enkentris* or *kentron*) was the emblem of their anger, and it somehow represents their qualification—why they have a special competence for judging politicians and other crooks. They earned it long ago by military service, and they see their continuing role in the courts as much the same patriotic duty. But the sting is also pathological, a symptom of their vindictive obsession. They swarm into court like wasps to the nest, and they use their sting to preserve that province by extracting fines and more painful penalties.

And then, at the end of this parabasis, the chorus demands some reform, to reserve jury service to those like themselves who have the right equipment: "There are drones that sit beside us, stay-at-homes who have no sting, who eat up the revenue without a care. This is most annoying to us, if anyone dodges service but gobbles up our wages. . . . So it is my conviction: henceforth any citizen who bears no sting must take no pay!" (1114–21).

It is tempting to suppose that this jibe responded to an ongoing debate (already in the 420s) on recasting the juries, but we have no direct evidence to confirm the suspicion. And, indeed, all indications from this era (from three comedies as well as historians and speechwriters) suggest that juries of the late fifth century were not subject to any restriction or lottery such as we find in the fourth century. Age was the one qualification that was standard in this period, perhaps already indicated by an official staff, *baktēría*:[3] when the chorus of *Wasps* complain that none should serve in court who brandish no sting, the audience would think of the walking stick that older men carried when they had far to go on rocky roads, a "third leg" that also served as a goad or cudgel.

So, by the late fifth century, the first qualification was already presumptive: the court belongs to the elders. But what of the other defining features, oath and allotment? To take the latter first;

Assigned by Lot

As Aristophanes tells us already in *Wasps*, there was funding for six thousand *dikastai* but, evidently, no procedure for balancing or limiting participation on any given day beyond the signal that courts were closed. Those who were old enough and eager enough crowded in, cheek by jowl. It seems to be a perfect model for those self-selecting factions that plague modern democracy as well.[4] When issues are decided by the constituents who are most angry or most invested, who carry the vote simply because they are the first to show up, again, this is the democracy we get.

In the fourth century, the courts seem to be insulated against such self-selecting factions. The literary sources tell us little about how and why this happened, but from the 390s down to around 350, we can trace the formative technology, and those innovations seem at least partly designed to dispel the angry swarming of the old democracy.

The jury-selection procedure of the later fourth century is described in great detail in the *Constitution of the Athenians* (*Ath. Pol.*), but it remains something of a puzzle. From the Aristotelian description alongside the extant artifacts, we can decipher the lottery devices (*klērōtēria*) and identification tags (*pinakia*) that were essential to the process. But it may still seem a baffling "rigmarole."[5] To make sense of it all, let us begin, again, at the end, and then try to discover the changes by which the contraption took shape.

In Aristotle's day the system worked as follows. On each court day, jurors came to their tribal area in the court complex where two *klērōtēria* were set up, each with five columns, numbered one to five (A to E) and six to ten (Z to K), together representing the ten sections of the tribe.[6] We may wonder, as Sterling Dow did, why two *klērōtēria* with five columns each and not one device with ten? But the way they worked seems clear enough.

From the 370s until sometime around 350, the jurors were given bronze *pinakia* (figure 2.1). Each man's *pinakion* showed his name and deme, preceded by his section letter: thus in the example, we find the section letter gamma to the left of the name Timophon of Paianía; at far right the owl of the triobol stands for his jury pay.[7] Most probably, these jurors' *pinakia* were originally wooden slats and then, in the 370s, reusable tags were issued in bronze. Sometime around 350, or soon after, the bronze tags became permanent identification for anyone in public service, and the jurors went back to using boxwood tags for the lottery machines.

As *Ath. Pol.* explains, the archon would insert balls or "dice" (*kyboi*) into a funnel at the top of the *klērōtērion* to feed out from the tube at the bottom: each

Figure 2.1. A *pinakion.* Courtesy of the Spurlock Museum of World Cultures, University of Illinois at Urbana-Champaign (1930.01.0001)

kybos, white or black, would decide for a whole row of *pinakia* (A–E or Z–K) *whether* those men would serve that day. Then each of the winners would discover *where* he would serve by plucking a bolt or "acorn" (*balanos*) from the water jar, each marked with a letter for the court site. Each juror was also given a staff, a *baktēría,* color-coded to match his destination. There he was given a seating token and, evidently, after the arguments were heard, he exchanged his staff for the ballots he would use to cast his vote.

Even from this outline I think we can see the system was not designed that way: what *Ath. Pol.* describes is a product of successive adaptations, replete with relics and misnomers. Some of the redundant features seem to have become purely ceremonial, but the pattern reveals an abiding purpose. The *dikastēs* (or "dikast") who finds his seat in court has survived a three-stage lottery: In the end he picked the acorn out of a jar to determine *where* he would serve; before that, the machine decided *whether* he would serve that day (whether his row got a white ball or black ball). But, even before that, he was subjected to a "prior lottery" (as Dow called it); for each section the *pinakia* were jumbled in a box and inserted under that letter in random order. Any jurors who ended up at the bottom of the better-attended columns were not ordinarily chosen; only the whole rows were allotted to the courts.

For illustration, consider this hypothetical distribution of *pinakia* by letter-section for one particular tribe (figure 2.2). In this sketch, each dash represents an inserted *pinakion* and shading represents excluded jurors. To fill (for instance) two courts, one panel of two hundred and another of five hundred, each tribe contributes seventy dikasts; to choose that contingent the archon inserts seven white balls in each *klērōtērion,* along with two black balls for the additional complete rows. For the rows that receive a black ball, the jurors are dismissed. The incomplete rows ("dangling") are also excluded, thus cancelling the high turnout for column Δ.

We can imagine that when turnout was low, the dangling dikasts were somehow combined to fill the vacancies, but the system was not designed for that. Dow

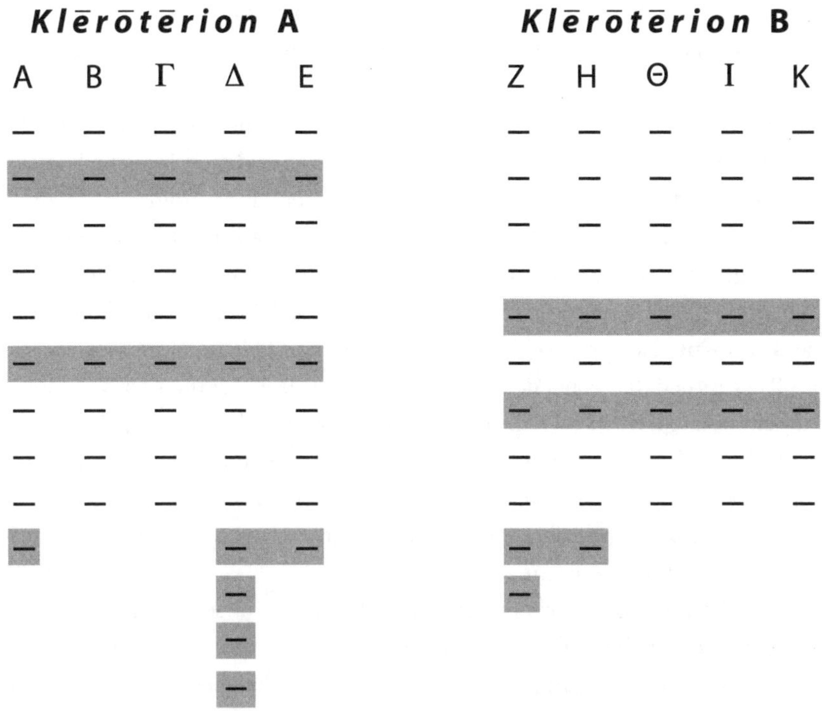

Figure 2.2. Hypothetical distribution of *pinakia* showing jurors excluded. Out of ninety-nine *dikasts* from one tribe, seventy are chosen to judge that day.

explained it as a tradeoff, sacrificing fairness for efficiency: as he put it, "injustice to a minority . . . to save minutes for the majority" ("Aristotle, the Kleroteria, and the Courts," 1939, 34). That may have been the rationale that made sense in midcentury, but this feature was also a legacy of reconstruction, when it seemed vital to bar self-selecting groups from dominating the jury.

In the year or so after democracy was restored, the old court system was suspended. That suspension may have been partly a response to financial exigencies, but it was also a precaution against vindictive prosecution. And when the jury system was reintroduced, there was good reason to recast it and avoid filling the courts with firstcomers. The Council of Five Hundred (the *boulē*), going back to Kleisthenes, would serve as a ready model: prospective jurors could be assigned to their sections-of-the-tribe according to the same scheme of regional balance that was built into the *boulē*. They had only to allot jurors for each deme in proportion to their *bouleutai*: twelve jurors per councilman for a full pool of six thousand.

After all, *Ath. Pol.* 62 mentions a broad reform by which certain offices came to be allotted in tribal meetings. Once upon a time, they were divided among the demes. Most officers were then chosen locally, not in one centralized process. Wilamowitz assumed that those deme-picked officers included *dikastai*, and he may yet be right. From surviving *pinakia* and other evidence, Mogens Hansen once calculated that the proportion of jurors and other officers from each region—inland, city, and coast—remained much the same as for *bouleutai*; somehow the same regional balance that was built into the council was approximated in the other offices. And some system for assigning section letters to council members was already in place by 409, as Alan Boegehold pointed out. More recently Jessica Paga argued that major deme centers served as hubs for their *trittyes*; a town busy enough to have its own theater was probably a regular meeting place for its third of the tribe.[8] And, I suggest, the distribution of section letters was probably shaped by that geography: in each *trittys* men were assigned to sections by deme, and that sorting was probably done originally in the *trittys* center, along the mustering route to the city (figure 2.3).

Later the process was centralized, and the *klērōtēria* served to allot jurors across the whole tribe on the same principle: members from any particular deme who found themselves "dangling," at the bottom of the longer columns, were simply excluded from the jury pool for that year. In this way each region within the tribe was fairly represented. And the same principle would carry over to the later use, when the *klērōtēria* allotted jurors for any given court day.

By this theory, what Dow took for an incidental inequity was designed so that no particular area could claim any disproportionate share of jury clout or jury pay. Of course in Aristotle's day any such adaptation seems largely forgotten, but in the early fourth century, scenes from comedy reflect an evolving process and an abiding concern for fairness, beginning with Praxagora's Reform in *Congresswomen*. Under her regime there will be no need for trials, so Praxagora will use all the old facilities for new purposes. Her man, Blepyros, wonders what she will do with the lottery machines (τὰ δὲ κληρωτήρια ποῖ τρέψεις), and she explains:

> *Praxagora*: I'll set them up in the agora, and then, convening beside Harmodios [the liberator's statue], I shall allot to all, so each gets his fair share and goes off glad to know what letter he's to dine in. The herald will announce that those with "Beta" go to the Stoá Basíleios; and those with "Theta" to the one beside it. And those from "Kappa" to the Grain-sellers'.
>
> *Blepyros*: "K" as in "Kram it in"?
>
> *Praxagora*: No, by Zeus, only to designate where they dine.

Figure 2.3. Attica, with mustering routes and *trittys* centers for four sample tribes; deme theaters are marked Θ. Based on Siewert, *Die Trittyen Attikas* (1982), and Paga, "Deme Theaters in Attica" (2010).

> *Blepyros*: But what about him whose letter ain't drawn? Do they drive 'em all away?
> *Praxagora*: That won't happen. . . . We'll provide for everyone and begrudge to none. (681–90)

Blepyros' first question, what to do with the *klērōtēria*, shows that they were already a familiar fixture, essential to the court-sorting process; but Praxagora's plan, to move the *klērōtēria* to the agora, shows that they were located elsewhere. In the new regime, the lottery would proceed in the court center and conclude with the lucky juror "glad to know what *letter* he's to dine in" (683). Matching letters to courts was a separate process, and it required no complex device; even in the Aristotelian rigmarole (in *Ath. Pol.*) it was done with acorns in a jar. Blepyros assumes that each section is assigned to its court en bloc; for those "whose letter ain't drawn," he fears, the whole section would go home hungry. Praxagora will remove that uncertainty entirely: in her plan, the *klērōtēria* will be used to guarantee that everyone is seated in one diner or another. The status quo did just the opposite—*klērōtēria* were used to assign some jurors to their section and exclude others.

The system in place in the 390s seems designed to restrain the swarming parodied in *Wasps*: in that setting old war buddies troop together into court, as many as can crowd in before the cutoff, for a case well anticipated, at a venue they already know. Those self-selecting juries were the angry face of the old democracy. Now, under the new regime, at the beginning of the year men who wish to be eligible for jury duty present themselves at a meeting of tribe or *trittys* with *pinakia* in hand.

These *pinakia* of circa 390 were probably wooden slats with the man's name and demotic. They put the *pinakia* in the columns corresponding to their demes, and those who won the lottery were given some official marker for the letter assigned to them, something harder to counterfeit than wooden slats. Already in the fifth century the Athenians had experimented with ceramic tokens for assigning other offices by deme,[9] and by the fourth century they had arrived at something handier for mass distribution, perhaps an "acorn" or peg to fix upon a juror's staff. Then, with those markers in hand, the jurors made their way to the agora to discover on each court day *where* their sections were assigned. The presiding archon matched section letters to court sites using tokens in a jar, and when each man arrived at court, he was given a matching token as his ticket for payment.

That scenario fits the picture in Aristophanes' *Ploutos* (or *Wealth)* in the early 380s. Near the end, the god Hermes hopes to join the happy household that plays host to the god Wealth (with his sight newly restored). The trickster god offers his services under many titles, and the wily slave, Karíon, remarks how useful it is also for a mortal man to have many eponyms to contribute to his livelihood: so, for good reason, court-goers "are eager to be inscribed in many letters."[10] That jibe suggests that, somehow, whether it was legal or fraudulent, *dikastai* could be eligible in more than one section:[11] if someone had the bad luck that Blepyros feared in *Congresswomen* and his letter was not drawn, he could simply use another one.

Ploutos also provides a clue to the path from local hub to central court. Earlier in the play, Karíon encounters the venerable chorus leader, and the old fellow assumes that the wily slave is up to no good, so he brandishes his *baktēría* (272). This sounds like the usual threat of a beating, but there is another implication in the joke that follows. For the Koryphaios threatens Karíon with shackles, and Karíon warns him that if he's passing judgment, he'd better hurry: "Your letter's been allotted to the Court of the Coffin [or in the Urn, *sorós*], and it [your letter-section] is judging there now. Aren't you going? Charon [pun on archon] is already handing out the *symbolon*" (276–77).[12]

The joke seems to suppose that the chorus leader is readily recognizable as a juror on his way to court—and so old and decrepit, he might as well go to his grave. Here we find that *symbola*, tokens of some sort, already serve to assign seating in court (as in *Ath. Pol.*). But each letter is assigned to its court en bloc, by a lottery in the court complex. Evidently that lottery, to determine which sections serve *where*, is done the old-fashioned way, with tokens in a jar. A juror would not know which case or which court his section was assigned to until he got to the agora and learned how the letters matched up.

So Karíon speaks as though the *baktēría* was the badge of a juror on his way to court, looking to discover where he would sit; and the joke seems to assume that the section letter was somehow displayed for Karíon to recognize. The real thing, the judge's official staff, must have been marked in some distinctive way, and the juror had to have some way of proving what section he belonged to; so perhaps that marker was somehow fixed upon his *baktēría*. Once he got to the agora, brandishing his staff, he would discover *where* his letter was assigned. And when he got to his venue, perhaps, he would trade his staff or lettered-marker for a *symbolon*, his voucher for pay (as in *Ath.Pol.* 65.2).[13]

About a decade later in Euboulos' comedy *Karíon the Riddler* we're told of a device that certainly sounds like a *klērōtērion* but still works rather differently from the ones in *Ath. Pol.*, and it may still be situated somewhere outside the court center. This is an "*agalma* standing up above, gaping at its base, bored clean through from head to foot, giving birth to men one by one from its butt; some are allotted portions sufficient for life; others wander away, each holding his own, calling 'On guard!'" Athenaios called it a *klērōtikón*, but for centuries it was assumed that this must be a ballot *jar* with a funnel on top. Dow showed, from the implicit shape and function, that it was almost certainly a *klērōtērion* like the ones *Ath. Pol.* describes, but perhaps with only one or a few columns.[14]

The difference is important: the Aristotelian lottery machine picked men for duty in rows of five at a time on each court day, and then each man plucked an acorn to determine where he would serve. In the comic prototype, the device chooses each man or excludes him "one by one" and rewards the winner with a portion of his livelihood. That description is a better fit for the initial process assigning citizens to their sections; a man's fated portion (*moira*) is his section letter, which guarantees a subsidy for the year, at least. But if so, how was it done?

It would be more efficient to assign *dikastai* to their sections deme by deme in *trittys* meetings than to use a random drawing among the tribe at large. At their regional centers the constituent demes would be assigned letters and then the lottery would chose men from each deme, each to receive a marker with a letter assigned to that deme. To see how that localized process would work, consider the following scheme for a fairly representative tribe, Akamantis, with a list of the largest *trittyes* for comparison (table 2.1). In small to average-sized demes with five or fewer representatives in council, such as Thorikos (Δ), all members of the same deme would have the same section letter. That would be the case for the majority of Athenians. Now among the *trittyes*, the smallest would need only two letters; but the largest, those with twenty-five councilmen (half of their tribal contingent), would have to have five letters.

Later, as the process was centralized, *klērōtēria* designed for the largest *trittyes* (with five columns each) were relocated to the city, presumably to the Theseion where other offices were assigned. That would help to explain why the process described in *Ath. Pol.* uses two *klērōtēria* with five letters each, instead of one device with ten. The two smaller machines were not just more portable, they were already available, relics of the old procedure. Institutions do not easily relinquish what they already have, and that conservatism suggests that assigning letters by deme would not be abandoned even when bronze *pinakia* were adapted for assigning offices at large (ca. 350) and day-to-day jury selection was done once again with boxwood slats.

By this view, Dow's "prior lottery," which effectively limited the number of jurors in any one section, was an adaptive feature that made the system less vulnerable to self-selecting factions. After all, the most remarkable change from the fifth century to the fourth was that no partisan groups could swarm the courts like wasps to defend their favorites or punish their enemies. And, just as

TABLE 2.1

Hypothetical distribution of **section letters** *(A–K) by deme for the tribe Akamantis*

CITY **A–Γ**	COAST **Δ–Z**	INLAND **H–K**
Cholargos (4) = **A**	Thorikos (5 or 6) = **Δ**	Hagnous (5) = **H**
Eiresidai (1) sharing **B**	Kephale (9) = **E–Z**	Kikynna (2) sharing **I**
Hermos (2) sharing **B**	Poros (3) sharing **Z**	Prospalta (5) = **Θ**
Iphistidai (1) sharing **B**		Sphettos (5) = **K**
Kerameis (6) = **Γ**		Eitea? (2) sharing **I** (or **B**?)

Larger *trittyes* for comparison:
COASTAL Aiantis (with 25 *bouleutai*) would need five letters (say, **Γ–H**)
COASTAL Antiochis (with 27 *bouleutai*), also five letters
INLAND Aigeis (with 24 or 25 *bouleutai*), five letters
INLAND Oineis = Acharnai (one deme with 22 *bouleutai*) four or five letters

Region assignments (city, coast, and inland) based on Traill, *Political Organization of Attica* (1975); number of councilmen for each deme from Whitehead, *Demes of Attica* (1986).

important, no particular deme or region could claim a disproportionate payday. Those dangling dikasts, with their *pinakia* at the bottom of the longest columns, were simply excluded. That disadvantage to a few was justified by the guarantee that every area have equal access to public service and a fair share of the city's largesse.

Of course this reconstruction is, admittedly, a theory built upon fragmentary evidence and what seem to me the most practical considerations. But the conventional model rests upon nothing more solid, and it is mistaken to treat it as anything but a comfortable assumption: we are to assume that letters were assigned randomly in the tribe at large simply because so much of the system resorted to lottery. *Ath. Pol.*, after all, never tells us how the letters were assigned; indeed, by circa 340, it probably made little difference. But fifty years earlier, some scheme for regional balance may have been vital, so that the urban plebs not overwhelm the farmers from outlying demes.[15] And if jury selection was construed in this way, it adds another dimension to the jurors' authority: more than any other institution of the democracy, this body represents the demos at large. For the courts include men of various classes (more fully than council) and yet cannot be dominated by the self-selecting factions that swarm into the assembly.

Before we proceed to the jurors' oath, it may be helpful here to outline the reconstruction thus far. The system that assigned the juries to their courts developed over the course of half a century, roughly as follows:

In the 390s jurors are assigned section letters each year on the model of council: for each deme (in principle) twelve *dikastai* are chosen for each *bouleutēs*. In this way all areas are proportionally represented in the jury pool. In this period, sections are assigned to courts en bloc (*e.g.*, sections Δ from all ten tribes proceed to one particular venue). There was probably some scheme to rotate the letters from one region to another, from one tribe to the next; and for major cases, seating multiple sections mitigated any imbalance. The *pinakia* were wooden slats, used only for the annual sortition on *klērōtēria* at *trittys* or tribal meetings. The men who were assigned to a jury section were given some official marker with their section letter (bronze or ceramic). These were collected, perhaps recast, and redistributed every year (or so). On court day, jurors made their way to the agora with staves in hand and lettered markers prominently displayed. In the agora, whole sections were assigned to courts by simple lottery (taking tokens from a jar). Surplus sections were dismissed without pay.

Sometime in the next decade (probably), *klērōtēria* were centralized for tribal lotteries, presumably in the Theseion. And beginning in the 370s, we see further changes that served (at least in part) to minimize tampering with the process. Bronze *pinakia* replaced the old wooden ones and every year or every few years these bronze tags were redistributed, the names erased and reinscribed; only the stamped letter remained unaltered. At some point, the *klērōtēria* were moved to the court area in the agora for the complicated lottery assigning jurors on each court day (as described in *Ath. Pol.* 63–69). In the earlier process, the larger *trittyes* had used *klērōtēria* with five lettered columns; two of these were now combined to sort the whole set of ten letters for the tribe. But the same principle applied: manning the courts with equal contingents from both *klērōtēria*—with the same number from each of ten sections—tended to assure that all three regions would be represented proportionately in the jury pool on any given day. For any section with higher turnout than the others (filling a longer column), the dangling *dikastai* were dismissed. Of those who remained, each juror plucked a lettered "acorn" from the jar to determine his venue, and thus the composition of each particular court was purely random.

The same selection process may have applied to the lawmakers, convened to enact new *nomoi*, at least in principle: they, too, should have reached their thirtieth year of age and, from that cadre, the panel to decide upon any given slate of legislation may well have been selected by a similar allotment process.[16] But let us leave that question aside until we have considered the last qualification.

Who Have Sworn the Judges' Oath

We are blessed or cursed with abundant evidence on the content of the dikastic oath.[17] The details sometimes conflict, but the essentials are solidly attested and all but indisputable: prospective jurors swore to vote according to the laws and not to yield to prejudice. The latter commitment was probably recast after the restoration of democracy: Andokides says that his jury in 400/399 had sworn an oath that included the pledge of amnesty, "not to recall wrong" (μὴ μνησικακῆσαι) (1.91), and Plato's *Apology of Socrates* (35c) suggests that some such rule against partisan recrimination was standard (though not in the same words). Amid this collection of evidence, one missing feature is most surprising: even after the new procedure for lawmaking (*nomothesia*) was established, there seems to be no dedicated clause in the jurors' oath regarding that duty. If, indeed, the *nomothetai* who enacted new *nomoi* were drawn from the cadre of eligible *dikastai*, we might expect some provision that recognized a basic commitment to that task: "In making new law I shall not allow conflict or contradiction," or something to that effect. But we are never given any indication of such a clause, even in cases where the litigant might have made much of it.[18]

The dikastic oath in some form was already established in the fifth century; Antiphon's testimony (5.85) comes only a few years after the jury profile in *Wasps*. And that is what we would expect: after all, the Greeks generally relied upon oath to seal any important commitment. But we should be wary of assuming too much from that trait.

There is perhaps an oblique reference to the jurors' oath in the Arginousai debate (discussed in the next chapter), but the referent is doubtful. There, where Euryptolemos envisions a proper trial for the defendants, he says thus the innocent will be spared, "and you will show reverence for the law and cast judgment true to your oaths (εὐορκοῦντες κρινεῖτε)" (Xen. *Hell.* 1.7.25). But that would be an odd way to draw the distinction, if he simply meant to say, "there, in court, you would be under oath; here, in assembly, you are bound by none." The usual way to make that distinction would be simply to say that in court they would make their decision as sworn (ὀμωμοκότες). On one level, he might mean that all Athenians *eligible* for jury service vowed to preserve the laws (as we consider below), and those who had so sworn could only be true to that oath in a proper trial. But the most straightforward meaning is simply that, by condemning men who had served the demos with distinction, they would be violating other oaths of service and solidarity.[19] That is, only by giving the defendants a proper trial can the men in assembly be true to their vows as citizen soldiers. In this way, he goes on to say, "you would not be joining battle on the side of the Lakedaimonians against men who seized seventy of their ships and won victory for us."

§2. Who Were the *Nomothetai*?

In Demosthenes' singular testimony (20.90–93), lawmakers of a bygone era were distinguished by their oath, but it is a lost or diminished distinction. He seems to suppose that *nomothetai* were, *once upon a time*, subject to the same oath as *dikastai*, but it was no longer necessarily so. Who then were the *nomothetai* that enacted new law?

The title itself tells us little or nothing about qualifications: *nomothetai* might describe any officers or assembly that framed the law.[20] Thus, in the restoration of the Solonian corpus and the enactment of new fundamental laws, *nomothetai* might refer either to the law writers (*anagrapheis*) who drafted the statutes or to the assembly that ratified them. So it is perhaps significant that neither in *Leptines* nor in *Timokrates* did Demosthenes refer to the jury as *nomothetai*, even though in each case the verdict that he was pleading for would reshape the corpus by restoring older statutes. Neither did he suggest that the jury at hand, whom he called upon to rescind the new law, were the very same personnel who approved it, though he insisted that the lawmakers *should be* the same "jurors (ὀμωμοκότες) who decide the other issues" (20.93). In the case of Timokrates' hastily enacted nomos, the judges may have been the very men whom the defendant and his associates had hoodwinked by their maneuvers; but the orator does not say so. It is not much to go on, but I think we can at least conclude that there was some significant difference between the lawmakers and the judges, that *nomothetai* were not necessarily or not simply *dikastai*.

The secondary tradition suggests, however, that the *nomothetai* indeed *qualified* as *dikastai* and were chosen from among their ranks,[21] and so scholars have taken it for granted that the qualifying procedures worked as we might expect: every year, when the incoming cadre of jurors were selected, they swore the dikastic oath *en masse*, in one body of six thousand;[22] and thereafter, from among that body, juries were chosen to serve as *nomothetai*, whenever that service was required. But there is respectable testimony that suggests a more open arrangement.

Harpokration gives the following notice on the hill called Ardettos: "A place above the Panathenaic stadium, in the lower deme Agryle; there they say *all Athenians* swore publicly the heliastic oath."[23] That last term, "heliastic oath," aptly describes a collective pledge by the citizen assembly, convened in a wide-open forum "under the sun" (*hēliaia*). The site called Ardettos was named for an ancient hero (of course), supposedly the one who was first to call upon (all) Athenians to swear.[24] And Theophrastos (F 647 Fortenbaugh) is cited specifically for the end of the practice: "Theophrastos reveals, in *On Laws*, that this practice had been undone." Pollux fills in the foundation myth with a mass swearing to unify the community in time of civil conflict, and other lexicographers present similar material alongside the reference to Theophrastos.[25]

So, it seems reasonable to suppose, Theophrastos reported that, previously, *all* eligible Athenians swore the judicial oath, but in his day that practice had been discontinued. That notice leaves us with various possibilities: conceivably, in the early to mid fourth century all citizens who were to serve as jurors that year gathered to swear the judges' oath; or perhaps each concerned citizen was only obliged to swear at least once, when or after he became eligible.[26] The latter seems to me the more likely explanation: every year, all those who had come of age would gather for the swearing in, if they were at all civic minded. It was *not a requirement* that each and every citizen *must* swear if he had no intention of serving in any official capacity. And not all who swore had any inclination to serve *as jurors*. Many men among the wealthy elite would have no interest in taking up jury duty; and, for that matter, many of the middle-class farmers from outlying demes might have no expectation of serving regularly at court in the city center. Theophrastos may simply have meant that sometime in the past, as the mark of a good citizen, it was expected that everyone, after he came of age for civic duties, would join the throng at Ardettos and swear the oath.

When there was nothing more to it than the swearing, it was probably impossible to confirm or disprove whether any given citizen had in fact taken the oath. So it was required that those who intended to serve as judges (or other officers) carry a token, an "acorn" or a staff, or even a "ticket" (*pinakion*) of some sort. Yet, among so many gathering from all the demes, there could not have been any systematic verification that every qualified citizen was present and took part, unless there was an elaborate enrollment process of which we hear nothing. Instead, the system seems to rely on face-to-face recognition (friends and fellow demesmen could vouch for those they saw there) and citizen initiative (to challenge those who pretended to rights they had not properly established). The jurors' tags as we find them, engraved with name, demotic, section letter, and triobol, as a ticket to court and jury pay could not be handed out at Ardettos but would have to be inscribed later and distributed elsewhere.

On this understanding, I suggest that those who attended that oath-taking in or after their thirtieth year were thereby *eligible* to serve as jurors (and in other offices as well) and, by the same token, qualified to serve as *nomothetai*. That broad cadre would help to explain how Aischines (in 330) could casually refer to an assembly scheduled "for *nomothetai*" (3.39): that is, (in principle) only those who had sworn the oath at Ardettos were supposed to convene in this *ekklēsia*; younger men or *idiōtai* who had not bothered to take the oath should not attend. On that day the assembly thus constituted would decide upon the decree for legislation and were therefore called "lawmakers," *nomothetai*. After all, *nomothetēs* is broadly used to describe anyone who authors or decides upon the law; and for most legislation, now on the fast track, the decisive vote was taken in the *ekklēsia*. Once the assembly decreed for *nomothetai* to convene and enact new law, ratification was often little more than a formality (as in the passing of Timokrates' surety law, described in chapter 6 §1). On the date prescribed in the decree, a representative body of men who once had sworn would convene as lawmakers in the strong sense, to *enact* the bill or reject it. In any event, Aischines seems to suppose that only those who were eligible, who were of age, and who had sworn the qualifying oath would present themselves at that session of the assembly. Any assembly of such citizens, convened for the purpose of authorizing new *nomoi*, would be properly called "*nomothetai*," even when their swearing in was a dubious formality.

Already in 355/4 Demosthenes suggested that the *nomothetai* of his day were no longer quite so qualified as those of a bygone era, "the earlier lawmakers" in the epigraph to this chapter. That decline has contributed to a worsening muddle in the body of laws (20.91–92). By distinguishing lawmakers of the past as somehow superior to those at hand, he might simply mean that the oath requirement had fallen into disuse, that citizens had come to take that duty rather casually.[27] To be sure, the fragment of Theophrastos (F 647) says that, at some point, the rule "*had* been undone" or abrogated (κατελέλυτο). The past perfect looks back from an era when the jury system ended altogether, when democracy itself was undone. As antecedent to that ending, perhaps he was referring to a time when the mass oath-taking was abandoned or converted into some other qualifying credential.

By circa 350, any citizen who served as an officer, in any capacity, would receive a bronze *pinakion*, such as formerly identified only court judges. In principle, presumably, the swearing in at Ardettos was still required of all, but in this era of the fast track, when *nomothetai* met only to hear the reading of the bill and ratify what the demos had decreed, the requirement that each of them had actually attended a mass swearing might seem incidental. If a citizen in good standing had received a *pinakion*, and no one who knew him had challenged him, his qualification as "sworn" would be simply assumed. And when almost everyone was presumed to qualify, the qualification lost much of its meaning. Perhaps in that era the grand gathering at Ardettos was replaced with a swearing ceremony at the tribal meeting when *pinakia* were distributed.

Be that as it may, in 346, Aischines insisted that *nomothetai* follow a higher standard than the courts, and one might suppose that he was referring to some specific pledge that lawmakers made. As he turned to the closing of the speech *Against Timarchos* (176–78), he advised the judges not to be distracted by extraneous considerations but to focus on their proper task: "Just as in horse-racing, drive on in the same lane." And, he goes on to say:

> If you do, you will not be an object of contempt but will show the same judgment that you show [elsewhere] as lawmakers, [here] as judges. If not, you will seem irascible, anticipating wrongs that have not happened yet, but indifferent to those that have already befallen. . . . Why do you think the laws are well made but the city's decrees are deficient, and verdicts in the courts sometimes cause consternation? It is because *you make the laws for justice in all regards, not for unfair advantage nor favor nor enmity, but intent up this object alone: what is just and in the public interest.*

These last duties—to make law for "justice in all regards" (ἐπὶ πᾶσι δικαίοις), without favor or prejudice, serving only what is right and in the public interest—seem to go beyond what we know of the jurors' oath. But Aischines did not say that lawmakers were bound by any distinctly nomothetic oath to guide them as legislators; he is probably referring to the same commitments but he means that *nomothetai* honor them more righteously. After all, he claims, "being naturally more astute than other men, naturally you make the finest laws. But in the assemblies and the courts, you are often misled by deception and cheap tricks, losing sight of the matter at hand" (1.178). So his point seems to be that judges and lawmakers are bound by the same commitments, but the latter are not distracted by partisan or adversarial arguments. This reading suggests, again, that with the usual fast-track legislation, *nomothetai* were not faced with a trial procedure (as later tradition imagined and modern scholars have often supposed) but voted on initiatives that were put before them without the debate that animated trials and assemblies.

Whatever their qualifications, the *nomothetai* who enacted new laws were readily identified with the people at large and not considered an elite body. The court reforms of the fourth century were initially inspired, at least in part, by the disasters of the old democracy, particularly the danger posed by self-selecting factions parodied in the angry swarm of *Wasps*. Thus the jury lottery of the fourth century seems designed for a more perfect union, as the courts of the people came to represent the polis more aptly than the assembly. That idea may be a consideration in the criteria for *nomothetai* as well. Only citizens chosen without prejudice from among those who had sworn to preserve the body of law shall have the authority to undo legislation (law or decree) in court and, by the same token, only those bound by the same obligation should convene to make new nomos.

§3. How Lawsuits and Legislation Meshed

For litigation against unlawful decrees (*graphai paranomōn*) the principle was adversarial: the prosecutor swore to prosecute the author of the bill and thereby blocked the decree in the assembly, either before or after it was put to a vote. Thereupon the measure was suspended until the court could decide upon the charges. If the assembly had already passed the decree, then the court gave a second and final decision on whether it would take effect. But if the proposal was challenged as a proposal of council (*probouleuma*), before the assembly could pass it, it was subject to limitation. If the case was not decided within that council's year, then the measure became moot, though the author was still liable (as in

Aristokrates' case). But if the case proceeded in due course and the jury voted in favor of the defendant, then the decree was confirmed. In such cases, the court enacted the decree.[28]

The lawsuit against unfitting legislation (*graphē nomon mē epitēdeion theinai*) was framed on a different premise, as a true constitutional safeguard. It was invented after the confirmation protocol gave way to a more expeditious process. The peculiar case against Leptines' law looks back to some such adaptation: in that case the author of the nomos was no longer liable more than a year after *nomothetai* approved it, though the law itself could still be undone in court; for it had been continuously under challenge and had not yet taken effect. The difficulties that Demosthenes and his colleagues faced in this case suggest that the remedy was designed to rescind aberrant legislation *within the year after it passed*, not to abrogate laws of longer standing.[29] We take up Leptines' case in detail in chapter 7, but here let us consider that piece of the evolving puzzle: At what stage of *nomothesia* should a new nomos be challenged and brought to trial?

In both of the cases where we have a speech to go by, it seems clear that the indictment came after *nomothetai* had ratified the nomos. The remedy seems designed for that situation, not for preempting legislation in progress. But there is another path implicit in the confirmation process: in the last scheduled assembly, the decree for *nomothetai* to decide upon the bill could be challenged by anyone willing, initiating a *graphē paranomōn* either before or after the decree was passed. In either case the bill would then be stalled until trial. Here the older *graphē* raises a knotty question: If the jurors decide in favor of the decree for the new law, is there any point in sending it back to the assembly or on to the *nomothetai*? The sworn have already given their decision in court. In the case of other decrees, the jurors either reject the bill or enact it. But in the course of lawmaking, the decree for *nomothetai* to convene might be challenged on grounds other than the merits of the nomos in question (e.g., qualifications of the mover). So, most probably, once the decree was approved, the bill would have to proceed to the *nomothetai* for yet another vote.

Be that as it may, the case of Demosthenes' Trierarchic Law of 340 suggests (as we consider in the next segment) that, at some point, the suit against unfitting law was adapted to this situation so that when law-in-the-making was challenged, it fell to the court to enact the nomos.

And it is that route to ratification that seems to be represented in the dubious document inserted in *Timokrates* at section 33. The source or inspiration for that concoction was, again, probably a later revision of the legislation law, not the original that Demosthenes' client included in his dossier in 353. After all, the lawsuit against unfitting legislation (νόμον μὴ ἐπιτήδειον θεῖναι) was not designed to repeal laws of long standing (see chapter 1 §5). The proper way to remove any old law was to replace it through the confirmation process. That old protocol did not provide any immediate remedy against a brand-new law in the months after it was enacted nor against the new bill in the very process of legislation; debate in the assembly (over the course of three meetings) should give full hearing to any challenge before the people would vote on the decree for *nomothetai* to ratify the law. Yet here (in Timokrates' case) the speaker calls for the reading of a statute that provided the immediate remedy of a lawsuit against a law newly enacted: that statute "expressly bars anyone from introducing (into the corpus) a law in conflict, and if anyone does so, orders him indicted" (32). The text intended would be the enabling statute for lawsuits against a law recently ratified or on the threshold of enactment, not a law of long standing.

Demosthenes says nothing to connect that remedy with the protocol for confirmation that he had just discussed (24.17–25). The enabling statute for the lawsuit against unfitting law is introduced thereafter, in connection with the text inserted in section 33. This insert recapitulates the main features of the confirmation process (for introducing new law to undo the old) and concludes with a cross-reference to the statute that created the remedy against unfitting legislation: litigation shall proceed according to a law that is already laid down (γραφάς εἶναι . . . κατὰ τὸν νόμον ὃς κεῖται, ἐάν τις μὴ ἐπιτήδειον θῇ νόμον). Again, if the compositor were simply inventing a document out of the clues that Demosthenes gave, he would come up with something more to the point: he had no need to cover the main provisions of the confirmation process, rehearsed in sections 24–26. If his aim was simply to fill in the gap with something to reassure his readers, he had ample scope to invent a law for this remedy, from Demosthenes' disquisition here and elsewhere. It would be something along these lines: "If anyone enacts a law that is in conflict with the standing laws or unfitting for the people, anyone willing is to indict him before the *thesmothetai*; the latter shall review the relevant statutes, conduct the hearings, and bring the case to trial." That original enabling statute for this remedy would, of course, give all the details, and an inventive compositor could surely have come up with something more convincing than a vague reference to the law that was already on the books. So the text inserted here (33), like the confirmation document (20–23), is not a pure fabrication (like those that adorn the Crown Case); it is patched together from historical material that seems relevant. But it is not what Demosthenes intended for his audience; it was included for readers of a later age, who probably appreciated the comparandum for what it was worth.

For this document (Dem. 24.33) the compositor probably drew upon some account of the later revisions to the confirmation process. As we noticed in chapter 1 (§5), the one substantive variant in the confirmation document (departing from the outline that Demosthenes gave), was the section on penalties against the chairmen and presiders if they fail to introduce the confirmation as scheduled (22). The details, as we have them, involve a textual problem or two, but the substance seems plausible enough: these would be clauses from a later amendment or addendum to the confirmation law, to hold officers to account for neglecting the confirmation vote. In the document to illustrate the remedy against authors of unfitting law (24.33), I think we have a similar product: the editor found or recalled some historical material from the later amendment, not the original law. It would not have made much difference to the ancient readers but, for our inquiry, the implications are significant. For this material refers to the application of *the old remedy in a new context.*

The suit against unfitting legislation was introduced, originally, to deal with laws enacted on the fast track; it was not designed to deal with products of the confirmation protocol. When the confirmation was conceived, no such remedy was deemed necessary; the new bill was matched against the laws that it would alter, with full publicity and debate in successive assemblies. Initially, the glare of that scrutiny was sufficient; there was no need to prescribe a remedy against a new law that might survive that process and yet prove repugnant to the corpus at birth.

The *graphē* against unfitting legislation was thus designed for laws that *nomothetai* ratified despite latent contradictions, through the sort of ad hoc legislation that passed Timokrates' law. Yet, in the inserted document (24.33), this remedy has been adapted from that use to another; it refers to the lawsuit as a remedy found in standing law (to address some other situation) now to be used against products of the confirmation process. In its new application, apparently, the lawsuit against unfitting law could be invoked even before *nomothetai* have given the law its second decision. Under the old arrangement, that ratification could be blocked by *graphē paranomōn* against the decree to submit the bill to *nomothetai.* After all, *graphai paranomōn* often served to obstruct a popular initiative, leaving the proposal to die of neglect (as illustrated in chapters 8–9). So, most probably, to assure that *nomothesia* not be subject to the same frustration, it was required that anyone who undertook to challenge a new law-in-the-making (a bill the demos had approved for *nomothetai* to enact) would now have to bring suit against it as "unfitting legislation." In such cases, the court would either enact the law or reject it.[30]

This reconstruction is admittedly complicated, so it may be helpful here to outline the bare bones of it, to be fleshed out in the concluding section (table 2.2).

TABLE 2.2

The sequence of adaptations in constitutional review

Legislative development	Remedy in litigation
The confirmation protocol is designed to "repeal and replace" laws of long standing.	Initially, no remedy is prescribed, as the rigorous process should prevent repugnancy. The only recourse to the court is *graphē paranomōn* against the decree for *nomothetai*.
Fast-track legislation is introduced to obviate the constraints of confirmation.	The more expeditious procedure leads to conflict; the *graphē nomon mē epitēdeion theinai* is devised in that setting for laws newly enacted.
Confirmation falls into disuse.	The law for confirmation is amended to penalize officers who neglect it.
The confirmation protocol is revived.	The *graphē nomon mē epitēdeion theinai* is made applicable to laws-in-the-making.

Legislating in Court

A decade after the cases against Leptines' law and against Timokrates, we come upon an important case that seems to illustrate the later adaptation, resorting to *graphē nomon mē epitēdeion theinai before* the bill goes to *nomothetai*. Among Demosthenes' legislative initiatives perhaps his proudest was the Trierarchic Law of 340, which replaced Periandros' law of 357 (Dem. 18.102–7).[31] His testimony suggests that the measure was approved by the assembly and was all but law when it was challenged and taken to court: the aim of the opposition was "so that these provisions be undone" (ὥστε δὴ ταῦτα λυθῆναι). In some sense, the law had already passed. So the lawsuit against Demosthenes' bill was not, strictly speaking, a suit against unlawful action, *paranomōn*, but one for unfitting legislation, *nomon mē epitēdeion theinai*. He pictures the wealthy opponents urging him to let the measure expire, not to proceed with it, once it was stalled by legal challenge. If the *nomothetai* had already ratified his law at that point, where the opposition tried to buy him off, we would expect him to mention that validation, at least to amplify the arrogance of his opponents. Instead he speaks of going to court *by decree*, but not of a lawsuit against the decree for *nomothesia*. Lipsius long ago concluded that Demosthenes drew up a decree to force the issue, for the orator describes it as "the decree by which I entered into the lawsuit," τὸ ψήφισμα, καθ' ὅ τι εἰσῆλθον τὴν γραφήν (18.105). This decree evidently provided for a trial to decide the fate of the bill, not simply to compel those who had challenged it under oath to follow through on their commitment.[32] The decree would call for a jury of, say, one thousand or fifteen hundred to convene on a scheduled date, and it would have to define the issue: the jury would decide between Demosthenes' bill and the standing law that it replaced.

If it were only a matter of forcing the prosecutor to proceed, there would have been no need for a decree; other remedies would suffice. In [Dem.] 58.6, we are told, the law assigned a penalty of 1,000 drachmas if a prosecutor initiated a public suit and then left it unresolved. We are not told how that could be enforced, but the ordinary rules should apply: if one took on a legal obligation that he failed to fulfill, he thus incurred a penalty and was himself liable to prosecution if he exercised rights that were forfeit until the penalty was paid (as illustrated in [Dem.] 58.43–9). The regular remedy would be "warrant" and arrest (*endeixis* and *apagōgē*).[33]

For a bill that was already approved by the citizen assembly and needed only ratification by a body of the "sworn," it seems pointless to require that, after the jurors in court decided in its favor, the bill must still proceed to the *nomothetai* for yet another decision by *omōmokotes*. Instead, just as the court might approve a *decree* in a *graphē paranomōn*, a court decision in favor of a *nomos* that the assembly had approved would enact it into law.

The case of Demosthenes' Trierarchic Law also illustrates a further complication, one that may be instructive for the whole edifice of constitutional review. As we noticed, the case proceeded to trial by decree;[34] the assembly, where the bill was introduced and debated, went on to prescribe in a *psēphisma* the arrangements for the court to decide the matter. Evidently, instead of the usual decree for *nomothetai* to convene and ratify the nomos that the people had approved, the assembly called upon the court to decide whether the bill would be law. In this way the court acted as a legislative body inasmuch as Demosthenes' law was enacted by the jury that decided in his favor.

Again, we know of no other case where that mode of *nomothesia* is clearly attested, but legislative intervention—the power of the assembly to dictate how the court will proceed—is certainly operative in the suits against unlawful decrees; so it seems reasonable to suppose that it was also invoked in suits against unfitting laws. Otherwise the sequence of proceedings gets rather awkward. In the case of Demosthenes' Trierarchic Law, Hansen supposed that the challenge took the form of a *graphē paranomōn* against the *decree* for convening *nomothetai*, and after the court approved the decree, the bill then went on to the *nomothetai* at last to enact the law. As we anticipated (at note 29), that might be how it had to work earlier in the fourth century. But if that was the only recourse, we are stuck with a four- or five-stage procedure: (1) council approves the proposal for *nomothetai*;

(2) the assembly debates it and, when challenged (3), the demos decrees for trial in court; (4) the court decides in favor of the decree; and (5) at last the bill goes on to the *nomothetai* for ratification. The Athenians were certainly capable of such convolutions, but the evidence suggests that sometimes in such cases they resorted to "cutting the knot," thereby reducing the tangle of procedure and substance to one final decision.

That principle seems recognized in the first case in the dossier, regarding the decree against the Arginousai generals. We consider this case in detail in the next chapter, but it will be helpful to foreshadow the feature that is relevant here: when the impeachment decree was challenged as *paranomon*, the challenger was threatened with a dire penalty for obstructing the people's will. A rider was proposed whereby the fate of the decree would be decided in court and, if it passed, he who attempted to block the measure with a lawsuit would be subject to the same fate as the generals targeted in the decree. Likewise, the last case in the dossier, the Crown Case (chapters 8–9), was probably brought to trial by decree: some legislative intervention was required to revive Ktesiphon's original proposal from years earlier, and that decree evidently specified an arrangement to punish the prosecutor beyond the usual penalties if the vote went against him.

Against this sort of shortcut scholars have often insisted upon a categorical rigor in Athenian proceedings, but that approach owes more to our own presumptions than to the evidence. After all, some propensity for cutting the knot is indicated in another mechanism devised or retooled in the early restoration era (soon after 403): the *paragraphē* that reshaped contract and settlement disputes. Anyone who was sued on a claim that should have been settled by a prior decision—or foreclosed by the Amnesty Agreement—could bring a *paragraphē* to put the onus on the plaintiff to show that his current claim was not covered by the earlier disposition of the matter. The conventional understanding of this recourse was much like the old model of constitutional review: the procedural issue must be settled separately, and then, if it cleared that hurdle, the main issue would require its own verdict. That is, if the court rejects the defendant's *paragraphē*, the litigants proceed to a separate decision on the plaintiff's claim. That model was based largely upon modern presumptions about how the rule of law should work. Even Paoli, who showed that there was no separate trial on the procedural question, concluded that there had to be a separate ballot. Yet, as I have argued and Mario Talamanca concluded from exhaustive study,[35] the evidence shows that the one verdict would resolve at once the *paragraphē* (defendant's claim that the matter is foreclosed) and the plaintiff's claim for damages; the court simply voted for one side or the other. After all, the substantive and procedural questions are often difficult to disentangle, so the Athenians sometimes saw fit to resolve them both at one stroke.

Of course constitutional review was a more momentous undertaking than the private suits that ended in *paragraphai.* Lawmaking by its very nature seems to require a second decision, but in that conclusion the same principle applies. A two-stage process was required not because there was a separate question of procedural integrity that had to be decided apart from the merits of the legislation. These cases affecting constitutional rules (rights, remedies, offices, and obligations) required a second hearing—after the assembly decided, then again among the sworn—because the sovereign people came to recognize the duty of sober second decision.

The model was found in the "scrutiny" of officers. In authorizing laws and decrees just as in selecting archons, there should a second vote by a body of qualified jurors. Thus the major officers were vetted first in council and then in court, where any charges or challenges should be resolved. The model for enacting new nomos seems to proceed along the same lines: council and assembly should approve the bill, and then it must be ratified by a separate body of citizens who have sworn to respect the laws, either by *nomothetai* or in court.

Thus in constitutional cases a second decision was required not because issues of procedure and substance had to be set apart but because a community that valued self-awareness saw the need to vote in good conscience all over again, in a more sobering setting and with better guarantees that the verdict would represent the demos.

§4. The Framework of an Adaptive Process

In light of these findings on the body that swore to preserve the laws, it may be helpful at this point to fill in some of the timeline (introduced in the previous chapter) connecting the adaptations in lawmaking and jury assignment, to be further developed in the chapters ahead.

> *In 403/2 or soon afterward,* the restored democracy proceeded with a scrutiny of laws to restore old statutes that the Thirty had undone; law writers produced the text for council and assembly to approve. Teisamenos' procedure (or one like it) provided a template for new *nomoi,* to supplement the Solonian corpus and implement the Amnesty Agreement. These new constitutional rules had to be enacted by a jury of *nomothetai* who seem to have been chosen in some representative fashion by demes.

> *Circa 390, most probably,* on the model of Teisamenos' measure (or one like it) was devised the confirmation of the laws, or "vote of confidence" (*epichei-*

rotonia), as an annual process such as Demosthenes described in *Leptines* and *Timokrates*. This protocol required that novel legislation—any that overturned standing law—be initiated in the first prytany of the year and follow a prescribed schedule for public notice and deliberation, with final decision by *nomothetai* who had sworn the "heliastic oath." That protocol was considered sufficient to assure the integrity of the corpus. There was, as yet, no specific remedy against unfitting legislation (νόμον μὴ ἐπιτήδειον θεῖναι). A contentious bill should be rejected in the assembly or blocked by a conventional lawsuit (*paranomōn*) against the decree to convene *nomothetai*.

In the 380s, probably, the fast-track alternative emerged in which *nomothetai* decided (δεδόχθαι) upon changes in financial allocation or other practical adjustments to standing law (bypassing the confirmation). The lawsuit against unfitting legislation (γραφὴ νόμον μὴ ἐπιτήδειον θεῖναι) emerged by the end of the decade as a remedy against abuses of the fast track. It was designed as a safeguard against new legislation that stood in conflict with the corpus and had not proceeded through the confirmation protocol. In this period judges were chosen in regional hubs, but each section was assigned to its court by random drawing at the court center.

In the 370s and 360s, as arrangements for the Second League complicated the allocation of funds and administration of justice, bronze *pinakia* were introduced to identify those who had sworn the dikastic oath and were eligible for jury assignment. It was probably in this period that the allotment devices (*klērōtēria*) were moved to the city center to chose jurors for the year in tribal meetings. In legislation the fast track became standard and the annual vote for confirmation of the corpus fell into disuse.

In the 350s and 340s, conflict in the corpus required a special committee to sort out the contradictions and prompted Demosthenes and his allies to reinforce the confirmation process: by amendment or restatement of the law, *prytaneis* and presiders were now penalized if they left it off the agenda (as indicated in Dem. 24.22). And after the revival of the confirmation (by 340), the suit against unfitting law was adapted to it, allowing an alternative path to the second decision: a lawsuit to block the bill *before* it went to the *nomothetai* now proceeded to court and it was left to the jurors to enact the law (or not).

"Unlawful Acts" (Paranoma) *and the Case of the Arginousai Generals*

It is a terrible thing . . . if anyone shall bar the people from doing as they will.
—Xenophon, *Hellenika* (1.7.12)

Thus far we have examined the Athenian constitution "writ large" in the assemblies that framed the legislation (in chapter 1) and the juries that made the final decision (chapter 2). In this chapter we turn to the predicament of the individual who set these bodies in motion for it was up to the concerned citizen, taking his stand in council or assembly, to initiate legislation or to instigate legal remedies against it. Citizenship itself was subject to some revision in the course of the long war with Sparta, the downfall of democracy and its reconstruction, but those ad hoc adjustments do not seem to have affected the prevailing views on what made any citizen's initiative lawful or not. From the fifth century to the fourth the problem remains essentially the same: What rights can any constituent claim against the sovereign power of the people? That calculation becomes critical in the offices undertaken by any qualified citizen. What safeguards, after all, did the public servant have against reprisals for his official actions that proved unpopular? We might expect to find that reckoning spelled out in statutes, but it seems to lurk in the penumbra of various remedies.

At the heart of this chapter is the most notorious case of that sort from the late fifth century: the impeachment proceedings against the generals who returned victorious from Arginousai in 406, only to be executed for failing in their duty to rescue the shipwrecked and bring home the bodies.[1] For that case captures the quintessential problem of due process as a constitutional issue: When does the citizen's right to a fair trial trump the power of the people to decide his fate?

The evidence is not unambiguous and the inquiry is complicated by some old assumptions. It seems clear enough that there was no particular statute that guaranteed a court trial to each of the defendants.[2] Yet, fifty years after Arginousai, in the case against Aristokrates' decree, some of the same issues reappear (as we consider in the next chapter), and there the case is based, indeed, squarely upon the reading of particular statutes. That parallel has prompted legal historians to read back much the same statute-bound rationale into the Arginousai case, but the contemporary witnesses saw the problem somewhat differently.

§1. The Emergence of a Constitutional Remedy

It was once supposed that the *graphē paranomōn* was introduced (in some form) by Solon.[3] As Wilamowitz argued, the sworn challenge (*hypōmosia*) against a decree was essentially a form of appeal that must go back to the birth of the council as a steering committee for the assembly; the most common threshold for that challenge was the lack of council's approval, when the measure was introduced by some speaker on his own initiative (*aprobouleuton*) from the floor of the assembly. In principle, Wilamowitz was probably right: there must have been some constraint against unlawful acts of maverick leaders long before it became a mainstay of the democracy. But it does not look as though the classical procedure was born fully formed from the brow of Solon. Scholars in the century or so before 1970 generally supposed that the democratic remedy emerged in the 460s with the reforms of Ephialtes and Pericles (or soon thereafter):[4] previously the council of the Areiopagos had controlled the accountings of major officers, but that role was taken from them and assigned to the courts of the people. Of course, if that was the origin of the *graphē paranomōn,* we might readily suppose that its acknowledged aim was to guard the laws as the Areiopagos had done.[5] But even as that notion became conventional wisdom, Ulrich Kahrstedt reduced it to a paradox (as we noticed in chapter 1 §1). We know of no case that can be securely dated earlier than 415, more than forty-five years after Ephialtes gave the court of the people jurisdiction over the city's officers. And, as Kahrstedt argued, the function much acclaimed in the fourth century, to protect the laws from aberrant decrees, could only have arisen after 403, alongside the more rigorous procedure for making and maintaining *nomoi,* for it was only this perspective that made *laws* superior to decrees. To retroject that rationale back to the earliest cases is to suppose that the safeguard was invented before the hierarchy of rules it was designed to protect. Kahrstedt suggested that the suits described as *graphai paranomōn* in the era before 403 simply had a different function than to safeguard higher law—there was no higher law than the people's decree. The original aim of this remedy was to punish leaders of the people who misled or abused that power.

Kahrstedt's paradox was quickly discounted by others but, a generation later, it seems to have prompted Hans Julius Wolff to rethink the problem: If *graphē paranomōn* was introduced as a means of controlling unlawful acts by reference to some higher law—even before *nomoi* were superior to *psēphismata*—we should be able to find that higher law or the path to it.[6] Wolff had to agree that the introduction of *graphē paranomōn* finds its most plausible context not in the overthrow of the Areiopagos but in the post-Periclean era, when the first cases are attested. And in the one early case with a record of the argument, he found much the same path to higher law that litigants would follow in the fourth century.

Wolff's insight is still crucial to our understanding of Athenian judicial review, and we return to his findings in the conclusion to this chapter (§6). But first, in the following sections, let us carefully reconsider what our sources tell us about this test case (so to speak) and its aftermath, beginning with what little we know of its precedents.

The earliest securely attested case comes in 415, in the midst of the witch-hunt for those who mutilated the Herms and profaned the Mysteries. Andokides' father, Leogoras, was accused of attending some such parody (or unsanctioned ceremony), and he initiated a suit for unlawful acts against the councilman who accused him, Speusippos. Andokides described his father's suit as decided at trial before six thousand judges. Kahrstedt suggested that he was referring to a lawsuit for official wrongdoing against the councilman for his handling of a hearing before the council.[7] Wolff dismissed that approach,[8] but I think Kahrstedt was right to argue that early *graphai paranomōn* were often much like this one: a remedy against officers or citizens who overreached in some official capacity, who used the cloak of authority to infringe upon traditional rules. The procedure was not construed in the abstract, as defending prior laws against a new decree that contradicted them, but as an adversarial remedy, against the mover of a decree who abused that prerogative. And an abuse of that sort might not be easily reduced to a particular violation of statute.

In order to prosecute profaners of the Mysteries, Andokides tells us (1.17, 22), the council was made *autokratōr*, with full authority to conduct the investigation and hand down their verdict to a special court for final decision. Leogoras apparently made no complaint about that constitutional maneuver—there was nothing illegal in council's undertaking to bring an indictment in this way. Instead, Leogoras seems to have argued that the councilman abused his official authority by departing from the traditional way of investigating and framing the charges.[9] At least Andokides suggests that Leogoras won the point by challenging Speusippos to question his own slaves, to contradict the slave who testified against him. This sort of challenge would ordinarily apply in preliminary investigation, so it suggests that Speusippos proceeded unlawfully by producing an indictment on improper evidence—the information of a slave without threat of torture and uncorroborated by traditional forms of proof. These evidentiary rules may not have been encoded in statute, but they were a vital part of customary practice. There is no sign of a conflict between one text and another.

The only other *graphē paranomōn* earlier than Arginousai is represented in the fragments of a speech that Antiphon wrote against the general Demosthenes. This would be Demosthenes of Aphidna (*PA* 3585), who was prominent from the 420s until his death in 413 (in Sicily). The case could be as late as 415 supposedly, the same year as Leogoras' case against Speusippos.[10] But on historical grounds it probably belongs in the 420s. From the various references it seems reasonably clear that Antiphon's speech was written for the defense in a case that Demosthenes prosecuted, πρὸς τὴν Δημοσθένους γραφὴν ἀπολογίᾳ;[11] it was presumably this speech for the defense that Pseudo-Plutarch called πρὸς Δημοσθένη . . . παρανόμων (833D). These clues suggest that Demosthenes was impeached in the assembly for misconduct or dereliction, he brought suit against the decree as unlawful, and the author of the *psēphisma* then enlisted Antiphon to write the defense speech.

A likely occasion arose a decade earlier than Leogoras' case. After a disastrous campaign against the Aitolians in 426, as Thoukydides reports, Demosthenes was "afraid to face the Athenians" (3.98.5); for the infantry he had lost, he would be impeached on a charge of *prodosia*. Thereafter he regrouped and found the prospect of returning to Athens "less formidable" (3.114.1). The following year he was denied the generalship but had somehow survived the inevitable recriminations: as "a private citizen" he served as adjutant to Kleon in the campaign at Pylos (4.2.4). So the winter or spring of the year 426/5 was a likely context for Demosthenes to face impeachment for *prodosia* only to block the decree with a suit for unlawful action. On this view, Demosthenes' case would be roughly parallel to the one Euryptolemos contemplated in defense of the generals twenty years later.

§2. The Arginousai Case

In autumn of 406 the mightiest fleet that Athens could muster, under the joint command of eight generals, came to Lesbos to relieve Konon, who was bottled up by the Spartan fleet at Mitylene. What followed was described as the greatest victory on record of those pitting one Greek navy against another (Diod. Sic. 13.97–99). But after the battle was won, a storm came up and the Athenians failed to recover the survivors and the bodies of their comrades. And so the leaders of that "greatest victory" came home to face no hero's welcome but instead a tide of recrimination.

As Xenophon tells us, the assembly that sat in judgment of the generals was stacked against them, and Kallixeinos drafted the impeachment decree because he was bribed to do so by Theramenes.[12] This resourceful character was eager to shift blame from himself by stirring up resentment against his superiors. So he took advantage of the Apatouria festival to organize a show of mourning for those who had been abandoned at sea. And that sense of loss and frustration dominated the assembly that would condemn the generals without a proper trial.

The Athenians later repudiated the decree as unlawful, but our sources are not very clear about just what made it *paranomon*.[13] As Xenophon describes it, the process was anything but arbitrary. The assembly debated the matter at length; the defendants made a brief statement, presented witnesses, and nearly persuaded the people to leave them free on bail. But when it was almost dark and impossible to count hands in a close vote, it was decided that the council should draft a measure defining "the manner in which the men should be judged." So it was that Kallixeinos, as a member of council, introduced a decree for the assembled demos to judge the defendants summarily and en masse: "Let the Athenians all decide, casting their ballots tribe by tribe."[14]

Now Euryptolemos, a kinsman of one of the defendants (Pericles the younger), tried to block Kallixeinos' decree with a *hypōmosia*. Ordinarily that challenge-under-oath would be sufficient to block the decree until the court could decide. But then Lykiskos, one of the backers of Kallixeinos' decree, proposed that those who challenged the measure be judged by the same ballot as the accused "if they would not abandon their suit." Before there could be a vote on that amendment to the decree, evidently, Euryptolemos withdrew his challenge.[15] Instead he offered a competing proposal: let the defendants be tried separately according to the decree of Kannonos, a measure notorious for its severity. A vote was taken and Euryptolemos won, but that tally was challenged and, on a second vote, Kallixeinos' measure prevailed: in short order the generals were convicted and those in custody were put to death. Some months thereafter Kallixeinos himself was condemned (by *probolē*) for his role in the proceedings. And a few years later, after the democracy was overthrown and then again restored, Socrates could remark, as though it were incontrovertible, that the proceedings against the generals had been unlawful and everybody knew it.

But just what made it *paranomon*?

Kallixeinos' Offense

To be sure, the procedure that Kallixeinos prescribed was somewhat irregular: the body of the people was to cast ballots tribe by tribe; there was to be no proper trial by a jury in court. But deciding such cases in the assembly was not in itself unlawful, and in this case there were at least minimal safeguards: the balloting would assure an accurate count, and casting their ballots under the watchful eye of fellow tribesmen would discourage voter fraud. There were certainly sufficient grounds for Euryptolemos to challenge the decree as *paranomon* but, if that case had proceeded, Kallixeinos might have been vindicated in the end. The suit for *paranoma* would go to trial before a jury, and their verdict would either quash the decree or enact it; then, if the decree survived the court challenge, the voting would proceed just as Kallixeinos prescribed. And this case would never have become such a landmark of injustice.

What seems to have made the case so notorious was not one particular defect but the series of maneuvers to disable the traditional safeguards. Ordinarily the bill would be stalled until the suit against it could be resolved in court, but in this instance, that delay was preempted by the threat of Lykiskos' amendment.

How would this countermeasure have worked if Euryptolemos had not been intimidated into withdrawing his challenge? One might suppose that Lykiskos simply threatened Euryptolemos with *the same charge* as the generals, but that is not what the evidence indicates. There is no description of *prodosia* that would apply and no sign in the other known cases of anyone charged with *prodosia* for obstructing legal or political proceedings.[16] The term *prodosia* naturally refers to betraying or "giving up" ships, soldiers, or other assets; the specific instances attested conform to that legal meaning. Kallixeinos' proposal (*Hell.* 1.7.9–10) adhered to that usage: he charged the generals with "failing to recover" their comrades (οὐκ ἀνελόμενοι). And, evidently, Kallixeinos and his backers could not simply dismiss the *hypōmosia* by holding Euryptolemos liable for something else; in fact, if they were prepared to proceed in defiance of the rules for *graphai paranomōn*, there was no reason to force the challenger to withdraw his challenge at all.

Kallixeinos' proposal would have been effectively blocked until the suit for unlawful action could be decided if Lykiskos had not found a way to resolve it without delaying the main issue: his rider called for anyone who challenged the decree "to be *judged by the same ballot* as the generals, if they would not abandon their complaint" (τῇ αὐτῇ ψήφῳ κρίνεσθαι ᾗπερ καὶ τοὺς στρατηγούς, ἐὰν μὴ ἀφῶσι τὴν κλῆσιν). That is, if the assembly approved the measure with that addendum and Euryptolemos would not withdraw his challenge, his case would be given a hearing but the verdict would decide at once the legality of the decree and the fate of the generals. And their defender, who challenged the decree, would face the same jeopardy. Thus the charge against Kallixeinos for *paranoma* would have been decided by the very vote that he had prescribed for the generals (with ballots and urns, tribe by tribe), and Euryptolemos would face the same penalty prescribed for them. But, of course, rather than face that jeopardy, Euryptolemos withdrew his challenge, Lykiskos' rider proved unnecessary, and Kallixeinos' decree was approved and carried out.

After all, if not for defying the sworn challenge, the legalities were largely in Kallixeinos' favor. There was nothing unlawful in giving council a mandate to investigate and hand down an indictment; the councilors certainly abided by their oath to condemn to death no citizen without a quorum of the people. Euryptolemos could not point to any language in law that expressly barred or preempted the procedure that Kallixeinos prescribed. The measure was unconstitutional only in the most broadly positivistic sense: it went against the whole edifice of laws that the people had constructed. But that was not yet a rationale that the Athenians could readily articulate for themselves. Indeed—it is the epigraph to this chapter—those who sided with Kallixeinos objected that it was outrageous for any individual to thwart the corporate will of the people.[17]

From this perspective, the most brazen illegality comes with the move to short-circuit Euryptolemos' lawsuit, but even here the irregularity may not have been patently unlawful. The assembly regularly dictated arrangements for impeachment by decree, and it was probably not unusual to meet objections as Lykiskos did, with a rider to fix the procedure.[18] To decide both the challenge and the main issue by one vote seems in keeping with the usual assumptions: when a proposal of council was blocked before a vote of the assembly, a verdict against the *graphē paranomōn* would enact the decree.[19] With much the same expediency, Lykiskos' rider would combine the two cases: if the rider had been approved, the legality of the decree and the verdict on impeachment would have been decided by one vote; and if the generals were condemned, the same sentence would apply to Euryptolemos. That explanation makes better sense of the tactics; it is not meant to legitimize them. Perhaps the most damning wrong is the intimidation that forced a concerned citizen to abandon the challenge he had every right to make or risk execution for defying the demos.

The same coercive charge, of obstructing the will of the people, was sufficient to intimidate the presiding officers (all but Socrates). Even after the challenge was withdrawn, Xenophon tells us, some of the *prytaneis* refused to put Kallixeinos' proposal to the vote, and so he returned to the dais and "made the same charge against them" (κατηρόρει αὐτῶν τὰ αὐτά). That complaint, the same he had made against Euryptolemos, was not *prodosia* but instead obstructing the will of the people. Technically the chairmen would be charged with wrongdoing in office; when Plato's Socrates recalled that turn of events, he says he was threatened with the remedies proper to that offense, *endeixis* and *apagōgē* (*Ap.* 32b–c).

So the damning illegality in this fraught sequence is better understood in this way: it was not simply that the generals were denied a court trial but that the lawful recourse to a second decision was blocked by intimidation.

Euryptolemos' Alternative

In the midst of his narrative, Xenophon provides us with an account of the speech that Euryptolemos gave for his competing proposal, and much has been made of the constitutional implications in it. The rationale he offered was certainly consistent, at some level, with the positivism that Wolff found there. But this was not, after all, a speech for the prosecution in a suit against unlawful action, and it is at least as important to be clear about the differences. So let us carefully reconsider Euryptolemos' argument and the constitutional principles that are *not* embraced as well as those that seem to be recognized.

First of all, there was, as yet, *no rule that standing law trumped a decree.* Euryptolemos began with the *psēphisma* of Kannonos and only then turned to the nomos for treason and sacrilege, with no suggestion that the older law on treason took precedence. On the contrary, his alternative was built on the relatively recent decree, as though it superseded or qualified the older legislation.[20] For his proposal essentially followed the procedure that Kannonos had prescribed, adding only that the defendants be *judged* separately.

That is not to say that each had to be given "*a separate trial,*" if that meant each defendant would have his own day in court.[21] When Euryptolemos first invoked the decree of Kannonos (19), he acknowledged that this precedent allowed for punishing the culprits "all together or separately" (κολάσεσθε ᾗ ἂν βούλησθε δίκῃ, καὶ ἅμα πάντας καὶ καθ' ἕνα ἕκαστον). That formulation suggests that the several defendants might be tried as a group, but each defendant would stand apart,[22] make his own defense, and be given his own verdict. Thus, under Kannonos' decree, the assembly would hear the case and then vote, whether to "punish . . . all together" by one ballot or give separate verdicts. Euryptolemos proposed, essentially, to follow Kannonos but to eliminate the procedural vote and take the second option (κατὰ τὸ Καννωνοῦ ψήφισμα κρίνεσθαι τοὺς ἄνδρας δίχα ἕκαστον). He argued for that option without citing any guarantee in statute, that each defendant be judged on his own and not be damned by association. If there were any such provision in standing law, surely Xenophon would have had Euryptolemos spell it out.

And let us be clear about the trial procedure that he endorsed: *it was not a jury trial.* The decree of Kannonos called for defendants to make their defense in the assembly (20), ἀποδικεῖν ἐν τῷ δήμῳ. In that respect Euryptolemos seems to have conceded the point to Kallixeinos, that the people were entirely within their right to condemn their officers in this angry gathering of thousands. So Euryptolemos asked for no change of venue, although the other legal authority he cited, the law for treason and subversion, called for trial in the jury court.[23]

To be sure, he seems to have acknowledged that proper judges should be sworn and constrained by their oaths: he framed his proposal (25) by saying that, in this way, "you [Athenians] will give your verdict according to the law, reverent to gods and true to your oaths" (κατὰ τὸν νόμον εὐσεβοῦντες καὶ εὐορκοῦντες). Now, it is not unlikely that the mass swearing of the judges' oath was already in practice in the late fifth century (chapter 2 §1); if so, many of those assembled to decide the fate of the generals had already sworn to judge by the laws. But what Euryptolemos seems to mean is that the assembled citizens were already bound by oaths they had sworn in the course of their careers as citizen soldiers. They could only be true to those commitments by proceeding as he proposed: by separate verdicts they will acquit those who served honorably and punish only those responsible for the betrayal. For, again, in the very next clause, he insists that, by his proposal, "you will not be fighting on the side of the Spartans against those victorious comrades who seized seventy of the [enemy's] ships!" The damning implication was that those who sided with Kallixeinos in condemning the victors would be guilty of the very charge they brought against them! So the oaths that would naturally come to mind were those they had sworn in the course of their military service.

On this reading, what Euryptolemos insisted upon was not that the trial should be transferred to a jury court (where they would have to be true to the judges' oath) but, rather, that by a more scrupulous reckoning they (or many among them) be true to the oaths they were already bound by. After all, most of those present in the assembly in 406 would have sworn the oath prescribed in 410 against traitors and subversives.[24] And it seems reasonably certain that these men, upon entering military service, had sworn some version of the ephebic oath: not to break ranks but defend the fatherland. So the citizen soldiers who decided the fate of the generals had burdens enough without taking up the juror's staff.

In sum, the violation of nomos that Kallixeinos perpetrated was to condemn these men indiscriminately, in a rush to judgment—"What are you afraid of, to be driven by such urgency?" (25–6, τί δὲ καὶ δεδιότες σφόδρα οὕτως ἐπείγεσθε;). It is not a matter of the defendants' rights so much as the people's vital interest to avoid costly mistakes. There was certainly no presumption of innocence if the defendants were to plead their case in shackles. But there seems to be a strong conviction that each defendant should receive a proper hearing in the literal sense that he should be allowed to say his piece and be heard. That principle is proclaimed in the three-part agenda that Euryptolemos outlined (23): "there must be one period for prosecution and another for the defense," and only then do the judges decide upon a verdict. For those familiar with the regular trial procedure, it went without saying that the opposing arguments must be given equal time. That is the context where Euryptolemos drew the stark contrast between due process with arguments on both sides, κατὰ τὸν νόμον, and Kallixeinos' proposal to decide by one vote, παρὰ τὸν νόμον.

§3. Evolving Principle

In the years following the Arginousai case there was certainly a profound sense of the injustice, but it was not easy to define. After all, there was no foundational text that guaranteed trial by a jury of peers as a constraint upon the sovereign, as in Magna Carta. Of course, there was a Solonian rule that shielded citizens from the arbitrary decisions of magistrates with the right of appeal to the court of the people, comparable to the Roman's right of *provocatio*.[25] But at Athens, at least as late as 406, the right of appeal was construed strictly as a limit on official authority, not as a positive right that a citizen might invoke even against the demos itself. Euryptolemos argued that each defendant should be judged on his own account and this was what the nomos required, but he did not present any particular text that said just that. Instead he cited two statutes and one notorious precedent to suggest a rough principle of due process. By constructing the higher law in this way he seems to anticipate the argumentation of the fourth century; at least by the 350s, we can see that constitutional principles were regularly extracted from a list of relevant rules. But, as Wolff himself conceded, the deliberative arguments in 406 (for one decree against another) may not represent the typical reasoning at trial in a *graphē paranomōn* of that era. And Euryptolemos' argument is the only evidence we have suggesting that, before 403, constitutional principles were constructed from the wording of relevant statutes by a method that would be standard in the 350s.

A rather different meaning is indicated in other testimony from the late fifth century, and it was not lost thereafter. Long after nomos was adopted as the proper term for general statutes of permanent validity, it retained an archaic sense of customary practice or traditional role. Nomos often seems to describe the familiar path or range of activity by which a person in power dealt with someone subject to it.[26] Fifth-century use of *paranomon* is largely consistent with this essential idea: it often describes a transgression *ultra vires,* beyond one's proper role. The issue is certainly larger than any particular conflict between old statute and new decree, but it does not necessarily involve the corpus of "all the laws," where later litigators would find the decisive nomos. The evidence is largely consistent with Kahrstedt's basic observation: early *graphē paranomōn* was directed against those who abused their law-given powers. The remedy was not conceived as a constraint on the powers of the sovereign demos—on the contrary, the assembly of the people in 406 found it intolerable that the lawsuit should obstruct their will.

After all, the old notion that the *graphē paranomōn* was conceived as a constitutional safeguard was largely based on the assumption that it was introduced to confer upon the people's court the role of "guardian of the laws" that the Areiopagos had played. Wolff discounted that connection but argued in the same direction, that *graphē paranomōn* was conceived as a safeguard imposed upon the sovereign's power in the era of unbridled democracy. Yet even after the democracy was overthrown and resurrected, the Athenians do not seem to have embraced that principle, that the demos must be subject to some law beyond themselves.

Law and Decree in the Restoration Era

Soon after the warring parties were reconciled in 403, they brought out the old weapons of political infighting. The champion of the democrats, Thrasyboulos, tried to introduce a measure extending citizenship to all those who had fought alongside them, only to be thwarted by a lawsuit. In this era, even at the outset of the new democracy, decrees could alter the law in fundamental ways. Thus in regard to citizenship, alongside Thrasyboulos' failed decree, there were two others that succeeded (evidently), one that changed the law and then another that changed it back. First Nikomenes restored the old law but added a statute of limitations: once again, only those whose parents were both *astoi*—with rights recognized in their phratries—could claim citizenship (as in Pericles' law of 451);[27] but there would be no challenge to those who had established that status as of 403/2. And then in the same year, apparently, Aristophon amended the law to disqualify anyone born to a noncitizen mother, whatever the date of his enrollment. The latter was described as nomos (in *Athenaios* 577c), but it was probably enacted by the people's decree, just as Nikomenes' was. One decree superseded another.

In this way, the Athenians continued to make law—even basic law defining citizenship—as they had in the old democracy, by a vote of the people that differed little if at all from ordinary decrees. In the course of the next twenty years (or so) the two forms of legislation would diverge and the difference became categorical: nomos would be created and altered only by a more rigorous procedure. But even in this legislative ferment, so far as we can see, there was no new law to define the *rights and protections* of citizenship. When those rules came into question, it remained for the court to decide. The old remedy against aberrant decrees, against a councilman or assembly leader for unlawful action, would now invoke the basic law that decrees must not conflict with *nomoi*. And thus to safeguard citizenship thereafter, the Athenians laid down a law restricting the honorary grant of that status: citizenship could only be bestowed by ballot in a quorum of six thousand.[28] And yet, even in the fourth century, there seems to be little recognition that the safeguards should constrain the sovereign people rather than the reckless politicians.

Court Sovereignty and the Author's Liability

The conventional view of this remedy involves two connected assumptions: (1) the court could overturn any decree at any time, but (2) the mover was liable *only if* prosecuted within a year of his proposal.[29] If the demagogue who authored an unlawful measure could go unpunished, supposedly, the proper aim of *graphai paranomōn* was to protect the constitution. But the only clear case we have for that limit on liability belongs to the fourth-century suit for enacting an "unfitting law," the *graphē nomon mē epitēdeion theinai*. For centuries scholars supposed that there was no distinct procedure for wrongful laws as opposed to unlawful decrees, but now we are reasonably confident of the distinction (we examine the suits against unfitting law in detail in chapters 6–7). After a new nomos was enacted, it could still be challenged as unfitting, but if the trial was somehow postponed for a year, the author of the law was no longer liable. Such was the case against Leptines' law.[30] But we have no clear case of a *decree* that was indicted in this way, one that became the sole target of the lawsuit when the author was immune.

Of course, the secondary tradition often seems to assume that the same rule applied in suits against decrees as in suits against laws: from late antiquity the hypothesis to Demosthenes' speech *Against Leptines* claims that "the author of a law *or a decree* is not liable after one year" (τὸν γράψαντα νόμον *ἢ ψήφισμα* μετὰ ἐνιαυτὸν μὴ εἶναι ὑπεύθυνον). But as Kahrstedt recognized, the author of the hypothesis was probably generalizing from the case at hand, a case against an unfitting law.[31] So Wolff himself acknowledged in a footnote: the prospect of prosecuting the decree alone, when the mover was no longer liable, is not quite so probable as usually supposed.[32] After all, the suit against unfitting law belongs to the era when *nomoi* and *psēphismata* were formally distinct. Demosthenes explained the rules to guarantee the integrity of *nomoi* in this way (24.35–36): as these were permanent rules that the court must apply uniformly over time, it was vital to remove any laws that made conflicting demands, whenever they were discovered—if the judges were to be true to their oath. By contrast, most decrees targeted by *graphai paranomōn* in the fourth century had a limited time span or applied only to certain persons (targeted for penalties or honors). So the old assumption that the same limitation applied in suits against unlawful *decrees* as in the suits against unfitting *laws* may be merely a simplification by the rhetorician who drafted that hypothesis. And even if he is right about the law of the 350s, we have no reason to suppose that the time limit applied to wrongful decrees before it was recognized in suits against wrongful laws.[33]

The principle of author's liability, that the lawsuit was aimed at the erring politician, is indicated in the rule regarding a *probouleuma* that was blocked before it could be passed by the assembly and then came to trial more than a year later. Ordinarily, after a year the measure could no longer be enacted, as we learn from Demosthenes 23 (in the next chapter): Aristokrates authored a *probouleuma* giving special protection to Charidemos, but the measure was promptly challenged and never took effect because a preliminary decree of one year's council could not be enacted by the next. Nonetheless, at trial a year or so later, Demosthenes demands that the jury punish the mover of the decree. And if the mover could still be punished for a wrongful measure that was moot, surely he was not shielded from liability for a measure that actually took effect.[34]

Yet scholars had readily supposed that the mover became immune after a year, while the decree could still be overturned, on the assumption that the remedy was conceived to maintain the integrity of the rules and punishing the unlawful actor was incidental. There may have been few such cases, but the likely explanation is just the reverse: there was no *statutory* limit on the mover's liability, but there was a *practical* limitation on quashing the decree. Most decrees enacted in the assembly were promptly implemented and, ordinarily, those enactments could not then be overturned in court. Indeed, many of the decrees targeted by *graphai paranomōn* would be irreversible once they were carried out—as in the case of the Arginousai generals.

As the early cases suggest, this remedy was designed to block the author of an unlawful act from putting it into action. And among the later cases, that is the best rationale in the one instance that suggests a time limit of some sort: Demosthenes in *Aristokrates* §§103–5 refers to a decree of the late 360s that undermined Athenian interests in Thrace; by the time the wrong was recognized, it was too late to undo the disaster by prosecuting the author of the decree.[35]

To be sure, there are two cases soon after democracy was restored where, supposedly, the trial came some months after the decree was implemented. The first was the suit against Thrasyboulos for his proposal to grant citizenship to all who joined the democrats in Peiraieus. If the decree had taken effect, only to be later overturned in court, that would explain how Lysias could act as a citizen against Eratosthenes (soon after 403) but hold no such status thereafter. But, in fact, Lysias did not have to be a citizen to make his complaint.[36] In the speech Lysias emphasized how he was victimized as a resident alien (a metic) and never suggested that his status had changed. Ps.-Plutarch's testimony (835F–36A), that Thrasyboulos' decree was quashed because it was *aprobouleuton* (without council's approval) would suggest that it was challenged at the first opportunity, immediately after it passed in the assembly, so the grant of citizenship never took effect.

The second case involved a decree most plausibly dated to the same year or soon after:[37] the *graphē paranomōn* against Theozotides for a measure benefitting the orphans of those who fought for democracy. Only "rightly born" sons (*gnēsioi*) need apply; bastards and adopted sons, *nothoi* and *poiētoi*, get nothing. In the fragments of Lysias' speech we find reference to a measure affecting the cavalry corps, a decision that had passed and taken effect sometime prior to the speech. Hansen supposed that the two measures were part of the same spending decree; so here again, supposedly, we have a decree prosecuted sometime after it was implemented.[38] But as Stroud argued when he published the inscription, the cavalry measure probably had nothing to do with funding for the orphans. Lysias mentioned the cavalry decree as a *fait accomplí*, not at issue in the current case but simply another example of Theozotides' arrogance. Thus, as the relevant fragments would naturally suggest, the suit *paranomōn* was directed against the orphans decree before it could take effect.

In sum, among the early cases there is no clear instance where the court overturned a decree after it was implemented. In the later fourth century there may have been cases where a decree was overturned after it was ratified and briefly became valid, but such action would succeed only against honorific decrees with limited effect. And if there were such cases in the later period, they would reflect the ideology of that time and not necessarily the original rationale. The early cases, where decrees were as potent as the laws, point to a different idea: the decree can only be overturned by attacking the mover in the very act of abusing that power.

Paranoma and *Hybris*

In the prosecution speeches, the author of the targeted measure was portrayed as unlawful, *paranomos,* in all his actions. This sort of offender threatened a constitution that encompassed customary roles—τὰ τῆς πολιτείας ἔθη, as Demosthenes called them.[39] These were seen as largely unwritten rules about asserting rightful authority. An "unlawful act" was an abuse of authority by an official who overreaches. And even fifty years after the Arginousai case, Demosthenes' arguments suggest that *paranomon* was still understood in this way: it was sometimes synonymous with *hybris.*

A similar standard can be found in the fragments of Lysias' speech *Against Theozotides,* within a year or so after the restoration of democracy. As we noticed, Theozotides proposed that the sons of those who fought to restore democracy be honored and supported by the polis, but that largesse applied only to the legitimate sons; illegitimate and adopted offspring were excluded. Lysias seems to argue that this would be contrary to custom and civic duty, οὔτε νομίμως οὔ[θ' ὁσίω]ς (line 7), as it was precisely the disadvantaged who deserved support. We have no way of knowing whether he took a more text-bound approach in lost sections of the speech, but there is a sign of his strategy in a section that survives largely intact (§2). Lysias' client could not quite argue that Theozotides' bill contradicted prior statute, but he did contend that "it will slander the finest proclamation in the laws and render it a fraud" (τὸ κάλλιστον τῶν ἐν τοὶς [νόμο]ις κήρυγμα . . . διαβαλεῖ καὶ ψεῦδος καταστήσει): when the herald proclaims at the Dionysia that "these are the boys whose fathers died in war," is the herald to explain that only the legitimate (*gnēsioi*) are represented, or will he lie and speak of "all the orphans"? "Isn't this *hybris* and a great slander [against the city]?" (Ταῦτα οὐχ ὕβρις καὶ μεγάλη διαβολή). Later in the speech Lysias charged that Theozotides had shown similar arrogance in his decree cutting pay for the cavalry (col. II), which had little relevance except to illustrate a lawless career. So the arguments that survive from this case are at least consistent with the line of attack against Androtion (in chapter 5): the lawlessness offends against a way of life.

And this construction seems largely consistent with the foundation that Euryptolemos built upon. It seems the only viable response when the people protested against his challenge, that it was "a terrible thing if anyone [person] shall bar the people [as a body] from doing as they will" (δεινὸν . . . εἰ μή τις ἐάσει τὸν δῆμον πράττειν ὃ ἂν βούληται). To answer that slogan, he argued that the people must look to their own interests and commitments and not be misled into grievous error.[40] Euryptolemos condemned the rush to judgment (26), but the nomos that he defended was not a barrier of text that the demos had imposed upon itself. He seems rather to have regarded it as an ethological imperative for the demos to be true to their character. That is to say, like any creature in nature, the body of the people has a characteristic set of behaviors: if they stray from that path, they blunder into disaster. It is an appealing argument, however often it ignores history.[41]

After all, as Ostwald observed, the early usage presents its own paradox. The nomos in *paranomon* naturally conveys the prescriptive sense that emerged with Kleisthenes: *nomoi* are statutes.[42] Yet, long after the Athenians typically thought of written laws as *nomoi*, even in the last decades of the fifth century, this positivistic sense of the word was largely overshadowed by the older value: "the nomos violated constitutes a general code of behavior."[43] This was the prevailing pattern of usage for Thoukydides and his contemporaries. Thus in Antiphon's speech *On the Murder of Herodes*—within a few years of the case against Leogoras—the defendant objects to what he regards as an improper procedure (insisting that the case should be tried by the traditional homicide court), yet he does not claim that any specific statute was violated; rather, the *paranomon* consisted in a procedure contrary to the customary recourse against accused murderers (12, 15). The denial of bail, which this defendant protests as "most unlawful" (*paranomōtata*, 17), did not expressly contradict any wording of law but went against customary practice.

This traditional sense of *paranomon*, as violating customary roles and rules, is probably the original value of that term in the law for *graphē hybreōs* (Dem. 21.47; Aeschin. 1.15) and in the law against abuse of widows and orphans (Dem. 43.75). For our inquiry it matters little whether the *hybris* laws were enacted under Solon or Pericles:[44] even as late as 430, *paranomon* would naturally convey an act contrary to customary practice, not necessarily a violation of statute. And it is that sense that complements the main designation of the crime: in each version, *hybris* and *paranomon* seem to be alternative descriptions of the same act, ἐάν τις ὑβρίζῃ . . . ἢ παράνομόν τι ποιήσῃ.

The debate over the moral range of *hybris* is beyond our scope, but I think the preponderance of the evidence suggests that, as an actionable offense, *hybris* involved the demonstrable intent to dishonor (as Nick Fisher argued); that is, the violator asserted his superiority improperly, aiming to humiliate the victim and take satisfaction in it. The law's description of the offense, "if anyone commits *hybris* or does something *paranomon*," has always been puzzling: if we assume that *paranomon* essentially refers to any violation of statute, it is tempting to regard it as a later addendum to the law. But if we recognize the overlap in these two traditional ideas, the wording makes good sense as a sort of legal hendiadys in the original formulation of a concept that was hard to define. Indeed, Hans van Wees has argued persuasively that "the 'law of *hybris*' was . . . the law by which Solon established the [*graphē*] procedure for a whole range of offences."[45] Thus *hybris* and *paranomon* together describe transgressions of customary roles and rules. In any such action a person of greater strength or authority abuses that advantage against a subordinate or vulnerable figure. Even in the mid-fourth century (as in the case against Androtion), speakers often invoked that linkage between the two terms.

This ethological sense of *paranomon,* as an act against norms of behavior, would fit the earliest cases of the *graphē* (of those securely dated). Much as Kahrstedt observed, the common element in Leogoras' case against Speusippos and Euryptolemos' challenge to Kallixeinos seems to be that the councilman who moved the decree was abusing his power by stepping outside the proper path for legal proceedings. Speusippos indicted a citizen upon the information of a slave, without the threat of torture or corroborating evidence that custom required. Kallixeinos would have the people decide the fate of their generals without allowing a proper defense. For a councilman to neglect traditional constraints in this way, to victimize those subject to his authority, was readily seen as *paranomon.*

In the speech Xenophon has given him, Euryptolemos built on this model but had to adapt it beyond its usual scope. As the *graphē* against Kallixeinos was withdrawn and the Athenians were faced with competing proposals, the charge of unlawful action, *paranomon,* was not formally at issue, but it remained the strongest weapon in his arsenal. The situation then required that he apply that argument to the Athenians as a body, largely disregarding the culpability of Kallixeinos. So, in his assertions about what was according to nomos or against it, κατὰ τὸν νόμον or παρὰ τὸν νόμον, he focused upon previous measures that illustrated the ordinary practice of the Athenians—what they had usually and properly done in trying citizens for treason and other high crimes. Much as Wolff observed, Euryptolemos constructed a broader principle from law and precedent, in a manner that prefigured the formative cases of the 350s.

§4. A Glimpse of the Constitution

In §23, Euryptolemos demands that the Athenians choose between two statutory models, the decree of Kannonos and the treason law.[46] By one statute or the other, he says, "let the men be judged *by the law.*" He never quite articulates the common principle; instead, he seems to take it for granted that his audience would recognize the nature of their obligation. And at the end of this argument he gives a clear indication of how that imperative was understood: "Keep guard over the laws that are properly yours—for it is especially on their account that you are [at your] greatest—and take no action without them."[47]

This is his clearest assertion that violating the law in this instance went against the "Rechtsordnung als Ganzes," as Wolff would call it. To describe this package of laws as an asset that was peculiarly their own (ἑαυτῶν ὄντας) suggests a property they held title to (cf. *Hell.* 2.4.38; 7.4.12). By contrast, a positivistic model, whereby the law is what the sovereign has asserted, was certainly recognized, but that was closer to the demands of Kallixeinos and his backers. The principle of restraint that Euryptolemos embraced was, rather, governed by tradition. The sovereign body must follow its own dictates, not because the law that is once laid down is forever binding, but because the people must maintain what belongs to them, as though obligated by some inherited estate or shared enterprise.

Leading up to this climactic formulation, Euryptolemos cited the one precedent of recent memory, the treason trial of Aristarchos (28). Aristarchos had been involved in the regime of 411 and was accused of betraying the border town Oinoe to the Thebans.[48] In that case, Euryptolemos recalls, "You allowed him a whole day to make his defense however he chose, and in other regards [as well] you disposed of the matter according to law" (κατὰ τὸν νόμον); but the generals "you will deprive of these very things." Now, the decision about how to try Aristarchos was itself a decree, a third statute that Euryptolemos might have cited if he were constructing nomos strictly from legal text. Instead he treated the decree as subject to some prior imperative. And it is that recent precedent that led to the climactic demand, "Keep guard over the laws that are properly yours . . . and take no action without them." That injunction suggests that the Athenians were guided by a code of rights and duties they could not abandon without betraying themselves. It was not the law because the people so decided; the people should so decide because it was their law.

In the decades leading up to this crisis the Athenians had violated that inherited principle of due process, but not without recriminations. In 411 the chorus of old men in *Lysistrata* besiege the women who have seized the acropolis, and they vow to punish instigators and followers alike, "by one vote" (*Lys.* 268–70). It is not a flattering portrayal and probably reflects upon familiar abuses. Thus Antiphon (5.69–70) some years earlier, mentions a rush to judgment in the case of imperial treasurers (*hellenotamiai*) who were executed (all but one) before evidence was brought to light proving their innocence. Both passages suggest that the Athenians regretted their rash decisions, though they could not yet hear the qualms of conscience that Socrates would give voice. Euryptolemos, urging the demos to preserve "the laws that are properly yours," did not dare to go beyond traditional ideas. Xenophon recognized how historic a moment it was, but what seems to have made Euryptolemos' construction memorable was the way he applied an old principle in a new way. An act *paranomon* was conventionally understood as a relational wrong, like *hybris*. It was the crime of a man in power abusing his authority over others; it was wrong because it violated the traditional rules that defined his role. Euryptolemos could only suggest that the same principle should apply to the sovereign people. By the 350s, that connection linking the ethological imperatives of the people to those of their officers would become a mainstay of constitutional argument.

§5. The Struggle with Due Process (down to 359 BC)

The impeachment procedure that prevailed against Euryptolemos' challenge would continue to be used in much the same way for decades. The proceedings often began in the assembly, with the "vote of confidence" (*epicheirotonia*) that was called in each prytany. Against generals or other public officials accused of treason, corruption, or deception of the people, any concerned citizen could introduce his charges in council or directly in the assembly and call for the demos there convened to decide the fate of those officers. They might properly decree for the case to be decided by a jury, but in many instances they heard the testimony (such as it was) and decided the case outright without court trial.[49] Such was the fate of Timagoras in 367, executed for his role as ambassador to the Great King. Likewise Kallisthenes, one of the generals of 363/2, was executed for treason (*prodosia*) in negotiating too generous a truce with Perdikkas of Macedon. More fortunate was his colleague Ergophilos, accused of betraying the Thracian Chersonesos: he was condemned in the assembly, without court trial, but sentenced to a hefty fine (in 362).

In some cases, of course, we do not know how the case was handled or how the defendants fared, though the connected cases do not bode well for them. Thus Autokles, one of the generals of 362/1, was indicted by Apollodoros of Acharnai on a charge of treason or dereliction in his official duties (*prodosia*). And Timomachos of Acharnai, a general of 361/0, was impeached in the assembly by his fellow demesman Apollodoros (the same who attacked Autokles) for betraying Athenian interests in the Thracian Chersonese, for which Kallisthenes and Ergophilos were condemned without trial two years earlier; Timomachos was sentenced to death in *absentia*.[50]

After 360/59, the catalog of known cases includes none where the evidence indicates summary judgment in the assembly (without a jury trial). Weighing the knowns against the uncertainties, it seems reasonable to conclude that in this critical period, whether by constitutional reform or simply by evolving practice, we witness a shift away from the autocratic principle that we saw in the Arginousai case. By the old path, impeachment led to execution whenever the demos so decided. In the new model, it was either prescribed by law or simply presumed that such cases required a proper trial before the court. As though coming to their maturity at last, the Athenian people seem to have adopted some restraint upon their sovereign power to punish the leaders who disappointed them.

§6. The Evolving Argumentation

So far as we can see, *graphē paranomōn* emerged in the era of radical democracy, when the people's assembly had unfettered authority. Over time it became a diagnostic tool to discover what the body politic required. As Wolff described it, the nomos that *graphē paranomōn* defended was the corpus of laws to which any particular legislation was integral, and the only way to discover what that body of law demanded was by interpreting particular statutes.[51] In the Arginousai case, for instance, the decree of Kannonos did not in itself prohibit the procedure that Kallixeinos proposed; it stood for a connected body of rules that had to be preserved. As Wolff explained it, the disparity between fifth-century and fourth-century arguments is largely a matter of technique. In the later period, the framing of higher principle became more sophisticated. But even at the height of their powers the fourth-century authors could not escape from the well-worn path: they must find the principle from a list of statutes. Demosthenes and his contemporaries never gained a footing beyond the litany of text at the level of constitutional rules, such as due process that one might invoke as a higher principle and then apply deductively to the case at hand.[52] After all, there was no body of legal experts to formulate such super-statutory rules. Instead in each case, the prosecutor of an unlawful measure had to construct his foundation anew, reasoning inductively from the particular wording and practical implications of relevant statutes (and some not so relevant).

> As surely as they could extricate themselves from bondage to the express wording, even so their conception of the *paranomon* remained fixed upon the idea of conflict with the particular provisions examined in isolation. Regardless of the fact that invariably the result was in each case the same and, moreover, always on similar grounds, they apparently knew no other method than to proceed from one statutory provision to another, in tiresome monotony, always describing how [each provision] stood in conflict with the indicted measure *ab initio* and without reference to the others. (*"Normenkontrolle"* 66)

This finding involved two adjustments to the older constitutional model: (1) The principles invoked by the Athenians against unlawful measures were neither constructed nor applied in quite the same way as modern judicial review; it was a rough approximation. (2) There was no real change in the rationale, but there was, as Wolff describes it, a *continuous development in argumentation,* from a more radical positivism toward rationalized control. Under the new regime the two remedies in tandem, against unlawful acts and unfitting law, "could develop into an instrument capable of realizing, to some extent, the ideas that support the judicial review of modern constitutional law."[53] In this perspective on the argumentation, Wolff's study remains compelling, and his way of defining the issue has been widely accepted and adapted.[54] He suggested that there is an essential continuity linking the arguments of 406 and the classic case of 352/1, Demosthenes' *Against Aristocrates.* In Demosthenes' speech the approach that Euryptolemos took is fully developed ("zu voller Entfaltung gelangt"). It is not different in kind but more advanced in technique. From its inception in the post-Periclean era, *graphē paranomōn* was meant to defend the law as an inviolable body of rules. In the fourth century that body of rules was more clearly identified with the corpus of all the laws (as reauthorized in 403 and expanded thereafter), but the juristic rationale was much the same as its original inspiration: it came of "the recognition that the Athenian democracy required, for its own preservation, a certain self-imposed restraint."[55]

But there is a distinction with a difference, as I have tried to show in this chapter and those that follow: In the earliest cases it looks as though the lawsuit against *paranoma* was seen as a remedy against leaders who abused their authority, a safeguard in defense of particular victims. It was only in the course of its later evolution that this remedy (and its sequel) came to be seen as a mechanism for "second decision," a safeguard to assure that the sovereign people thought twice about what their rules and traditional roles required.

PART II

THE CONSTITUTIONAL WINDOW

CHAPTER FOUR

Privileged Characters

Aristokrates' Shield for Charidemos

> If anyone among you knows which is the house of Themistokles or of Miltiades or any of the famous figures of their day, he can see that it is no more impressive than the homes of most of us. But the city's buildings and facilities [of that era] were of such size and quality as to leave no scope for later generations to outdo them. . . . In those days the demos was lord over the politicians; now it is their underling. And the ones responsible are the authors of decrees like this one, training you to despise yourselves and admire one or two persons.
>
> —Demosthenes, *Against Aristokrates* (207–10)

Fifty years after the Arginousai case, the Athenians were once again trying to salvage a foundering empire and they resorted to dubious decrees to deal with their disappointments. Just up the coast from Lesbos, the peninsula called Chersonesos (on the European side of the Hellespont) had long been crucial to the Athenian grain supply and to naval operations in the north Aegean. As the Second League fell apart, the Chersonesos fell prey to Thracian princes, and the Athenians found allies wherever they could. One such "friend indeed" was Charidemos, a mercenary leader from Euboia, whom the Athenians employed with some success, then made a citizen (ca. 357),[1] and thereafter elected general (*stratēgos*). At some point in this sequence, Aristokrates proposed an especially protected status for this mercurial and well-connected character: in effect, anyone who might kill Charidemos anywhere within the alliance could be forcibly arrested and brought to Athens for retribution, and any person or community that refused to give him up was ousted from the alliance.[2] Evidently the decree did not specify what proceedings would follow upon the arrest,[3] and that vagary opened the door to a lawsuit.

There were no express guarantees that anyone who killed Charidemos justifiably (or accidentally) could claim the protections of law, and thus the decree might be construed as an open-ended license to deal with the killer summarily, without proof or due process. It seemed to override a host of laws, those regarding the treatment of known and suspected homicides as well as the rules regarding the reach of legislation, that no decree can supersede a law and no law can privilege particular persons. But that construction is probably not what Aristokrates intended or what most Athenians would have assumed. On any straightforward reading, this was an imperial decree of the people asserting jurisdiction in what they still regarded as their province; it was especially directed to those *poleis* or disaffected parties among the alliance who might shelter an enemy of Athens. And, on that reading, it is tempting to dismiss the arguments that Demosthenes devised for the lead prosecutor, Euthykles, as pandering to a particular faction. Indeed, even Wolff had to acknowledge that the political baggage in this case might have outweighed the legalities.

The points of law require a fair reading on their own, and it will be helpful to bear in mind the overarching concern: what Wolff described as "the unalterable principle which affords to every defendant the right to have the questions of fact and penalty decided at trial."[4] That is the question of due process that has loomed so large since the Arginousai case, and yet now, more than half a century later, it becomes all the more clear: there was no constitutional statute that guaranteed to every defendant a court trial, even in capital cases, if the people in their assembly decided otherwise.[5] Once again the principle has to be constructed from a litany of provisions on particular instances where the original intent and lasting implications are often obscure. We take up that exegesis in the main sections of this chapter (3–5), but to lay the groundwork, let us begin with two connected puzzles: (1) piecing together the career of Charidemos to understand the timing of the lawsuit, and (2) sorting out the composite text of this speech, to see how the patchwork came together.

§1. The Sequence of Events

The date of the speech is reported by Dionysios of Halikarnassos in a professorial essay on the development of fourth-century rhetoric:[6] he assigned the case to the same year as the *First Philippic*, 352/1. That date follows comfortably upon the events discussed in the speech itself, and it is important for understanding the way Demosthenes' argument took shape. But our inquiry is complicated by the dubious sequence of Athenian decisions affecting Charidemos in the course of his remarkable career. The basic question is whether he rose to the highest office in one spectacular leap or several giant steps. In modern scholarship it has been sometimes assumed that he was made an Athenian citizen and chosen general in short order, as much as eight to ten years before the case against Aristokrates,[7] circa 361/0. The more recent and more reasonable conclusion is that he was enfranchised circa 357/6 and elected general a few years later. The later date for citizenship seems solid, but the sequence of events before and after remains doubtful, and the connection between those other honors and Aristokrates' decree may be crucial to the argument.

The Charidemos in question is a character to inspire the imagination.[8] He was not a favorite son of the Athenian elite who might expect to play a prominent role in their affairs. He was not even an Athenian by birth but a native of Oreos in Euboia, and he was (allegedly) a *nothos*, not the offspring of lawful marriage, who may never have acquired citizenship in his birthplace. In his early career he hired on as a mercenary among the light-armed and lower-class warriors, slingers, and peltasts, in the era when this agile force was used with such success by Iphikrates. Thereafter Charidemos operated somewhat more profitably as a pirate, plundering the allies of Athens—or so Demosthenes said (23.148–49). In the 360s, he was hired by Iphikrates himself and served under him for three years in the north Aegean (down to 364). It was then, when Iphikrates was replaced by Timotheos, that Charidemos gambled on a risky alliance with Thracian leaders: rather than serve with Timotheos, he released the hostages that Athens held for leverage at Amphipolis and promptly went over to the Thracian king Kotys (lord of the Odrysai). It may have been at this juncture (late 360s) that Charidemos married into the royal family (as Iphikrates did) and became brother-in-law to Kotys' son and successor Kersobleptes.[9]

The maneuvers of this Charidemos become all the more obscure thereafter, and none of the documents that might have shed light upon this period are preserved in the speech. In 359/8 we find him in control of some towns in the Troad, opposite the Chersonesos, but besieged by the Persian satrap Artabazos. In that predicament, Charidemos sent a letter to the Athenian commander Kephisodotos offering to restore all of Chersonesos to the Athenians in return for their assistance.

It was then (presumably later in the year 359) that Demosthenes' client, Euthykles of Thria, made his mark in the court battles over Thracian policy. He had been a trierarch under Kephisodotos and now promptly prosecuted him for *prodosia* over some failing in the course of that campaign; he may have argued that negotiating with Charidemos was somehow a betrayal.[10] It was in this case, evidently, that the alliance between Euthykles and the speechwriter began, as the young Demosthenes joined the prosecution as *synēgoros*. But, if they did attack Charidemos at this early stage, their arguments on that score were not nearly so successful as they were against Kephisodotos; for the Athenian general was convicted and fined five talents, narrowly avoiding a death sentence, whereas Charidemos was rewarded with citizenship in 357/6 and conspicuous distinctions thereafter.

The award of citizenship was no small honor in itself and, from the end of the fifth century, the Athenians had adopted more rigorous constraints against freely dispensing that status. As Apollodoros would put it (about a decade after the case at hand), the question of granting citizenship was one that especially focused the Athenian sense of constitutional restraint: "The Athenian people, though possessing absolute authority over everything in the city and able to do whatever it wishes, believed that the grant of Athenian citizenship was such a noble and solemn gift that it imposed laws on itself defining terms on which one must admit a man as citizen, if they so wish."[11] In the case against Aristokrates we meet with similar sentiments on the sanctity of the franchise (esp. 200–201), and Euthykles has to anticipate the objection that if he felt so betrayed by Charidemos, he should have spoken up against granting him citizenship. Those reflections only go to show that the case at hand must have come after he became a citizen, when that status was no longer at issue. The privilege that Euthykles attacks is the special protection.

So, Aristokrates' decree, to shield Charidemos from assassination, came sometime after the grant of citizenship, but it is not so clear how long after. Demosthenes introduces his narrative by recapping the rivalry between Kersobleptes and the other Thracian princes, who had their own champions (8–14). It was at that juncture, amid the jostling for power after Kotys died, that an interested Athenian, Aristomachos of Alopeke, spoke up for Kersobleptes and his commander Charidemos, claiming that only the latter could restore Amphipolis (west of Chersonesos) to Athenian control. To this end Aristomachos proposed that Charidemos be made general, and Demosthenes suggests that the scheme for protected status was somehow connected to this promotion. The council's *probouleuma* was drafted on that occasion, but the proposal was promptly challenged, before the demos could ratify it; after that council's year ended, the bill became moot.[12]

It is often supposed that the decree for special protection came *after* Charidemos was elected to the generalship, as that sequence seems to fit the tenor and focus of the speech: from beginning to end, Demosthenes rails against this privileged status as the last and most dangerous step toward abdicating what was left of the people's power and dignity. But that sequence—supposing that the privileged status came *after* Charidemos was made general—goes against Demosthenes' express testimony (§14) and defies the logic of such honors.

In fact, the view that Aristokrates made his proposal in 353/2 (the year before Dionysios' date for the speech) seems to be based largely on the assumption that the indictment must have come *no more than* a year after the proposal; for the speech threatens Aristokrates himself with severe penalties, and it has been commonly assumed that the mover of a decree became immune to prosecution a year after his measure was introduced (as the author of a nomos was). But that assumption is based upon late-ancient confusion: the limitation, making the author immune after a year, clearly applies to *nomoi,* laws in the strict sense;[13] it proves doubtful whether or when the limitation applied to decrees. And in this very case Euthykles insisted that he was out to punish Aristokrates and make an example of him for trying to dupe the people in the interest of a well-connected group, even though the decree itself was no longer viable. In this respect, the suit against unlawful acts (*paranomōn*) was still essentially a weapon against the wrongful actor.

After all, the logic of such honors would suggest that the bill to protect Charidemos must have come *before* he became general. Demosthenes, as he frames the issues in the prologue, indicates precisely that sequence: the faction allied with Kersobleptes "were looking for some way to compel his rivals to keep quiet, [so that] . . . Charidemos, acting as an officer for Kersobleptes (Κερσοβλέπτῃ πράττων τὴν ἄρχην), might subject the whole area to him." To that end they conceived a two-stage campaign: "*First* there should be a decree of the people (ὑμέτερον ψήφισμα), 'if anyone kill [Charidemos], he be subject to arrest'; and *second,* if Charidemos were elected general by you [the demos], neither Simon nor Bianor would readily take up arms against him as your general."[14] Demosthenes suggests that the two initiatives were part of the same plan, to make Charidemos an unassailable instrument of Kersobleptes and his Athenian backers. But it seems rather more likely that they seized upon the generalship when the first gambit failed, for the second option makes the first superfluous: once Charidemos became general, none of the other commanders active in this Thracian conflict, neither Bianor and Simon (serving Amadokos) nor Athenodoros (serving the sons of Berisades), would dare to assassinate him as they were also Athenian citizens, subject to regular review and eager to keep the city's backing.

The imputation, that the advancement of Charidemos was all about weakening the rivals of Kersobleptes, was (as we shall see) crucial to the strategy that Demosthenes devised. Here, in introducing that idea, he treats the proposal for protected status as prologue to the generalship: the competitors would not want "to face the charges framed by Aristokrates' decree, which was clearly aimed at them."[15] Thereafter he introduced Aristomachos as an Athenian acting as "ambassador" for a particular faction of the Thracians, urging his countrymen to promote Charidemos to the generalship, assuring them that only he could win back Amphipolis (13–14). Demosthenes pictured that campaign for the generalship amid the early hostilities among Thracian rivals, and that should take us back sometime before 353/2. The decree of Aristokrates must have been introduced even earlier.

That timing is also indicated later in the speech, where Demosthenes tries to justify prosecuting what might seem a pointless lawsuit: even though it was quashed, Arisokrates' *probouleuma* so favored Charidemos as Kersobleptes' champion that it intimidated those serving the rival kings, rendering the latter weak and the former the stronger (103). Thereupon, for contrast, Demosthenes recalls the decree that threatened Miltokythes (after he rebelled against Kotys, 362/1), a measure that was *not* blocked but was enacted and implemented: when the reckoning came, "the time for a lawsuit against the mover of the decree had passed, and the damage to the city's cause had been done" (104). This passage is often cited as the one clear instance where the author of a decree became immune after a year, but that conclusion misses the point of the comparison—and relies on some dubious scheduling.[16]

The decree against Miltokythes worked against Athenian interests, and the Athenians had to reverse course: Autokles, the general who was sent against Miltokythes, was deposed from office and punished by *eisangelia* (as noted in chapter 3 §5). But by then it was too late to undo the setback to Athenian arms and influence. That sequence of events does not require the delay of more than a year that scholars have seized upon to save their assumptions: ordinarily, a general deposed from office (by *apocheirotonia*) would be promptly indicted, and that would put the case well within a year of the decree that sent Autokles on his ill-conceived campaign. After all, the best sense of Demosthenes' cautionary tale is simply that the policy was reversed and at least one of those complicit was punished, but it was too late to block the decree and prevent the damage. The earlier example thus served to vindicate the lawsuit against Aristokrates, which did indeed quash the decree before it could do more damage to Athenian interests.

There is much omitted in that comparison (103–5), but it is at least clear that the decree to shield Charidemos was proposed when he was acting for Kersobleptes (τῷ μὲν ἡγουμένῳ τῶν Κερσοβλέπτου πραγμάτων ἀσφάλειαν διδόν) and not yet installed as a general for Athens. For that scenario, the best window of opportunity would come in the mid-350s, along with the grant of citizenship. To be sure, Demosthenes treats the two subsequent honors, generalship and special status, as items on the same agenda; yet, more likely, the one was seized upon when the other failed. The decree for privileged status was quashed, but the second option, the campaign to give Charidemos the generalship, ultimately succeeded.

So I suggest that Aristokrates' decree for privileged status was part of an earlier plan. Sometime before Charidemos was actually elected to the generalship, perhaps soon after he was enfranchised, Aristokrates proposed that he be given special protection against any assassin. That sequence also seems to be assumed in the first epilogue (discussed in §5 below), where Demosthenes protests that the shield of inviolability (would have) rewarded Charidemos as Kersobleptes' general (192). We cannot determine precisely when this singular honor was proposed; whenever it was approved in council, it was promptly derailed by Euthykles' challenge-under-oath. But it was only thereafter that Charidemos and his backers settled for a less extraordinary promotion, electing him general in the regular process. They may have been slow to seize upon this option because Charidemos was already acting as their mercenary commander in the field, and his citizenship had been conveyed as an honorary status, not with the expectation that he would actually share in the offices and obligations of a *politēs*. But when Aristokrates' decree to shield him failed, they seized upon the second option, to get him elected general. After all, in principle, as a citizen properly vested in deme and tribe, he was as eligible as any Athenian. Moreover, in 357 Euboia had joined the Athenian alliance and thereafter it may have seemed all the more comfortable to treat this Euboian native as a full partner at Athens, fit for the highest office.

If Charidemos himself were disappointed not to have gained inviolability, he could take comfort in the cloak of generalship, which would convey much the same protection that Aristokrates had proposed. Anyone who attacked an Athenian general in the performance of his duties would certainly be subject to forcible arrest, killed, or extradited to Athens, and any community that harbored the assassin would be considered hostile. After all, Demosthenes acknowledged the point in passing (12), that the other Athenians serving Thracian rivals would be as much deterred by the general's rank as by the special status that Arisokrates proposed.

But if the proposal was such a dead letter of legislation, why would Euthykles and Demosthenes undertake to revive the lawsuit when they did, in 352/1?[17] Bear in mind, Dionysios synchronized *Aristokrates* with the *First Philippic* (or. 4, later the same year), and that connection gives a clue to the strategy.

In the *Philippic* we see how complacently the Athenians have come to rely on outsourcing their wars.[18] Struggling against the tide of recent policy, Demosthenes pleads for a modest contingent of Athenians (just a quarter of the manpower) to serve and supervise in person, among the throng of mercenaries deployed against Philip. Demosthenes himself had served as trierarch in the early 350s, along with Euthykles, who became lead counsel in the case against their general, Kephisodotos. But, evidently, the current way of war often involved little patriotic investment, and Demosthenes blamed the failures of their Thracian policy on Athenians who dodged their duty.

The *Third Olynthiac* is an even more passionate appeal in the same vein a few years later. Here we learn that Demosthenes' *Philippic* had met with some success but that, nonetheless, thereafter Charidemos was assigned to sail north with "empty ships," taking only the money to man them.[19] He is still the poster boy for a failing strategy, adept at fighting wars with hirelings, bargaining on his personal connection to Kersobleptes as surrogate for the wealthy elite of Athens who would rather not serve in person. And that comfortable arrangement prompts a version of the commonplace with which this chapter began (~ 23.207–10). In stark contrast to the current state of affairs, Demosthenes reminds them, in the aftermath of the Persian Wars the Athenians balanced their public and private assets rather differently:

> [They] finished fine buildings and works of art at public expense, . . . in such number and such quality as to leave no scope for later generations to outdo them. But in private life they were so sensible and so firmly committed to the *ēthos* of the constitution that, if anyone among you knows which is the house of Aristeides or Miltiades or any of the famous men of that time, he can see that it is no more impressive than its neighbor. In those days the demos was lord over the politicians and master of all their goods . . . now, just the opposite: the politicians are masters of [your] goods and manage everything, but you the demos are rendered gutless, deprived of money and allies, demoted to the lot of an underling or appendage. (Dem. 3.25–31)

This is the "political issue" that outweighs the legalities in Aristokrates' case. To be sure, conflict between standing law and the decree in question is prerequisite—without it there would be no case.[20] But I think the prominence of those legalities in the first part of the speech has encouraged scholars to see this case as primarily a legalistic dispute and to diminish the political issue in that light. If we approach this case without such categorical assumptions, we can see that the two issues are tightly entangled: after fifty-odd years of retooling the democracy, even at the end of a series of cases in which the constitutional issue was masterfully articulated, the suit for "unlawful action" is still an adversarial weapon, to strike down overreaching politicians.

In any event, we have in the case against Aristokrates another like the *graphē paranomōn* against Ktesiphon (to which we turn in chapters 8 and 9): a prosecution for "unlawful measures" that was prosecuted sometime after the council's *probouleuma* should have become moot. However long it lay in abeyance, it was plainly a lawsuit to punish the wrongful actor, one in which the unlawful decree was not the target but the principal evidence. The speech we have makes a singular impression with the presentation of that evidence in the first portion, but it should not overshadow the other issues that must have carried as much weight with the original audience.

§2. The Composite Speech

The text of *Aristokrates*, as we have it, is an exceptional artifact of rhetorical enterprise. Whether the case succeeded or not, the speech became one of Demosthenes' most celebrated masterpieces, largely because of what was done to it after the legal issue became moot. For Demosthenes developed at length the diatribe against Charidemos and the policy he represented, and it was the interplay of that invective with the legal argument that made the case so impressive.

In the major manuscripts, we find a second "hypothesis" or preface (after the one by Libanios), which may go back to Menander (in the third century AD). It was this second preface that told how Charidemos was first crowned and made citizen (in 357/6) and was later singled out for special status in Aristokrates' bill.[21] This second preface also provides plausible testimony on the recasting of the speech, for it tells how Euthykles (experienced litigator that he was) challenged the bill and effectively quashed it, but then, in preparation for taking the case against Aristokrates to trial, he hired Demosthenes to write up the speech. And here the preface indicates a dramatic change in strategy: "the orator"—that is, Demosthenes—recognized that the straightforward legal argument was strong but the merit of the honorand was likely to outweigh it, as many Athenians might think Charidemos worthy of the distinction. And so, as the preface puts it (5), Demosthenes, out of his own ingenuity, "devised another case" or a second line of attack (ἑτέραν ἔξευρεν ὑπόθεσιν), which he wove together with the more straightforward argument on the law. Now Demosthenes claimed that the bill was proposed "on a pretext" of serving the city's interest, and he "attacked the (defense) case for (securing) the Chersonesos, . . . claiming that Aristokrates had written the decree as a ploy, to intimidate the other Thracian lords, so that none would dare kill Charidemos for fear of Athens; and thus he would save the Chersonesos for [their ally] Kersobleptes."

One could argue that the prefator's conclusion might simply derive from the speech itself, but he proceeds somewhat elliptically, as though relying on some authority. Moreover, his notes on the turn of events provide reliable details that we would not know otherwise. So I think it only reasonable to suppose that the preface drew upon some historical account, and its implications are likely to be right: the argument was composed in two stages as the case developed, and there may have been more than a year between the first stage and the second. Aristokrates introduced his *probouleuma* sometime in the middle of the decade, but Euthykles promptly challenged it under oath in the assembly, presumably with a speech that laid out the obvious conflict between the decree and the laws. That challenge was sufficient to defeat the proposal as Aristokrates did not see fit to answer the challenge and so the *probouleuma* died of neglect. But then in 352/1, Euthykles decided to proceed with the case against Aristokrates himself, to make an example of him and to discredit the faction that backed Charidemos. So he called upon Demosthenes to develop the double-edged argument.

As the prefator suggests, it was Euthykles who devised the basic legal attack, drawing the obvious conflict between the decree and standing laws; it was Demosthenes who developed the adversarial argument (to punish Aristokrates and his backers) and "wove the two issues together" to great effect. The feature that really made the case was that last part of the legal argument where Demosthenes went beyond the conflict of particular provisions to extract the big idea: what most offended the Athenians was not the clash of one statute against another but the fact that this privileged character should be given wider retribution than other citizens could claim.

§3. The Laws in Evidence

There is a singular feature of this text that has made commentators all the more inclined to focus on the clash of conflicting rules: the documentation, the way those very statutes were inserted into the legal argument to substantiate the points of law. *Aristokrates* is not unique in having such inserts, but they are unusual in their focus and reliability: the only documents that were included in the manuscript are the statutes that proved the illegality of the decree, and these texts of law appear to be largely authentic, not simply concocted from the orator's comment or the editor's imagination.[22] By contrast, in the latter part of the speech Euthykles called for the clerk to read to the court a great many documents—decrees protecting other benefactors, letters and agreements involving Kersobleptes and others, testimony from the trial of Kephisodotos, and so on—but nothing representing those documents was included in the manuscript.[23]

The documents that are preserved in the speech represent the requisite evidence in cases of this kind. In suits against unlawful decrees, *graphai paranomōn* (and in suits against unfitting *nomoi,* as well), the targeted measure and the laws that stood in conflict with it were arranged in parallel on planks (*sanides*) and presented at trial, writ large enough for at least some of the court to see. In the course of his delivery, the lead prosecutor would call for the clerk to read the relevant law from the plank, to verify each point in the indictment. And the prosecutor might call on the jury to demand that the *defendant* also read the laws in evidence and refuse to hear him if he did not comply.[24]

This presentation of the statutes in conflict, *paragegrammenoi nomoi,* was standard in any case against a law or decree, and there can be no mistaking the importance of this device. In the epilogue to *Aristokrates* (as we have it), after the long-winded diatribe against Charidemos and the policy he represented, the prosecutor dutifully returned to that catalog of *paragegrammenoi,* as though to acknowledge that this evidence of illegality was *sine qua non.*[25] A copy of that exhibit would have been kept with the speech among the client's important papers and the speechwriter's records, and it was probably passed on in family tradition.

But how did the excerpts from that attachment, originally quite separate from the text of the speech, come to be written into it? From a remarkable convergence of evidence we can make a fairly confident conjecture: an enterprising editor saw fit to integrate the *paragegrammenoi* into the argument early in the tradition, at that stage where the text was adapted for large-scale copying. It so happens that the documents in *Aristokrates* were largely included in the line count (or "stichometry"), whereby every block of a hundred lines was counted off alphabetically in the margin.[26] That line-count edition may go back to the third century BC, when original documents were still readily accessible. At least some of the documents inserted in that first edition are reliable and not concocted from the argument; in those instances we can see that the document differs from what the speaker says to summarize the law, yet those divergent details ring true or seem more plausible than the speaker's explanation.

The Legal Argument

In *Aristokrates* the list of laws begins well enough with the Solonian rule establishing the jurisdiction of the Areiopagos council for charges of deliberate killing or wounding *ek pronoias.*[27] The point of emphasis is the very fact that such charges must go to trial (*dikazein*), and historically the point seems solid enough. But the next few provisions come from the Drakonian law on treatment of those exiled for homicide, and we can hardly rely on the historical perspective that the prosecutor offered. Euthykles aimed to prove that a proper trial was the inalterable foundation of the system, but these venerable statutes do not always fit that model.

The first of these *nomoi* or *thesmoi* says that homicides (*androphonoi*) may be killed or arrested in the homeland, but (if arrested) they must not be subjected to torture or extorted for blood money; if any avenger does so, he will be fined (28). This document includes procedural details beyond what the speaker describes, clauses specifying the remedy and the penalty, and these seem reasonably reliable: the violator was to repay twofold the damage he had done; anyone willing could take his case to the competent magistrate, depending on the nature of his claim (damage, assault, or abduction); and the *hēliaia* would decide the case.[28]

The next *nomos* (37) matches the inscription of Drakon's law (*IG* i³ 104.26–28): so long as the exiled killer stayed clear of border markets, communal games, and festivals of the religious coalition called Amphiktyones, anyone who killed him was subject to the same penalties as one who killed an Athenian fully possessed of his rights. In such cases the committee of Areopagite judges called *ephetai* would decide the avenger's fate. In such provisions Euthykles insisted that the very term "manslayer" (*androphonos*) must mean that the killer has been tried and "convicted" by ballot-vote of the court.[29] That condition is nowhere indicated in the inserted documents, but the disparity is one more sign of their authenticity. Euthykles interpreted the text with the natural understanding of his day, though probably not the original meaning. The aim of the law in Drakon's time, in the seventh century, was to limit reprisal against those who had gone into exile voluntarily rather than face the victim's family at trial. But for our inquiry that anachronism is all the more telling. By the 350s it had become a standard presumption of the Athenian legal system that for a man to be held liable for some penalty, he must be given a proper trial by a jury with suitable qualifications. That is, the accused was entitled to due process.

It was not always so—or the principle was not always embraced so wholeheartedly. As we saw at the end of the previous chapter, impeachment proceedings against generals and other officials were often decided by vote of the assembly—as in the Arginousai case. This was true as late as the late 360s, scarcely a decade before Aristokrates' case. From that perspective it seems reasonable to question whether Euthykles' argument represents the assumptions of most Athenians in 352/1, so soon after the cases of Kallisthenes and Ergophilos, both condemned without court trial in 362.

Not only was the killer in exile secure in life and limb, but as we learn from the next law in the series (44), his property was protected from depredations. Interpreting this provision, Euthykles naturally assumed that the protection could only apply to those who were exiled for unintentional killing, as the rule applied in his day—and once again there is good reason to doubt whether that distinction applied in the seventh century. But here at least the speaker does not insist that the killer (*androphonos*) be duly sentenced by a court; he concludes that the exile is self-imposed.[30] So, despite Euthykles' earlier insistence, *androphonos* does not always mean "one convicted" (ἑαλωκώς).[31]

In most respects, Euthykles was reading the law, understandably, with the assumptions current in his day. But he also made a point (49) that is solid historically though less acknowledged, for the summary arrest in Aristokrates' bill would have opened the door to lethal violence.[32]

After all, summary arrest (*apagōgē*) by its very nature put the accused at risk. The persons who undertook to make the arrest had to be prepared to use force, to take control of the accused if he resisted. In fact, that violent recourse was expressly protected in certain situations, as we learn in the very next statute that was read to the court (51): those who arrest an exiled killer, when he intrudes in the community, may act with impunity if they first inform against him. That is, if they went to the Eleven (the magistrates in charge of most criminal cases) and gave a credible report that the intruder was indeed a known killer, they were (in effect) given warrant for the arrest and could claim justification if the accused resisted and was killed in the process.

Euthykles treated that law on *endeixis* as yet another precaution against the sort of license that Aristokrates' bill might have given. And in this regard it fits closely with the next two laws on the list, from the general statute on justifiable killing: "If one kill [another] in athletic contest unwillingly, or overtaking him on the road or in warfare unwittingly, or [catches him] with his wife, mother, sister, daughter or concubine . . . , the killer is not to flee [or face exile] for such killing" (53). And "[i]f one kill (another) in the act of defending against violent and unwarranted theft or abduction, there is no recourse for the killing" (60). The first of these (53) shows, once again, a small but significant deviation from what the orator said in his argument, and it seems most probably true to the law at some stage in its development. The vague phrase "overtaking on the road" (ἐν ὁδῷ καθελών) received no comment from the orator and baffled the ancient commentators. But it may have dealt with a fact of life that we would expect to find somewhere in the law: traffic fatalities, where one man runs down another with his horse or cart. As a rule declaring such casualties justifiable, it would have favored the horse-driving elite and, in the democratic era, that archaic rule was probably not the most popular relic of Drakonian justice.[33] So Euthykles would readily pass over this phrase, without comment, precisely because it was an obscure term whose original meaning had fallen from favor.

The other clauses in these statutes (53, 60) are more straightforward, and Euthykles put them to good use: Suppose that Charidemos himself might someday reside at Athens (or sojourn there) and rape another man's wife or commit some other crime that would justify lethal response. In that case, nonetheless, was the killer of Charidemos to be arrested summarily as Aristokrates prescribed?

And then as though to conclude this part of the argument, Euthykles recites the entrenchment clause, the provision that sealed the Drakonian *thesmos* against any change (62): anyone, public official or private citizen, who proved responsible for confounding the statute or changing it, would be "rightless" (αἴτιος ᾖ τὸν θεσμὸν συγχυθῆναι τόνδε ἢ μεταποιήσῃ, ἄτιμον εἶναι). That is, the offender, who tampered with the statute, would have no legal recourse against anyone who took action against his person or property.

On that note (ironically) Euthykles turned to the panorama of homicide courts, whose rules appear to have altered the Drakonian *thesmos* in many particulars.[34] It is beyond our scope here to retrace his path; it's sufficient to say that this vision of the legal landscape, looking down from the Areiopagos to the peripheral sites, was meant to bring home the big idea. The series of venues, each with its peculiar rules, was conceived to make due process a reality: whatever the social dynamics—whether the case involved one family demanding retribution from another, the killer admitted culpability or insisted upon his justification, or an exiled killer pled to return—there had to be a trial in its proper place.

That rationale was even applied, oddly enough, to the provision for hostage-taking (82–85): as Euthykles understood it, if a wrongful death occurred and those implicated were unwilling to stand trial or to surrender the persons responsible, the aggrieved family could take hostages—but not more than three! That statute would seem to undercut Euthykles' complaint against summary arrest; the recourse recognized in this provision was originally an extrajudicial remedy. But he argued away the contradiction, insisting that even this relic of vendetta was a fixture of due process; the hostage-taking was construed as a way of forcing the culprits to face trial.

In sum, Euthykles insisted that the decree was unlawful for failing to require that the accused be brought to Athens for trial in the proper court (90–91): aside from being at odds with a host of laws on particular points, this was the damning defect, that Aristokrates nowhere provided for any trial at all: τὸ δεινότατον πάντων ἐστί, τὸ μηδεμίαν κρίσιν ἐν παντὶ ποιῆσαι τῷ ψηφίσματι (90). "For [Aristokrates] has written, 'If anyone kill Charidemos, he is subject to arrest, and if any city or private person withhold him, they shall be excluded from the treaty,' not 'If anyone refuse to surrender *for trial*' the man they have withheld."

That point of emphasis—that the body of law for this ancient jurisdiction requires, in each case, a trial—is recalled in the epilogue (215–20) where the *paragegrammenoi* are summarized. And that focus on the list of laws in conflict has made a great impression upon modern readers, as it seems to fit our own rationale for judicial review of legislation. But let us not lose sight of the less legalistic principle that must have been at least as effective with the original jury: they would be most provoked not because they were loathe to see due process denied to a foreign assassin but because Charidemos was given a special status that none of them could claim.

Rules and Principles

In this case Demosthenes gave a compelling demonstration of the inductive method, extracting the principle from a host of particular rules. How much of that technique was novel? Wolff concluded that this exercise, from the 350s, is essentially the same approach illustrated in Euryptolemos' argument more than fifty years earlier. Of course, Wolff's interpretation is persuasive, so far as it goes. Euryptolemos' argument (as Xenophon recalled it) addressed the assembly on the choice among competing proposals—he never had the chance to address a jury to decide the lawsuit. Wolff scrupulously acknowledged the distinction but largely dismissed it:[35] if Euryptolemos did not capture the principle, that was for lack of technique, not a sign that the concept was yet to evolve.

But, by my reading, Demosthenes' method may represent a rather different way of thinking about the disparity between one measure and another, for Euryptolemos set forth a set of alternatives, any of which was preferable to the summary procedure that Kallixeinos proposed. To be sure, he seems to suppose that nomos embraces traditional ways of justice *in sum*, that the particular contradictions posed by Kallixeinos' decree amount to a broader violation of "all the laws." But he never *articulated* the principle common to the statutes he cited. And so, in the Arginousai case we are left to argue over which defect is really the most damning.[36]

The way Wolff framed his assumptions and traced the development has largely shaped subsequent discussion, so it will be helpful here to be clear about how he interpreted this technique (*"Normenkontrolle,"* 1970, 52–54): What is most remarkable is not the list of obvious contradictions, the clash between the indicted measure and the particular wording of the standing laws. As Wolff saw it, the real aim of this technique was "to ground the claim of *paranomon* upon the fundamental incompatibility (*Unvereinbarkeit*) between the proposed measure and *the pattern that is discovered in explicating those laws*" (52, with my emphasis). The method probably became popular in response to the lawless proceedings of the Thirty, and by the time of *Aristokrates*, it had become standard, embracing "the unalterable principle which affords to every defendant the right to have questions of fact and penalty decided at trial."

But, in order to understand how this argument would affect the ancient audience, let us also consider what Aristokrates and his defenders had to say against it. They would argue, almost certainly, that the further proceedings of due process would be undiminished, by virtue of the very rule that Demosthenes has just rehearsed, that no decree shall supersede a law (87). The arrest and extradition of the assassin must lead in due course to the procedure that law prescribes—it goes without saying. Indeed, it may be partly because he did not wish to pave the way too smoothly for that looming defense that Demosthenes made so little of what would seem the most essential statute among the *paragegrammenoi*: the rule that no decree prevail over law, ψήφισμα δὲ μηδὲν . . . νόμου κυριώτερον.[37] If Aristokrates' bill would indeed overturn the many procedural laws that Euthykles listed, this rule would seem to be the very crux of the case. And so perhaps it was, in Euthykles' draft.

But in the speech we have, that statute was introduced in support of another argument: not that Aristokrates' decree would indeed overturn a host of laws but that it would break the rule against laws *ad hominem*. That is, insofar as the decree worked *with* the laws, Arisokrates made the laws serve the privilege of this one individual. Even if Charidemos' assassin was to be given a proper trial, he was to be apprehended anywhere he could be found in the alliance and brought forcibly to Athens, or extradited from any community that held him—and any that refused to give him up would share the enmity of Athens. No one else in the ranks of Athenian citizens was protected with the same long arm of retribution. In that respect it violated the most basic constitutional rule, that each citizen shall have an equal share in the constitution (86).[38]

That principle comes into focus at the end of the legal argument, in transition to the diatribe against Charidemos and his backers. After the last of the homicide laws (the old rule for hostage-taking), the speaker summarized the argument thus far with a list of procedural guarantees that were violated, supposedly, because Aristokrates neglected to specify that these rules still applied: there must be a trial; victims must have remedies; the accused should have some humane avenue of exile; and a neighboring community must not be damned by the presence of the accused among them, while the immediate accessories, "among whom the injury occurred," may be spared.[39] It is at this point that the speechwriter turned to the two restoration-era laws, "to make no law against anyone, if not the same for all Athenians," and that "no decree be superior to a law" (86–87). This is the link between the litany of repugnancy and the second half of the speech, the long harangue against Charidemos and his backers. The strategy that the prefator described as the mark of Demosthenes' peculiar genius, the weaving together of legalities and policy, depends upon this principle. As Demosthenes explained,

> [T]he author of the law [against laws *ad hominem*] supposed that all must share equally in the laws, just as each has an equal share in the constitution (πολιτείας ἶσον μέτεστιν ἑκάστῳ). . . . And so, since it is agreed that one must draft decrees in accord with the laws, the fellow who drafts such a measure as this, for the advantage of Charidemos personally and not for all of you, would be plainly proposing a law contrary to this statute [that bars laws *ad hominem*]. (86)

Then, to illustrate how that principle applied even to decrees honoring foreign benefactors, Demosthenes called for the reading of measures that include the proper formulation: "Let the same retribution apply in his behalf as in the killing of an Athenian" (88–89). That clause illustrates the principle that all shared equally in the *politeia* and no one was entitled to rights and remedies that other Athenians could not claim—not even a kingmaker. That principle was one indisputable tenet of the *patrios politeia*, the "ancestral constitution" that became the rallying cry of reformers and reactionaries alike:[40] "equality before the law."

At this turn of the argument Demosthenes moves beyond the list of laws in conflict, the *paragegrammenoi*. The manuscript has no document inserted, and we have no indication what particular decrees were read to the court. But we can be reasonably certain of what he did *not* introduce into the dossier, and that gap is another sign of the timing: he made no reference to any statute protecting officers in the course of their duties. Of course a more far-reaching retribution cloaked Athenian generals than ordinary citizens, but that could be squared with democratic principle because every Athenian citizen in good standing was eligible for that office. So, if the special protection had been proposed *after* Charidemos became general, we might expect the speaker to anticipate the objection, that the shield is merely honorific because Charidemos is already protected as *stratēgos*. In the prologue Euthykles acknowledged that making him general made Charidemos just as intimidating (11–12), but he made no mention of that equivalence in the legal argument. That is probably because Aristokrates had offered his decree for privileged status *before* Charidemos was made general. And now, *after* Charidemos had become general, Demosthenes must keep his focus upon the injustice that *would have been done* if that privilege were given when Charidemos was a citizen not yet cloaked in the highest office.

So the most compelling argument was not that Aristokrates confounded procedural rules but that the mainstay of the democratic community, *isonomia* itself, was undone. Within the legalistic framework, Euthykles appeals rather persistently to something more basic and dearer to the hearts of his jury. Great benefactors must be honored, of course, and should be fairly rewarded for their service; but those privileged characters must be subject nonetheless to rules that preserve the *politeia*.

§4. The Case against Kephisodotos and Its Aftermath

The greater part of the speech as we have it is devoted to the questions of policy and merit: whether Aristokrates' decree and other measures it might inspire were really in the city's interest, and whether Charidemos in particular was worthy of such distinctions. The two issues are tightly interconnected but there are programmatic cues suggesting where one ends and the other effectively begins. Just so, after insisting yet again that the people must disavow this decree to end its malign example (138–40, with a cautionary tale at 141–43), Euthykles seems to pick up where he left off in the case against Kephisodotos. A new section is introduced, "to examine in brief the actions of Charidemos" and the arrogance of his backers (144). It is here that we learn of his early career, how he started out in the ranks of light-armed mercenaries, turned to piracy, and was then employed by Iphikrates until Timotheos came to replace him (148–49). It was at that juncture that Charidemos revealed his talent for disrupting Athenian policy, by freeing hostages that Athens had kept for leverage, and by appropriating ships that he was hired to command. The first maneuver (allegedly) cost Athens control of Amphipolis and the second (apparently) won for Charidemos a warm reception from Kotys and the Olynthians. So, we are to suppose, Charidemos was already in cahoots with Kotys when he began to bargain over the Chersonesos. In the segment that lays out these implications (153–69), Demosthenes seems to rely on documents from impeachment proceedings against Timotheos and against Kephisodotos (in the years 360–359). Bear in mind, in the latter Euthykles was prosecutor and Demosthenes was co-counsel; so, it seems reasonable to suppose, much of this harangue against Charidemos was adapted from that case.

Sometime after their first disappointment, when Charidemos had frustrated their grasp at Amphipolis and Athens was at war with Kotys, the renegade commander sent a proposal to the Athenian general, "in which he promised to bring the Chersonesos over [to Athens], while he decided to do just the opposite." At this point, when Timotheos was still in command, Charidemos was besieged at Abydos (on the Asian side of the Hellespont), but then, after furtive negotiations, he was allowed to cross over to Sestos, which was under the control of Kotys. Demosthenes' narrative suggests, plausibly enough, that the promise to deliver the Chersonesos was already part of the bargain and that this was the consideration for which Charidemos was allowed to cross over from Abydos to a secure position with Kotys. That maneuver, moving unopposed from one side to the other, showed that something was promised, and the outcome reveals that Athens was cheated.

Now in proof of that charge, the speaker called for the reading of documents that were evidently preserved from one impeachment or another (159–62): first the letter that Athenian officers sent back to Athens, evidently describing the deal they had made; then the letter that Charidemos himself had sent to Athenian officers in the Chersonesos; and finally a series of missives from those officers confirming that Charidemos had, in fact, hired on with Kotys and was helping him steal the rest of the region that Athens claimed as her own.

After Kotys was assassinated (360/59) Charidemos seems to have revived his offer to deliver the Chersonesos (§§163–68). The Athenian general in command of Thraceward operations was now Kephisodotos, and it was to him that Charidemos addressed "that letter," to the effect that he would now fulfill what he had promised. But "for seven months" he continued operations against the Athenians: he commandeered some of their ships, when the crew was still at breakfast, and killed those who resisted (165); and later he defended the pirates' harbor at Alopeconnesos against an Athenian blockade (167). And yet Kephisodotos saw fit to write up what Charidemos had repeatedly promised and reneged on, in the form of a treaty (*synthēkai*) for the demos at Athens to approve. This text was, evidently, exhibit A in the case against Kephisodotos: the Athenians were so outraged at what they saw as collusion in a patent fraud that they deposed the general and fined him five talents, after very nearly sentencing him to death. And as though to emphasize the link between that case and this, Demosthenes remarked upon the disparity: for the very same transaction one party was cruelly punished "but the other is honored as a benefactor even now" (168).

After yet another betrayal by Charidemos (as Demosthenes tells it),[41] his rival Athenodoros brokered a deal among the Thracian kings: they were to share power, dividing the realm into three sectors, and Athens was to recover her territory in the bargain. Chabrias was now the Athenian commander, and he lent his good name to the deal. But Kersobleptes evidently disavowed what he had agreed to with Athenodoros and, at Charidemos' urging, made yet another agreement, with Chabrias—"a deal even more daring [or ingenious, *synthēkas deinoteras*] than the one with Kephisodotos" (171). The Athenians in assembly insisted on a more formal commitment: Ten ambassadors were elected to meet with Kersobleptes to witness his oath; or, if he refused, they were to conclude the agreement with the other two kings and close ranks with them. But the embassy accomplished nothing.

In the meantime Athens intervened in Euboia, and Chares, who had led a mercenary force in that campaign,[42] was sent north to demand that Kersobleptes comply with the promise Charidemos had made more than once, to restore the Chersonesos to Athens. Then, at last (357/6), a treaty was concluded. Demosthenes does what he can to diminish the contribution of Charidemos: he only did what he was cornered into, after he had delayed and evaded his commitments for so long, with no intention of doing anything straightforward or equitable.[43] To prove that strategy of subterfuge, seven documents were introduced (174–78), including letters from the principal parties and covenants from two stages of the negotiations. Some of this evidence was probably preserved from the case against Kephisodotos, who earned a grudging note of sympathy (178).

It was thereafter that Aristokrates proposed his decree to create a privileged status for Charidemos. The speech does not say how long thereafter but it describes the sequence as follows: So long as Athens maintained a force in the Hellespont, Charidemos played along, but as soon as Athenian forces were withdrawn, he went to work trying to eliminate the two partners in power in order to consolidate control for Kersobleptes. He realized that he could not defy Athens and break the treaty with impunity until he had disposed of the other Thracian kings, and it was in aid of that subversive strategy that Aristokrates' bill was introduced (179–80): "So as to accomplish this aim all the more easily, he hit upon a decree which, once you had enacted it, would plainly have injured the other two kings and stifled their commanders . . . with fear of predatory prosecution (*sykophantia*)—were it not for the indictment that we brought against the bill!"[44]

§5. The First Epilogue

As Demosthenes comes to the closing of this argument, he tries to capture the essence of the offense in terms that will enrage the audience. Scholars have often dismissed this first epilogue as purely emotional appeal, but I think it connects rather strongly with the core issue of this and other cases for unlawful acts (*paranomōn*): how to weigh the favors of benefactors in the tradeoff that defines the community. It is the subversion of that principle that constitutes the crowning insult: Aristokrates and the backers of his bill for Charidemos "would have made *you his* guardians . . . and, if we had not brought this very indictment, the city would be acting as hireling to *him*, keeping watch over Charidemos! Wouldn't that be a fine mess . . . that the very man who once defended your enemies, hiring on as their spearman, ends up guarded by your decree!" (186).

Euthykles must anticipate the obvious objection that Athens should not be vindictive once they have resolved old wrongs with new alliances (191–93);[45] on that principle of reconciliation they have even sided with Spartans and Thebans and (recently) with Euboia. That argument would have some merit, he insists, only if Athens had achieved "just such a treaty of mutual assistance with Kersobleptes and Charidemos" (191–92). But Athens was bound by no such convention, and reconciliation did not extend to those who were preparing further injuries, "intending to make [Kersobleptes] all the more powerful by a grant of immunity (*adeia*) for his generals." If someone was once an enemy but had a change of heart, claiming now to be a friend, the principle might apply. But in the case of Charidemos, it was just the reverse: it was when he pretended to be a friend that he had been most deceitful (193).

And then the argument against privilege concludes with a disquisition on asymmetric obligations, the precarious balance between privileged characters and the people who rely on them. It runs on at length (196–211) but deserves close reading, beginning with the following (196–98):

> It is worthwhile to consider . . . how men of old dispensed honors and privileges to their true benefactors. . . . If you see that their way was better than yours, it would be well to emulate them; if you find your way is better, it is up to you to carry on with it.
>
> First, for Themistokles, who won the naval battle at Salamis, and Miltiades, the leader at Marathon, and for many other benefactors, incomparable beside the generals we have now, the men of that day did not lavish adulation or set up bronze statues—not because they were not obliged to those who did them some good turn. They felt it strongly but they repaid that debt in a way that was worthy of themselves and their benefactors. As men who claimed much respect themselves, they gave preference to those men as their leaders. For men with self-restraint and a strong sense of true worth, it is far greater recompense (*timē*) than any brazen image, to be chosen first among men of character and conviction. For they would not deny themselves a share in any of those accomplishments: no one would say that the battle at Salamis belonged to Themistokles but to the Athenians, not that the battle at Marathon belonged to Miltiades but to the city. But [now] many say just that, that Timotheos took Corcyra, and Iphikrates cut down a whole Spartan regiment, and Chabrias won the naval battle at Naxos. So you seem

to relinquish any claim to those deeds by bestowing such an excess of honors on each of them.

Of course that critique applies to homegrown heroes, not to outsiders such as Charidemos. In what follows Demosthenes turns to that side of the equation, how *xenoi* who have done great service to Athens were sufficiently rewarded with citizenship alone, "an honor prized among all mankind, . . . but now so cheapened that many of those who have won it have gone on to do more harm to you than your admitted enemies" (199–200). By contrast, even the heroes of the Persian Wars were made to answer for their crimes: Themistokles died in exile, and Kimon, the son of Miltiades, was saddled with a fine of fifty talents (205).[46]

And on that note we return at last to the theme with which we began, pitting the great men who were once content with modest recognition against the privileged characters who demand ever more exalted status:[47] "If anyone . . . knows which is the house of Themistokles" (206–8). And yet nothing that these latter-day heroes accomplished can match what those men of old did for their fellow citizens—least of all Charidemos with his double-dealing for the Chersonesos: "In those days the demos was lord over the politicians; now it is their underling. And the ones responsible are the authors of decrees like this one, training you to despise yourselves and admire one or two persons" (210).

§6. The Second Epilogue and Further Perspective

Much of the historical sequence remains doubtful, but in many respects the speech *Against Aristokrates* may be our best evidence on how constitutional review was supposed to work in the 350s. Exactly what was at issue and when or whether the case came to court are still somewhat doubtful questions, but the argument may serve as a model. Here we find the full presentation of *paragegrammenoi,* the list of laws in conflict read from the painted boards; it is the clearest example of what seems to be standard procedure. And the second half of the speech is also exemplary for the way it links policy and legal principle, up until the second epilogue that recaps the list of laws.

Encouraged by that second epilogue, scholars have focused on the first section of the speech, dealing methodically with the legalities, and we tend to gloss over the longer argument as, well, argumentative: a rant on feckless policy and sinister personalities. Thus Wolff seized upon the legal argument as much the same finding-of-principle that emerged in the Arginousai case, and he largely ignored the greater part of the speech. Even MacDowell, who acknowledged the balance of law and politics, treated the greater part of the speech dismissively and pronounced it a ruse or a failure (*Demosthenes*, 206). After all, the original audience probably understood that none of the laws listed as conflicting with the decree would be undone by it; if the hypothetical killer was brought to justice at Athens, he would get just that, trial and punishment as the laws of Athens prescribed.

But, as an ancient commentator recognized in the second preface, the legal argument was not just an exercise in drawing contradictions; it may have begun that way (in Euthykles' draft), but Demosthenes wove it together with the charges against Charidemos and his backers, and it was thus that the argument takes on its most potent implications. For the crux of the case was the rule against laws that target any individual or group, a standard near to our own sense of "equal protection." The rule against laws *ad hominem* would be recognized in the Roman Republic and in the US Constitution. In the latter, of course, bills of attainder are barred (Article I, Section 9) and "equal protection of the laws" is guaranteed explicitly in section 1 of the Fourteenth Amendment. At Rome the authors of the Twelve Tables framed the principle more broadly as a bar to laws affecting particular persons—*id est enim privilegium*. As Cicero put it, "What could be more unjust than that, when this is the very essence of Law, that it be decided or binding for all" (*De Legibus* 3.19.44). For the Romans the original concern was to bar punitive measures against particular persons, and such also was the original force of the Athenian rule against laws ἐπ' ἀνδρί. Demosthenes saw that any unrestricted warrant, such as Aristokrates proposed to protect Charidemos, amounted to the same injustice, as it could easily become an extrajudicial sentence of outlawry against any of his adversaries. By this reckoning, the same rule that bars punitive *privilegia* must also prohibit any disproportionate advantage, "privilege" in the familiar sense.

That equivalence may not have been quite so obvious in the decades before Demosthenes developed this argument in the 350s. Here, in *Aristokrates*, we have only the last and most elaborate formulation of his theory of privilege or "asymmetric obligations." Much of the speech as we have it was probably drafted before Charidemos was ever elected general. The only indication that Charidemos had advanced to the highest office was patched into the prologue. So, I suggest, the case was revived and the speech circulated in connection with the outsider's promotion to general: not to dispute the legitimacy of his election but, rather, by revising the more cut-and-dried case against Aristokrates' bill, to discredit the privileged character and the backers of his Thracian rapprochement. In this later iteration, it is the last of the four major speeches against unlawful legislation from the 350s, what I have called "the constitutional window." The inner argument captures the issue of asymmetric obligations much as it emerged earlier in the decade.

In the next chapter we turn back to the earliest speech in that set, *Against Androtion*, a less detailed exercise in argumentation on "unlawful acts" but one that illustrates much the same concern with inequality as a threat to the *politeia*.

Outrage

The Case against Androtion

> If you agreed to be a city of slaves—not of men who claim the right to rule over others—you would not put up with the outrageous acts of this man, the abuse that he has inflicted upon Athenian citizens and foreign residents indiscriminately, throughout the city center, arresting men and tying them up, shouting out in the assembly from his perch at the speaker's platform, slandering men who are better than he, sons of better fathers than his, calling them slaves and sons of slaves, asking if the jailhouse were built for no purpose.
>
> —Demosthenes, *Against Androtion* (68)

Within the span of a few years, 355 to 351 BC, we have an extraordinary window on Athenian constitutional thinking. In the last chapter we began with the last of those diatribes and found Demosthenes' method perfected. In this chapter we turn back to the opening of that window, where the argument seems rather less polished and the outcome was, initially, less successful. Against the faction led by Androtion and Timokrates, Demosthenes wrote at least twice for the same client, Diodoros, in the course of a campaign that involved two other major cases that we know of. The speeches that we have probably did not win conviction, but they serve to illustrate the divergent functions of the two remedies, the suits against unlawful decrees as opposed to those against unfitting laws. In the second instance, *Against Timokrates* (in the next chapter), we are given another tour de force in arguing from the "laws in evidence," the *paragegrammenoi* (as in chapter 4). But, like *Aristokrates*, *Timokrates* is also a "first speech," where the lead prosecutor must lay the groundwork. The earlier essay, *Against Androtion*, is a "second speech," written for Diodoros as a supporting speaker. Here his role was to amplify the issues, not to define them, and so, in this chapter we are not given a step-by-step lesson in the laws. Instead, Demosthenes puts on display his skill for stirring a sense of outrage.[1]

There is a legal argument of sorts, but it may have appeared dubious to the ancient audience. The main thrust of the speech we have is an aggressive attack on Androtion's character. Among the charges or slanders against him was the claim that, as a young man, he engaged in prostitution (21–24); that charge must have seemed doubtful both as to the fact, whether it was actually so, and the law, whether it had anything to do with this case. But it darkens the profile of a character who seems to have no sense of the integrity that citizens cherish.

The first speaker, Euktemon, had introduced the formal charge, along with laws-in-evidence to support it. Diodoros refers back to that dossier, though without much emphasis; rather than dwell upon the contradictions his colleague had laid out, he proceeds with another aspect of equal rights under the law: the notion that plaintiffs must have a choice of procedures to suit their capabilities and risk tolerance (25–30). It may seem to us misleading, to suggest that some "Solon" drew up a comprehensive set of overlapping remedies, but it was probably not meant quite literally. Rather more broadly, Demosthenes wanted the jury to acknowledge a justice system that had grown responsive to citizens who lacked the resources of the wealthy. That concept frames the argument that he crafted for Diodoros: Androtion has led a life of lawlessness, his arrogance has played out in a series of crimes worthy of an arsenal of remedies, but the proper weapon to combat them all is the *graphē paranomōn.*

This approach is sometimes dismissed as an aberration: the legalistic reckoning in *Aristokrates* and the Arginousai case, supposedly, shows the true nature of this procedure.[2] But, we should bear in mind, both of those comparanda were themselves anomalous. The defense of the generals, as we have it, was in support of a competing proposal, not an indictment of Kallixeinos. As for Aristokrates' decree, the mover was liable but the case only came to trial after his proposal had become moot; so, even in the first speech, the bulk of the argument focused on the schemes of Charidemos and his backers. In neither case was there much to gain by demonizing the author of the decree, as Demosthenes did in Androtion's case.

A less legalistic perspective may help us to make sense of this odd indictment, one that sometimes reads as though it were patched together by committee. Much of the speech we have was padded with common passages in a later edition for circulation (outlined in §3 of this chapter), but even if we strip away the padding, there is much that seems out of place. Along with the charge that he was once a kept man, there is also the claim that Androtion should be barred from public office and from authoring decrees because he inherited a debt from his father that he never paid (33–34). This claim, which the prosecutors have no notion of substantiating, was meant to remind the jury of Androtion's family ties to the oligarchic movement, and to suggest that, despite those ties to wealth, he came to manhood impoverished and schooled in the arts of swindling and seduction. That character, a man who brings to politics the skills of a hustler, is the figure that unites this otherwise haphazard harangue.

For it is that profile that should disqualify Androtion from making legislation: as Diodoros would insist, democracy is the form of government most antithetical to clever and unscrupulous politicians who thrive on shameful acts. Conversely, for good folk of the rank and file, the laws that disqualify anyone for deviancy are no intrusion in their lives; as they have no designs on high office, their bad behavior is their own business. The greater hazard is that a sleazy grifter may overthrow the people altogether by persuading them to tolerate his outrage.

Now, to us it may seem a despicable tactic, to impeach someone with such allegations, and for what it's worth, it doesn't look as though the Athenians were taken in by it in this case. Yet, for our inquiry, the tactic is nonetheless suggestive: Demosthenes expects his jury to regard *paranoma* as actions that are not just against the law but repugnant to the very character of the demos. Before we take up that thread of the argument, it may be helpful to draw a profile of the defendant from the range of historical evidence, as a frame of reference for the various allegations.

§1. The Son of Andron

The main target of this campaign is Androtion, the son of Andron, of the deme Gargettós.[3] The father, Andron, was active in the interim regime that succeeded the Four Hundred (411/10); he authored the decree against Antiphon and others when the short-lived oligarchy unraveled ([Plut.] *X orat.* 833E). At a later date, Demosthenes insists, Andron was jailed for failing to pay his obligations but somehow skipped out.[4] Aside from that testimony, we have no clue as to how his story ended. His son Androtion, however, was active in Athenian politics and League governance from an early age and carried on for forty years, apparently inheriting no disqualification from his father's debt.[5] No doubt, he took advantage of his offices, and yet he hardly seems to deserve the insidious persona that Demosthenes has put upon him.

Androtion served his first term in council when the League was established: he is named as *epistatēs* in a decree of 378/7. It has been supposed that his tenure as tax collector goes back to the early years of the League (say, mid-370s),[6] but Demosthenes' argument proceeds as though the abuses were not so long ago. On balance it seems more reasonable to suppose that this tax-gathering activity, which is given so much scope in the two speeches, belongs to the same period as his second tenure in council. Before that second term, Androtion was implicated in another revenue scheme going back to 365/4, when he authored a decree to dispose of golden cups (processional props) and was, apparently, responsible for assessing their value.[7] Perhaps subsequent to that duty, Androtion was to blame for melting down golden crowns that honorands had dedicated to Athena (22.70; 24.177). That liquidation provoked comment but rather less consternation at the time.[8]

Not long thereafter Androtion won a crown of his own: in 357/6, he was honored by a decree of the people of Arkesine on the island of Amorgos (RO 51), to receive a crown worth 500 drachmas "for his merit, just-dealing, and good will" as governor of this outpost. Apparently he earned this gratuity by loaning the money to bankroll the garrison there when the city was unable to cover its obligation to the League, and he decided to forego the interest (*tokos*) that was owed to him. The decree acknowledges that the charge would have amounted to 1,200 drachmas; so the loan must have been at least 10,000 drachmas.[9] This singular benefaction proves his standing among the wealthy men of his generation.

Abuse of Office

Androtion's second term in council is dated, with reasonable confidence, to 356/5, the year after his crowning at Arkesine.[10] It was an honor he proposed at the end of this second term in council that provoked the suit for unlawful action, the *graphē paranomōn* for which Demosthenes wrote the speech we have (or. 22). The issues in this case are examined in detail in sections 2 and 3 of this chapter, but here suffice it to say the crime seems surprisingly benign. The crucial offense that triggered the lawsuit was a proposal that Androtion made in the assembly on his own initiative (without *probouleuma*), that the council of which he was a member be honored with crowns. That measure was at odds with a standing law that barred the council from requesting such honors when they had not built any warships (as, evidently, they had not). Despite Demosthenes' emerging genius for making much of a trivial case, the prosecution evidently failed. And that reversal must have been especially disappointing if Androtion's aggressive tax collecting belonged to the same period; the arrogance of his illegal decree would then seem all the more damning to those he had extorted. Such, at any rate, was the majority view of historians in the nineteenth century, and more recent work brings us back to that conclusion.[11]

In the same year when he was charged with *paranoma* (355)—and almost certainly acquitted—Androtion was chosen to serve on an embassy to Mausolos, the dynast of Karia, with the aim of improving relations.[12] On the return voyage the warship conveying Androtion and his colleagues encountered a merchant vessel from Naukratis in Egypt, and they seized the cargo. Egypt was in revolt from the Persian king, Mausolos' overlord, with whom Athens was officially friendly; so, reasoning that the ship hailed from a hostile state, the ambassadors and shipowners thought they could simply appropriate the assets. But it was later determined that the cargo belonged to the polis: Euktemon, the lead prosecutor in the present case, introduced a decree to hold the ship captains accountable for the proceeds, and they in turn could recover whatever the ambassadors had gotten. Androtion and his colleagues challenged Euktemon's decree with a lawsuit, but the court acquitted and thus ratified the measure; Androtion and company were required to repay proceeds amounting to nine and a half talents. At the end of the year the debt doubled, and those in default would be jailed; it was to address that exigency that Androtion's ally Timokrates introduced his law to allow such debtors to find sureties and avoid incarceration. The indictment against that law (in 353) is the subject of Demosthenes' second speech for Diodoros (or. 24), to which we turn in the next chapter.

Androtion's diplomatic reach and his ties to Timokrates again converge in a decree of 347/6 (*IG* ii^2 212) honoring the rulers of a kingdom in the Black Sea region. The sons of Leukon promised to protect Athenian grain shipments, just as their father had done and his father (Satyros) before him. In return, the sons of Leukon were to enjoy the same privileges as their father and to be crowned at the Panathenaia; money owed to them would be repaid. To this bill Polyeuktos, the son of Timokrates, added a rider that a third son of Leukon should share in these honors. Not long thereafter Androtion went into exile in Megara and it was there, presumably, that he published his important history of Attica, his *Atthis*.[13]

How such a resourceful character was driven out, we can only guess. Jacoby and others have readily supposed that Androtion followed the anti-Persian agenda of Isokrates, and he was discredited for opposing an embassy from the Great King. That theory hangs by a tenuous thread,[14] as there is no evidence of a decisive measure against him. But, it stands to reason, the series of lawsuits led by Euktemon and Diodoros may have taken their toll. In 346/5 Aischines alludes to the charge of prostitution that Diodoros had made against Androtion to justify similar allegations against Timarchos.[15] Androtion had become a familiar face to put upon such turpitude.

This son of Andron is sometimes seen as just the sort of oligarchic racketeer that Demosthenes would make of him. Conversely, Phillip Harding discounts any party affiliation and insists that Androtion was just a well-meaning participant in Athenian governance, with no partisan agenda in foreign policy; there is no explicit bias in his *Atthis* (such as commentators have often found between the lines). Largely in keeping with that profile, this chapter should not be taken as an argument that the claims of Demosthenes and his clients ring true. Demosthenes was developing a tactic that was essential to this sort of litigation: the prosecutors portray the defendant as a career offender, one who regularly abuses his official authority. After all, the remedy was a suit for "unlawful acts," plural; it was triggered by a particular violation of statute, but the prosecutor had to prove a pattern if he was to prevail upon the jury.

Modern discussion has neglected this dimension of the *graphē* in large part because the legal argument—the parsing of contradictions between the bill and the standing laws—was given priority in the other speeches, and it seems more straightforward and satisfying to those who approach these problematic texts with assumptions shaped by modern judicial review. This study argues to the contrary: the attack on Androtion as a serial offender was typical of the genre. This profile in *paranoma* was probably true to the origins of the remedy and remained crucial in such cases to the very end of the democracy.

The Baggage of "Groundless Prosecution"

Before we turn to that profile, there is a prior case that casts a shadow over Androtion's legal defense. Early in the prologue (Dem. 22.2–3), Diodoros complains that Androtion had brought a suit for impiety (*asebeias*) against his uncle (unnamed), in which the prosecutor failed to win one vote in five. He does not mention the consequences, but from other evidence, we can only suppose, Androtion should have been subject to penalties for groundless prosecution. We have credible testimony elsewhere that such abuse of prosecutorial license brought a fine of 1,000 drachmas and a penalty of *atimia*; the latter should have barred him from public prosecutions to some extent. But more than a year later, in *Timokrates* (Dem. 24.13), the speaker tells how Androtion was party to the *graphē paranomōn* against Euktemon's decree (to recover the assets that were seized from the Egyptian vessel); so, clearly, at that point he faced no barrier to legal recourse. One scholiast (on Dem. 22.3) settles for the explanation that the offender paid his fine and would face no other disqualification (until the third offense).[16] But a second scholiast notices Theophrastos' report that in such cases the reckless prosecutor was subject to disbarment, quite apart from the fine. Dilts (1983) printed the text as follows:

> Ἀθήνησιν οὖν ἐν τοῖς δημοσίοις ἀγῶσιν, ἐὰν μὴ μεταλάβῃ τις τὸ πέμπτον μέρος, χιλίας ἀποτίνει καὶ ἔτι πρόσεστί τις ἀτιμία οἷον τὸ ἐξεῖναι μήτε γράψασθαι παρανόμων μήτε φαίνειν μήτε ἐφηγεῖσθαι.

At Athens in public suits, if anyone fail to receive the one-fifth share [of the ballots], he pays a thousand [drachmas] and there is yet in addition a loss of rights, such that he is barred from bringing suit for unlawful acts or from denouncing [property] or from leading officers to make an arrest.

In this form the note seems competent in most respects, especially in comparison to the variant in *Lexicon Cantabrigiense* (considered next). But what we read as γράψασθαι παρανόμων is a correction (by Reiske long ago) for what the scribe wrote as γράψασθαι παρανόμον (*sic*).

Harris insisted that the original reading is preferable and would mean that the offender was barred from prosecuting any *graphē* against any illegality whatever.[17] But the odd orthography παρανόμον (with misplaced accent) almost certainly points to παρανόμων, not to παράνομον (with regular accent). After all, the scholiast probably relied upon aural memory, not the sort of visual impression that guides most of us in copying or comparing one text to another. Rather than seeing the text in his mind's eye, he read it to himself and copied from that pattern. In later tradition the acute accent was no longer a rise in pitch but a true stress, and the scholiast was less likely to misplace that marker; he was more likely to mistake the final, fading syllable, thus to write -ον for -ων.

Of course that sort of mind reading is doubtful by itself, but in this instance the conclusion is confirmed by the preponderance of the evidence. First there is the variant in the marginal notes to the Cambridge manuscript of Harpokration, the so-called *Lexicon Cantabrigiense*.[18] The manuscript (as Dobree first reported it) reads as follows, beginning with a missing letter and lacking subscripts (with emphasis added):

[π]ρόστιμον ἔκειτο τῶ μὴ μεταβαλόντι (*sic*) τὸ πέμπτον μέρος τῶν ψήφων, ὡς Θεόφραστος ἐν πέμπτω περὶ νόμων· ἐν δὲ τοῖς δημοσίοις ἀγῶσιν, ἐζημιοῦντο πρῶτον πρὸς ἀτιμίαν, ὥστε μὴ *ἐξεῖναι μετεγγράψασθαι παρὰ νόμων, μήτε φαίνειν, μήτε ὑφηγεῖσθαι·* ἐὰν γραψάμενος μὴ ἐπεξέλθῃ, ὁμοίως· περὶ δὲ τῆς εἰσαγγελίας ἐὰν μὴ μεταλάβη τὸ πέμπτον μέρος τῶν ψήφων, οἱ δικασταὶ τιμῶσι.[19]

"There was an additional penalty imposed on one who fails to receive [assuming μεταλαβόντι for μεταβαλόντι] a fifth share of the ballots, as Theophrastos [reports] in the fifth book *On Laws*." That much seems clear enough, but then for the critical provision, the text as it was written makes no good sense.[20] Yet, if we set the two versions side by side, the original, from which both derived, is practically irresistible: ἐξεῖναι μήτε γράψασθαι παρανόμων μήτε φαίνειν μήτε ἐφηγεῖσθαι. It was not permitted to prosecute for *paranoma*, to denounce (assets forfeit to the polis), or to call upon officers to make an arrest. The variants in *Lexicon Cantabrigiense* would be errors of the ear of another sort, misinterpreting a text read aloud: μήτε γράψασθαι was misheard as μετεγγράψασθαι; παρανόμων as παρὰ νόμων; and ἐφηγεῖσθαι as ὑφηγεῖσθαι.

Nonetheless, Harris may be right to conclude that the additional penalty was a broad disbarment from all public suits.[21] In the fragment, Theophrastos (or an intermediary) mentioned the three procedures (*graphē paranomōn*, *phasis*, and *ephēgesis*) not because the disbarment was imposed *only* in those cases, but because they were among the most abused. In other words, the rationale for barring a citizen from all public suits (however broadly construed) was simply illustrated with three that were notorious tools of litigiousness.

Be that as it may, this prior case—the groundless prosecution of Diodoros' uncle—is at best an indication that the additional penalty of disbarment (beyond the *atimia* that came with public debt) was not yet part of the law: for Diodoros would surely have protested that Androtion should be *atimos* on that account, if the *prostimon* already applied. At this point, the scholiast and his sources are probably right to conclude that Androtion had no further liability once he paid the fine.[22]

§2. The Legal Basis for Euktemon's Case

The argument revolved around two accusations: that the decree was repugnant or at odds with standing law, and that the author usurped official authority only to abuse it.

Repugnancy

Some contradiction between the targeted decree and standing law is required; without such conflict there is no lawsuit. In this case the legalities seem wretchedly tenuous, as the *paragegrammenoi nomoi* are given only minimal treatment in this speech; but, again, that is largely because it is a supporting speech, not the arguments of the lead prosecutor. So here we are given no reading of the relevant laws and barely a glimpse of them, but the offense amounts to this: Androtion has proposed, from the floor of the assembly, that the council of which he was a member be honored with crowns. Any measure proposed in this way, without a decision of council (*aprobouleuton*), was open to challenge. And this particular maneuver was at odds with a law that barred the council from requesting such honors if they had not built warships. Technically, Androtion dodged the law by proposing his decree as a citizen's initiative, not as a petition from council. But, in substance, the defendant seems obviously guilty and, to our way of thinking, the issue ought to matter: the obsession with unearned honors does not bode well for democracy.

The Athenians would not have seen it in quite that way. After all, vital offices, such as council, were not sought-after prizes of electioneering, nor well paid, and yet every servant of the people was accountable to them for any failing or corrupt practice in office. The honors that officials might claim for their services were thus considered reasonable recognition, and in this particular case, Androtion and his colleagues had every reason to claim it. As we gather from what Diodoros did not want to admit, the council's efforts to build up the fleet fell victim to an unforeseen disruption: the treasurer had absconded with funds that they had labored long and hard to recoup. That description is generous, but we can safely assume that Androtion and company would present an even more sympathetic picture of themselves as public servants struggling to carry on with the people's business. In response, Diodoros argued that Androtion's whole career had been a series of insults against the very dignity of the demos.

Stealing Citizen Rights

An important part of the case appears to consist of charges that Androtion had exercised the right to public office and to participate in the city's business when he should have been barred because of past history. The way in which this part of the case is presented does not inspire confidence, and the fact that so much of Diodoros' argument was devoted to it is perhaps an indicator of how flimsy a case Euktemon had.

Again, there is the allegation (mentioned in the preface to this chapter) that Androtion was once a "kept man" (21–24). This tactic was not such a dead end as we might like to think—Aischines, as we noted, would soon use it successfully against Timarchos. But in this case it was less damning and may even have been regarded by the jury as a sign of desperation.

Diodoros takes up this morals charge as though on guard against Androtion's response: inevitably, the defendant will claim that the prosecutors are committing outrage against him,[23] that the charge is entirely bogus; if there were anything to it, someone should have charged him on that account, not simply bundled it together with his case against the decree. To undermine that defense, evidently, Euktemon was able to find someone who could verify the prostitution with a document of some sort:[24] if Androtion insisted that it was false testimony, let him bring suit against that witness; otherwise, they had every intention of launching a separate case against him for exercising rights that he forfeited by his lawless lifestyle. That was probably pure bluff or rank distortion: any such document would probably be (or purport to be) a "gentleman's agreement" between Andron and his son's admirer when Androtion was a boy. As such, it would not weigh heavily against him. In fact, Androtion appears to have been acquitted in the present case and free of any such disability as Aischines put upon Timarchos.

For our inquiry, the allegation is nonetheless revealing: tenuous as the charge must seem, Diodoros carried on with it to show that the case at hand involved more than an isolated instance, rather a career of unlawful acts. That is how Diodoros justified the charge (24): "If the contest at hand is a suit for unlawful acts (*paranomōn*), and the laws bar from public discourse even lawful proposals by those who have lived this way, yet we show that he has not only proposed what is unlawful but also led an unlawful way of life (βεβιωκότα παρανόμως), how can it be improper to speak of this law by which these [sins] are proven?!"

Perhaps he protested too much. He certainly seems to anticipate some consternation among the jury, many of whom might regard this charge of youthful prostitution as immaterial to the case at hand. But the decision to bring it into the case suggests that a lawsuit for unlawful acts (*paranomōn*) would take as its proper target not just a single incident but the character it revealed.

In support of that strategy, there follows (25–30) a disquisition on the flexible application or "open texture" of the Athenian laws for procedural remedies, a concept that has stirred much debate.[25] For our inquiry at present it hardly matters whether this description of law in action is correct from a legalistic perspective; the importance of this theme is that resourceful speechwriters would expect it to resonate with the layman jury.[26]

> The Solon who laid down these laws . . . did not provide for action against each of the many wrongs by only one path for those wanting to take retribution from the wrongdoers, but in many ways (πολλαχῶς). For he knew this, I think, that for people in the city to be all alike, clever or confident or moderate, just won't happen. And so, if he made the laws simply sufficient for moderate folk to find justice, he realized that there would be many villains acting with impunity; and [if he made law] for the confident and capable speakers, private citizens (*idiōtai*) would not be able to take retribution in the same way as they did.
>
> (26) He thought that no one should be deprived of his access to justice, as each is capable of it. How would this come about? If he should provide many avenues by way of the laws [for the injured] to take action against those who have done them wrong. For instance, against theft: [suppose] you are strong and

> self-confident, arrest the thief, the risk is a thousand drachmas. [But, suppose] you are too weak to do it yourself, lead the officers [to arrest him]. You are afraid even to do this; write up an indictment.
>
> (27) You find yourself indigent, without a thousand drachmas [to cover the fine if you fail to win over one-fifth of the jury], then take your case for theft to an arbitrator, and you take no risk. None of these cases is quite the same. Likewise for impiety (*asebeia*), it is possible to arrest, to indict, to take your claim to the Eumolpidai or bring information to the *basileus*. For all the other offenses there is nearly the same range of recourse.

That principle—that any offense should be actionable in various ways—served to justify the broad scope of *paranoma*: if a wrongdoer was charged with various offenses and he tried to get off by claiming that his accuser should really have followed proper procedures, that ruse should be laughable (28). By the same reckoning, Androtion must not be allowed to evade the charge that he was ineligible to propose his decree because the original offense had its own remedy (29).

Furthermore, Diodoros insisted, the original offense should have disqualified Androtion precisely because such criminals, with no integrity in their personal lives, were often the gravest threat to democracy (31–32):

> The lawgiver knew—*for certain*—that there is a *politeia* most opposed to men who have lived shameful lives, one where everyone has the right to name their shame. And what is that *politeia*? Democracy! He did not think it safe if there should ever be, in any period, gangs of men clever and daring with their skillful speech but thoroughly tainted with evil and shameful acts. The demos would be often seduced by them into making mistakes, and those men, indeed, would try to overthrow the demos altogether—for in oligarchies, even if some have lived more shamefully than Androtion, it is not permitted to speak ill of those in office—or [conversely, in democracy, the debauchees] may try to lead the people on to be utterly immoral, so as to be just like themselves. So the lawgiver prohibited such men from giving counsel, lest the demos be swindled by them into making some mistake. This fine upstanding fellow has shown contempt for that principle and not only presumes to make proposals and draft legislation, when he has no right, but to do so even in violation of the laws.

Much the same principle should apply to the other disqualification, the claim that Androtion should be barred from public discourse because of his father's unpaid debts. Again Androtion would object that they should follow the correct procedure to disqualify him, but here Diodoros insisted that Androtion bore the burden of proof and must show that the debt was actually paid (33–34).

On another front, Androtion was bound to claim that it was unfair to deny all the councilmen their reward based on allegations against him alone, and he would call others who served in that body to defend their crowning. But that tactic only made the issue more urgent: each councilman's protest was self-serving since Androtion's decree would protect them against accountability (35–39).[27]

At the conclusion to this patchwork of anticipation, Diodoros proceeded at last to the most substantive issue at the heart of this case: Androtion would claim that he was being persecuted for his rigor in collecting back taxes, and if he was punished for doing his job, the tax dodgers would be all the more daring in future (42). Diodoros, of course, could point out that the jurors have sworn to decide upon the legality of the decree, and the case should be simply a question of whether the decree met the requirements of the law. But he had to add that the moral calculus was out of kilter if Androtion could claim justification for committing more serious offenses because the tax dodgers he targeted did some small wrong to the city. After all, an illegal decree of the demos was a much greater injustice than any individual's failing to pay his modest contribution (43). Remember that for all his claims of acting in the public interest, Androtion collected barely half of the fourteen talents that were past due (44).[28] And so, Diodoros insisted, the jurors must be mindful of their oath and focus on the indictment: what was at issue was not the virtue of recovering back taxes but the very sovereignty of the laws, εἰ δεῖ κυρίους εἶναι τοὺς νόμους (46).

In the next breath, he turned to the approach that would dominate the rest of this speech, weaving together the issue of legality and the more compelling case against a career swindler-in-office, a character "utterly unsuited to participate in a democracy."

> First let us examine what he is most proud of, the collection of revenue, not distracted by his bragging but focusing on what really happened. He claimed that Euktemon [his predecessor in that office] was in possession of revenue that belongs to you and he would prove it or pay the sum himself; and on this pretext, by decree, he overturned an office that was duly allotted and insinuated himself into the collection of revenue. (22.47–48 = 24.160–61)

This outrage against Euktemon was introduced in the prologue as a blow to all the laws (1, παρὰ πάντας τοὺς νόμους Εὐκτήμονος ὑβρισμένου): Androtion had used an irregular decree to create the special commission for collecting back taxes, which he then directed at his own discretion, with the Eleven as enforcement officers making arrests on his order.

This would be the focus for the rest of this speech and for much of the second argument in *Timokrates* as well: the way Androtion installed himself in an extraordinary office and then used it arbitrarily. The grievances of Euktemon, the lead prosecutor in this case, are signal: he had been chosen to fill the regular duty of tax collector (*eklogeus*) in the ordinary way (by lot among prequalified candidates) but was ousted from it by decree, apparently on the grounds that he was withholding some of the collections. Androtion never made good on the charge but proceeded to victimize others at will, as though his motive was "not his enmity for Euktemon but hatred of *you*." Rather than extract the large sums owed by major offenders, Androtion went about systematically extorting relatively small sums from others, and he arrested people to secure payment.

It was that reign of outrage that prompted the most impassioned harangue of the speech; it was so compelling that Demosthenes (or Diodoros) would copy much of it into the speech *Against Timokrates*. He began (22.51=24.163) with the most obvious reason (*procheirotaton*) why anyone would prefer to live in a democracy: that obligations are enforced "more gently" (*praotera*), without the harsh methods of autocrats, the very path that Androtion had followed to extremes. The whole passage (52–57) merits close attention as a disquisition on outrage and lawlessness, *hybris* and *paranoma*, as opposed to what is fitting (*epitēdeion*) in a democracy.

> When, of all times, was the situation in the city most dire? Everyone would say, under the Thirty. And yet, it is sometimes said, no one put his person at risk if he hid himself in his house;[29] we condemned the Thirty rather because they led men away unjustly from the agora. But this character [Androtion], acting under a democracy, has so far exceeded their viciousness that he has made for each man a prison in his own home and even led the Eleven to invade their houses. And yet, what do you think of it, men of Athens, when a poor man or even a rich fellow, having spent a lot and somehow, understandably, short of funds, has to climb over the roof to his neighbors' or hide under the bed, so as not to be seized bodily and dragged off to jail, or submit to other indignities such as slaves might suffer, not fitting for free men—and doing all this where his wife has to watch, the woman to whom he made his engagement as a free citizen?! The one responsible for all this is Androtion who is disqualified even from bringing suit in his own behalf, let alone prosecuting for the city, by the things he has done and the life he has lived!
>
> (54) Yet if anyone should ask him whether the taxes are owed on one's property or one's person, if he's willing to tell the truth, he would say "property"; for those are the assets from which we pay our taxes. For what good reason, then,

did you [Androtion], abandon the practice of confiscating land and listing houses and the like [under lien for past debts] and turn to arresting people and abusing them (*hybrizes*), both citizens and long-suffering metics whom you have treated more abusively (*hybristikōteron*) than your own servants?

(55) If you want to consider what is the difference between being a free man or a slave, you would find the biggest difference is this: that, for any wrongs they do, slaves are accountable with their very bodies; but free men, even for the greatest errors, can keep themselves safe from this [corporal punishment]. From free men it is fitting to exact justice, for most offenses, in cash. But Androtion took retribution against their bodies, just as if they were slaves.

(56–57) He was so shameless and self-serving in his dealings with you that he thought it right for his own father [Andron] to skip out when he was jailed for debts to the state, without paying or standing trial, but if any other citizen found himself unable to pay, [Androtion] dragged him out of his house off to jail. And what's more, as though he was free to do anything whatever, he seized Sinope and Phanostrate "for security" (προσενεχύραζε), women who are prostitutes but owed no taxes at all. Even if it seems fitting for those women to suffer, the way it was done doesn't seem fitting at all (ἐπιτήδειαι 'κεῖναι παθεῖν, ἀλλὰ τὸ πρᾶγμά γ' οὐκ ἐπιτήδειον), for some men to be so self-important, seizing upon the opportunity, to walk into the homes of others who owe nothing and carry off their furnishings. One might see many instances where it seems fitting for many persons (πολλοὺς ἐπιτηδείους ὄντας) to be targets of such treatment, but it is not called for by the laws or the customs of our constitution (τὰ τῆς πολιτείας ἔθη) which you must preserve. Those customs embody compassion and forgiveness, all the consideration that free men deserve.

This severity toward some is matched with a perverse leniency toward others. Androtion tried to justify his irregular tactics on grounds of public interest to recoup the missing revenue, but Diodoros countered with a tally of pittances: Leptines of Koile gave up 34 drachmas; Theoxenos of Alopeke, 70 or so; and others on the same scale, none more than 100 drachmas (§60). Androtion had spoken up in the assembly to justify these extractions by denigrating those persons as servile or slave-born, prostitutes or sons of prostitutes, and so on. Scholars have assumed that these small sums are to be regarded as further examples of the same extortion that Diodoros decried in the preceding segment (51–59), but there is bound to be some irony in the explanation: "Do you [really] think that each of these men [who were taxed so little] hates him and wars against him on account of this tax assessment? Or because he said in the assembly, with all of you listening, that one of them is the son of slaves and ought to pay the one-sixth along with the metics, that another has children by a prostitute," and so on. The truth is, despite Androtion's slanderous talk, however offended they were by his drunken abuse, "each of them regarded his payment as a 'necessary expenditure'"—which is to say, they were grateful not to be charged more. To be sure, Diodoros did not say that those who benefited from Androtion's unevenhanded extractions were in collusion with him, but he made it clear that these sums were not proportionate. From the same list, Satyros as dockyard supervisor had previously assessed and collected a very substantial sum for maintaining the fleet, thirty-four talents, and yet that officer was not so reviled as Androtion (63). Those who got off lightly hated him for the outrage they suffered from his drunken arrogance (ὑπὲρ ὧν ὑβρίσθη καὶ ἐπαρῳνήθη), not because of the taxes he took. And the others, who were most victimized, had all the more reason to protest. After all, Androtion's arbitrary methods violated the most essential principle of democracy, then as now: equal protection of the laws.

§3. The Conclusion Shared with *Timokrates*

At this point, having demonized Androtion the tax collector, Diodoros anticipates the argument that he acted in the public interest. In response to that claim, Demosthenes framed an extensive passage that also appears in the speech *Against Timokrates* (22.65–78 ~ 24.172–86). We shall have to reconsider much of this material in the next chapter, but first let us try to sort out the contamination: the passages that some officious editor seems to have taken from the later adaptation and roughly retrojected into the original argument.

The stock material raises up the standard of community, as though the scales of justice are balanced upon it. Beyond the dictates of statute, there must be a reckoning of what citizens in various stations contribute to the shared endeavor and how their respective failings should be weighed.

> If anyone should ask him who he thinks guilty of the greater wrong to the city—those who work the land on a tight budget, who have come up short on their taxes because they have to raise their children and pay for household needs and for other civic duties [on top of their taxes], or those who steal the money from others who pay willingly and from the allies and make away with it—I don't think even he, shameless as he is, would be so bold as to claim that those who fail to pay what is theirs do greater injustice that those who pilfer from public funds. (65)

And yet Androtion had never taken part in prosecuting those greater offenders, in all his thirty years of political activism, despite the long list of leaders who cheated the polis and were condemned for it in court. It was only when he had the chance to punish so many lesser offenders all at once that he showed, at last, some interest in righting civic wrongs (66).

Of the passages in *Androtion* that seem to be interpolated from the version in *Timokrates*, the next section is perhaps the most problematic and yet critical to the common argument (22.67 = 24.174). In both speeches the shared passage proceeds from the last complaint, that Androtion spent his career in public life and yet never took up the righteous cause against leaders who wronged the people; instead, he stepped up as a concerned citizen only when he could injure the many. Here (22.67) the speaker promised to explain why that was so, but much of the tradition preserves a text that seems almost unintelligible. Most of the manuscripts have plural verbs, agreeing with the implied subject in the later speech (both Androtion and Timokrates); that text of *Androtion* was probably adapted from the later version. The original text for circulation (if not for trial) was probably somewhat shorter and kept verbs in the singular, much as we find it in two of the earliest and most reliable manuscripts.[30] That text fits the argument better than the version recast from *Timokrates*. Here the older version of the problematic text is represented in italics with implications in brackets.

> Let me tell you the reason [why he prefers this unpopular role]: *what he steals from certain persons [is not enough] because of his insatiable habits; [so] he takes twice as much from city coffers. For it is no easier to be hateful to the many, who do small wrongs, than the few who do great injustice; it is surely not a more popular position (dēmotikōteron), to focus on the wrongs of the many than those of the few. He knows that he himself is one of the wrongdoers [as guilty as any],* but he regards you [ordinary citizens] as worthless and treats you that way.

That seems to be the sense required by the argument. For it is this confused but crucial passage that leads into the rant that serves as epigraph to this chapter: "[Even] if you agreed to be a city of slaves . . . you would not put up with the outrageous acts of this man, the abuse that he has inflicted upon [you] . . . slandering men who are better than he, sons of better fathers than his, calling them slaves and sons of slaves, asking if the jailhouse were built for no purpose." Answering that question, with matching irony, Demosthenes says, "I would have to say, no"—the jail was, indeed, built for nothing—"since your father walked out to join the parade at the Dionysia, dancing out of his shackles." Then Demosthenes brings his theme to a close: "The count of his outrageous acts (ὅσ' ὕβρικεν) is more than one could say, so many in number. Take retribution today that is equal to the sum of his wrongs and make an example to the others, to make them show some restraint."

The original text for trial may have ended with that thought experiment in the "city of slaves" (68).[31] The last ten sections of the speech (69–78) seem largely adapted from the rambling argument in *Timokrates* (176–86), including at least one passage that does not fit the present context (74). Indeed, it is tempting to suppose that this last section (69–78) was originally drafted in the interim, perhaps in defense of Euktemon's decree to recover the nine and a half talents that Androtion and his colleagues had appropriated. It begins on a turn of thought that seems to fit that situation, when his defenders would argue that so devoted a public servant should not be crippled by one mistake: "there are other matters that he managed well." To which Demosthenes seems to reply with exasperation, "Where to begin?" In this context Demosthenes added the story of how Androtion liquidated the ceremonial crowns and cups, practically as an afterthought (22.70); it would be amplified in *Timokrates*.

§4. Making Sense of the Composite Text

At the conclusion to this chapter and transition to the next, let us focus on what is likely to be the original ending to this speech, the passage that stands (in the text we have) at the juncture of two segments largely shared with *Timokrates*. These two segments form the latter part of *Androtion* (47–78), where we are faced with a patchwork of material that was either copied into *Timokrates* or adapted from it. These sections amount to eleven pages in standard editions, more than a third of the earlier speech as we have it. So, if we are to understand the case against Androtion, we have to ask, how much of that long conclusion really belongs to this speech?

In *Androtion* these two parts cover sections 47–68 and 69–78. Much of the latter (as we noticed) seems to have been copied or corrected from a version better suited to the later case, against Timokrates; but, even there, the formulation does not quite fit its context. In fact, introducing this passage in *Timokrates*, Demosthenes acknowledges that it was adapted from earlier arguments (24.159): "What I have to say is nothing you have heard before, unless some of you were present at the trials of Euktemon." The plural "trials" suggests that we have here material from Euktemon's defense against the *graphē paranomōn* that Androtion and company brought against him a few months before Timokrates' law was passed and challenged, as well as what was introduced two years earlier, in the first case against Androtion.

That acknowledgement of material borrowed from Euktemon's other cases was probably the clue that led the early editor to expand the borrowing: he took note of the cross-reference in *Timokrates* (159) and saw that what follows (160–73) closely matched the earlier argument in *Androtion* (47–66). He assumed that the remainder also belonged in the earlier speech (or would make an attractive expansion), and so he copied into *Androtion* additional material from *Timokrates* that amplified the theme of self-dealing, even including a passage that only suits the later context.

Thus in *Timokrates*, the first segment (24.160–73) shows occasional adjustments, adapting invective that was originally directed against Androtion alone (22.47–66) to target Timokrates as well. The revisions are sufficient to show that the later version was adapted from the earlier by someone mindful of the differences and with better competence than the compositor who added the bulk of *Androtion* 69–78. For example, in regard to the tax-collecting operation, where *Androtion* introduces the defendant's promise to recover what was missing from Euktemon (the outgoing *eklogeus*) or deposit the sum himself (22.50), *Timokrates* omits that bit of drama but notices how Timokrates was co-opted by Androtion to serve in his behalf, with the excuse that Androtion himself was unwell (24.160–61); but then the two of them together led the search into the homes of their targets, which none of the other board members joined in (162).[32]

Also omitted in *Timokrates* is the dramatic scenario picturing a hapless victim of Androtion's intrusion, a fellow who has to "climb over the roof to his neighbors' [for refuge] or hide under the bed, so as not to be seized bodily and dragged off to jail, or submit to other indignities such as slaves might suffer, not fitting for free men—and doing all this where his wife has to watch, the woman to whom he made his engagement as a free citizen" (22.53). *Timokrates* describes the hapless target simply as "not only afraid to venture into the agora but not even feeling safe to remain at home" (24.165).

And then, expounding upon "the difference between being a free man and being a slave," *Androtion* has the stronger distinction: "For free men, even if they face the greatest misfortune, there is this saving grace, that for the most part the judgment against them should be taken from their property," not exacted upon their persons (55). *Timokrates* has merely "for free men to be punished [in person] should be the last resort" (167).

The most substantial adaptation is a passage regarding "the customs of the constitution" (τῆς πολιτείας ἔθη) or the "the city's character" (22.57–59 and 24.169–71). The earlier version has the odd note of pathos describing how even prostitutes were distrained, and it compares the more productive tenure of Satyros, when much more revenue was brought in. The later version is effectively fitted to the later case: Timokrates, whose law allowed his wealthy cronies to arrange for sureties to cover their debts, permitted no such reprieve when he was tax collector; anyone in arrears had to pay double or go to jail. Androtion, Timokrates, and their backers would claim that it was all in the city's interest; but anyone relying on that defense should show that they matched the city's character (τὸ τῆς πόλεως ἦθος), with compassion for those who are disadvantaged, not for the powerful and their lackeys.

By contrast the later portion in *Androtion* (22.69–78 ~ 24.176–86) has no adjustments of that sort.[33] In fact, the editor seems to have copied the later material back into the earlier speech without regard for the differences. The most striking divergence comes right at the juncture between the two parts (22.68): there the earlier harangue concluded with that searing comparison, likening Athens under Androtion to a "city of slaves." The corresponding passage (24.175) has only a lukewarm injunction, not to relent in their wrath: "You must remember and take into account what wrong each offender does, and punish him when you catch him, not ponder the time, if the deed is long past, but [simply] whether they did it!"[34] If lenient now at what once provoked them, the jurors would seem to have condemned the offenders out of spite and not from a true sense of the wrong done to them. That was a rare distinction among court arguments, where it was standard to call for righteous wrath, without much qualification. The substitution—casting the jury bound by precedent in place of the "city of slaves"—confirms what we might have suspected: the original conclusion to *Androtion* was not well received.

CHAPTER SIX

Overthrowing the Court

The Case against Timokrates' Surety Law

> Those that have decisive authority in all cases are the courts (*dikastēria*). . . . I think all would agree, to render the courts' decisions invalid is a terrible and damnable step toward overthrowing democracy. For our city is administered by laws and decrees, but if anyone can introduce novel legislation to undo what the ballot decided, where will it end? How can it be right even to call it a "law" and not "lawlessness"? . . . For this [Timokrates] deserves the extreme penalty, not just because he brought in this law, but because he also shows the way to others, to overthrow the courts, to bring exiles back home and bring on other terrible consequences. For, if he gets away with enacting such a law, what is to prevent another legislator from undoing some other fixture of the city's security by means of novel legislation? Democracy was overthrown once before, I hear, when lawsuits against unlawful measures were first undone and the courts lost control.
>
> —Demosthenes, *Against Timokrates* (151–54)

The speech *Against Timokrates* is a stout defense of court control. That theme resounds from the opening sections to very near the end. But the text is a patchwork, perhaps the most difficult to disentangle of any in the Demosthenic corpus. Following the pattern of *Aristokrates,* the editor has inserted a set of documents representing relevant legislation. Some of these items seem reliable, others not so much, and what we make of the legal argument depends in large part on how we assess this secondary material. Scarcely does the patchwork of documents conclude before the reprise of old arguments begins, cobbling together material from earlier cases in the continuing battle of Diodoros (and his allies) against Androtion (and his). Bear in mind, in the last case Diodoros was second speaker for the prosecution; now in the case against Timokrates he is cast as the first speaker, thus to bear the burden of addressing the legalities. Much of the material borrowed from *Androtion* may not have fit well at trial against Timokrates but would have been readily added to the version for circulation addressed to another audience. And, as though the text were not ponderous enough, there is an epilogue that seems more of a response to Isokrates than an effective conclusion to the issues at hand. Each of these features is significant in its own way but, in the midst of them, it is easy to lose sight of the central argument or reduce it to an abstraction.

In essence, Demosthenes argues that Timokrates' law undermines the very edifice of the laws by creating a loophole, allowing those sentenced by the court to post bond and thus evade the additional penalties that juries may impose and those that accumulate when fines are not paid on time. The target of the last case reappears in this one, as Androtion and his colleagues owed a huge sum to the polis and might have owed as much again for failing to pay up. So Androtion's harsh tactics as tax collector, forcing payment from more modest offenders, are rehearsed as a lesson in outrage. And the footing for the later case, *Aristokrates*, is laid out in this one, as both suits defend the bar against laws ἐπ' ἀνδρί, legislation for particular persons. But the central issue is the more crucial to the constitution: Timokrates' law would undermine all the verdicts and penalties that juries have handed down, in effect overthrowing the very principle of court control.

To give the defendant the benefit of the doubt, Timokrates can count to his credit an earlier law reinforcing citizen rights in cases of impeachment by council (63–64). By that law, the accused must be brought from jail to trial within thirty days; it is at least a step into the realm of *habeas corpus*. In the case at hand, Demosthenes deftly casts that earlier measure as repugnant to this later legislation, Timokrates' surety law. But on any straightforward reading, the two laws share the same aim: to leave citizens at liberty.

Demosthenes' speech may also be responding to Androtion and his associates on another level; for here, it has been said, he mocks or "mimics Isocrates . . . insisting that the laws, not foreign policy, should have the highest priority."[1] The dueling passages—pitting Demosthenes' *Androtion* against Isokrates' *On the Peace*, and *Timokrates* against *Antidosis*—are not compelling; it may be too much to insist that one specifically responds to the other. But there should be little doubt that the issue loomed large in the late 350s, as foreign entanglements threatened the integrity of the law (considered here in §1). From that perspective, this case involves a clash of elite opinion and alliances of convenience against reasonable distrust of foreign influence. Still, for many among the jury, this was a case about the power of their ballot (outlined here in §2): for Timokrates' law "breaks (λύει) and renders it worthless," and his aim was "not to serve the city's general welfare"; how could this statute serve the greater good when it "renders invalid the cumulative penalties that laws have set upon the crimes?!" Instead, its obvious agenda was "so that certain persons be exempt from paying for what they were caught stealing, what has been pilfered and plundered from *you*."

§1. Background to the Case

The case at hand goes back to the incident involving Androtion and his colleagues on an embassy to Mausolos, the ruler of Karia, in the fall of 355, not long after the earlier suit against Androtion. Both Athens and Karia were, at the time, friendly or compliant to the Persian king; Egypt was rebelling against him. And so, when Androtion's vessel encountered an Egyptian cargo ship from Naukratis, the Athenians seized it. Upon returning to Athens, however, the ambassadors kept possession of the cargo (or its proceeds), even as emissaries from Naukratis came to petition for the return of their property. The assembly decided that the cargo was seized from a hostile party and therefore property of the polis; on that reckoning, the captains (trierarchs) of the Athenian vessel were to hand it over. But, it soon became clear that Androtion and his colleagues had taken possession, so the burden of reimbursement should fall to them (not to the trierarchs). Timokrates' law was designed, evidently, to spare them the cumulative penalties for failing to pay off their debt by the ninth prytany of that year (spring of 354).[2]

Their liability came to light when Aristophon proposed a decree in the assembly to choose investigators (*zētētai*), and anyone with knowledge of public money that was being withheld should inform those officers. Euktemon came forward and implicated the trierarchs in council where he initiated a *probouleuma*; thereupon, in the assembly, Euktemon recounted how the cargo had been seized and was later declared property of the polis (12–13). The assembly was then clearly inclined to approve Euktemon's proposal, holding the two trierarchs accountable for the sum of nine and a half talents. At that point Androtion and the others "jumped up . . . shouting their protests and abuse (against Euktemon); they took the blame from the trierarchs, admitted that they had the money and insisted that they themselves were the proper targets of the investigation." To resolve this complication Euktemon "gave his opinion" (as a rider to his decree) that the trierarchs remain liable but have lawful recourse against those who actually had the money in their possession; any dispute over who owes what would be resolved by judicial assessment (*diadikasia*), and whatever the parties were assessed, they owed to the city.[3] With that addendum Euktemon's decree seemed sure to pass, but it was promptly challenged, with a *graphē paranomōn* lodged against him. At trial he was vindicated, and the court thus ratified the decree.[4]

> At this point what should have happened? The city should have the money and should punish the one who took it—there was no need for any further legislation, none whatever. Up to this point Timokrates here had done you no wrong; but thereafter he took upon himself the role that has been told, and he turns out to have done you wrong after all. For he has hired himself out to serve their devious designs and thus brought their wrongs upon himself. (14)

In the timeline that follows, there is a hint of the development that may have proved fatal to the case against Timokrates (15–16). The suit *paranomōn* against Euktemon had dragged on into the last month of the year (Skirophorion), and even then (as Diodoros complains) Androtion and company were not prepared to do the right thing (οὐδε παρεσκευασμένοι τὰ δίκαια ποιεῖν). At that juncture they announced that they were ready to pay the original sum but could not pay the penalty (which doubled the debt). Diodoros insists that this public relations campaign was all an "ambush," preparing the ground for Timokrates to sneak his bill into law, in the first prytany of the next year. Presumably, convinced that the defendants were willing to do right, the lawmakers would be sympathetic when the surprise solution was presented to them. And the proof that it was all such a ploy is that "they deposited not a single drachma *in that period*," but (thereafter) tried to undo the additional penalty (for failing to pay on time) by introducing Timokrates' law as a Trojan horse. Late in the speech (187), Diodoros has to admit that, before Timokrates' case could come to trial, the original debt had actually been paid. In the early narrative, he dodges that detail, but the jury would not be misled for long.

§2. The Legislation Laws and the Dubious Documents

As we turn from that narrative to passages that frame the legislation protocol, we should bear in mind what Diodoros (as first speaker) would make of this material. He has just described Timokrates' law as "the most daring and shameless of any that was ever enacted," as this one law invalidated most of the rules about additional penalties that the court may impose (16). That is the perspective that leads into the next segment (17–27), the discussion of old legislation laws "that have been on the books a long time" (24). These are laws that particularly apply to *new legislation that contradicts standing law.* He does *not* say that *all nomoi* must be enacted in this way; in fact, he proceeds as though most of the jury would find this protocol less familiar than the fast track that Timokrates had used to enact his surety law (see chapter 1 §§2–4). If we keep that perspective in mind—these are the rules that strictly apply to new statutes that effectively overturn and replace old laws—the argument will be easier to follow and we can sort out the inserted documents with rather less confusion.

It is this replacement procedure (beginning with the vote for confirmation of the corpus) that is limited to a particular window of opportunity: it must begin at a set time in the official calendar and then requires thorough publicity, with notices posted at the heroes' monument near the council house "for anyone willing to examine," and debate over the course of three assemblies. The new bill must conform to the rule against privilege, "that the same law apply to all," and that issue will bear considerable emphasis in the later argument. But the most essential requirement comes last in the list: the rule that old laws in conflict with the new bill must be undone, λύειν τοὺς ἐναντίους (18).

Demosthenes concludes this initial description with reference to the remedy: "if anyone violate *one* of these rules, anyone willing is to prosecute." That does not mean that the text to be read at sections 20–23 includes the very remedy that Diodoros and his allies have invoked (or not necessarily). Apparently the enabling statute for the lawsuit against unfitting legislation (*nomon mē epitēdeion theinai*) would have to wait for other documents to be read first; he finally calls for that statute providing the remedy at hand at section 33. And neither in preface nor in comment after the laws are read (24–26, 32–34) does he specify how or at what point the prosecutor should proceed. Instead, he emphasizes how Timokrates has violated many of the legislation law's provisions (legislating at the wrong time, without publicity, etc.) and could have been prosecuted for any one of those infractions—he does not say how. In violating *all* the relevant rules, the offense is all the more damnable, and, we can only suppose, the remedy at hand is suited to that omnibus offense.

To be sure, the claim that the law's author has violated "all the laws" sounds like the usual amplification. But it may also help to excuse an obvious lapse on the part of the prosecutors. The provisions that are now to be read to the court (for which we have, instead, the dubious document at §§20–23) seem to rely on anyone willing to bring suit against the legislator, at some stage of the process, where he violated one or a few of the procedural rules. In the original confirmation statute, that remedy, which would interrupt the legislative process, was probably the older recourse, *graphē paranomōn*. The prosecutor would challenge the proposal in the assembly in order to block the decree for *nomothetai* to ratify the bill, thus to derail any legislation that did not adhere to those rules. That old remedy was available to Diodoros and his colleagues but the decree for legislation was passed without any warning of where it would lead. And so, as though to illustrate that subterfuge, after the confirmation protocol was read and briefly explained, the decree of Epikrates, which convened *nomothetai* to rubberstamp Timokrates' law, was read in turn (27) and condemned for facilitating this travesty. It is only thereafter that we finally get to the law that provided the remedy invoked in this case (33): the suit against introducing a law that does not fit, *nomon mē epitēdeion theinai.*

The old legislation rules required that substantive changes, effectively replacing old laws with new, must follow the confirmation protocol in the first prytany of the year. And what Demosthenes seems to say is that if anyone violated any of these rules—if he introduced such a measure at any other time and not in connection with that regular review in the first prytany, or if he did not allow for the period of public comment, or if he offered a bill that conveyed some privilege—some concerned citizen should challenge the legislation in progress. That challenge would take the form of a *graphē paranomōn* against the decree for *nomothetai,* before the bill was submitted to them.

On that reading there is all the more reason to regard the inserted document with caution: Demosthenes described the laws to be read at sections 20–23 as including a remedy of some sort against anyone who violates those rules and tries to introduce legislation improperly. But the only remedies recognized in the document apply against the *officials* in charge of the proceedings, if they shirk their duties: if they do not open the confirmation procedure or fail to provide for the legislative session, the chairmen or presiders (*prytaneis* or *proedroi*) are fined, and if they do not pay voluntarily, they can be denounced to the proper magistrates (by *endeixis* to the *thesmothetai*). And if the *thesmothetai* do not take the case to court, they are barred from advancing to the Areiopagos council (where former archons in good standing would continue for life). If they have any historicity, these penalty provisions probably derive from later revisions to the legislation law (as argued in chapter 1 §§2–4). Whatever we make of it, as so often with such inserts, it has little to do with the provisions that Diodoros would call for at this stage of his argument.

On this theory, what was actually read to the court at this point in the prologue was a set of rules where the remedy was the more familiar one, a lawsuit against the unlawful decree: a *graphē paranomōn* to block the proposal for *nomothetai* to ratify the bill. If that is so, then there is a much clearer connection to the next item read to the court (27): the decree of Epikrates that provided for the session of *nomothetai* where Timokrates' law was introduced and enacted without warning. The effect of introducing the decree at this point, after the reading of the confirmation law, is to emphasize that there was simply no warning to trigger the remedy prescribed in the law. Epikrates called for legislation to deal with funding for the upcoming Panathenaia celebration, and thus *nomothetai* were promptly convened. But if the content of Timokrates' bill had been properly publicized, the citizens in assembly would have known that it would change the rules for paying penalties but not appreciably affect funding for the festival, which was Epikrates' pretext. It would have been obvious that the decree was in violation of the protocol for replacing old laws and therefore should be challenged as *paranomon*. Instead, as it happened, there was no way to know that Timokrates' bill was unlawful or unfitting until it was actually laid before the lawmakers.

That scheme, to sneak in new legislation, regardless of the contradictions, is followed in detail and with great consternation after the reading of Epikrates' decree (28–31). And when that protest against the bait-and-switch is finally finished, then Diodoros presents the legal basis for the proceedings at hand: the statute that provided a remedy against the unfitting law itself, followed by the documents that should make the case, the *paragegrammenoi nomoi*.

The Statute That Enables the Lawsuit

Before turning to the litany of laws that Timokrates contradicted, Diodoros had another law read out to the court, the one that prescribed the very procedure that he resorted to in this case: the enabling statute for the suit against unfitting legislation, *graphē nomon mē epitēdeion theinai*. He introduces it as follows, marking the shift in focus from procedural abuses to the substance of Timokrates' law:

> Not only did he do wrong on this account [in procedure], that he violated the timeframe prescribed in the laws, did away completely with the period for public comment and deliberation and brought forward his legislation during a holiday, but also on that account [in substance], that he has introduced a law that contradicts all the standing laws, as you shall now learn in detail.
>
> Take and read for me this law first, the one that expressly forbids introducing any contradictory law [into the corpus] and calls for a lawsuit if anyone does introduce such a law. διαρρήδην οὐκ ἐᾷ νόμον οὐδέν' ἐναντίον εἰσφέρειν, ἐὰν δέ τις εἰσφέρῃ, γράφεσθαι κελεύει.

This is the last of the prefatory materials, items from the dossier not posted on whitened boards; and so Diodoros instructs the clerk to take up the law and read it to the court. By contrast, when we turn to the list of laws that were cited in evidence of specific contradiction, he simply calls for the clerk to read the next item on the board. So this particular statute, the one called for at section 33, was crucial to the case but not part of the evidence that would be posted on *sanides*. This is the law that prescribes the remedy that Diodoros has actually invoked, the suit against a legislator who somehow succeeded in enacting a law in conflict with other standing laws.

The provisions that we find in the inserted document (33) may be substantially accurate, but it reads as though it was patched together from accumulated scholia, much like the text for the confirmation itself (20–23). This composition, like the other, does not really match the speaker's description. It begins with the rule that *standing* laws (*keimenoi nomoi*) can *only* be "undone" in a meeting of *nomothetai*, which does not describe the case at hand. What Diodoros would call for at this point in the speech is the enabling law for the remedy against unfitting legislation, and that is not what the document provides. He had already handled the legislative mechanism to repeal and replace old law (17–27); here he is calling for the law that prescribes a lawsuit against a measure that conflicts with standing laws but has been nonetheless enacted. That remedy (at least as late as 354) dealt with laws ratified by the fast track. But the document, as we have it (33), seems to describe a later adaptation of the rules; for it simply refers to a law already on the books and therefore gives no instructions on how the lawsuit should proceed.

The first part of the document (33) is simply a restatement of the confirmation protocol, and then the brief reference to the lawsuit reads like an amendment to that protocol, not the enabling statute for the remedy that Diodoros called for. By this amendment, evidently, the prosecutor could initiate his suit against unfitting legislation at the conclusion to proceedings in the assembly, *before* the law could be ratified by *nomothetai*. Under the old rules the bill could be blocked at this stage by *graphē paranomōn* against the decree for *nomothetai* to convene. But by the 350s, that recourse proved cumbersome, and in the decade thereafter, I suggest, the lawsuit against an unfitting law was adapted to take the place of the old remedy against the decree. The prosecutor still had the early option to challenge the bill at that first decision in the assembly (rather than wait for *nomothetai* to compound the error), but by this new recourse the jury's verdict would either ratify the law or reject it. In this way the *graphē nomon mē epitēdeion theinai* took the place of the *graphē paranomōn* as a bar to legislation in progress. That later amendment seems to be the inspiration for the document inserted in section 33.

Be that as it may, the compositor seems to suppose that *nomothetai* operated just as the assembly had done, by show of hands in favor of the standing law or the new amendment (ὁπότερον δ' ἂν χειροτονήσωσιν οἱ νομοθέται). That procedure is, again, plausible enough and can be reconciled with the epigraphic evidence, at least in principle. The usual formula for legislation by the *nomothetai* (δεδόχθαι τοῖς νομοθέταις) suggests that they were called upon to ratify or reject a proposition that the assembly had approved, and that ratification could be more efficiently managed by show of hands rather than balloting. But none of the epigraphic examples with that formula involve the replacement of standing law; they are simply adjustments to the allocation of funds or practical expedients. In the case of Timokrates' bill, Epikrates' decree had authorized a legislative session of that sort, to deal with financing for the Panathenaia, and the new law was submitted (however deviously) as just such a measure for *nomothetai* to approve (as described in 27–31).

Only in the last clause of this document (33) do we find reference to the remedy: If anyone follows the prescribed procedure, removing statute(s) that would conflict with the new law, and yet the new law is unfitting for the Athenian people or yet in conflict with other law, then, the document declares, the author of the bill is subject to prosecution under law that is already on the books, "the standing law, if anyone enact unfitting law."[5] This provision seems credible as an amendment to the confirmation described in sections 17–26, and it responds to the speaker's cue in the broadest terms—at least it recognizes a lawsuit against "unfitting law." But the feature that seems most reliable is the last detail, adapting a remedy that was already on the books, precisely because it does *not* fit the speaker's description but fills a critical gap in the history: Diodoros called for the enabling law that introduced this remedy, but the statute that inspired the insert (33) was not the original law for *graphē nomon mē epitēdeion theinai*; it belongs to a later amendment where that procedure could be simply cited in older law.

Diodoros (with Demosthenes' speech to guide him) had begun the background to these citations (17) by promising "to explain in detail the standing laws that authorize such lawsuits as these" (μικρὰ διεξελθὼν περὶ τῶν κειμένων νόμων, καθ' οὓς εἰσιν αἱ τοιαίδε γραφαί). And here at last he cites the very statute that he had followed to introduce his suit against unfitting legislation. But what he claims to rely on is old law of long standing.[6] In that respect the provisions in section 33 are, again, culled from the wrong source. Yet, for our purposes, the fact that it belongs to the wrong statute actually lends some credibility to it. If the editor who inserted this document were fashioning a text from whole cloth, he would not have invented that disparity; he would simply reconstruct what the speech describes. Instead he went looking for a text that matched the description, and he found something relevant in what he thought was a reliable summary. That secondary source was probably an historian (such as Krateros) or one of the commentators on major rhetorical work (such as Didymos).

Demosthenes concludes this procedural preface by summarizing the whole set of rules (34): "Consider how just and earnestly democratic is its framing." He offers no suggestion that they might have brought their suit against the bill itself, before it was enacted, though that is what the inserted document implies. At this point (in the 350s), there was probably no specific provision for bringing suit against a *bill* as "unfitting law," before *nomothetai* had ratified it. The older *graphē paranomōn,* against the decree (convening *nomothetai*) would have served to block the bill, if its content were known, and that option was probably revealed in the document that was actually read to the court in lieu of the insert in sections 20–23. But the measure cited at section 33 had to be one that prescribed the suit for unfitting legislation (*nomon mē epitēdeion theinai*), and the compositor of the documents naturally supposed that it had to be an integral part of the protocol for confirming or revising the corpus that Demosthenes had just described. What he found to answer that description was an amendment to the confirmation protocol,[7] not the enabling statute for the remedy that Diodoros called for.

Without the original documents to go by, these adaptations are bound to be confusing, so it may be helpful to recall the competing procedures, as laid out in chapters 1–2 (table 6.1).

Repugnancy and the Clash of Principle

The passage that follows (35–38) deserves closer reading than it has gotten, as it links two principles essential to the democratic constitution: the integrity of the law and the sovereignty of the people as its guardians. Why, after all, was the legislation law so framed as to bar contradiction?

> First of all, so that you [in the jury] could cast your ballots in good conscience (μετ' εὐσεβείας). For if there were two laws in conflict when litigants were disputing some public or private business, each side could claim to prevail by exhibiting disparate laws—and you could not very well vote for both of them! So what then? Neither could you vote for one or the other and be true to your oath [as *dikastai*], for the verdict [following one statute] would go against the opposite law, which is just as binding. And so these provisions were drafted in your behalf, to save you from this conundrum and, moreover, with the aim of making you guardians of the laws. For the lawgiver knew that the other safeguards that law prescribes can be often evaded: even the supporting speakers that you elect can be persuaded to keep silent.[8] So he orders that the bill be posted so that everyone have prior knowledge, [and yet] it might happen that this safeguard fail, if some who oppose the bill foresee its pitfalls but others ignore them.
>
> (37) To be sure, it is still open to anyone to indict, just as I have done [against Timokrates]; yet even here the city is driven off course if someone can change the

TABLE 6.1

Two tracks to legislation and the respective remedies, as revealed in Timokrates' case

The old legislation law described in Dem. 24.17–27	The fast track, by which Timokrates' law was passed	The proper remedies
In the first prytany of the year presiders in the assembly introduce the confirmation vote for anyone willing to challenge standing law with a new bill.		
	In any prytany of the year the assembly is open to proposals to make law for financial adjustment or expedients consistent with standing law.	The proposal is open to challenge, either as *probouleuma* or decree, by *graphē paranomōn.*
The bill and relevant laws are posted and the issue is debated in three successive assemblies. Advocates (*syndikoi*) are elected to defend standing law. In the third session, assembly votes a decree for *nomothetai* to decide upon the new law.		The decree (for *nomothetai*) may be challenged by *graphē paranomōn,* but most often, the rigorous procedure obviated that recourse: any case against the bill should be argued by the *syndikoi* before it proceeds to the *nomothetai.*
	The *nomothetai* convene according to the decree and vote on the bill, up or down.	
By the 350s the *nomothetai* simply vote to ratify (or not), on the model of the fast track. If the law is enacted, its author is liable for the first year.	If not challenged, the law takes effect. Its author is liable for the first year.	Once the nomos has passed, it can be challenged by *graphē nomon mē epitēdeion theinai.* The remedy was originally designed as recourse against products of the fast track but, with the revival of confirmation, was adapted to it.

prosecutor's mind for him. What then is the only just and secure safeguard of the laws? You, the great majority. For no individual could take away from you the capacity to examine and decide for the best, nor could anyone, by influence or corruption, persuade you to enact a worse law in place of the better.

(38) For all these reasons the lawgiver blocks every path of wrongdoing, thwarting those who plot against you. All of these provisions, so rightly framed, Timokrates has done away with, he has erased them in so far as he could, and introduced a law in conflict with all the laws we have, *so to speak,* without public reading, without removing contradiction, without giving you the choice or doing any of the due diligence.

The last paragraph (38) may put us off with its adversarial fervor and what seems like hyperbole: "*all* the laws," really? But most of the ancient audience, having sat through the lesson thus far, would naturally understand that, in context, he means "all the laws" relevant, those that should govern the legislative process but which Timokrates has evaded. For any jurors (or readers) who might take it too literally, the prosecutor adds a scrupulous qualification at this first instance: all the laws, "so to speak" (ὥς ἔπος εἰπεῖν). Initially he refers to the rules governing *nomothesia*, those that provided for public comment and other safeguards: any law that violates that framework undermines the body of law that was built on it.

In the course of the argument, the scope of "all the laws" will broaden to include all those that conflict with Timokrates' scheme to keep his friends out of jail. The bar to such repugnancy is a formative principle in the modern development of constitutional review, as in Blackstone's "Tenth Rule," regarding acts of parliament: "if there arise out of them collaterally any absurd consequences, manifestly contradictory to common reason, they are, with regard to those collateral consequences, void."[9] In one respect the parliamentary parallel is especially apt because, as in the British polity, the Athenians had no prescriptive constitution; so the ordinary assumption is that new legislation simply supersedes the old. Such systems have to develop a set of principles by which to dispose of legislation that is not specifically barred but is ultimately at odds with indispensable rules. In British tradition, any such collateral absurdity was rejected as "repugnant to reason," and in our case Diodoros seems to be reaching for a similar principle. For the contradiction between Timokrates' new rules and the older statutes will take some explaining.

In this case, it is argued, Timokrates' law, which allows state debtors to post surety and go free, comes in conflict with the standing rules that add on late-payment penalties and jail those who fail to pay. It may not be easy to see what this disparity has to do with the constitutional quandary that Demosthenes and Diodoros have conjured up (34–36), where jurors are baffled by conflicting laws. When they convict a man in a criminal case (say, for theft of public funds), they decide on a particular penalty, the one proposed by the prosecutor or the alternative offered by the defense. Ordinarily there is no deliberation over the further question of what will happen *if he fails to pay*. That question is decided automatically by the laws regarding such liabilities (as Diodoros explains in the latter part of the speech).

Timokrates' law addressed the situation that Androtion and his colleagues faced, where a law or decree imposed the additional penalty of imprisonment automatically; the new law gave them the option of posting bond, to remain at liberty. One could certainly argue, as surely Timokrates would do, that there was really no contradiction; the new law simply added another feature to the accumulated rules, and it might even succeed in recovering more of the money that was owed to the polis. Androtion and his colleagues would argue that the money was guaranteed (by their sureties), they were meeting their obligation, and so there was no contradiction between the recourse that Timokrates gave them and the other laws regarding fines and additional penalties. But, evidently, in the text of his law, Timokrates' had not asserted that principle very clearly; obviously, if he had spelled it out, the entanglement with other laws would invite just the sort of debate and delay that Androtion and company would like to avoid.

But the judges' quandary was complicated by the situation that might arise if some concerned citizen tried to enforce the older laws against state debtors exercising rights they had relinquished: one might list property to be seized in payment; or, when Androtion ventured into the agora or the assembly, some personal enemy might presume to arrest him forcibly. After all, those laws were still on the books for anyone willing to take action against those who were in debt to the polis but exercising rights they had lost until they paid.

Such considerations come to mind for the ancient jury more readily than they occur to us, but it seems nonetheless surprising that Demosthenes did not yet explore the implications as fully as he would do in *Aristokrates*. Perhaps he does not make those connections clear seriatim in order to avoid distracting from the real burden of his argument, for the repugnancy at the heart of his case is more than collateral absurdity. It offends against the most fundamental rule of the ancient democracy, the sovereign authority of the people in court. They must not be swindled by self-dealing lawgivers.

That grand perspective on popular sovereignty (35–38) makes the crucial connection between the procedural preface and the legal argument proper. In what follows we have the point-by-point account of conflict between Timokrates' bill and the older body of statute.

The Laws Listed in Opposition

Many of the documents presented in this segment of the speech (39–71) seem largely reliable, and the stichometry suggests that most of this material was included in the first edition for wide distribution.[10] These are the statutes crucial to the case, and their presentation in *Timokrates* seems to anticipate the rigorous treatment in *Aristokrates*. But the differences are also significant: we find many more documents in this speech than in the companion piece, and those that fall outside the legal argument seem especially suspect; many of these were not in the line-count edition, and much of their content does not match the orator's comments quite so closely. That disparity points back to a crucial stage in the early transmission of the text, when the dossier of evidence in the case was readily available: much of the documentation in the legal argument corresponds, for the most part, to the texts that were attached to the *graphē* itself, the *paragegrammenoi nomoi*. These were the statutes adduced to show that Timokrates' law was in conflict with the corpus, and much of this early documentation is consistent with the orator's comments. By contrast, the material that appears to have been added in subsequent editions does not bear so directly upon the conflict between the targeted measure and the older body of law, and those later addenda do not match quite so closely with the orator's summary.

The insert for Epikrates' decree (27) appears to be an exception but actually confirms the pattern. This measure, convening the special session of legislators where Timokrates' law was enacted, matches the orator's comment closely and was probably concocted from it by a later hand. It is not indicated in the line count, and much like the later inserts (after the legal argument), Epikrates' decree, revealing as it is, does not bear upon any specific conflict between the targeted law and the others; it does not belong among the *paragegrammenoi*. Among documents that fit within the line count there is another anomaly: the text of Diokles' law (42) goes well beyond what the orator has to say, and we shall take up that historic text in the following paragraphs. But perhaps the most notable difference between this composition and *Aristokrates* is the treatment of the targeted measure itself. For in this case Timokrates' law was read in full to introduce the comparison with older measures (39–40), and it was read again (at least in part) after the laws in conflict had been covered (71).[11] As Canevaro concludes, both readings were probably represented in the *Urexemplar,* the major edition that set the line count for later manuscripts. Some of the intervening material sprawls beyond the stichometry, but it looks as though these two readings of the targeted law stood like bookends at the beginning and conclusion of a section where the early editor tried to collate the *paragegrammenoi* into the text of the speech.

The first reading of Timokrates' surety law (39–40) seems largely reliable and falls within the line count, and right after it we find another text that fits that description: Diokles' law on the application of statutes in the early restoration era. Laws enacted under the old democracy were again valid, those that were enacted and recorded in Eukleides' archonship (403/2) were valid from that date, and those that were enacted thereafter were not retroactive but valid "from the day of enactment, unless a starting date was attached." The inserted document then concludes with a plausible provision for the council secretary to make systematic notation in the standing laws as to which time frame applies. Of all these rules, Demosthenes gives a paraphrase only for the clause requiring that laws be valid from the day of enactment unless there is a time specified; he wants to suggest that the rule is thrown into confusion because Timokrates' law ignores such distinctions. But the critical conflict seems to be that Timokrates made his surety law without *any* limitation; it would alter the application of old laws and might mitigate penalties prescribed long ago. Demosthenes points out the conflict (44) but gives no summary of the old law that this contradicts.

Whatever text Demosthenes and his client actually included here, it must have indicated some principle of statutory limitation. There was no more famous statute of limitations than the one that was vital to the restoration of democracy in 403/2: not to apply public remedies to any offense before that year of Eukleides.[12] So the ancient editor would naturally look back to that era if he did not have the actual document in hand. If he had any doubt of the context, the restoration-era laws cited later in this argument (54, 56, and 59) would point in that direction.

Thus in Diokles' law we have a solid case for a document that (1) was included in the line-count edition,[13] and (2) could not have been concocted from the orator's comment, but (3) belonged to a set of laws that was particularly well known and readily accessible. How, then, did the early editor come to introduce this document?

Here, again, it is certainly possible that the editor had access to a copy of key documents from the indictment itself. That full text of the *graphē* would include the targeted measure and the laws in conflict with it; copies were preserved for many years in the officers' archives and, perhaps for generations, among legal papers important to the client and his family, if not also in the speechwriter's collection. Perhaps in the course of gathering a corpus, that set of supporting material was attached to its speech. Then, at some point in the third century BC, an early editor saw fit to write those documents (or significant excerpts) into the main text. Small deviations might result from careless or officious hands in the later tradition. That scenario seems to me a reasonable possibility in the case of *Aristokrates*. But in *Timokrates* there are more troublesome disparities, and these seem sufficient to disprove any direct access to the *paragegrammenoi* as assembled for the official record.

In the targeted law itself, Timokrates' surety law (Dem. 24.39–40 and 71), the content is problematic at the beginning and end. In the first reading, the document concludes with an unlikely flexibility: those in debt by the ninth prytany are to pay (or have their sureties pay) by "the ninth *or* tenth prytany of the next year." And in the second reading (71) a name is added in the prescript for the chairman of the presiders who put the matter to a vote, and that name (most probably) shows some error or corruption.[14] That flaw in the formalities seems trivial, but it is still a puzzle why the editor would include the prescript (identifying officers and the presiding tribe) in the second instance and not in the first.

These two readings of Timokrates' law suggest one of two explanations: either the documents were haphazardly added into the edition that set the line count or significant alterations crept in with later tradition. The latter hypothesis seems the more likely, and we find evidence for it in the intervening documents (after Diokles' law), especially in §§50–63; these inserts fall within segments E and Z (representing lines 401–600 in the original) where the manuscripts show a notable expansion beyond the line count. Evidently, both for Timokrates' law and for other documents in this part of the legal argument, the first edition for wide distribution drew largely on reliable material(s); in later transmission dubious padding was added.

Whatever our reservations about the inserted text, Demosthenes himself confirms the two provisions of Timokrates' bill that seemed to him and his colleagues most plainly repugnant to standing law. It is, in effect, an *ex post facto* law as it alters the application of earlier sentences under older laws. And it sets aside a major group of state debtors whose liabilities are not affected by the new law—tax farmers (under contract to collect taxes from others), lessees of state assets, and the sureties who guaranteed payment for them. That exclusion makes it all the more obvious that Timokrates' law was designed to benefit another group.

That second provision may be the more damning, as it seems to confirm the charge that Timokrates' bill was a brazen attempt to benefit a few privileged characters: it goes against the fundamental rule that laws should be the same for all. But the first principle—against *ex post facto* law—may have been as important to the Athenians under the restored democracy as it was to the framers of the US Constitution.[15] In this case the concern is not that later law may reach back to punish those who were not charged or penalized under older law; it is rather designed to reprieve those whom older law had punished. But the principle seems to be valued in much the same way, for *ex post facto* laws (of both sorts), by their very nature, affect a defined class and not all citizens equally. And thus the first provision, like the second, violates the principle of *isonomia*, equality before the law.

The next statute in the list gives an historic dimension to the rule against *leges postfactae*: Diokles' law (ca. 403/2) was a measure to put the lawbooks in order after a decade of revolution and reform. The secretary to council was instructed to make notations upon the old and current laws, sorting them into three sets.[16] Those that were enacted before the new regime but which remain valid and fully applicable to events before 403 were labeled to that effect. Those that were enacted or reenacted in 403/2 were labeled "valid from (the archonship of) Eukleides." And laws enacted thereafter were valid from enactment unless there was a starting date specified. For each of these sets, respectively, the secretary was to make note at the top of each text: before Eukleides, from Eukleides, or indicating the prytany when the law took effect.

But the way Diodoros explains this principle seems baffling to us, and it suggests a significant disparity between the inserted text and the provision that was actually read to the court. He says nothing about the historic divide between laws before and after Eukleides' archonship; instead he focuses on the rule about "starting dates"; for, as he explains, many laws come with the note that "the law is to be valid from the next archonship" and do not take effect at enactment—and certainly not retroactively. A fortiori:

> Consider how repugnant to the rule is the law that this fellow has laid down. The old rule orders that a prescribed time or the day of enactment be valid; but Timokrates has prescribed, "If an additional penalty has been assigned," referring to past events. And neither does he specify an archon-date as the statutory limit [as in Diokles' law], but instead he has made his law valid not only from the day it was enacted but even reaching back before any of you were born. (44)

That last perspective confirms that Diokles' law or some corollary from the early restoration era is indeed the law that Diodoros would cite. In any case, if Timokrates insisted on overturning that historic legislation, he was obliged to undo it (ἐκεῖνον λύειν, as the legislation law required) and "not throw the whole business into confusion" (πάντα τὰ πράγματα συνταράξαι).

The laws that follow (50–59) are all meant to substantiate that charge: the first statutes prohibit any reprieve or privilege that would undo the verdict of the court, and the last is the cardinal principle that the same law must apply to all citizens; it is the essence of democracy that each have an equal share in the package of rights and remedies in the constitution, πολιτείας ἴσον μέτεστιν ἑκάστῳ. This is, of course, the same principle that would guide the argument in *Aristokrates* two years later.

The following tables match the list of laws from the speaker's summary, in the left column, with the summary of Timokrates' statute and its repugnancy on the right: first regarding privilege (table 6.2), and then regarding the laws against reviving settled cases (table 6.3).

The statute inserted at section 54 (between the two tables) bars anyone from appealing or reopening a case decided by the court; the gist of it is confirmed by

TABLE 6.2

Matching the rules on reprieve and privilege against Timokrates' law

(46) This is another law that prohibits making a motion concerning *atimoi* or state debtors or putting it on the agenda to release them from their debts or restructure them, unless immunity is granted [to the mover] with no fewer than six thousand voting.	(46 cont.) But [Timokrates] has written in express contradiction, "If any state debtor is assessed the added penalty of imprisonment," he is to obtain release by providing sureties, . . . without any grant of immunity or any prior motion whatever.
(52) Wanting to leave no pretext for the state to suffer any harm, [the lawgiver] thought that those convicted by trial at court must not take advantage of your good nature and their misfortune to make an appeal; instead he absolutely prohibited him [once convicted] or anyone else from appealing or making any motion on behalf of such persons.	(53) If anyone should ask you whether you would rather do what people *ask* or what they *order*, I know you would say "what they ask"; for this is the response of men with integrity, the other of cowards. And yet the laws all order what one must do, while those who make appeals are asking. And so, where it's not allowed to appeal for something, is there any room for a law [such as Timokrates'] that makes it an order?

TABLE 6.3

Ne bis in idem

The laws against reviving settled cases	Repugnant provisions in Timokrates' law
(55) The law prohibits reconsidering any business that the court has decided once and for all.	But (Timokrates) wrote that "if penalty is added by law or decree," the demos shall reconsider the business, so what the court has decided will be undone, and the one liable shall post sureties.
And the law forbids any of the officers from putting it to the vote.	And he wrote that the presidents be required to bring up the matter (of allowing surety), . . . "whenever anyone wishes."

the speaker's comment, but the insert is probably the editor's own construction.[17] That is important for understanding what the ancient editor was up to and what he was up against. We might expect that law (along with those that follow in the same vein, 56) to be central to the list of laws in conflict with Timokrates' surety law; for the latter would effectively cancel or mitigate penalties imposed by the court, thus (arguably) contradicting the old rule that settled cases not be revived. And yet it looks as though there was no documentary text of this law available for the line-count edition, and so the early editor was left to his own devices.

In the next two provisions (in 56) the editor found himself in the same predicament but with rather less guidance from the speaker's comments. The inserted provisions confirm what other evidence tells us: legal decisions from the old democracy (before 404 BC) remained binding under the restored democracy; all dispositions and legal decisions under the Thirty were invalid. Demosthenes' comment (57–58) reveals that the law in question did indeed annul the acts and decisions of the Thirty, but he makes no explicit reference to the positive provision, reaffirming the verdicts of the old democracy.

> Tell me, what would you say is the direst disaster you've heard of, and what would you most pray against? Isn't it this, that what was done under the Thirty never happen? I think so. And so this very law—a measure well considered, in my view—has barred the acts of that regime from taking effect. And yet this fellow [Timokrates] has condemned what was done under democracy as though guilty of the same lawlessness that you condemned in [decisions of the oligarchs]; for he makes them equally invalid.
>
> But what will we have to say, men of Athens, if we allow this law to take effect? Is it that the courts, which are manned by sworn jurors under democracy, commit the very same injustice as those tribunals under the Thirty?

The first of the inserted documents—declaring that "lawsuits and arbitrated settlements, decided by law under democracy, shall be valid" (56)—is certainly a plausible corollary to the clause abrogating decisions of the oligarchic regime, but the editor had to be guided by his familiarity with other sources to come up with it. Demosthenes focuses upon the principle, not the particular repugnancy, and he tightens that focus with the next statute in evidence.

The document inserted in section 59 is doubtful on the details, but the gist of it is spelled out by the speaker: it prohibits any law that does not apply to all citizens on the same terms.

> That is a truly democratic rule, for just as each has an equal share in the constitution in other regards, so, too, in this respect the law demands that each have an equal share. But you know as well as I do, on whose account he introduced this law; . . . he as much as admits that he has authored a law that is not the same for all, as he has stipulated that it does not apply to tax collectors and lessees and their sureties. Surely where he has excluded certain groups, he could not have made the law the same for all.

In other words, by excluding certain obligations that any citizen might undertake—as tax collectors, or those who have leased assets from the state, or *their* sureties—Timokrates reveals that he has drafted the law for a particular clientele. In that respect the law violates democratic principle.[18]

Timokrates' *habeas corpus* law[19] is a second instance (after Diokles' law) where the inserted document (63) goes well beyond the orator's explanation, and the additional information lends credibility. Of those under impeachment (*eisangelia*) by the council, all who were currently under arrest or in custody but not yet remanded to the *thesmothetai* for trial, the Eleven were to bring to court within thirty days or as soon thereafter as practicable; anyone willing might prosecute, and if the defendant was convicted at trial, the people's court (*hēliaia*) was to assess whatever penalty he deserved to suffer or pay. "*And if a fine is assessed, he shall be imprisoned until he pay whatever judgment has been given against him.*" This earlier law by the same lawgiver is cited only for that last clause, to pose a conflict with the targeted law: the latter would allow those burdened by fines to post sureties and remain at liberty; the earlier law left them in jail. Indeed, Demosthenes has that last provision repeated for emphasis (64) and says nothing more about the other content of that earlier law.

That clash of two laws by the same legislator was used to introduce a crucial turn in the argument: here the litany of contradictions is linked to the basic question of whether Timokrates law is "fitting" or not (66–76). In the end, that was the question the jury had to decide, and the way Demosthenes framed it deserves close reading.

> That Timokrates has made law in conflict with these laws and the ones mentioned earlier—*I could nearly say, contrary to all the laws in the city*—is quite clear, I think, to all of you. I am amazed that he dares to say anything at all in that regard. For he won't be able to show that his law is not in conflict with the others, and he can't claim that he missed it because of inexperience, as though he were simply a private person. For he has been visibly active for quite some time, drafting and introducing laws for hire. (67) And he can't just admit the wrongful act and make some claim on your sympathy; for it's plain that he did not draft the law unwillingly or on behalf of kinsmen or relatives who met with misfortune, but intentionally for clients who have done you great harm, who are no relation to him at all—unless he claims to adopt the men who hired him!
>
> (68) And now I shall try to show that the law he has introduced is neither fitting (*epitēdeion*) for you nor in your best interest (*sympheronta*). For I think you all agree that a law that is properly framed and likely to benefit the majority must first of all be written in plain language that is intelligible to all, and not allow one man to think this and another think that. And second, the actions required by the law must be practicable; for, if it should be well conceived but describe something impossible, it would function as a prayer, not a law. (69) In addition it must not appear to give relief to any criminal. If anyone objects that it is democratic for the laws to be gentle, let him also consider, for whom? If he is willing to look at it squarely, he will find that it serves those *awaiting a verdict*,

> not those who have been *convicted*. For in the one case it is unclear whether the accused are being slandered unjustly, but, in the other, there is no room to deny that they are criminals.
>
> (70) Of these criteria that I have now described, the law [of Timokrates] plainly meets none at all but contradicts them one after the other. This could be shown from many angles but best of all by explicating the law he has made; for it's not a case where one part is well framed and another goes wrong, but the whole thing, from the first clause to the last, is framed against you. *Take the indictment itself* and read as far as the first section of the law.[20]

The second version of Timokrates' law, which is inserted at this point, is more doubtful than the first (as we noticed in note 14). The line count shows that most of both inserts was included, but for this second reading (71) there is room for a small expansion, and that may account for the extra line identifying the chief presider.

The way Demosthenes frames this second reading gives us as revealing a glimpse of Athenian constitutional thinking as any we have. There is, of course, conflict in the law, which is actionable in itself. But to make his case, what Demosthenes really has to show is that those contradictions constitute a wrong against the sovereign people. If the law in question is not written in plain language that laymen can interpret, and impossible to enforce without violating other, equally binding law, but written in such a way as to favor the guilty by sowing confusion, then it is "unfitting," contrary to the character of the demos and against their best interest.

One side of this formulation was introduced early in the legal argument (35–36), where Diodoros insisted that laws-in-conflict compel the jurors to violate their oath; for they cannot decide a case in accordance with the laws if two rules governing the same case are at odds. Here (73) the threat to jury justice comes from "introducing a law that will undo what was final, what the court has decided." Demosthenes is beginning to focus on the connection between that sabotage of the rules and the more insidious threat: he aims to show in this case, much as he argued in the first installment (Dem. 22), that Androtion and his backers are writing legislation to favor their own group at the city's expense, to give them a get-out-of-jail card for debts past and future. And that outrage gives direction to the remaining sections of this speech, haphazard though they often seem.

§3. "City of Slaves" Revisited

As we have anticipated, Demosthenes and Diodoros were not prepared to revisit the shaming scenario from the earlier case, where citizens run and hide to escape the long arm of Androtion. Evidently the specter of a "city of slaves" had not been well received. Here instead we find a respectful call to arms against those who put themselves above the law.

> (75–76) If one should consider, what is the difference between law and oligarchy and why it is that men who are willing to be governed by laws are considered sensible and reliable (σώφρονες καὶ χρηστοί), while those under oligarchies are cowards and slaves (ἄνανδροι καὶ δοῦλοι), he would find that this is really the most obvious difference: in oligarchic regimes the members have authority to undo what has been enacted and to arrange for the future as they see fit; but [in democracy] laws prescribe for the future what must be done, rules enacted with the conviction that they will serve the interest of those who abide by them. Timokrates, however, while the city is governed by the demos, has borrowed the injustice of the oligarchy for his own legislation and arrogated unto himself greater authority over past decisions than the judges who made them.
>
> (77) And this is not the only note of arrogance in what he has done, but he has also prescribed, "if hereafter, in addition to a fine, a penalty of imprisonment is imposed on anyone, let him provide sureties, bound by oath to pay what he owes, and be released." Yet, if he thought imprisonment is awful, he ought to have framed the law [prospectively] to "add imprisonment to the sentence of no one who provides sureties," not taking advantage of the situation where you have [already] sentenced a man to prison, so that then the convicted man can arrange his bond, after you have made an enemy of him. Now, instead, he has introduced a law of this sort, as though making it a show [of his own liberality], that if you [the jury] decide to imprison a man, [Timokrates] will set him free.

This last turn of thought may seem "invidiously argued," as though the point is simply that Timokrates' get-out-of-jail guarantee is an embarrassment to the democracy.[21] But the practical implications were more serious: Timokrates not only arranged for his clients to evade the *automatic* penalty of imprisonment (when their debts to the polis were not paid), but also forestalled any sentence of the court that *specifically* prescribed imprisonment. In other words, if prosecutors specified imprisonment for default and the court decided in their favor, Timokrates' law allowed the defendant to go free in that case as well—if the assembly accepted his sureties. In this respect, once again Timokrates was subverting the court's traditional authority (78):

> Do you think such a law will be to the city's advantage, one that is superior to the verdict of the court and orders that *decisions by jurors under oath be undone by the*

> *unsworn* [vote of the assembly]? . . . If the constitution matters at all to you and each of you believes that his own judgment must be decisive in cases where he casts his ballot under oath, a law of this sort must be undone and must not be allowed now to prevail.

This is the dominant theme in the remainder of the speech: rendering the court powerless, τὰ δικαστήρι' ἄκυρα ποιῆσαι (79), is the direst threat to the *politeia*, the bundle of rights and obligations shared by all citizens. The ramifications may be summarized as follows.

The ruin of the constitution begins by eroding the division of authority between sworn judges and the ordinary assembly of citizens (who convene without swearing). Timokrates' law leaves it to the assembly to decide whether sureties will be accepted and the debtors can go free. In addition Timokrates' law cheats the treasury of penalties for fines past due (82–84). The defendant has only to *propose* sureties to evade the surcharge; if his first nominees are rejected, he can stay out of jail simply by claiming that he will nominate others—the clause is a magic charm (ἀλεξιφάρμακον) for those wanting to do wrong (85). Thus Timokrates is reversing the legal order: "he has released those who appropriate your property, in your despite, and might as well give them the right to bring a lawsuit against the judges who impose the penalty of imprisonment!" (86–87). There is no penalty for those who put forward unreliable sureties whom the assembly is bound to reject, and in this way the wrongdoers can postpone the reckoning indefinitely. In the provision to imprison the sureties and disseize from them (if not paid by the ninth prytany), he as much as admits his hypocrisy; putting others at risk and treating wrongdoers "like benefactors, he has given them the choice whether to pay the penalty or not" (88–89). "In sum, how could there be a law worse disposed to you or more against your interest?" Timokrates' law overturns past decisions, preempts further penalties in future, "secures a reprieve for debtors who fail to pay what they ought, and exposes the futility of all that you do under oath, as you judge and pass sentence in anger. *If Kritias, one of the Thirty, were introducing legislation, I don't think he would draft it any different from this!*" (90).

As a result, Timokrates' law cripples the city's financing for war and for peace. Funding depends on adherence to "the laws and decrees that require some citizens to contribute [*eisphora*] and others to fit out a warship [as trierarchs], some to sail out [in person], others to handle other requirements." The performance of these duties relies upon the juries who imprison those that break the rules (91–95). The administration (*dioikēsis*) is disrupted if such penalties are not enforced, notably those against tax farmers in default (96–101). Under "the laws that Solon laid down," there are additional burdens for thieves, those who abuse their parents, and those who fail to enlist for military service.[22] Timokrates has provided an exemption for all, and for that he deserves to be executed—let him legislate for the damned in Hades' realm (102–4).[23] Timokrates has made his law for the benefit of criminals, and he would never have introduced it if the *graphē* against Euktemon's decree had not failed (116–18).

Diodoros has proposed the extreme penalty and he justifies it by the notorious Lokrian rule (139): "If a man wants to enact a novel law, he legislates with his neck in a noose." Otherwise, "if you don't take vengeance . . . *it won't be long before the majority is slave to these predators.*"

This is as close as he gets to the "city of slaves," and the speaker quickly pivots to a proper constitutional argument (144–48). From the oath of council, to imprison no one who provides three sureties (except in cases of treason, subversion, etc.), he draws an important distinction: Solon made the *council* powerless to imprison, "for he believed that the *court* must have supreme authority over all."[24] After all, overthrowing the court is the first step to subverting the demos (152–54). And after adapting the common passages from *Androtion*,[25] Diodoros turns back to the sentencing in Timokrates' case:

> [Timokrates is bound to argue] (a) that it would be awful for him to suffer some harm for legislating that no Athenian be bound [or imprisoned], and (b) that it is especially to the advantage of those without clout (*adynatoi*) that the laws be as gentle and moderate as possible. . . . When he says "so that no Athenian be bound," don't let him get away with lying to you. For this isn't what he has enacted but that *you* [*the court*] *be powerless* to impose additional penalties; and so he reopens the closed case, where you had cast your ballot under oath after debate and deliberation. (190–91)[26]

Timokrates would wrap himself in the clauses that sound most humane (*philanthrōpotata*), but Diodoros warns the jurors not to conflate the rules for dealings among themselves with those that govern obligations to the polis. In the former, compassion serves them well; in the latter, the laws should be rigorous and unforgiving (192–95).[27]

Severe punishment is all the more deserved for one "who introduced a law to damage the majority." An ordinary thief harms only his victim and brings shame only to himself:

> [B]ut if someone introduces a law that gives license to those who would harm you, he wrongs the city and shames us all. For when a shameful law is in force, it is a

> reproach to the city that made it and harms all those that apply it . . . On this reckoning most of all, one would realize the scope of what [Timokrates] aims to do in writing this law and how repugnant to the constitution as it stands, if one should consider that all *who undertake to overthrow the demos in a revolution do this first of all: they release those who had incurred the penalty for some violation* (205–6).

In fact, Timokrates is a one-man revolution, setting free not only those the courts have sentenced to jail heretofore but all those who face the additional penalty of jailing hereafter. If there were a jailbreak, people would lend a hand to stop it. And if someone should say that this fellow here is the one responsible, they'd sentence him to death without a second thought.[28] But as it is he acts openly and more destructively: He tears down the prison and the court as well (209).

§4. Solon's Example

The speech, as we have it, concludes with a demand for righteous vengeance against those who corrupt the corpus with vicious laws. The call to wrath is, of course, standard in Athenian legal argument—there is no pretense of being dispassionate. And, as though to legitimize that willful emotion, he conjures up an apocryphal tale casting Solon himself as prosecutor against the author of an unfitting law (212–14): The ancient lawgiver reminded the jury of the law against corrupting the currency, for which the penalty was death; yet currency (*nomisma*) is but legal tender for transactions among persons, while law itself (nomos) is the very currency of the polis. So any man who corrupts this currency earns the enmity of his fellow citizens all the more. For cities often recover from a devalued coinage, but when the laws are corrupted, there is no redemption. As usual, the speaker does not elaborate on the metaphor itself (to which we return in the conclusion to this study), but the analogy suggests that laws provide hard rules of equivalence to govern the transactions that citizens must make with their community.

The passage that follows this parable (215–18) reads like an afterthought and may well be a later addendum, tacked onto the version for circulation after the lawsuit was abandoned.[29] But it is a fitting sequel to the outrage expressed in that warning against a currency debased, and it is tempting to suppose that jurors in the case, or readers who had served in that role, would imagine the owls on Athenian coinage, worn with usage, tested to verify authenticity.[30] And they would naturally reflect upon the owls that validated their own *pinakia* and tokens for jury-pay as the tangible symbol of their most vital transactions with the polis.

However they visualized the metaphor, the core meaning is clear enough: the body of laws is a coinage in the image of the people, and the power invested in those emblems is all well and good unless and until their character is corrupted. That moral lesson is very much in keeping with the preceding chapter: when they are seduced into laws or decrees that betray their rights and obligations for the benefit of a privileged few, they become rather like a "city of slaves." These cautionary images are effective precisely because the deeper obligation is not extraneous; there is no higher law enthroned in the archive to overrule the people's errors. The principle that controls laws and decrees is found in the *ēthos* of the community, in the exercise of their rights and obligations; it changes with them, for better or worse. This ethological principle was not always congenial to modern thinkers, and so (as we saw in the introduction) court control of the laws at Athens has often been the butt of consternation, from Hume to Wolff, whether we insist upon laws as an inheritance, framed by class and precedent, or search for some approximation to *Grundgesetz*. At Athens, for the century that ended with Demosthenes, there was no body of law independent of the people's character.

Breaking the Bargain

The Case against Leptines' Law

> The *law* is not on trial here, whether *it* is fitting or not, but *you* are under scrutiny, whether hereafter you are fit to be well treated, or not.
>
> —Demosthenes, *Against Leptines* (83)

In the same summer when he wrote the diatribe for Diodoros to deliver against Androtion (355 BC), Demosthenes himself spoke for the first time in a major public prosecution in the odd case against Leptines' law. In his own voice he took a very different tone but conveyed much the same message: the people must judge the laws and decrees by the standard of their own character. If they are willing to be bullied and extorted by self-dealing politicians, only to reward them with unearned honors, then they practically brand themselves "a city of slaves." But if the people cheat their benefactors of rewards they have given rightfully, they are only passing sentence upon themselves.

In Leptines' case, the young speechwriter had to dig into the lawbooks (so to speak) to find the foundation he would build upon in his later career as litigator and legislator. Ancient testimony tells that he won the case,[1] and modern readers may readily assume, as the ancients did, that it was bound to succeed, as though the argument were already accepted by most of the jury. But the basis for this suit was drawn from an old legislative protocol that was, evidently, unfamiliar to many of the jurors. The prevailing theme, which made that obsolescent procedure vital again, is an old standard of *integrity* that must have seemed a bit unwieldy on the newcomer's shoulder. But even as he proved feckless on foreign policy,[2] Demosthenes became the master of this quintessentially democratic technique: holding up a mirror to the face of the people.

The plea for integrity follows in the path of historic figures: it is reminiscent of Pericles warning against weakening resolve, or Kleon in the debate on Mitylene, or Alkibiades insisting that an aggressive people cannot change its character without courting disaster. In those instances the champion of the people turned upon them defiantly, protesting that he was standing his ground while they had abandoned their convictions. That approach may seem strange to us; after all, in modern democracies demagogues demonize the opposition and dare not impugn the people at large. It seems readily assumed that few would keep their following if they blamed the misguided throng and said flatly, "You are only condemning yourselves." But it is probably a posture as old as the citizen-soldier assembly and may have been a familiar tactic even in the 350s: Isokrates ventured upon a similar approach in *On the Peace* (14, 69, 102), within a year of Demosthenes' variation in *Leptines*.

In this speech Demosthenes is adapting that old approach to an odd predicament and, to make the best of it, he seems to be reviving a more commonplace meaning for the critical term "fitting law" (ἐπιτήδειος νόμος).[3] For, in this case, as later in *Timokrates*, that term of law is reduced to the functional sense of ordinary usage: the laws should be *epitēdeioi* in the same way that kinsmen and relatives are so called, not just "suitable" or "expedient" but closer to "belonging, like one's own."

In this chapter we begin by setting the stage (§1), proceed with the legal argument (§2), and then return to this peculiar construction of constitutional integrity (§3).

§1. Background to the Case

Leptines' law was prompted by recent reversals. Scarcely two years earlier the Athenians were facing, once again, the loss of their empire. The web of alliance had been stitched together with pledges of autonomy, but was constantly frayed by competing interests; and now, twenty years after it began, the League was unraveling. The rise of Thebes seems to have alienated many among the allies, and others were lost to Mausolos, the enterprising satrap of Karia. In 357 Athens faced major defections at Khios, Kos, and Rhodes, and one of Athens' veteran commanders, Chabrias, gave his life in the all-but-lost cause. Chabrias was already a hero (for recovering Naxos in 376), and he bequeathed to his son Ktesippos his exemption (*ateleia*) from the otherwise obligatory civic services called "liturgies" (λειτουργίαι).[4]

That sort of privilege—to be exempt from the expensive obligations to fund a chorus or other civic event—is the target of Leptines' law, and the exemption for Chabrias and son will serve as a case in point. Demosthenes presents himself as a friend of Ktesippos and defender of his inherited privilege. And among the defenders of Leptines' law, we find Leodamas of Acharnai, who originally tried to quash the decree for Chabrias and was now given a chance to rehearse some of those arguments.[5]

A year after the death of Chabrias, Leptines had introduced his bill to cancel exemptions such as Ktesippos inherited. The purpose clause (127) makes the aim clear enough: so that the wealthiest bear the burden of civic services, no one shall be exempt (except for descendants of the tyrannicides). That is, there would be no exemption from the obligations that rotated among the propertied class, for them to pay for the festivals that all citizens enjoyed. Leptines' law included an entrenchment clause of sorts, barring such exemptions in future, and, evidently, a rather rigorous procedure was specified against anyone who might try to introduce any such privilege: he is subject to immediate arrest and confiscation, then to be tried by the procedure against those who take office illegally (156). For much of his argument, Demosthenes takes aim at the relevant rules, such as would affect Ktesippos; if Leptines' law is upheld, neither the son of Chabrias nor others among the propertied class could claim exemption from burdensome expenses, as producer (*chorēgos*) at the Dionysia or director of athletics at the Panathenaia (for instance). But Demosthenes also does his best to cloud the issue, insisting that the statute makes no clear distinction between liturgies (such as the *chorēgia*) and other duties, taxes, or tariffs from which benefactors might also be exempt (29).

The purpose clause—"so that the wealthiest perform the civic services"—seems straightforward; it sets the scope of the main clause "no one shall be exempt" (μηδέν' εἶναι ἀτελῆ). The aim is that wealthy Athenians share the burden equally, and the proper scope of that rule is liturgies in the usual sense of revolving duties to fund a festival performance or the like. For, regardless of Leptines' law, no one was exempt from wartime obligations (to fit out a trireme or pay *eisphora*); and, evidently, honorees should continue to enjoy any exemptions from taxes or commercial fees. But noncitizens were also affected, and their predicament opened the door to wider implications.

And so, from the outset, Demosthenes isolates that operative phrase, "no one shall be exempt," and he proceeds as though it might be construed absolutely, as though the targeted *ateleiai* might include exemptions from other obligations such as port fees and commercial duties.[6] Thus he directs an extended argument against the injustice if foreign benefactors were cheated of their rewards. The Bosporan ruler Leukon[7] and his successors would be denied recompense for privileges that they had given Athenian shippers along the grain route from the Black Sea—and it would be costly to the Athenians if *their own* privileges were cancelled in return. From this emphasis it was once supposed that Leptines' law would, in fact, cancel exemption from taxes and tariffs; after all, if the law had nothing to do with such expenses, Demosthenes' defense of Leukon would seem pointless.

But on balance, this example conforms to the strategy that guides this argument from beginning to end: as Demosthenes puts it, the provision that "no one be exempt, neither citizens nor privileged residents (*isoteleis*) nor foreigners, does not distinguish *from what* each is not exempt, whether producing a chorus or any other duty" (29). From that vagary, Demosthenes can proceed as though Leukon and sons might be called upon to fund any of the regular services that citizens must undertake. And that scenario is made to seem a little less preposterous, considering that the law has to take its course: in principle, a wealthy Athenian could challenge one of the sons of Leukon (as a fellow citizen) to render a civic service in his place or exchange property with him (by *antidosis*) (40). And, if Leptines' law is broadly interpreted, perhaps, one could even bring suit against Leukon or his agents, for importing goods without paying the proper fees (prosecuting by *phasis* or the like). To be sure, the purpose clause suggests that it was not meant to be applied in this way, but from the other features the ancient jury may have been easily persuaded to make sweeping assumptions about what the law allowed or the slippery slope would lead to.

What Is at Stake

For most of the speech Demosthenes keeps his focus on the broken bargain and what it will cost. If citizens and foreign benefactors are simply denied their honorific exemptions and thus conscripted to fund choruses and the like, he asks, how can the modest gains offset the shame Athenians must face for revoking the rewards they have given? The ranks of liturgists might gain a handful of foreign residents and, say, twice as many citizens—for the sake of argument, call it thirty in all. Their added contribution is hardly worth the disgrace that comes with cheating those who have done Athens some greater good. As an alternative to Leptines' blanket cancellation of benefits, Demosthenes and his colleagues have drafted a replacement bill, and it is included among the items in evidence; this alternative would take away exemptions only from the undeserving. In all, the resources gained by Leptines' law are made to seem trivial, but perhaps there is more at stake than Demosthenes admits.

Mirko Canevaro concludes that the stakes were, indeed, rather higher: Leptines' law canceled *all* exemption from liturgies, even the automatic "respite" that a wealthy Athenian won for serving as trierarch and for the year after a major civic service.[8] By law, men were exempt from liturgies for the year when they took on the costly duty of equipping a warship and for the following year or two to recoup some of that expense. On that count (for trierarchies alone), as many as five hundred wealthy Athenians were exempt in any given year. Add to that the one hundred or so who enjoyed a similar reprieve for the year after funding a *chorēgia* or the like. So, if Leptines' law affects *all* exemptions, not just the honorific awards, out of a pool of around twelve hundred, about half would now face the additional expense of successive services—producing a chorus, a sporting event, or a banquet in the years when they would have enjoyed a respite. Such would be their burden if the judges let Leptines' law stand, or so Canevaro concludes.

But if Leptines' law contravened the rules granting a respite after trierarchy and civic services, we would expect that to figure prominently in Demosthenes' argument as a direct contradiction of statute and custom. There is nothing of that sort. Instead, Canevaro's reading depends rather precariously on one incongruous phrase in a much smaller calculation, where Demosthenes counted the cost "if the law stands" (20): scarcely five metic contributors would be gained and (let us suppose) "no citizen would be exempt because of trierarchy." Canevaro takes that as an admission, in passing, that Leptines' law would end the respite for those already burdened with the expense of a trierarchy, and Demosthenes promptly changes subject to divert attention from that fact.[9] But if it were really a question whether several hundred of the propertied elite must lose their respite and be liable for civic services every year (or even every other year), surely that would enter into the calculation: the cost to noncitizens is balanced by the hundreds of Athenians facing a greater burden. In any event, in the course of the argument, it seems clear that Demosthenes is referring to the trierarchic respite not as a cushion the wealthy would lose but as another factor *diminishing any gain* that Leptines' law would bring.

Again, the calculation begins with what Leptines would (supposedly) claim, that the law would add many to the roster of foreign residents (metics) liable for liturgy.

> If he can show *five*, I will admit that I'm babbling. Then again (τοίνυν), let's assume what is not the case, that among the metics even more than these will undertake liturgies, if the law stands, and [assume that] *among citizens no one will be exempt because of trierarchy;* [even so] it will prove hardly worth the disgrace it brings.
>
> (21) Look at it this way: among the foreigners resident, I'll assume there are *ten*—and by the gods, as I just said, I don't think there are *five*; indeed, *among*

> *citizens* there are not more than *five or six*. So of both [citizens and metics, call it] *sixteen*. Make it *twenty* or, if you like, *thirty*. Now how many undertake scheduled liturgies each year, as producers for choruses, athletic events, and banquets? Perhaps *sixty or a few more* altogether.
>
> (22) Therefore, so that *thirty* more may take on liturgies for us hereafter, we should make everyone lose faith in us?!

To start with five metics and five or six citizens and posit thirty as the upper limit, he must be counting only those who would become liable because of losing a formal grant of exemption. The totals make no sense if Leptines' law would have ended the respite for trierarchy—the numbers of citizens added to the tally would be many times higher. Instead the reference to "*citizens . . . exempt because of trierarchy*" is added to simplify the calculation and reinforce the implications a fortiori: assume (for the sake of argument) that, for any given year, those who lose their formal exemption are *not already exempt* for trierarchy (though some inevitably would be); even so the gain is trivial. His point is that, every year, some of those citizens whom Leptines would deprive of their honorific exemption would still be exempt from festival liturgies because they served as trierarch that year or the previous year; thus the gain from Leptines' law is all the more minuscule.

So, in my view, that elliptical reference to the respite from duties during and after a year as trierarch only confirms the implications of the argument overall: the targeted provisions of Leptines' law simply canceled formal exemptions (*ateleiai*) that the demos had given in honorary decrees. The case is, after all, much ado about a change in the rules with little practical effect. The issue is really more a matter of character. The weighing of small gains against the greater discredit is not a diversion; it is the crux of the case.

Leptines and his colleagues would defend the law on a rather different rationale than the one Demosthenes foists upon them: their purpose is not to shift the burden from the less wealthy to the uppermost elite but to provide incremental relief for the whole liturgic class. If those who formerly enjoyed an honorary exemption (such as Chabrias' son) now join the pool of contributors, others in that pool would be called upon for civic services a little less often and would thus be better able to shoulder the costs of defense.

Demosthenes seems to be answering that argument in section 26.[10] The backers of Leptines' law warn that some who enjoy honorary exemptions stand to prosper from their respite (ἀναπαυομένους τινὰς εὐπορήσειν), and Demosthenes insists, "I shall show that (their prosperity) serves your need (εἰς δέον ὑμῖν); for surely you know that no one is exempt from trierarchies or war-time contributions (*eisphorai*)." Evidently the advocates would argue that because those who have honorific *ateleiai* are free of costly obligations more often, they get rich from the respite that others rely on to recoup their expenses. That is, the honorees were already exempt from civic services, so the regular respite after funding a trierarchy allows them to save money in those years. Demosthenes turns that argument around: the savings of those honorees remain an asset for war-funding. If the community gains by leaving more money in the hands of the propertied class to fund the weightier obligations of defense, the same applies to those who enjoy honorific exemption from civic services: What you give up in one column you get back in the other (27), ὅσον ἐνθαδ' ἀφίετε, ἐκεῖ κομίζεσθε.

The replacement bill, which Apsephion introduced, evidently said nothing about restoring the automatic respite (which would be crucial if Leptines had taken it away) but specifically confirmed old law that Leptines would overturn. After reading the restoration-era law that "grants given by the demos shall be valid," Demosthenes says, "Isn't that in conflict with the provision, '*No one shall be exempt*,' among those to whom the demos has granted exemption? Surely it is. Yet there is no conflict in the bill that Apsephion is introducing, but what you have given shall be valid" (97). Thus the old law that Leptines' had undone would be reaffirmed, and to take the place of Leptines' categorical cancellation, a new procedure would be created, recognizing grounds for legal action against "those who misguided you (in winning their exemptions) or did you wrong thereafter or prove altogether unworthy" (97). In all, Apsephion's replacement bill seems to make no change in any privileges other than honorific exemptions granted by the demos.

But there is probably one more clause of Leptines' law lurking behind the long discussion of honorific decrees (35–87). It was standard procedure, of course, to publish such decrees on *stēlai*, at Athens and elsewhere,[11] and no less routine to erase those decrees when they were rescinded. In principle any inscription in the public sphere should be read aloud and might be felt to have some binding force. So when a decree was annulled, it was ordinarily required to erase any notice of it; otherwise some concerned citizen might presume to act upon whatever injunctions spoke to him from the stone.[12] More likely than not, some such clause concluded Leptines' law: let the secretary see to it that the relevant decrees are erased. Demosthenes does not say so himself, but he twice refers to Phormion's discussion (in the speech that preceded his), and he proceeds to describe a series of decrees that were published not only at Athens but also elsewhere. Perhaps Phormion protested against erasing those honors in Attica, and it now fell to Demosthenes to emphasize the shame it would bring to the Athenians when they canceled all those well-earned honors at home but the copies beyond their jurisdiction stood as a monument to their perfidy! That is the likely implication where Demosthenes describes the *stēlai* honoring Leukon as equivalent to a contract or treaty (*synthēkai*) with copies not only in Peiraieus but also at the Thracian ports, Bosporos and Hieron (37–38). Demosthenes refers to them without explanation, only to remark, "how much more disturbing it is, if those [contracts] you reneged on remain standing."

The Status of Leptines' Law and Its Replacement

Demosthenes gives every indication that Leptines' measure had passed and would be the law of the land, if not for the lawsuit.[13] The law had not yet taken effect only because it was promptly challenged and seems to have been kept in abeyance for over a year as one prosecutor after another took up the case. Initially a concerned citizen named Bathippos (otherwise undistinguished) had brought suit, but he died before the case came to court. Demosthenes tells us that two other prosecutors had taken up the case but dropped out (145). Then, more than a year after the bill was passed, Bathippos' son Apsephion took up his father's cause with support from Phormion and Demosthenes. This team of litigants had to deal with a complication that the first prosecutors had not faced, as Leptines' measure was now regarded, technically, as standing law: it was no longer a new measure enacted in the past year.[14] That development meant that Leptines himself was no longer liable. The measure would be defended by public advocates with nothing but their reputation at risk, and in that role Leptines himself stepped up to defend the law that he authored. He was joined by some of the most prominent politicians of this era. Against this team of champions, the prosecutors faced a further disadvantage in the very status of the law in question: there was no ordinary procedure, as yet, to repeal standing law with a lawsuit rather than replace it through legislative revision. That was the problem that prompted Demosthenes to dredge up the old legislation law.

Apsephion's replacement bill was probably devised to bolster the case, but Leptines would argue that it was merely a ploy.[15] After reading the old legislation law, Demosthenes listed the key provisions and insisted that he and his colleagues followed it "in all respects," but he seems to protest too much. After all, he introduced the old rules as something of a relic that the jurors would find unfamiliar. Apsephion had *not* followed the confirmation ritual to undo Leptines' law, and that failing seems to need no explanation because that protocol had fallen into disuse. So Demosthenes and his colleagues had to explain essential requirements of the old legislation law in order to maintain that they were complying with those venerable rules *in principle*, whereas Leptines did not abide by the law at all.

Demosthenes identifies the key provisions of the old law in order of importance, not following the sequence of procedure (93–94):

> First, the final decision must come before a body of "jurors," men who have sworn, ὀμωμοκότες.
>
> Second, laws in conflict must be undone, "so that there be one law on each subject" and no profusion of laws to befuddle the layman.
>
> And prior to that decision, the bill must be posted at the heroes' monument and read out in successive assemblies, "so that each of you has heard the text repeatedly and taken the time to deliberate on the issue, before he makes law."

After this summary, Demosthenes condemns Leptines for fulfilling "not a one" of these requirements; "if he had complied, you would not have been persuaded" to pass the law. And he quickly adds, "but we . . . [have done] all" that the legislation law requires, ἡμεῖς δὲ . . . πάντα. That grand claim, pronounced in passing, should not be taken too literally: it may mean merely that the prosecutors have met the parameters by challenging Leptines' law in the assembly and vowing to offer a replacement bill. It is quite clear that they did not do quite exactly as the legislation law required, or Demosthenes would have made much of it, insisting that they had introduced their replacement bill at the confirmation of the corpus, posted it at the heroes' monument, and debated its merits in successive meetings of the assembly. Demosthenes would surely have reminded the jury of every step in the process. Instead, he presents Apsephion's bill to the jury (97–98) as a new proposal. Evidently he cannot say that they had heard it read in the assembly or seen it posted for some time. And, at some length (99–101), he has to insist upon the commitment that he and Apsephion have made to introduce the bill at the next session of *nomothetai*—which Leptines dismisses as a scam.

The Syndics

Even though Apsephion and his colleagues had not followed the old legislation law to the letter, by relying on it to justify their lawsuit they seem to have opened the door for the opposition to invoke a key provision of that old protocol: to have public defenders of the law chosen in the assembly. And these *syndikoi* are formidable adversaries.

Leptines himself was a venerable figure, famous for his rationale in supporting Sparta after the defeat at Leuktra (in 371 BC): he would not let Athens stand idly by and watch while Hellas was bereft of an eye (Aristotle *Rhet.* 3.10, 1411a).

He is assumed to be the Leptines of Koile who heads the list of men from whom Androtion extracted trivial sums;[16] that same Leptines from Koile (evidently) served as trierarch in 366/5.

Leodamas we have noticed (at note 5), and his involvement probably goes back to the case against the decree for Chabrias—his grievance may be personal.

But foremost among the syndics was Aristophon, who had been active in patching the League together and was recently prominent in the impeachment trials of Iphikrates and Timotheos.[17] Late in his long career, he seems to have become a major defender of the faltering alliance, punishing the rebels and the generals who failed to subdue them. The fact that he himself had been honored with exemption only makes him a more convincing advocate for canceling that privilege.

A close second in influence was Kephisodotos (*PA* 8331), an orator second to none, as Demosthenes describes him (150). He was on the same side as Leptines in 371, supporting alliance with Sparta against Thebes, and perhaps his backing for Leptines' law represents a similar commitment to defense. But the only motive Demosthenes acknowledges is personal enmity: "It would be better to use his skill to punish those who injure *you* . . . ; if he has to be at odds with anyone, I think it ought to be those that wrong the demos and not those that do us some good." That personal hostility against a particular benefactor would be continued, perhaps, in Kephisodotos' attack on Chares in 349 regarding the defense of Olynthos.[18]

Finally, Deinias (*PA* 3163) belongs to the upper echelon of the wealthy elite,[19] notable for trierarchies as well as festival liturgies. Demosthenes suggests that he should earn some honors himself rather than jealously deny them to others (151).

With some among these advocates Isokrates may have been influential, but it is unlikely that he inspired their case. Leodamas is named among his students ([Plut.] *X orat.* 837d), but on the other hand, a more prominent associate of Isokrates, Timotheos, was targeted by Aristophon, and the latter's conciliatory approach to Thebes may also have put him at odds with Leptines and Kephisodotos. On balance, it seems doubtful to explain the backing for Leptines' law as a matter of partisan loyalty. From Demosthenes' treatment (146–53), it is unlikely that these five represented any faction or unified position. We cannot even be sure of the selection mechanism, whether they all volunteered to defend the law or were nominated in a more representative process.[20] Three of the five seem to have no public position against the law, and Demosthenes is left to his own devices to conjure up their arguments.

Before turning to those issues, however, we should sort out the rules regarding these public defenders. Demosthenes insists that each of them has served as *syndikos* before, and he produces a statute that would bar anyone from serving as *syndikos* twice (152–53). He vaguely acknowledges that "the law was not enacted for these [cases or persons?]" (οὐκ ἐπὶ τούτοις τεθείς). By the conventional understanding, he means that the measure in question did not target these particular politicians.[21] But I think the tactic here is of a piece with the main strategy: Demosthenes seems to be extracting a broader principle from a law devised for a different situation.

Lene Rubinstein sorted out the implications along these lines:[22] either the rule against repeated service was formulated for another duty (e.g., in *apographai* and other financial claims); or, more plausibly, the restriction affects "syndikoi who were elected by Assembly to represent the *polis* in certain public actions such as apophaseis or in disputes involving other poleis." But, "no matter what its original meaning," the law was regularly interpreted more broadly and could apply to what seem comparable roles.

After all, Demosthenes mentions this law with something close to an acknowledgement, that the law was not enacted for situations like the case at hand but for another function of *syndikoi*. "The law was not devised for these [cases], but so that the practice [of serving as *syndikos*] not become a business or the basis for *sykophantia*" (152). Of course the old legislation protocol and the remedy against unfitting law were never expected to be prolific areas of litigation, where some restriction would be needed to prevent enterprising litigators from making a career of it. So the most natural implication seems to be this: the law barring reiteration was not enacted for such cases as these (defending the laws against repeal or replacement) but to govern more common and corruptible litigation (*apophaseis, eisangeliai, endeixeis,* etc.) where public counsel were regularly elected to represent the city against other *poleis* or their own indicted politicians.[23]

§2. Reviving the Old Legislation Law

The legal argument proper is limited in scope (88–101),[24] and the division of labor largely dictates that restraint: the speaker who initially presented the case (Phormion, if not Apsephion himself) began by sorting out the laws in evidence, the *paragegrammenoi* (as in speeches 23 and 24). Demosthenes' job was to deal with the broader issue, but in order to make that perspective persuasive, he had to delve into legislative procedure. The law that governed the amendment of standing law (more than a year after enactment) required that a new law replace the old one. To comply with that rule (at least in principle), Apsephion drew up a replacement bill, complete with a remedy against those recipients who seemed unworthy while preserving those exemptions that were deserved. In so doing, Demosthenes claims that he and his colleagues are studiously following the old law that Leptines disregarded (88). And Demosthenes wants the jury to know that by promoting the new bill in this way, "nothing we say is meant to confuse or befuddle you." But he had to be concerned that the old legislation law (to be read at 92–93) would seem indeed confusing because, the truth is, they were not following it to the letter.

> (89) In all of this there is nothing that we invented and nothing novel, but the old law, which [Leptines] violated, called for legislation along these lines: if anyone thinks that one of the standing laws is not right, let him write it up [or "indict" it] and *introduce another in its place, one which he enacts while undoing the other.*[25] And after hearing the arguments, you are to chose the better law.
>
> (90) For the "Solon" who devised this method of lawmaking did not think it right that the *thesmothetai*, chosen by lot to enforce the laws, be twice scrutinized before taking office,[26] vetted in council and [again] by you in court, but the laws themselves, by which the officers serve and all others exercise their citizen rights, are enacted on the spur of the moment, whenever occasion arises, and take effect without being scrutinized.

Demosthenes takes the double scrutiny as a model to vindicate the procedure that he and his colleagues have followed: what they were attempting was consistent with the old way of lawmaking, in contrast to the prevailing fast track that led to Leptines' law. From their own experience, the jury probably found the current legislative process not so haphazard as Demosthenes claimed,[27] and many may have never taken part in the elaborate procedure that Demosthenes outlined here (89–90). So they perhaps regarded his claims with some suspicion, until the law was read to them at the end of section 92.

As though to answer their suspicions, Demosthenes complains that politicians hijacked lawmaking long ago and the current process of legislation has produced a mass of contradictions, constantly under review and with no end in sight (93). From that complaint MacDowell concluded that the old legislation law was actually abrogated; but that conclusion is misleading, as Demosthenes clearly invokes the old law as one still on the books.[28] To be sure, there may have been a later legislation law, with its own enabling statute (as MacDowell supposed), perhaps in line with the administrative reforms of the 370s. But the confusion at hand seems largely the result of adaptive practice, for Demosthenes does not expect Leptines to read out any statute to vindicate the procedure that he had followed.[29]

And Demosthenes claims to be confronting the case for the defense rather squarely. After the reading of the old legislation law (92–93) and the old guarantee-of-grants that Leptines' contradicted (95–97), he returns to that focus:

> (98) [Leptines] says that this law [which Apsephion proposes] has been written into evidence (παραγεγράφθαι) as a deception, and if the law Leptines has made is undone, this one [of ours] will not be legislated (οὐ τεθήσεσθαι).[30]
>
> (99) But I contend that, by your ballot, when that law of his is undone, the old law clearly calls for this measure that we offered in its place to be valid (*kyrios*); by that rule the *thesmothetai* wrote it into evidence for you.

He makes that pronouncement as though it is perspicuous, but it has been read as an obvious contradiction. As Wolff interpreted the argument, Demosthenes claims (here and elsewhere) that the replacement bill will be *automatically* enacted if the jury votes to repeal Leptines' law—and that is sheer trickery.[31] In fact, the speaker has to acknowledge the reality that the replacement bill will have to be submitted at the next session of *nomothetai* (137–38). And if the jury were paying attention to the argument and the documents, there may have been very little confusion on their part.

There are two considerations that must have been clear to the ancient audience from the relevant documents. First, when Leptines' law is repealed, *there will be an automatic effect on the laws in force*: the restoration-era rule (95–96), "grants given by the people shall be valid," will be the law of the land once again and the exemptions that Ktesippos and others enjoyed will be secure. So that part of the replacement bill will be, indeed, confirmed by a jury verdict canceling Leptines' law. But if that were all there was to it, the substitute bill would be superfluous.

The second and more awkward implication would have been clear from the reading of the old legislation law itself: standing law could not be simply repealed without new law to replace it. Therefore the prosecutors wrote up their own version: to end unworthy exemptions but keep the rest. That change would appeal to the jurors' sense of fairness, but as Demosthenes insisted, the replacement law was not just more equitable it was *required*. And it was in compliance with that requirement that the *thesmothetai* included the replacement law in the list of statutes posted on planks as part of the body of the evidence.

Yet there is a significant deviation from the prescribed protocol that Demosthenes never deigned to explain: rather than repeal and replace in the same process (as the legislation law required), they resorted to repealing Leptines' law first and pledging to enact their replacement afterward. It involved a sort of "bait and switch": pointing to the legislation law, Demosthenes said that a new bill was automatically enacted with repeal of the old, but then he had to admit that the substitute bill in this case would have to wait for enactment at the next legislative session. Having just heard the reading of the old legislation law with commentary (92–94), the jury would recognize that the mechanism to repeal and replace belonged to that protocol and not the proceedings at hand. And veterans among them probably understood that the lawsuit against unfitting legislation was invented for a different predicament, to block new law in the year when it would otherwise take effect. The old legislation law, by contrast, *required a replacement bill in order to make any change in the corpus of long-standing laws.* What Demosthenes seems to be telling them is that the rule is honored in principle, even though they resorted to a different remedy.

That is the best sense of the convoluted sentence at section 99: the old legislation law clearly dictates that, when Leptines' law is undone by the jurors' verdict, the replacement bill is approved; in accord with that law, the *thesmothetai* have included Apsephion's bill among the documents in evidence.[32] In this case, of course, enacting the replacement bill will not be a done deal. But, having just heard the old legislation law, the jurors would understand that—in that procedure—repealing the old law and replacing it are two aspects of the same decision: by one vote the sworn *nomothetai* will either enact the new bill or reject it. That is not the procedure at hand—Demosthenes is addressing the court, not the legislature—but the legislative model serves to justify it.

Conversely, if the proceedings at hand truly adhered to the old protocol, we might suppose that the rules required anyone intent on amending old law to repeal it *before* introducing the new bill,[33] as though the working principle of the old legislation law was to "repeal and *then* replace." But, as we saw in the last chapter, the confirmation protocol was designed to undo standing law with a bill to supersede it. That mechanism emerged from the experiments of the early fourth century. After democracy was restored, the law writers went to work restoring the body of law that the renegade regime had canceled, and new laws were enacted to supplement that body. The new legislation of that era does not seem to have been subject to any requirement to repeal and replace: *old* laws were reauthorized and reconciled with the Amnesty Agreement, and new constitutional rules were enacted the old fashioned way, by the demos directly.[34] The need for a protocol such as Demosthenes describes was not recognized until the next decade or so, when the chaotic situation that Aristophanes parodied in *Congresswomen* led to a new control on legislation. That is the predicament that called forth the old legislation law that Demosthenes would invoke first against Leptines and, again, against Timokrates. It was designed to prevent or eliminate contradictions in the longstanding law and, to that end, required a studious protocol: in order to undo or amend a standing law, the lawgiver had to introduce a replacement bill and fully publicize the changes (not try to sneak something in, as Timokrates did). And then, if the new bill were approved by the demos and poised to supersede the standing law, any concerned citizen could still challenge the *decree* for *nomothetai* to ratify the bill with *graphē paranomōn* (see chapter 2 §3).

It was only thereafter that the *graphē* against unfitting law emerged. When the old legislation law prevailed, no law that stood in the corpus could be repealed (or substantially altered) except by a replacement to cover the same ground. But then, to bypass that requirement, a more expeditious procedure was adopted (on the model of decrees) for laws that dealt with financial adjustment or other expedients that did not alter the *politeia*. The lawsuit against unfitting legislation was framed to deal with errant laws of that sort, to challenge the novelty in the year when it was to take effect. It was not designed to remove a law from the corpus, more than a year after enactment, but in Leptines' case the remedy had to be adapted to that predicament.

That reconstruction makes better sense of Demosthenes' conundrum. He has to explain an old legislation law that his audience may not remember but are bound to respect, a protocol that does not quite fit the case at hand but whose principle nonetheless applies: *standing law* must not be overturned without new law to replace it.

The Reprise in Timokrates' Case

Now, to be sure, in a year or so, Demosthenes and his allies seem to have succeeded in reviving the replacement protocol, and a confirmation vote was scheduled in the first prytany of the year. So when Demosthenes returned to this lesson in legislation law in *Timokrates,* he treated it as a more familiar paradigm: in Timokrates' case the laws for *nomothesia* were confidently described as "all established for quite some time now and often proven to your advantage."[35] But these tried and true statutes still required a primer on the details. So that the jury might better comprehend the rest of the argument (17), Diodoros proceeded, step by step, to show how Timokrates violated every safeguard. And after the legislation law was fully presented, he called for the clerk to read the law that provided a remedy: "Take this law first and read it for me, the statute that specifically bars anyone from introducing a law in conflict or, if anyone does, to indict him" (32).

In *Timokrates,* Demosthenes speaks of this remedy as though it is part of the legislation law.[36] But he is not referring to a remedy against an old law that somehow poses a conflict; it was devised as a way to rescind a law like Timokrates', one newly introduced. The crime is described in the present aspect, εἰσφέρειν, ἐὰν δέ τις εἰσφέρῃ, and the exegesis (34) shows that the lawsuit should commence when new law is "brought in," not after it has become a fixture among the standing laws. Those two features of the orator's description suggest that the remedy against unfitting legislation (νόμον μὴ ἐπιτήδειον θεῖναι) properly applied to laws recently ratified, not a year or more later.

So, as I have argued in the last chapter and those laying the groundwork for it,[37] the remedy against unfitting legislation was not part of the confirmation of the corpus at its inception. The latter was a protocol that allowed addenda or amendments to the standing laws only in the course of a rigorous review in the first prytany of the year. The lawsuit against unfitting nomos was created in response to abuses of the fast track (by which *nomoi* could be introduced at any time). It was originally a remedy after the fact, against the author of a statute within the year after its enactment. But sometime after 354, perhaps inspired by Demosthenes' arguments, the remedy against unfitting legislation was added to the revised version of the legislation law that is represented in the incongruous documents, Dem. 24.20–23 and 33. In that restatement of the law, penalties were prescribed against officers who neglect the confirmation protocol, and the fast-track remedy was adapted to the confirmation process. By this adaptation, the suit against unfitting law could be used to challenge a lawgiver who was using the confirmation to introduce a statute that was nonetheless at odds with others.

Both of the speechified cases came before that adaptation. Neither Leptines nor Timokrates had enacted his law through the confirmation process. Both laws appear to be products of more expeditious proceedings, and both were challenged with the remedy that was devised for abuses of that fast track. In each case there was an odd turn of events that made that remedy awkward, and that predicament led Demosthenes to invoke the old rules for confirmation.

Thus in *Timokrates*, as Diodoros waxes eloquent on the virtues of the old legislation law, he invokes the popular majority as guardian of the laws: the confirmation process gives the people the power to reject any bill that would pose a conflict, to quash it outright by their vote in the assembly. After all, even the appointed advocates may be silenced (he says), "so who stands as the one righteous and steadfast defender of the laws? It is you, the many!" (τίς οὖν μόνη φυλακὴ καὶ δικαία καὶ βέβαιος τῶν νόμων; ὑμεῖς οἱ πολλοί) (37). That describes the role of the people at large as first-deciders in a double-decision process. Timokrates had bypassed that first decision and evaded the requirements for public debate. And so Diodoros cannot be blamed for failing to block the bill before it was enacted: Epikrates moved his decree for *nomothetai* to decide measures for festival funding, and there was no warning that it would serve as a pretext for Timokrates' surety law.

By contrast, the old protocol scheduled a vote in the third assembly (24.25) for the demos then to decide whether the bill would go to the *nomothetai*. That procedure was not followed in either Leptines' case or Timokrates'—it probably would never have occurred to either lawgiver to wait for that opportunity. Timokrates' law was not debated or subject to any decision at all in the assembly. Instead, by Epikrates' decree evidently, the people passed an open resolution for *nomothetai* to enact financial measures to meet an exigency, and under that heading Timokrates snuck his bill in. So it was not debated and approved by the assembly before it was sent to the lawmakers for ratification, and that is the point of Demosthenes' objection (24.37–8): Timokrates' bill bypassed the demos.

Leptines' measure had not been enacted in quite the same way as Timokrates' would be, under cover of an open resolution for funding. There must have been spirited debate in the assembly, before the bill was remitted to *nomothetai* and ratified; so Bathippos was on guard to block the new law. But his death and the derelictions thereafter delayed the trial until the law was no longer a proper target for the remedy against fast-track legislation. It was that predicament that prompted Demosthenes to dredge up the old legislation law in Leptines' case, and that paradigm would prove all the more instructive in *Timokrates*.

Something more expeditious than confirmation appears to be the normal course of lawmaking in this period. On this fast track the role of *nomothetai* was often perfunctory: when the assembly passed the bill, it was as good as law. This way of lawmaking seems to have developed without any repeal of the old legislation law; the replacement protocol that Demosthenes describes was still on the books for him to invoke in 355/4. But that procedure was simply too burdensome for a productive agenda, so proponents of new law would naturally avoid it, if they could; they would proceed on the comfortable assumption that their measure posed no conflict. And that complacent legislation on the fast track seems to have prevailed even when, as in Leptines' case, the new bill would make a momentous change in the civic responsibilities of many.

What, after all, makes a law "unfitting"? Demosthenes reflected on this problem (20.91) and insisted that so long as the city adhered to the old arrangement, they laid down no novel or new-fangled laws, καινοὺς δ' οὐκ ἐτίθεσαν. That does not mean that they made no *new* laws at all but only that they made none that were disruptive—*kainos* is a disparaging word. And the obvious implication is that Leptines' law is just such a νόμος καινός, as it changes long-standing rules of civic obligation. The fast track was designed for that happy time when the only new laws were not disruptive but congenial or readily "fitting" to the body of law and custom. Leptines had taken that well-worn path with a measure that was anything but fitting to the character of the demos (as Demosthenes portrays it). But, before we proceed to that character study (in §3), it may be helpful here to review how the constitutional remedies came about and where this speech fits into the sequence.

Legislation and the Lawsuits to Control It

The lawsuit against unfitting legislation (νόμον μὴ ἐπιτήδειον θεῖναι) was not devised to repeal standing law but to abrogate what was recently enacted. That it is properly a lawsuit of this sort is indicated by (a) the legal description itself, *nomon mē epitēdeion theinai*—not against the law alone but the act of making it law—and (b) the fact that the author of the pending law is himself liable in the year when the law is newly enacted (as in Timokrates' case), but a year later the author becomes immune (as in Leptines' case). Conversely, (c) the rule that *syndikoi* be chosen to defend the standing law properly belongs to the old legislative review or confirmation, regarding laws that were framed by some "Solon" long since immune. There are no such *syndikoi* in Timokrates' case; they seem to be required against Leptines' law only because, more than a year after enactment, it had to be treated, technically, as standing law.

After all, the suit against "unfitting legislation" was not simply a special application of the older *graphē paranomōn*. We find no reference to any such remedy in Nikomachos' case (398 BC) or in *Congresswomen* (392 BC), though both sources point to the need for some such safeguard.[38] The earliest cases attested take us back only to the late 380s. So, most probably, the remedy against unfitting legislation was not part of the original mechanism for confirmation and amendments to the corpus. The confirmation protocol was never meant to govern all legislation; it was only required for the troublesome situation where a standing law had to be undone or substantially altered. Before Nikophon's Coinage Law (375/4) it looks as though financial expedients were largely governed by decrees enacted expeditiously in the assembly. So it was no great leap to enact such measures as *nomoi* on a fast track, without waiting for the confirmation. When such rules had to be ratified as laws, they were treated as supplementary, adding to the corpus and not correcting it, even where the new rule overturned some venerable conventions, as both Leptines' law and Timokrates' would do.

As for the change that brought this about, Demosthenes says, rather cryptically ("*as I learn*" from older witnesses), that certain politicians managed to take control of legislation, enabling them to make laws at will, as the occasion arose.[39]

That treatment suggests that the prevailing procedure developed through casual adaptation, not by any historic reform. If there were a fundamental law of, say, the 380s, codifying the fast-track process, Demosthenes would expect the *syndikoi* to cite that law in answer to his insistence that confirmation was required. So the enactment of Leptines' law, like most of the nomothetic decisions known to us, seems to have followed a simple procedure that was adopted without any monumental change in the legislation law. So long as the new bill seemed consistent with standing law on the face of it and posed no obvious contradiction, there was no need for the burdensome protocol in the first prytany.

Demosthenes had to reckon with the old procedure, to repeal and replace standing law, only because of the peculiar situation in Leptines' case. To be sure, Leptines' law had been challenged soon after it was enacted, but the lead prosecutor had died, others dithered and abandoned the suit, and more than a year had passed; at that point Leptines' law had to be treated as "standing law," *keimenos nomos,* to be defended by public advocates, *syndikoi.* So Demosthenes turned the old protocol to his advantage. He could reasonably argue that Leptines should have followed the rules to dispose of the old law, "grants given by the people shall be valid," though everyone knew its context and implicit limitation. To make that charge meaningful, Demosthenes insisted that his colleagues were doing as Leptines should have done: rescinding the aberrant law with a replacement bill in the works.

§3. *Ēthos*, Integrity, and Second Decision

Reviving the law for legislative repeal gave the lawsuit its guiding principle, but whether the case succeeded or failed would depend on how readily the jurors saw Leptines' law as "unfitting" for the character of the community. That criterion may have seemed self-evident in the enabling statute for the lawsuit against "unfitting legislation," but for Leptines' peculiar case, it had to be discovered or reconstructed from the confirmation protocol. In that mechanism Demosthenes found the same principle that governed the scrutiny of officers: a second decision was the mainstay of democratic integrity.[40]

From a historical perspective, it seems all too obvious that decisions driven by some passionate reaction or particular crisis are likely to prove shortsighted. But even a novice must realize that it is only self-defeating to blame the people for their own mistakes. And so Demosthenes comes as close as he dares: He portrays the demos as an honest character, but he warns of the slippery slope that the people stumble toward if they once begin to renege on their commitments (120–24). And then, after considering what makes their community superior to the oligarchies around them, he blames Leptines and his co-counsel for leading the people down from that high standard to serve their own spite.

All of the advocates who defend Leptines' law have turned against Athenian values, Demosthenes argues. The culture of honor and privilege is essential to the Athenian community, yet these syndics seem eager to deny such honors to others categorically, evidently to injure their enemies without having to attack them on the merits (137–38).[41] And on that note Demosthenes warns the jury of being tainted with the same suspicion (139–40): If this law is put into effect—denying men their rewards without proving they are undeserved—"you will appear to be acting out of jealousy" (δόξετε φθονήσαντες). And, of all failings, jealousy is the surest sign of viciousness in one's nature (φύσεως κακία).[42] It is a sin with no excuse, alien to a community that strives to remain above reproach. That righteous character that knows no envy is found in the city's funeral orations for the heroes who die defending her, in the celebrations for athletic victories, as well as the countless rewards for public service. Those practices define the community, and it is unfitting to undermine them with Leptines' law (141–42).

What follows takes a more combative tone, and I suspect that these concluding sections were added in the version for circulation. To make the syndics now more vivid to the readers, Demosthenes singles them out; he assigns some particular motive to each and thus puts identifiable faces on that insidious jealousy that would taint the people, if they let the law stand.

First he urges Leptines' to renounce his own law and not cling to rivalry (μηδὲν οὖν φιλονίκει, 144), and then he turns upon the other defenders (introduced above in §1), as though to accuse them all of colluding in a campaign of personal enmity. Leodamas was not content to challenge the decree honoring Chabrias, but now he tries again to take away the hero's reward—in defiance of the rule *ne bis in idem* (146–47). Aristophon should have renounced his own exemption when it was given, if he finds such honors improper, rather than now deny the same rewards to others (148–49). Kephisodotos should make enemies of those who injure the demos, not those who do them some good (150). Deinias should claim his own rewards, for all the good he does, rather than begrudge them to others (151). And they should all be wary of the law that bars elected *syndikoi* from serving twice in the same role, a statute framed to prevent self-dealing against the public interest (152–53).

So, to make the case for the old law as a barrier to self-inflicted disasters, Demosthenes shifts the blame from the people to their politicians: the leaders are the ones driven by envy, and they try to take advantage of a less rigorous legislative system to push through their spiteful initiatives. That is why the old procedure has to be revived: requiring a rigorous decision in the assembly after a proper sequence of public notice and informed debate, and then giving the bill a second decision by those who have sworn the judges' oath.

Demosthenes does not try to justify this procedure by some higher law; he simply invokes the (supposedly) Solonian model of official scrutiny (90). That is, the laws that the people choose to govern them must face a second vetting, just as the executive officers do. But the subtext seems to be something along these lines: Without a second decision, such as archons must face, the body is vulnerable to the crisis at hand. Whatever group is most motivated by spite or vested interest will dominate the meeting on any given day. At such moments the people may yield to their worst instinct, φύσεως κακία (140), and there will always be a politician eager to rouse their evil nature for his own reasons (141–53). Ordinary public notice may prove insufficient because the body of the people may not take the consequences to heart until they have stumbled down one path or the other. It is only with a second decision, by a body under oath, that the people can see beyond the front men to what the bill really represents.

The law canceling exemptions, in itself, would have no profound effect on the security or prosperity of the polis, but it does infringe upon a host of rules and interests. Taken literally, it violates the older law that "grants given by the people shall be valid." In principle, it breaks the rule against laws ἐπ' ἀνδρί inasmuch as it targets the personal enemies of the lawgiver and his backers. There are financial implications: if their exemptions are revoked, citizens and metics will have less of their wealth to spend on more vital needs, and if the Athenians renege on the benefits they have given foreign benefactors (such as Leukon), they can expect no more favors from them. But, above all, this case is a test of character: in all the wrangling over who else is worthy of rewards, "Don't do anything *unworthy of yourselves!*" (μήθ' ὑμεῖς ποιήσητε μηδὲν ἀνάξιον ὑμῶν αὐτῶν) (101).

That compelling "character" (ἦθος) is invoked early and often. It dictates the benefits that the demos deserve.[43] It is wrapped in good repute (δόξα χρηστή) with a wary eye on what it will cost to lose that banner of honor (10). And there is a broader obligation that those labels cannot quite capture. The good that benefactors do and the privileges they receive are not defined by particular transactions but linked in a "chain of reciprocity" or a web of shared advantages.

Yet the argument is not just a warning that Athenians may lose the good offices of some and the respect of others if they renege on the honors they have given; it is also a plea to preserve a deeper sense of obligation, to uphold the commitments that they have made in their own right but also to abide by their inherited duties. By Solon's inheritance law, a man was entitled to reward his benefactors, and his heirs were bound by that disposition; likewise the people have rewarded their benefactors by a sovereign right, which Leptines' law would revoke (104–5).

In this light, the case of Ktesippos (inheriting his exemption from Chabrias) finds an unfortunate parallel in the "reward" that was given to Lysimachos, the son of Aristeides. Some may say that heroes in the past were not so grandly honored, to which Demosthenes replies that they gave honors in proportion to "their customs at the time" (τοῖς τότ' ἔθεσιν). But if anyone was expecting him to concede that those heroes of a bygone era were content with more modest rewards, the answer here is a surprise: for he introduces a dubious decree of Alkibiades as though it bestows a lavish grant upon Aristeides' son Lysimachos, for no merit of his own but only for his father's contribution (114–15). Demosthenes either misconstrued the context or fell for a forgery.[44] That he would resort to such evidence only shows how committed he was to this line of argument.

He introduced that theme in the prologue: the authors of those inherited bargains may be long gone but the obligations are still binding (11–14). A law to renege on those commitments is the overthrow of the Athenian *ēthos* (τοῦ ἤθους τοῦ ὑμετέρου κύριον ποιῆσαι τοιοῦτον νόμον). That sense of deeper obligation, beyond what one freely contracted to do, was alive and undeniable in the aftermath of restoration in 403/2. Athenians united paid off the debts of the oligarchic regime: "the demos chose to contribute and share in the expense, not to undo any part of the agreement . . . to pay for the ones who had wronged you, not to prove false" to themselves. Again the pious example distorts the history: faced with Spartan intervention, the Athenians may have had little choice at the time, but it was remembered as a moral imperative.

In that prologue, Demosthenes was intent upon something deeper than contractual obligation: we pay more than we owe in order to preserve something more vital than the quid pro quo. He put that principle as plainly as he could (13–14): "The city's character (ἦθος), in fact, in many other instances such as I've described, would prove honest and reliable, not looking for the most profitable payoff but to do the right thing." It is more "the right thing" to do and satisfying to the moral sense for Leptines' to be guided by the jury (voting against the law) than for them to follow him; after all, however respectable Leptines is, "his *ēthos* is not superior to the city's."

To describe that standard of integrity, at times Demosthenes resorts to contractual models: the bond between Athens and her benefactors is a settlement or a treaty of sorts (*synthēkai*). But this bond goes beyond defined obligations; it is the linchpin of Athenian democracy (15–17, 121–22). Under tyranny or oligarchy, rewards are cheap—the regime may easily enrich its backers. But honors won in democracy have incalculably greater value as they are given willingly by men who enjoy no privilege but equal freedom to speak their minds; and, implicitly, their partners in the bargain expect the same attitudes in future. That implied consideration is all the more important, he insists, as for any form of government, the power to reward those who support the regime is no small protection.[45] Without that balance of rights and rewards, the *politeia* stands teetering on the slippery slope:

> Leptines will make some such argument as this, I suppose, that his law will not take away the statues and banquets from those who received them, nor deny to the city its right to honor [in that way] those who are worthy. . . . But whenever you take away anything that you have given to anyone previously, you put all the rest of the rewards in doubt. For what is there in a statue or an honorary feast that is any more secure than an exemption, once you are seen to have taken away what you have given?! (120–21)

Those commitments were all the more vital to the ancient democracy precisely because it was *not* egalitarian (like the *homoioi* at Sparta) but distributive; ideally, it was a system where each was rewarded in proportion to his worth (122). In defense of that character, Demosthenes built his case against Leptines' law not by defending exemption in itself but on the grounds that breaking such commitments would engender a vicious trait that puts all endowments of the demos at risk.[46]

§4. Looking Back on *Leptines* from the Modern Vantage

Demosthenes' defense of the old legislation law has had a perverse effect on modern commentary. His pleading often reads as though he and his audience would embrace a text-based constitutionalism rather like the American paradigm (which we explored in the Introduction). But he appeals to the character of the community more than the letter of the lawcode. To be sure, the lawsuit must show some direct conflict between the targeted bill and the body of statute, and the other studies in contradiction suggest that conflict in the text is critical. But, on that reckoning, the case against Leptines' law is almost without foundation. There is, of course, the old restoration-era law, by which "grants given by the demos shall be valid," but that proves to be a flimsy threshold. Everyone knew that the old law was meant to restore what was lost under the oligarchic regime, not to bar the people from altering their dispensations in future.

The crux of the case is the balance of privilege and obligation that gave Athenian democracy its peculiar character. Can the sovereign people arbitrarily abrogate the special status they have granted to their benefactors and bar such privilege ever after? David Hume, in 1742 (*Essays* no. 10), declared those clauses "absurd," as "the legislature vainly attempted to bind itself . . . from an universal sense in the people of their own levity and inconstancy." Demosthenes had to put it more politely: the critical question was whether the community would abide by its character. Their *politeia* depended on a particular sort of bargain: certain rights are *granted* or vested in one family or another in exchange for singular contributions. That construction is at odds with modern parallels on two dimensions: the place of the one among the many, and the way the rules stack up.

In the modern discussion we are likely to focus on rights that seem *inherent* in the individual, independent of any bargain with the group. That distinction was drawn by Benjamin Constant (de Rebecque) in 1819.[47] Constant discounted the traditional reliance on classical models: the latter had fostered both the conservative faith that guided the Anglo-American development—preserving rights and properties like an entailed inheritance—and the "collective will" that de Mably and Rousseau conjured up for the French Revolution.[48] In Constant's estimation, modern liberty belongs peculiarly to the individual as a creature of the marketplace; after all, commerce changes the very nature of property and gives the entrepreneur greater freedom from tribe and tradition. Of the ancients, Athens came the closest to that liberty, but her agora was still a long way from our predicament. In Leptines' case we see the differences laid bare. The kind of dispute that defines their *politeia* is not about individual rights but how the "customs of the constitution" set the balance of largesse and privilege. To alter that equation is to change the very character of the demos.

Our modern liberty, with its commitment to individual rights, is allied with representative government and a brand of constitutionalism constrained by the text. If our greatest fear is a tyrannical state intent upon denying our freedoms, then we find a bulwark in the written rules by which the community has bound itself to respect those rights. And, in modern democracies, those rules are framed by delegates of the people who must find a form of words to capture the will of their constituency. But in ancient Athens, of course, the rules are made by direct democracy, channeled through huge committees of citizens sworn, where the *dikastai* and *nomothetai* were not representatives but formed a critical mass of the demos itself. They spoke for themselves, and their deepest concern was the failure of community, overwhelmed by its own dysfunction or undermined by a foreign adversary. In that setting the rule of law is not guaranteed by statutes *per se* but by the shared values and characteristic practices that frame the body politic.

In his quest to get above the text, Demosthenes seems to be arguing for something like Ronald Dworkin's model in *Law's Empire*, but here again the difference is telling. For Dworkin, constitutional integrity relies on a coherent ranking of principles, and the gravest threat to the regime is revealed in "checkerboard statutes" that recognize rights in one quarter but deny them in another. Such were the original rules in the US Constitution favoring the slave-holding states, giving them disproportionate clout in Congress and the electoral college. From such cynical prescriptions, the Constitution emerged as a patchwork of rules, some to accommodate one region, others another, which we have struggled to sort out ever since.[49]

When it comes to ranking the rules, of course, there is a great divide between government guided by a prescriptive constitution and any direct democracy such as Athens'. But for our inquiry, perhaps the most instructive difference lies in the level of abstraction. Demosthenes never arrived at any canonical set of principles, beyond the priority of *nomoi* over *psēphismata*. We might expect him (or his rivals) to recognize certain fundamental laws as the standard by which lesser *nomoi* are measured; perhaps certain laws that were laid down at the founding or at the restoration should trump any that infringed upon them. From the preceding chapters, we could easily list them in a ranking that satisfies our own assumptions: citizens are entitled to due process, not to be denied by intimidation; no one is above the law and the rules that regulate his office; the verdicts of the court cannot be altered arbitrarily; and implied contracts are binding even upon the sovereign people. But for Demosthenes and his juries, in each case the standard has to be constructed anew. The corpus is conceived as a coherent body of rules only insofar as it fits the image of the community. And so, when unfitting law comes to trial, the issue is cast as a matter of self-awareness, whether the people will confirm or condemn themselves.

PART III

THE CROWN CASE AND ITS ANTECEDENTS

The Aftermath of Chaironeia

"Did you write a proposal to free the slaves?"
I did, so that free men not be enslaved.
"Did you write that exiles be restored [to their rights]?"
I did, so that no one else be driven into exile.
"What about the laws that prohibit such measures—didn't you read them?!"
I could not, because Macedonian arms blocked them out.
—Hypereides (frag. 27 [Kenyon] = Rutilius Lupus 1.19)

After the disastrous defeat in 338, the factions that dominated Athenian politics jockeyed for position, in line with the Macedonian juggernaut or against it, and that rivalry led to a series of decrees and lawsuits against them. There were at least four major cases of unlawful action involving Hypereides (Demosthenes' ally at the time) that unfolded in the few years after the disaster. These cases are known to us from persistent testimony and substantial fragments, and they will be the focus of the first two sections of this chapter. Then, in the third section, we take up the initial complaint in what was to be the most famous case in the dossier, the indictment that Aischines brought in 336 against Ktesiphon for the measure that he proposed in Demosthenes' honor.

§1. Hypereides on Defense

The Emergency Decree

Facing the loss at Chaironeia and the example that was made of Thebes thereafter, the Athenians had some serious second thoughts about their own *politeia*. Years later, Lykourgos gives an intimate glimpse of their experience as he describes the setting for Hypereides' emergency decree (*Against Leokrates* 36–41): women were cowering in their doorways desperate for news of their husbands and sons; old men no longer fit for military service were girding themselves to fight for survival. Facing an existential threat, Hypereides proposed a desperate measure beginning with what had been unthinkable: to free the slaves and enfranchise foreign residents, if they would fight for the Athenian cause. He would also restore citizen rights to those who had lost them, move the council down to the harbor town of Peiraieus, and relocate the women and children to that avenue of escape. Lykourgos tells us that Hypereides' measure passed in the assembly, so seriously did the Athenians take the threat. But evidently—though Lykourgos does not say so—Aristogeiton promptly challenged the measure as unlawful (*paranomon*). Luckily for all concerned, the emergency decree became moot when Philip stopped short of besieging Athens and, instead, imposed a precarious peace. Later tradition insists that Hypereides stood trial and won his acquittal with stark images of enslavement and barbarians at the gate.

Lykourgos does not mention the trial, where Hypereides defended his proposal to "liberate the slaves . . . so that free men not be enslaved"; it would only have distracted from his case against Leokrates. But the fragments of Hypereides' defense probably go back to a version for circulation, from which later authors may simply have assumed that the case was decided in court.

Be that as it may, years later Hypereides recalls the desperate situation in defense of another decree of rather less moment, one that was drafted before the disaster and indicted in the aftermath by an ambitious young litigator named Diondas.[1] And, in the course of that reassessment, Hypereides calls upon the Athenians to recognize how dysfunctional their remedy against unlawful action might be in the wrong hands: "*I am on trial for what you have already decided.* And yet, gentlemen of the jury, just as you think you must punish those who write decrees, if anyone authors anything against the interest of the demos, so, too, you should hold to account those that bring the indictments [in those cases]. For it is no less a wrong *to obstruct what is in the people's interest* by trumping up charges than it is to draft unlawful acts"[2] (145r. 3–9).

Against Diondas

Until a decade or so ago, the case against Diondas was known only from a few oblique references.[3] Now a substantial fragment of the speech has been recovered from palimpsest and subjected to meticulous study. Some questions remain but the key findings are fairly solid: this case involves a decree to honor Demosthenes that was blocked by the lawsuit, left in abeyance for more than two years, and then somehow came to trial with the consequences undiminished. That is to say, both the fate of the decree and the liability of the litigants are for the jury to decide. Unlike Aristokrates' case, where the *probouleuma* was blocked and died after a year of neglect, in this case the assembly passed the measure before it was challenged, and now, if the jury approves it, that decree will finally take effect. And there can be no question but that the author of the measure faces a serious penalty—Hypereides insists that he is on trial for what the demos has decided.

The conclusion to this case, when it finally came to trial, can be dated no earlier than winter or spring of 335/4.[4] The beginning is more doubtful. In later testimony Demosthenes mentions the case as though it targeted his cousin Demomeles as well as Hypereides for a decree honoring Demosthenes for his efforts on the eve of Chaironeia (Dem. 18.222–23); and, he tells us, Diondas lost that case conclusively, winning fewer than one-fifth of the ballots. Demosthenes had been honored by proposals of this sort on several occasions, so, conceivably, Diondas may have been involved in lawsuits against more than one. But the vote tally in this case probably means that it would have to be his last lawsuit *paranomōn*; evidently, after Diondas lost by that margin, he was barred from prosecuting other cases of the same sort, if not from all public suits.

Why would he take the chance? Hypereides describes Diondas as an extortionist litigator of the worst sort, a *sykophantēs* who brought many lawsuits but used them to force payment or other compliance, often without risking a trial. The case at hand appears to be the last such gamble before Diondas vanished from the legal-and-political scene. Horváth suggests that Diondas revived the case when he expected to leave Athens and join Alexander's campaign in Asia, so he had little to lose. That consideration may have factored into his decision, but it cannot be the whole story. He must have known that public opinion was largely hostile to Macedon and her sympathizers, and he must have realized that if he revived the case and then lost it, the crowning of Demosthenes, which he had thwarted thus far, would succeed at last. So it seems to me rather more likely that it was Hypereides and his group who forced the issue: they revived the decree when it suited their agenda, and Diondas was compelled to proceed. But how would that work?

There was legal recourse against a litigator who swore to prosecute and then failed to proceed,[5] but it seems to have been rarely invoked.[6] Perhaps, nonetheless, that risk figured into the calculation that prompted Diondas to approach the *thesmothetai* and at last set a date for trial. And there was certainly a compelling turn of events that would stir up the litigators on both sides (below at note 9). In any event, it seems to be a regular tactic in this era to initiate a lawsuit and leave the defendant in jeopardy until a favorable moment presented itself. It is that tactic that prompted Hypereides' complaint against a campaign of obstruction by the pro-Macedonian group, but there is no sign that Diondas was threatened with arrest or indictment on that account.

Hypereides is the one in jeopardy, and yet it looks as though his liability somehow goes back to a decree of 338/7 that Hypereides himself was not the first to propose. For it was Demosthenes' cousin, Demomeles, who initiated the proposal on the eve of Chaironeia to honor Demosthenes at the next Dionysia. Then, sometime after the defeat, Diondas challenged the decree before the honors could be proclaimed at that high-profile gathering in the spring. Later (in 330) Demosthenes speaks as though Demomeles and Hypereides were authors of one and the same measure, and this was the act that Diondas had challenged. From that testimony scholars have supposed that Hypereides added a rider to Demomeles' decree. But ordinarily the principal author would be defendant in the lawsuit against the decree, and yet Hypereides, in 335/4, proceeds as though that decree of 338 is the legislation at issue and he is somehow the one defendant who will be answerable for it.

The most attractive solution, at least one that fits all the evidence, is that sometime after 338/7 Hypereides proposed to revive the decree of Demomeles that Diondas left for dead. As for the circumstances that inspired this revival in 335/4, we should be wary of grasping at historical moments when the Athenians might actually think they could cast off the Macedonian yoke, or when Diondas might think the Athenians were cowed by Alexander. The more compelling context may be the threat to their autonomy that emerged in the winter of 335/4. The evidence we have points to that period and a campaign to preserve due process against the demands of the overlord.

Hypereides puts the backdrop to this case amid political maneuvers at Athens after the revolt of Thebes was crushed and Alexander demanded the surrender of Demosthenes, Lykourgos, and other spokesmen of the opposition. Diodoros tells us (17.15) that Phokion called for Demosthenes and the others to sacrifice themselves for the salvation of the city, just as the martyrs of early Attica had done; but the people shouted him down.[7] Then Demosthenes delivered an inspiring speech, and Demades (pocketing a bribe) came forward with an "artfully composed decree" (ψήφισμα γεγραμμένον φιλοτεχνῶς) to answer Alexander's demand with a more tolerable concession: the men whom Alexander accused of insurrection would face Athenian justice and the court of the people would "punish them according to the laws, if they deserved retribution" (κολάζειν κατὰ τοὺς νόμους, ἂν ὦσιν ἄξιοι τιμωρίας). Evidently, Demades' artful arguments persuaded Alexander that he had more to gain by fostering litigious infighting at Athens than by making martyrs of his enemies. That scene is the best setting for the revival of Demomeles' decree, and there are passages in the pages we have that seem to allude to pressure from Macedon to deliver up Demosthenes and his allies. But that context comes with complications.

Before the new fragment was found, scholars had supposed, from Demosthenes' brief mention and a few other clues, that the target of Diondas' lawsuit was a decree authored by Demomeles *and* Hypereides; presumably, the former had proposed it and the latter added a rider. But the new fragment makes that theory doubtful or inadequate, for Hypereides insists that he is the one on trial, and he never mentions or alludes to Demomeles. To be sure, what we have is but a fragment of a substantial speech, but if the aged cousin of Demosthenes were a co-defendant in this case, we might expect Hypereides to indicate that complication somewhere, as he follows the threads of litigation entangling this case.

The fragment frames the issue as follows: "In every hazard one must attribute the first steps and the planning to those who take action, but the outcome to Chance. Yet Diondas insists on the opposite: not to praise Demosthenes for his policy (*proairesis*) but to make *me* accountable (εὐθύνας δοῦναι) for Chance" (137v = Carey et al., "Fragments of Hyperides," 2008, p. 2, lines 2–8). Hypereides then recasts the history as a hypothetical: if anyone had promised *beforehand*, that he would persuade Thebes to make war on Philip and ally themselves with their old enemy, Athens, "would anyone have spoken against praising him and not for giving the greatest rewards to one who achieved such aims? So isn't it strange to promise everything to one who makes the commitment, before it comes true, and then, when he has made good on it, to prove thankless?"[8]

And then the speaker seems to acknowledge the recent demand, to surrender Demosthenes and others, including himself. He recasts it into the past, when Philip was still alive and plotting against Athenian interests, as another hypothetical:

> Consider, surely, men of Athens, if we had been seized and brought to trial before Philip, what would he have accused us of? Not that we blocked him from taking Byzantion, led Euboia to revolt, demolished the alliance he had with the Thebans and made them our allies? What retribution would we have faced from him? Wouldn't we have been put to death? I, for one, think so. And so isn't it strange, men of Athens, if on the same charges, we must be put in jeopardy [twice], at the hands of our adversaries [in Macedon] and before you [in court]? (17–26)

Of course it is Alexander who has, only recently, demanded the surrender of his adversaries; despite the hypothetical recasting, the jury would have to recognize the situation at hand. In fact, Hypereides goes on connecting the past and the present in the issue of democratic integrity: "Philip himself not only honored those who acted for him against you but also agitated for them to be honored among us[9]—so *they* are inscribed as *proxenoi*—but *we* are barred from confirming the honors that we have given some among ourselves!"[10] (27–31).

The "double jeopardy" of Hypereides and his allies—facing trial in Athens and execution in Pella—only makes sense in the context that Diodoros reports: Alexander has demanded that Athens surrender Demosthenes and others, to take retribution for their troublesome opposition. We might expect the speaker to indicate recent events more plainly, but consider how he alludes to the fate of Thebes and the consequences at hand: there are Theban refugees present in court, with nothing left to do but listen to the arguments—"I would it were not so," he says, to soften the bitter reminder. And on that note he cautions the jury: "If you reject this lawsuit, [the Thebans present] will rightly conclude that the accuser is out of his mind, raving mad, but that *you* are sticking by the same [commitments you made] . . . But if you convict, *they would have every right to charge you*, as you condemn yourselves for wrongdoing in the very cause that you called them to join" (173v. 8–176v. 1 = Carey et al. 5.25–6.1). That is to say, Demosthenes was singularly responsible for the alliance in 338; the Athenians must not now betray their commitment to that cause. Demosthenes and his group may have agitated in support of the Theban rebellion in 335, but Athens had not joined in the insurrection, so the fate of the Theban refugees does not affect this case except to make the moral burden more compelling.

Putting the various motives in perspective, one may reasonably suppose that Diondas was willing to revive his prosecution against the old decree because the Athenians were under pressure to hold their troublesome politicians to account—and perhaps because he expected to join the Macedonian force in Asia and thus evade any consequences at Athens (as Horváth suggests). But that scenario does not quite explain how the old decree in honor of Demosthenes came at last to trial with Hypereides as defendant and not Demomeles. From the pages preserved in the palimpsest we might rather conclude that, in response to Demades' artful proposal—to rally support against any impeachment of Demosthenes and his group—Hypereides revived the old decree honoring Demosthenes, and so Diondas had to take up the cold case. By this tactic Hypereides reminds the Athenians of their debt to Demosthenes and undermines the case against them both.

By this time, after all, Demomeles seems to be out of the picture (*APF* 3597, IIIB, p. 116). He had been at least in his sixties, perhaps seventy or so, when he proposed the measure in 338; he may now be deceased or no longer active. Some such turn of events would explain why Hypereides seems to be the target when the original author should be defendant.

Now (as we noticed), it seems clear that the original decree was indeed passed in 338 and then challenged after Chaironeia, before the crown could be presented at the Dionysia. Ordinarily any decree of the demos that was challenged would be ratified when the court confirmed it. But we are not well informed about what would happen in a case such as this, where the measure comes to court some years after its original enactment. The case against Ktesiphon is only a partial parallel but perhaps indicative (as we consider in the next chapter). In that case the council's proposal, the *probouleuma*, was challenged before passage in the assembly and, ordinarily, the viability of any such proposal ended with that council's year; and yet, evidently, the *probouleuma* was somehow revived in 330. Conversely, in Diondas' case, the decree actually passed in the assembly but was then challenged, only to be revived years later. But the most likely assumption, it seems to me, is much the same: the moribund decree was not likely to be resurrected in court without legislative intervention. None of the other cases cataloged in Hansen's *Sovereignty* indicate any delay of more than a year for decrees approved by the court after passage in the assembly; no such delay was suspected in this case until the new fragment was published.

And in favor of the defense renewing the decree, there is this consideration: Alexander has demanded the surrender of Demosthenes and the others, and it improves their situation considerably for the people to reaffirm their support and not rely on a proposal dimly remembered from years before. On this rationale, Hypereides probably proposed that the old decree, what they "already decided," at last be carried out. And amid the divisive politics of the time, he may have anticipated the legal challenge that would not go away: if anyone should try to quash this measure again, the case must at last proceed to trial—it must not be thwarted by the same tactics that blocked so many initiatives in the people's interest. Faced with a decree to this effect, Diondas may have had no better option than to take his chances with the penalties for frivolous prosecution (if he failed to win one fifth of the ballots)—and pack his gear for a long tour of duty with Alexander. After all, he was an ideal target for growing resentment against those who obstructed the people's decisions.

The Pattern of Obstruction

After the passage where Hypereides insisted, "*I* am on trial for what *you* have already decided," we find a list of complaints against Diondas for his litigious career. First these:

He indicted (ἐγράψατο) Charidemos, whom he now extols, for not doing what he was rewarded for [with citizenship] by gift of the demos; but, as [Diondas] was willing to make some money out of it, he failed to prosecute any of the charges. Lykourgos he prosecuted (ἐδίωξεν) not only for *paranoma* [to the *thesmothetai*] but also for religious wrong (*asebeia*) to the *archon basileus*. Demosthenes he has indicted more than fifteen times. But *against me he brought in three indictments the same day,*[11] and now his shamelessness has come to this, that he does not allow you to use either the measures that I proposed and the demos supported[12] or the court's decision. (145r/144v=Carey et al. 3.17–27)[13]

As Hypereides tells it, this campaign of litigiousness was simply obstructive: Diondas challenged legislation or otherwise preempted public business and left it to die of neglect (unless he was paid off). The three indictments against Hypereides, in the same day (3.23–27), are obscure to us, but the tactic seems to be this: on the same day when Diondas brought two other charges against him, Hypereides evidently proposed a measure to honor or appoint men who shared Hypereides' policy (on the anti-Macedonian side), and Diondas challenged the measure but has not yet brought it to court. Hypereides continues in that vein:

Now my accuser makes pronouncements about the decrees that were made before the battle and slanders them and says, let them be forgotten as soon as possible.[14] But I pray to the gods that we be released forthwith from what we are decreeing *now* and let that be forgotten as soon as we can. Those [earlier measures] are in step with the decrees of our forefathers, but these [concur] with the dogmata of Megarians and Corinthians. His vicious insanity has come to this, that *he* indicts *us* regarding the *politeia*. (176v=Carey et al. 6.19–26)

We are left to guess at the referents because the jury needed no explanation. The more recent measures, "what we are decreeing now . . . [to match] the dogmata of Megarians and Corinthians," presumably involve some gestures of compliance. The earlier measures, "in step with the decrees of our forefathers," would be acts of defiance. At least that sort of opposition fits the following:

Then again, whenever Diondas poses as righteous champion in the courts, saying that he has brought fifty indictments, if someone should ask him, "Have you ever won any?" he will prove to have won none at all. So surely he must have prosecuted [all those] fifty suits against the city's interests?

For the aim of an extortionist litigator (*sykophantēs*) is to stir up many disputes; the duty of a law-abiding citizen, to resolve them in the courts. But before you [Diondas] are twenty-five—though the law forbids anyone to proceed

> to court before he's thirty[15]—you've brought in twice as many lawsuits [as you have years], acting as front man for others who do not dare to bring suit lest they be exposed but take advantage of your recklessness
>
> Diondas was a volunteer [for the corps that Philip demanded] and received money from his demesmen and from the city [to help with the expense], and he says he is grateful to the demos that assigned him to serve . . . And if [that] expedition had actually come about, leaving behind the court contests against me, which he says were entered in your behalf, he would have gone off to join Philip and profit again from him for the contests he was fighting here on [Philip's] behalf.
>
> Only consider, gentleman of the jury, why you should trust in him and cast your ballot against me: Is it because he ever seemed to have anything [productive] to say in the past? Or is it because he is well known among you as a *sykophantēs*? But by Zeus [some might say] his relatives, whom he works for, are like-minded [or supportive]. As for the others I have nothing to say, but his [father] at the hearings in every case asks him to desist and says he doesn't like what Diondas is doing but [the son won't obey his own father]. Nonetheless [Diondas] accuses me because I wrote a decree to free the slaves that fight alongside the demos [as though *I* subvert *their* obedience?]·· (174v–174r = Carey et al. 7.27–8.32)

Here, as though to cap his counterattack against obstruction, Hypereides puts the case at hand in the shade of his emergency decree (after Chaironeia) that would have taken Athens on an inexorable course of defiance. A line is lost at the bottom of the page, which the editors reconstruct from Hypereides' famous saying: "It was not I who wrote the decree but the fight at Chaironeia" (frag. 28 Kenyon). But the theme seems to be solidarity: Diondas wars with his own father yet he condemns Hypereides for rewarding those who fight for Athens.

In sum: what we have preserved in the palimpsest is but a fraction of a longer text, but as a more or less random excerpt,[16] it gives us a measure of what was at issue. And in that calculation the charge of obstruction looms large, involving roughly 20 percent of the text we have.[17]

Our reading of this case is complicated by the looming penalty for groundless or "vexatious" prosecution. Demosthenes reports (18.222–23) that Diondas lost his case by the critical margin, four to one; and, most probably, he was therefore subject to some bar to legal recourse, in addition to the fine of ten minas. How or when the additional penalty (*prostimon*) applied remains uncertain, but it seems likely that, in this case, Diondas was subject to some disbarment.[18]

In any event, Hypereides' attack upon Diondas belongs to a set of cases contributing to something like a crisis of faith in the system, when the remedy itself seems subverted. The question loomed large, whether to let the procedural mechanism function as it had or allow the people to intervene to limit the damage done by partisan obstruction. The demand that Alexander made of the Athenians, after the destruction of Thebes, seems to have given clarity to their dilemma: Would they sacrifice the leaders of the opposition or insist upon due process?

Framing the issue in that way, Hypereides appealed to the distinctive character of the Athenian demos as a law-governed body. That seems to have been a standard strategy for the defense against charges of unlawful action, and it lent itself especially to cases such as this, where the defendant could pose as a champion of the people against the existential threat.[19]

§2. Hypereides for the Prosecution

The other major cases of this era seem defined by the same division, between the Macedonian sympathizers and those who claimed the righteous cause of defiance. And, of course, when a decree would give the other side the advantage, Hypereides argued to block it as unlawful. Of these the suit against Demades was most notorious in antiquity.

The Case against Demades

For the case against Demades we have to rely on a few famous passages, but even among the snippets, we see that partisanship can make much of trivial matters. Obstruction, of course, is often in the eye of the adversary: so might Demades have described Hypereides' suit against him for a decree honoring Euthykrates of Olynthos for his service as *proxenos* and granting (or restoring?) citizenship at Athens.[20] Hypereides' speech was well remembered for its scathing irony, as he recasted the language of Demades' decree to fit the reality as he saw it, mocking the conventional language of such honors:

> Be it decided that [Euthykrates] be *proxenos* because he speaks and acts in Philip's best interest [not ours]; because, when he commanded the Olynthian cavalry, he betrayed them to Philip and in so doing was responsible for the downfall of the Chalkidians [not that he rendered Athens any service]; because he acted as assessor of the captives [setting a price on his compatriots] when Olynthos was taken; because he acted against the city [of Athens] concerning the Delians' temple; and because, when our city was defeated at Chaironeia he neither buried the dead nor ransomed the captives [as any true friend would do].[21]

Also famous in antiquity was another purple passage that seems to capture the divisiveness of the time: "Speakers are like serpents, as all serpents are despised; but some of them have the capacity to injure human beings, and [at least] the copper-colored ones devour the others" (Harpokration, s.v. παρεῖαι ὄφεις = frag. 80). Swollen with venom against the aiders and abettors of the enemy, presumably, Hypereides cast himself in the species that strikes at other snakes. He might as well have admitted that his own suit against Demades' cynical concession was largely a strategy of obstruction against the inevitable.

After all, honorific measures for foreign benefactors, much like the honors voted for Demosthenes and other Athenian leaders, seem important for their *effect* on public opinion as much as they are an expression of it. In the case of Demades' decree for Euthykrates, the Athenians were to acknowledge that this ally of Philip would be the new face of their relations with the Chalkidike. But, in Hypereides' description, that rapprochement would be nothing better than surrender.

Against Philippides and Its Context

The case against Philippides[22] also represents that strategy: rousing the intransigents against the collaborators. Philippides proposed to honor the presiding councilmen (the *proedroi*) with a proclamation of praise (*epainos*) "for their justice toward to the Athenian people and for presiding by the laws" (Hypereides 4.6). And the singular service that earned this praise was a motion by these officers to bring a pro-Macedonian measure to a vote in the assembly, arguably in defiance of recent rules about how those presiders must proceed. The measure to crown certain Macedonian worthies was a significant gesture; it was approved by the demos in the face of what must have been vociferous opposition.[23] The decree to honor the *proedroi* for facilitating that obsequious act seems trivial in itself; its purpose was to undercut any charges against those officers.

The dating of this case is not altogether certain, but a terminus of some sort is indicated in this passage: "You have assumed that one person will be immortal, while condemning so great a city as ours to death—failing to recognize the fact, that no one among the tyrants ever came back to life after he died, but many cities that were utterly destroyed have once again become strong."[24] The present-perfect, "You *have* assumed" (ὑπείληφας), suggests, perhaps, that Philippides *currently* supposed Philip to be immortal, and that would give us a *terminus ante quem* in summer 336, to precede the death of Philip (Diod. Sic. 16.94–95). But the reading is uncertain,[25] and the tenor of the whole passage is rather curious: it should respond to some provocative statement(s) that Philippides made. Perhaps at some point he suggested (a) that Philip was *practically* "immortal," having survived injuries that would kill a lesser man, or (b) that whatever his reversals, his power would ultimately prevail (as it did). That sort of talk would not necessarily be silenced when Philip's death was first reported; his admirers might even deny the report. At the occasion of this speech such denial could be past but relatively recent.[26] And since Philip himself is not named or unambiguously indicated in this passage, it might even respond to the rumor that Alexander had died, soon after his father; perhaps Hypereides was taken in by it. After all, this was the news that prompted Thebes to rebel, for which Alexander held Demosthenes and his group responsible (Arrian *Anab.* 1.7–10). So, it seems best to concede that we cannot set the date any more precisely than 336 to 335.

In this case, as in the suit against Demades, there is great stress upon *kairos,* the critical moment. The ironic reference to tyrants, presumed immortal yet vulnerable to unforeseen events, touches on that theme. There is also the patriotic reminder, how Athens responded once upon a time: "[Remember] under the Thirty, how [even then] with outside forces arrayed against her and collaborators within, she survived. But you [Philippides et al.] have proved to be *opportunists keeping watch* on the city, waiting for the opening to speak or act against the demos. And yet, at the opportunity, you will promptly have the audacity to say that you are *on guard against the crises* that challenge the city" (8–9).

This theme—that those opposed are self-serving opportunists—works as well for the prosecution as for the defense (as in the fragment against Diondas). It is the natural response to those who defend the decree and claim that the prosecution is nothing but obstruction. And Philippides may have claimed to be the victim of obstruction all the more urgently, because this decree, if found unlawful, would be his "third strike" (11), disqualifying him from any further activism.

The Judgment against Polyeuktos

Among the known *graphai paranomōn* involving Hypereides, we have still to consider the curious case of Euxenippos against Polyeuktos. It is of interest here as ironic testimony on the divisiveness of the 330s and because the outcome suggests how charges of obstruction and self-dealing factored into the outcome in many cases, even when the stakes may seem trivial: "[E]ven the children just out of school know the speakers (*rhetores*) that are paid by [the enemy] and those citizens that receive guests from Macedon, greeting them when they arrive and taking them into their homes" (Hyp. *Eux.* 22).

In these proceedings the prosecutor proposed a penalty for the author of the decree to pay, often a crippling fine; if convicted, the defendant proposed an alternative. In weighing one penalty against another, the jury might want to show

how little they respected the prosecutors' motives. In this case Polyeuktos, though convicted, paid no more than a pittance, 25 drachmas, for a proposal by which tribal interests stood to lose a valuable asset.

As prosecutor, Euxenippos probably proposed a substantial fine, but then, in the penalty phase, Polyeuktos had the nerve to offer next to nothing, and the court sided with him. Now, after losing so little in the *graphē paranomōn*, Polyeuktos responded with an impeachment (*eisangelia*) against Euxenippos, and it is Hypereides' speech defending Euxenippos that gives us an account of the earlier case against Polyeuktos (in which the speechwriter probably assisted the prosecution). The impeachment case belongs to the period 330–324;[27] the suit for unlawful action, somewhat earlier.

That suit, the *graphē paranomōn* that interests us, had to do with the disposition of property that Macedon ceded to Athens after the Theban rebellion was crushed (in 335). The Athenians disposed of this boon by dividing the real estate among the ten tribes: each tribe was paired with another and each of the five pairs was assigned (by lot) one parcel of the property. Apparently there was some debate over the disposition of property attached or adjacent to the shrine of Amphiaraos in Oropos; this property was part of the parcel assigned to the tribes Akamantis and Hippothontis.[28] The Athenians had chosen Euxenippos and two others to seek divine guidance on the question of what to do with that property. Euxenippos slept in the sanctuary of Amphiaraos and reported a dream that evidently led the Athenians to abide by the original disposition they had made when Alexander gifted them with this contentious asset. Polyeuktos, however, proposed that the land be given to the shrine of Amphiaraos; revenue from the land would go to the cult. Evidently he argued against what he saw as sacrilege. To make good what the two tribes stood to lose, he proposed that compensation should come out of the largesse of the other eight tribes. That generosity with other people's money may have counted against him as much as anything else. Whatever the jurors' reasoning, they ruled against Polyeuktos' decree but settled upon the modest fine, one quarter of a mina. It is perhaps possible that Euxenippos and his backers had proposed so painless a penalty in a show of piety, but it is far more likely, I think, that Polyeuktos himself proposed the token fine and on this second question the jury sided with him.

Emboldened by that outcome (and backed by Lykourgos), Polyeuktos resorted to impeaching Euxenippos for corruption, claiming that Euxenippos ingratiated himself with Queen Olympias and the Macedonians (20–21). The evidence against this pious figure seems slim, but it points to a time when such suspicions might do some damage.

In the sequence of historic events, it is a case of little consequence, but it is important for our inquiry because it helps to gauge our unknowns. There were bound to be many cases now unattested, turning upon questions of no greater consequence than this, but driven by fear and suspicion of Macedon. It also illustrates how little we know of the sentencing parameters in *graphai paranomōn*, which will be critical in the next section and the following chapter.

§3. Aischines against Ktesiphon: The Crown Case in 336

Amid the barrage of partisan initiatives in this period (337 to 336), Ktesiphon proposed to crown Demosthenes yet again, including some of the same language as in the decrees of Aristonikos, Demomeles, and Hypereides. Aischines saw fit to indict him for it. The speech that Demosthenes was to compose in support of Ktesiphon became, of course, the most famous oration in the corpus; it is a tour de force in finding principle to match the character of the people. And, as we saw in the last two chapters, Demosthenes was remarkably successful at refashioning the very institutions of the law-bound community. He emerges as a figure true to his name, the strength of the demos. There was obvious resentment against this domineering agenda, and Aischines relied upon that public sentiment in blocking the further honors in 336. In the end, ironically, the outcome (in 330) shows that, in fact, the mantle of *dēmotikos* ("man of the people") would fit Demosthenes well enough. We examine the arguments at trial in the next chapter. In this section let us consider how the original indictment arose in the aftermath of Chaironeia.

Late in the year 338/7 Demosthenes carried a measure to expedite repairs to the fortifications of Athens.[29] Each tribe was to choose an officer to be responsible for their share of funding, and Demosthenes himself was chosen "wall builder" (*teichopoios*) for his tribe Pandionis. He was already serving in a very important position for the city, as director of the Theoric Fund. This fund was conceived as a "lockbox" for subsidies that allowed every Athenian to attend festivals and civic functions, but its manager oversaw much of the city's financing. In this role Demosthenes received ten talents for fortification; and, as wall builder for his tribe, he added 100 minas, out of his own pocket. In response to that patriotic gesture, Ktesiphon, as councilman, brought forward a *probouleuma* to crown Demosthenes at the Dionysia. This tribute must have focused on his personal contribution (the 100 minas), to justify yet another laurel on the heap. But it also praised his career of service in language borrowed from earlier honors, as "he carries on saying and doing what is best for the city."[30] And it was that reference to Demosthenes' weightier duties that opened the door to the legal challenge.

The timing of this case has always posed a problem. How could a lawsuit that seemed so straightforward when it was initiated (in 336) be abandoned for nearly six years and then somehow be brought to trial with undiminished consequences when the legalities were no longer compelling? Later tradition complicated the problem, obviously confused by the proliferation of honors and lawsuits: so Plutarch mistook Ktesiphon's case for an earlier one, dating the indictment to 338/7. And the two speeches that survive pose a puzzle of their own, as Aischines includes an attack on Demosthenes' role in events after 336, which Demosthenes himself does not answer.[31] So, in this section, let us try to sort out what we can make of the case he had initially, when Aischines brought his indictment.

The threshold for this remedy was, of course, contradiction between the targeted decree and the standing laws. In this case that conflict arose from the provision to honor Demosthenes for official duties, before he had faced his accounting. To make of that more than a technicality, Aischines gave the following explanation as to why it was important not to preempt accountability: "In the past certain men serving in the highest offices and in charge of revenue, each of them corrupt, had the backing of speakers in council and assembly and thus gained an advantage, before their accountings, in the form of public praise and acclamations. And so, at their accountings, their accusers were utterly baffled—and worse affected were the judges" (9–10).

Having once honored an officer for his service, the people were bound by their sense of decency or "shame" to vindicate that officer in his accountings. Aischines does not quite say that it was shame for being fooled; the polite sense is rather that, once they have given approval, they were honor-bound by it. To avoid such commitments, he says, a law was enacted to prohibit crowning before accounting. Yet arguments were devised to get around the rules, "*logoi* stronger than the laws" (11–13). Politicians pretending to have some scruples added a proviso, that the honorand *would be* crowned *when* he had rendered his accounts. Or they would argue that a public servant appointed by decree had no "office" subject to accounting but a "charge or duty" (ἐπιμέλειά τις καὶ διακονία); strictly speaking, "offices" (*archai*) were those that the *thesmothetai* alloted (among the tribes) in the Theseion and those that the people voted upon in ordinary elections. That distinction was probably one that Ktesiphon could seize upon in 336 as he honored Demosthenes particularly for his extraordinary contribution as wall builder for the tribe.

But, Aischines would insist, the law had closed that loophole by combining "elected offices and those in charge of public works . . . and those who undertake any of the city's business for more than thirty days and those who take on the leadership of a court," as did all those in charge of public works. For those overseers were not ordered simply "to serve" (*diakonein*) but "to hold office after confirmation . . . and to transcribe an accounting for the secretary and the auditors (*logistai*)," just as other officers must do. And on that note, after having the laws read to support his argument, he demands that the people must be all the more outraged at any expert in criminality (*kakourgos sophistēs*) who shamelessly outargues the laws (16).

In his defense, Demosthenes will resort to the "inescapable argument" (ἄφυκτος λόγος) that he is not accountable for what he contributed out of his own pocket. Aischines answers that "no one in the city . . . is *un*accountable for proceeds that come into the treasury by any means whatever" (17–18). So it is that priests are accountable, who receive only "perquisites"; and trierarchs, who fit out the ships at their own expense "and have spent the family fortune to earn your honor" (19); and even the Areiopagos council who serve as *emeriti*, without pay (20).

In what follows we find a revealing description of Demosthenes' major duties for the year in question, and Aischines remarks upon an important change in the rules thereafter. In that year (337/6), the director of the Theoric Fund held consolidated power over much of the state, but then Hegemon's law altered that arrangement and divided up the various duties. Aischines wants to suggest that this redistribution of powers was a conservative reform, restoring a level of accountability that had been lost; so he introduces it by saying that, once upon a time, the "comptroller" (*antigrapheus*) was elected at large and gave an accounting in the assembly every prytany. But, "before Hegemon's law was enacted, because of the trust that Euboulos inspired, those elected to manage the Theoric Fund controlled the comptroller's office and the 'receivers' (*apodektai*); they oversaw the shipyards and built up the armories, they were road-builders and maintained nearly the whole financial administration of the city" (25). Then Hegemon's law broke up that nexus of authority.

Schaefer long ago put this in perspective: in 340 Demosthenes succeeded in undermining the old limitations on war funding with his Trierarchic Law; by 338 Lykourgos was "comptroller" and thus in a position to put the funds where needed for defense; and then (337/6) Demosthenes himself was in charge of the Theoric Fund and so at least formally in control of all those agencies, as well as director of the shipyards.[32] Then Hegemon's law came in response to that concentration of powers. But it was more than an institutional reform; Hegemon's law was a reaction against the war party, and it fell in line with the *graphai paranomōn* against decrees honoring Demosthenes.

But something seems to be missing in the argument we have. Aischines wants to emphasize that Demosthenes held multiple offices for which he was accountable when Ktesiphon proposed to crown him in 336 (26). He was accountable in some way for the service to which Ktesiphon gave particular recognition, representing his tribe in the wall building, and he was certainly accountable for various duties in connection with the Theoric Fund. Indeed, as noted, the elected directors of the Theoric Fund once held preeminent authority over many sectors of Athenian finance, before Hegemon's law diminished that authority. And so Aischines can say, with no more than the usual exaggeration, that Ktesiphon proposed to crown Demosthenes (before his accounting) "when he held *all the offices at Athens altogether.*"

The point seems to be that Demosthenes was, indeed, in a position of singular dominance in Athenian government in the aftermath of Chaironeia, and Ktesiphon's proposal was a "coronation" of the more offensive sort. But in the speech we have, Aischines never says very plainly that the decree was originally actionable because Demosthenes was accountable for his management of the Theoric Fund. Something seems lost in adaptation. When Aischines drafted his speech for trial in 336 (or for publication in lieu of trial), Hegemon's law was a subject of current debate or a recent memory; Aischines could suggest that the law was prompted by the very dominance of Theoric Fund managers such as Demosthenes. But by 330 that argument has lost its edge (as we consider in chapter 9 §2)

A similar shift in perspective may help to explain the oddly legalistic argument that follows (37–40), where Aischines insists that there can be no contradiction in the laws (some allowing the crowning, others forbidding it) because the regular correction (as he calls it) must have resolved all repugnancy (see chapter 1 §1). Anyone in the ancient audience who had witnessed legislative battles of the last generation (from the 350s down to the 330s) must have recognized the irony in this pronouncement: laws were caught up in a constant process of amendment as, ordinarily, the later law superseded the older. The scenario that Aischines conjures up for us must have been a very rare occasion, if it ever happened, that any law was simply rescinded to resolve a contradiction. So Aischines was speaking tongue-in-cheek when he insisted that there could not possibly be conflicting laws in the corpus, because the annual correction demanded that any repugnancy be resolved. That mockery would have been rather more effective in 336, when the audience would readily remember the recent career of Demosthenes exploiting the old rules to repeal and replace prior law (see chapters 6 and 7). After all, it was Demosthenes himself who resurrected the old legislation law, with its confirmation protocol, in order to revive the case against Leptines' law. Shortly thereafter, either at trial or in publication, Demosthenes drew on that same model to challenge Timokrates' law. And then a decade later Demosthenes would draw upon the same set of rules (or some adaptation of them), as he introduced his Trierarchic Law and then defended it in court (chapter 2 §3). That triumph came in 340, so the parody that Aischines made of the procedure in 336 would strike a familiar note.

Of course, in 336 Demosthenes seems to have retained broad support. Aischines would expect to rely on the legalities and insist upon contradictions between the decree and the law. By 330 he had more of an opening on policy: the dogged campaign of defiance has proven a disaster, and Demosthenes himself seems to be in some jeopardy. Within the fabric of the speech we have, we can see threads of the original argument most clearly where it is fraying at the seams.

In the original complaint Aischines probably focused more closely on the statutes that barred crowning before accounting. The second count, against crowning in the theater, would have greater weight in 330, when the crowning was no longer presented as an honor from the tribe. And what would be the crux of the case in 330, that the honorand is simply unworthy, would be given less scope in 336, without the benefit of hindsight from the "fourth critical period," from the destruction of Thebes to the defeat of Sparta. Conversely, when the case came to trial in 330, Aischines no longer had much of a case on accountability, yet he must begin again from that threshold, stubbornly calling upon the laws as his only supporting speakers, his *synēgoroi*.[33]

The Crown Case Comes to Trial

They make slaves of private citizens and make much of their own *dynasteia; they dissolve the trials that laws prescribe and set trial by decrees decided in anger.*

—Aischines *Against Ktesiphon* (3)

In late summer of 330 BC the famous Crown Case finally proceeded to court. Six years earlier (as we saw at the end of the last chapter) council had approved Ktesiphon's proposal to crown Demosthenes for his contribution in the aftermath of Chaironeia, but Aischines had blocked the proposal, swearing to prosecute for unlawful action. At the end of that council's year the case had not come to trial and the proposal became moot. And so the matter stood until, six years later, the case was revived and came before a jury who enacted the measure at long last. The procedural moves that led to this outcome and the reasoning behind it are of great importance for our understanding of Athenian constitutional review, but the ancient sources give no explanation. The surviving speeches for both prosecution and defense expect Demosthenes to be crowned if the bill passes, and that prospect suggests that the measure had been somehow revived in the council of 330/29.[1] But there are also indications in both speeches that Aischines forced the issue.[2] So who took the initiative?

Why this litigation halted and then proceeded as it did is a question overshadowed by the rise of Macedon, and the momentous events in that historic process sometimes seem to dictate the course of the lawsuit. In 336, we are to suppose, the report of Philip's death convinced Aischines to put off the case against Ktesiphon; and then, in 330, after the Spartan rebellion was crushed, Aischines regained enough confidence to revive his case. But little that is political happens for only one reason, and in this instance, I think, it is misleading to suppose that Aischines went to court in triumph at the news of Agis' defeat. After all, Aischines had a shaky case in 336, he may have had no intention of ever taking it to trial, and until the moribund decree was somehow resurrected, he had nothing to gain by reviving his lawsuit.

So let us reconsider the evidence on this singular case from the perspective of the preceding chapters. In the first section we try to untangle the procedural complications. Then, in the succeeding sections, we examine the way the prosecutor's argument was adapted, from 336 to 330 BC, and conclude with perspective from the parallel case *Against Diondas.*

§1. How the Case Was Revived

In 352/1 we found the relevant rule stated unequivocally: the law makes decrees of council viable only for that council's year.[3] For that reason Aristokrates' *probouleuma* was moot when the case came to trial a year after it was approved. Demosthenes and his colleagues proceeded with the case nonetheless to punish the advocate of so lawless a proposal and make an example of him. We have no sign of any alteration in the relevant laws in the interim, so in order for Ktesiphon's crowning decree to be carried out years after the council that approved it left office, there must have been some exception or ad hoc decision by the demos.

The Council of 330/29 Takes Action

In Aischines' argument, in fact, we find a persistent protest against recent disruption in the way the remedy was supposed to work. In his prologue, leading to the epigraph for this chapter, Aischines is irate about some irregular maneuver by the *prytaneis* and presiders who managed the proceedings in council and assembly:

> Now some men readily author unlawful proposals, and these measures are put to a vote by others who serve as presiders, who were not allotted that office rightfully but whose selection was rigged (ἐκ παρασκευῆς). And if one among the other councilmen, who was really allotted the presidency, tries to announce the tally of your votes, he is threatened with impeachment by those who regard the constitution no longer as common property but their own personal asset. They make slaves of private citizens and make much of their own *dynasteia; they dissolve the trials that laws prescribe and set trial by decrees decided in anger.* (Aischines 3.3)

This passage is usually read as a rant against systemic dysfunction with no particular relevance,[4] but it describes just the sort of rule-bending that would have been required to bring Ktesiphon's proposal back to life: it had the support of a faction in council who managed to control the presidency of the assembly, violating protocol and threatening to prosecute anyone who objected. So Aischines goes on to complain that deliberations of the demos are "no longer controlled by the laws or the *prytaneis* or the *proedroi,* nor even by the tribe in prytany." In such circumstances, there is only one fixture of the constitution remaining—the suits for unlawful action: "And if you dissolve even these safeguards—or give permission to those who are busily undoing them—then, I tell you, little by little you will abandon the constitution without even realizing it" (5).

Thus Aischines insists that the remedy itself is under attack, and it seems reasonable to suppose that he is referring to his own case. That connection gives a particular relevance to the otherwise tedious disquisition that follows (6–8): As everyone knows, there are three forms of government; the important difference is that democracies are governed by their standing laws, while tyrannies and oligarchies govern by the disposition of those in control. The suit against unlawful action is the chief safeguard against those who are eager to bend the constitution to their will: "Let no one among you fail to recognize that, . . . when he enters the courtroom to decide a *graphē paranomōn,* on this day he will cast his ballot on the very freedom of speech," the right to speak out against those who abuse their authority. Yet, he claims, the proper functioning of the procedure itself is being undermined by recent maneuvers, and it was precisely to guard against just such erosions that the lawgiver put it first in the judges' oath: "'I shall cast my ballot in accord with the laws.' For [the lawgiver] knew well that, if the city keeps watch over the laws, it will also keep the democracy secure." The jurors must keep that principle in mind and stand their ground, as guardians of democracy.

After his argument is largely concluded, Aischines returns to his protest against irregular proceedings in a section that seems specifically adapted to the situation in 330 BC (191–94). He has just argued that the culture of self-promotion is out of hand, comparing the modest and often nameless memorials of the past (178–85), concluding with Archinos' decree for the heroes who restored democracy in 403 BC (187). For comparison, he has the clerk read out Ktesiphon's decree once again (188). It is the worst sort of fraud, he insists: this crowning for "saying and doing what is best for the city" rewards the very man who should bear the blame for the greatest disaster, and it diminishes the honors for those who restored democracy in the time of their fathers. Rather, let their story be a lesson: the first step in establishing oligarchy is to suspend the suits against unlawful action.[5]

The history lesson may be simplistic but the relevance should be clear enough: the recent legislative maneuver to revive Ktesiphon's proposal, long after it should have died without a vote, is the same sort of prelude to autocracy that their (grand)fathers witnessed. After all, his challenge to Ktesiphon's decree in 336, should have killed it for good, but that quietus has been somehow disturbed.

There was a long tradition of protest, however, against any obstruction of the people's decisions, and what he says next (192) is a response to that complaint. As Aischines tells it, his aged father recounted how he had witnessed regular recourse to *graphai paranomōn* in the early restoration era, in which juries were quick to convict for only a single defect; they did not reserve their wrath for measures that violate "all the laws," as now. These days "the secretary reads the unlawful proposal and the judges, as though they are hearing an incantation . . . have their minds on something else."

> And now, by the artfulness of Demosthenes, you are taking up a shameful practice in the courts. For the city's justice proceedings are turned around: *the prosecutor becomes defendant and the defendant prosecutes*; and sometimes the judges forget what they are there to decide, compelled to cast their ballot on claims they were not called to judge.[6]

Of course "the prosecutor becomes defendant" is practically a cliché,[7] but here it seems especially suited to the case at hand. Somehow, after blocking the proposal for six years, Aischines saw the tables turned, and now he has taken his case to court, only to put himself in jeopardy.

For Demosthenes calls upon the jury to take proper retribution against Aischines. He seems to refer to that prospect in his prologue (18.13), where he envisions some measure to silence the obstructionist once and for all, to repay him for all the calculated malice that he brought to the city's deliberations.[8] He makes the point more plainly in response to Aischines calling him a paid mouthpiece (82–83): "[Aischines claims] *I* keep quiet when I've gotten something and shout [for more] when I've spent it. But not *you* [Aischines]; you shout when you've gotten [paid for it] and won't ever stop, unless these [judges] stop you today and deny you the right" (παύσει δ' οὐδέποτ' ἐὰν μή σ' οὗτοι παύσωσιν ἀτιμώσαντες τήμερον). Again, it is often supposed that Aischines would merely face the regular consequences of failing to win one-fifth of the votes: a fine of a thousand drachmas and limited disbarment (as we saw in chapter 5 §1). But Demosthenes is insisting upon a more radical loss of rights—for if Aischines faced only the usual penalty, it would hardly silence him in the assembly and in trials by other procedures.

Following this thread of the argument we might suppose that Aischines was cornered by the maneuvers in council and proceeded with his case under compulsion; it was not he who forced the issue but others who forced it upon him.

After all, having sworn to prosecute, Aischines remained in jeopardy, in principle, so long as he failed to proceed with the cause he had sworn to. There was no statutory limit on the lawsuit, and just as the author of the proposal was never immune from prosecution, neither was the prosecutor.

Aischines at Last Proceeds with His Challenge

And yet Demosthenes insists that Aischines had seized upon recent reversals to renew his attack (after keeping quiet for some years), and Aischines himself seems to admit as much. Demosthenes describes his tactics as follows: "[Aischines] bides his time until you [Athenians] are fed up with the man who is constantly making proposals, or misfortune has delivered some reversal or some other difficulty (ἐναντίωμα παρὰ τῆς τύχης ἢ ἄλλο τι δύσκολον) has befallen you—many are the setbacks in human experience—and then at this moment of crisis, suddenly the orator appears, like wind after the calm" (18.308). Cawkwell concluded that this passage "seems to dispose of the notion that it was Demosthenes who brought on the case in 330, and invites speculation," that it was the defeat of the rebels that prompted Aischines at last to proceed (see note 2). To be sure, Aischines was a vindictive character who would target Demosthenes' allies in order to deflect any threat (as he acted against Timarchos). But was he so blind to public opinion as to resume prosecution when he had little likelihood of punishing Ktesiphon and nothing to gain against Demosthenes?

Aischines seems to acknowledge the complaint against him as an opportunist litigator and to concede that he had taken up the case out of the blue when he had left the public eye:

> [Demosthenes] begins his harangue with the claim that I brought this indictment not for the city's sake but as a demonstration for Alexander, to gratify his hatred for him. . . . And he will ask why I presented the indictment censuring the sum of his policy (*politeia*) and did not try to block each particular or bring suit in each instance, but only after delaying and not constantly coming forward on what affects the *politeia*.[9]

But he goes on to insist that he initiated the suit before Philip's death so he could hardly have done it to gratify Alexander—unless he had the same prophetic vision Demosthenes claimed then (219). Irony aside, that response suggests, at least, that his decision to proceed with the case in 330 was dictated by the obligation he undertook in 336.

So, are we to suppose that Aischines revived the case in order to rid himself at last of the jeopardy he had incurred by failing to proceed? Theophrastos reported, evidently, that failing to proceed in cases such as this brought the same penalties as failing to win one-fifth of the votes at trial.[10] But there is little evidence to confirm Theophrastos' testimony (if it is his). Harris has given a careful analysis of what the offense would amount to: if the prosecutor proceeded as far as arranging the *anakrisis* and then failed to attend, or if he was given a court date and then failed to appear, his punishment would be the same as if he had proceeded to trial and lost four to one (or worse). But Wallace has shown that, in fact, we have no clear confirmation of the rule for failing to proceed, and he suggests that the penalties applied only if the offender was proven to have taken payment. The one clear case (where a defendant is held liable for failing to proceed), against Theokrines ([Dem.] 58), seems to support that explanation. But that singular case is also consistent with the older view, that the disbarment only held until the fine was paid. In fact, at the time of Theokrines' case (ca. 339), there may have been no such rule as Theophrastos attested thereafter. The most reasonable hypothesis (it seems to me) is that the additional penalty of disbarment for failing to proceed—quite apart from liability for the fine—was introduced sometime after Theokrines' case, perhaps as a reaction against the partisan tactics of the 330s.

Nonetheless, from the indications on both sides, Aischines had a difficult choice to make in 330. Evidently, he could have withdrawn his challenge and acquiesced in the coronation, but he felt obliged by the oath he swore in 336, and so he took up the obligation that he had neglected for so long. For that decision Demosthenes condemned him as an opportunist and threatened him with dire consequences.

Facing a Special Penalty

As we noticed, Aischines protested that "the prosecutor becomes defendant and the defendant prosecutes" (193). But just what was his jeopardy? The conventional understanding is that Aischines faced the fine of ten minas for failing to win one-fifth of the ballots;[11] and perhaps, as a further consequence of losing the suit by that margin, he would be barred from litigation of the same sort. But that disability hardly seems severe enough to drive him into exile, and there is a thread of ancient commentary that indicates a more compelling penalty.

On the one hand, we are told that Aischines was fined and could not or would not pay the fine; under *atimia* on that account, he went into exile and ultimately set up shop in Rhodes. Ps.-Plutarch begins with that version of the story in *Lives of the Ten Orators* (840C–D): after failing to win one-fifth of the votes, Aischines fled to Rhodes "refusing to pay the thousand drachmas charged to his defeat." But the author adds that "other sources say, an additional penalty of *atimia* was assessed and he left the city unwillingly," setting out for Ephesos to meet with Alexander. The last detail is consistent with other reports,[12] and the implication, that he was driven into exile by an assessed penalty, also finds support in later tradition. The *Life of Aischines* attributed to Apollonios has this account: "*Having specified an additional penalty* if he failed to prove the measure *paranomon*, as he lost the case, because he was unable to pay the *judgment that he himself had specified*, he resorted to exile."[13] That tradition was followed by Photios: "[Aischines] himself set the penalty he would face, if he failed to prove the act unlawful, and as he failed to prove (his case), as he promised, he went into exile."[14] That testimony is at least consistent with indications in the two speeches that Aischines was threatened with radical disfranchisement, to be stripped of all rights. So let us consider just how—by what method and what rationale—that reversal came about.

The justification may owe something to Demosthenes' persistent demand (carried over from the Embassy Case), that Aischines must be punished as a traitor (*prodotēs*). Spengel's treatment remains notable in this regard: much of his essay deals with the litany of accusations against Aischines, but he reduced it all to a *non liquet*.[15] Even the most compelling of Demosthenes' charges, that Aischines was to blame for all the advantages Philip had gained—by the Peace of Philokrates (32–49) and later by Aischines' initiative at the Amphiktyonic Council (142–53)—provide no proof that Aischines actually conspired *to that end*.[16]

For modern readers, of course, intentions are crucial. But in the Athenian assembly, proving a traitor's purpose was not required to establish *prodosia*. The fate of the Arginousai generals is a case in point: the charge against them was not that they abandoned the casualties out of malice but simply that they failed to do as duty required. By the same standard, Aischines may have been blamed by many in the assembly for acting with reckless disregard of what he was giving up to the enemy.

In impeachment (*eisangelia*), in this period, the arrangements for trial would be prescribed by decree, taking account of any special circumstances.[17] In the earlier period, of course, the assembly might decide the case outright, without convening the court. But even in the most famous instance, the Arginousai case from 406, we are given an important clue as to how a decree for trial might depart from the ordinary procedure. As we saw (chapter 3, §§1–2), as Xenophon tells it, Kallixeinos had brought forward a decree of council for the assembly to decide upon the generals' impeachment without a proper trial.[18] When Euryptolemos demanded due process and challenged the decree as unlawful (*paranomon*), Lykiskos offered a solution, that the case against the impeachment decree be decided by the same ballot that would decide the fate of the generals. Euryptolemos wisely withdrew his challenge, but if he had not, the two cases would have been effectively joined, with the prosecutor in the *graphē paranomōn* subject to the penalty prescribed for the *prodotai.*

In Ktesiphon's case, to be sure, there was no formal indictment against Aischines for "treason," but such accusations may have shaped the decree for trial. In effect, by one verdict the court would decide both complaints, the suit for unlawful action against Ktesiphon and the recriminations against Aischines for "betrayal" and obstruction. In effect, the rule that Theophrastos attests for *eisangelia* was adopted for these proceedings: an assessed penalty, which threatened Ktesiphon, would loom over Aischines as well.

Some such ad hoc procedure is probably indicated in the sequel to that passage where Aischines protests that "the city's justice proceedings are turned around: the prosecutor becomes defendant and the defendant prosecutes." For he goes on to complain of the license with which decree-mongers point to some other offender, as though it legitimizes their own misdeeds:

> [T]he *judges forget what they are there to decide,* compelled to cast their ballot on claims they were not called to judge [lit., what they are not judges of]. So the defendant says—if he ever deigns to deal with the matter—not that his decree is lawful but that, for some time now, another fellow has authored such measures and got away with it. That is the argument, I hear, that gives Ktesiphon such confidence.[19]

And to magnify the injustice in this, he holds up the notorious example of Aristophon, who prided himself on facing charges of unlawful action (*paranomōn*) seventy-five times, never once convicted.[20]

Aristophon had constantly faced *graphai paranomōn* and escaped unscathed: he was proud of succeeding with his agenda in the face of prosecution, but he also succeeded in undermining that vital safeguard of the democracy. And it would not be surprising to find that Aristophon had achieved that record by branding the prosecutors as obstructionists—as Hypereides did in the case against Diondas and Demosthenes would do in the case at hand. By contrast, Aischines insists, Kephalos was a better model of the democratic citizen (*dēmotikōtatos*) and proud that he was *never defendant* in a *graphē paranomōn*. And in those days, "it was not only political adversaries who brought suit for unlawful acts against each other, but even friends against friends, if one committed any infraction against the city." This more democratic, less partisan principle is illustrated by Archinos indicting Thrasyboulos, one of his colleagues in the restoration: for Thrasyboulos had proposed to enfranchise metics and former slaves who fought alongside the democrats; and yet, despite his patriotic credentials, he was convicted of unlawful action. So, Aischines concludes, a verdict in defiance of the legalities should not be a reward even for heroes.

And then he turns to a more subtle point: when defendants such as Ktesiphon call upon generals and other distinguished backers, to "argue for dismissing suits *paranomōn*" or to excuse the unlawful actor,[21] "you should rightly consider them ungrateful. For anyone who has won some distinction in a democracy, yet dares to support those that draft unlawful acts, overthrows the very constitution that honors him."[22] What follows may seem another standard tactic for preempting the adversary's arguments, but again it seems to have special relevance to the irregular proceedings that have resurrected this case:

> Whenever a suit for unlawful acts comes to court the day is divided into three portions: The first waterjar runs for the accuser, for the laws and the democracy; the second, for the defendant in the case and those who speak on that very issue [whether guilty or not]; and whenever the unlawful act is not [?] undone on the first vote, the third waterjar is poured for the sentencing and assessing the magnitude of your anger. Whoever asks for your vote at the sentencing is [properly] pleading to soothe your anger. But one who pleads for your vote [on the penalty, already] in the first speech is begging [you to forfeit] your oath, your law, and your democracy, which no one is ever right to ask nor to surrender to another. . . . So tell them to let you cast your first ballot according to the laws and [only] then proceed with sentencing. (197–98)

Here Aischines anticipates arguments for the defense that properly belong to the penalty phase, as though his audience would readily expect it. To be sure, he does not mention his own predicament; he is invoking the model of ordinary procedure. But the way Aischines describes the second vote is puzzling enough to have confused the ancient editors: the main manuscript tradition says that the penalty phase will proceed, "if the unlawful act is *not* undone." What that might have meant (to those who kept the negative) is that, in many cases, the penalty phase serves to rectify an injustice that was *not* undone by simply rejecting the decree; the one responsible must be punished in proportion to the wrong.[23] Be that as it may, Aischines seems to have phrased this description ambiguously so as to allow for his own predicament (much as later tradition reports it): the jury might be called upon to weigh the penalty on either side, against the defendant if he lost (by whatever margin) or against the prosecutor if he lost by the damning disparity of four to one.

In such proceedings, there was a separate debate after the verdict, before the jurors voted on the penalty, but both parties would naturally anticipate the penalty phase in their arguments on the main issue. The prosecution would emphasize the consequences of the crime to justify the penalty they had proposed, and the defense would urge the jury to spare the defendant that jeopardy. What is unusual in Ktesiphon's case is that the defenders called upon the jury to punish the prosecutor himself with the utmost severity. That is in fact what Demosthenes demanded and it seems to be the strategy that Aischines anticipated here (197–98). That adaptation may reflect the same rising resentment against obstructionists indicated in Theophrastos' report (see note 10) that penalty assessment against frivolous prosecution became standard in impeachment proceedings (*eisangelia*). Evidently the decree for trial in Ktesiphon's case also adopted this recourse.

And so, as though seizing upon the break with conventional procedure, Aischines proposes his own amendment to the rules to limit the sort of tampering that has gotten him into this fix: "All things considered, I am tempted to propose *a law solely affecting graphai paranomōn*, barring the defendant as well as the prosecutor from calling upon advocates (*synēgoroi*). For justice is not indeterminate but defined in your laws" (199). It is that turn of thought that leads to the instructions on how properly to argue a case against unlawful action: Ktesiphon must read aloud the posted text of the indictment and the laws in evidence (on the *sanis*), and the judges should regard that billboard as a *kanōn*, a measuring device of what is lawful and what is not (200–1). We return to that formulation in the conclusion to this study.

§2. How the Charges Have Changed

From the evidence considered thus far, the most likely setting is this: a measure was introduced in the assembly in 330 to decide upon the old decree *de novo*. The current council seems to have adopted the old *probouleuma* as their own, and in the course of debate it was specified (presumably in a rider) that, if anyone challenged the measure as unlawful, he would be subject to the same penalty he proposed. Under that threat, Aischines could have withdrawn his challenge or simply kept silent. Instead he insisted upon taking the case to court, probably because he felt an obligation to his party and saw an opportunity, even if he could not prevail, to embarrass Demosthenes in the glaring light of recent events. But this reprise of the cold case would require some adjustments.

Crowning before Accounting

The first count in the indictment was that the decree would honor Demosthenes before he had rendered his accounts. Aischines gives a good explanation why that maneuver was made illegal: so as not to prejudice the jury when the officer had to face his reckoning for any failings on the job (9–12). In 336 that rationale seemed straightforward, but by 330 Demosthenes had long since met that obligation. Technically, Ktesiphon might still be liable, but for many among the jury, this crucial piece of the case would now seem pointless, unless there was some liability as yet unresolved.

Demosthenes said little about that aspect of the case, and we might suppose that he thought it more effective simply to dismiss it.[24] But Demosthenes acknowledged that he had evaded accounting in one particular, the donation he made in his tribe's behalf. His defense was simply that he gave it as a gift, and no one should have to account for what he gives outright. So he admitted that he made that donation in the course of public duties for which he was accountable, but he never gave an account of that funding. And that gap in the record left an opening for Aischines to suggest that Demosthenes still had something to hide.

After all, Ktesiphon's decree gave particular recognition to Demosthenes' service in the wall-building project in 337/6, and in that year there were two offices or levels of responsibility that Demosthenes held in regard to that project. As director of the Theoric Fund he was in charge of the fortification project for the city as a whole; in that capacity, he was accountable for the sum of ten talents (or more) that was collected and expended in that year. But he was also the *teichopoios* for Pandionis, called upon by his tribe to collect their part of the funding and see that it was put to good use. In the latter capacity, he seems to have contributed the whole sum of what was owed for his tribe out of his own pocket.[25] How was he accountable for that?

Aischines gave particular emphasis to the range of public works that Demosthenes had managed as director of the *theorikon,* insisting that he was accountable for even the least of those ministries.

> Those elected to manage the Theoric Fund, before Hegemon's law was enacted,[26] controlled the comptroller's office and the receivers (*apodektai*); they oversaw the shipyards and built up the armories, they were road-builders and managed nearly the whole financial administration of the city. . . . The lawgiver prohibited crowning anyone accountable for any one office, (even) the least important, before his accounting. But Ktesiphon did not hesitate to propose crowning Demosthenes when he was *in charge of all the offices at Athens altogether.*[27]

Aischines went on to reveal that it was Demosthenes himself who created the board of tribal *teichopoioi* when he authored the decree for the wall-building project late in the year 338/7. Before reading the decree (27–28), Aischines emphasized the date of it and described its general content: on the next to last day of Thargelion, Demosthenes proposed that in the first few days of the next month (the last in the year), there should be a convention of the tribes for them to choose their *teichopoioi,* to act as stewards and overseers of the work on the walls (in 337/6).

These *teichopoioi* were charged with fund-raising and advising about builders and resources, and they probably held little responsibility for major construction decisions;[28] each would collect the contribution for his tribe and see that it was put to proper use. That is certainly the sort of duty for which there should be an accounting, and the decree included a purpose clause to make that explicit: "so that the city have persons accountable, from whom to receive a report of what is spent" (ἵν' ἡ πόλις ἔχοι ὑπεύθυνα σώματα παρ' ὧν ἔμελλε τῶν ἀνηλωμένων λόγον ἀπολήψεσθαι) (27). But how or to whom were they accountable?

The general oversight of that project seems to be squarely within the province of the theoric director, the high office that Demosthenes held when the project was carried out. As Aischines introduced the decree, he emphasized that bureaucratic arrangement: "That he held the office in charge of the wall builders (τὴν τῶν τειχοποιῶν ἀρχὴν ἦρχεν) when this fellow [Ktesiphon] wrote his decree, and [Demosthenes] managed public funds and imposed fines, like other officers, and held judicial competence to preside in court, I offer Demosthenes himself as a witness" (27). Thereupon the decree of spring 337 was read to the court, and the likely implication is that the tribal *teichopoioi* were directly accountable to the director of the project, as it was within his jurisdiction to assess fines or call them to court for any failing.

Aischines went on to anticipate Demosthenes' reply in a way that is also revealing about this arrangement: from the evidence of the decree Demosthenes may argue that he was not allotted or elected by the demos to the post of *teichopoios* for his tribe, hence not accountable as regular officers were (28). After all, Demosthenes, as wall builder, was chosen by the tribe and not by the people at large. Yet those ten *teichopoioi* were persons accountable in some way (ὑπεύθυνα σώματα), and Aischines made a point of the fact that such officials, appointed by tribe or deme, faced an initial "scrutiny" or confirmation in court, as did officers chosen by the demos. But he did not say that their end-of-term accounting was handled in the usual way (involving accounting officers, *logistai* and *euthynoi*), presumably because it was not so. The arrangement, under Demosthenes' own decree, seems to be that tribal *teichopoioi* were accountable to the director of that project.

Of course the director of wall building in 337/6 was Demosthenes himself (τὴν τῶν τειχοποιῶν ἀρχὴν ἦρχεν), and in that capacity he should have been accountable even for the money that he personally contributed as wall builder for his tribe. Aischines does not make the point as clear as we would like, but his audience in 330 would have heard the decree and other evidence in detail, and some would remember the events for themselves.

Nonetheless, since Demosthenes had to have passed his accountings for his major offices in 336, it would seem absurd to insist that he was still accountable when the case came to trial in 330, for what he had donated six years earlier. But Aischines seems determined to make something of that old complaint, and the opening he found was this: that Demosthenes never made any formal accounting for his lesser duty, as *teichopoios* for his tribe. Demosthenes insists that there were others who had been honored for their largesse while subject to accounting for major offices (114), as though their precedent should excuse him from accounting for his gift.[29] But in the lead-up to that list of comparable honorands, he as much as admits that he had never given a proper accounting as *teichopoios* for his tribe. He protests that Aischines sees wrongdoing in generosity:

> I donated the money when I was in charge of the Theoric Fund, [and Ktesiphon] proposed the honor while I was subject to accounting. But [the honor] was not for any of the duties for which I was accountable, but for what I donated. . . . Yet [Aischines will say] "you were *teichopoios*." Yes, and on this account I was rightly honored, because I donated the expenses [for my tribe] and *did not enter it in the accounting*.[30]

Demosthenes objects that he covered those expenses out of his own pocket and therefore gave no account of it. That is, in his capacity as manager of the project, he made no separate receipt for that 100 minas, to show that, as tribal *teichopoios*, he had fulfilled his obligation. But for that very reason Aischines can claim that there was a separate duty for which Demosthenes had never faced any accounting, as it was not documented in his accounts as theoric director. And that distinction seems to be enough to make the old and otherwise obsolete complaint still viable, long after Demosthenes had passed his accountings for that year.

Crowning at the Dionysia

In the passage that we just examined (113), it is also important to notice what Demosthenes says about the focus of the decree that Ktesiphon proposed: he claims quite insistently, that this crowning was "not for any duties for which I was accountable, but for what I donated."[31] That focus is overshadowed later in the speech, as Demosthenes turns to defense of his policy as a whole. For Ktesiphon broadened his praise to embrace Demosthenes' leadership in general, claiming that Demosthenes "carries on saying and doing what is best for the polis." In that regard, as Demosthenes tells us (223), Ktesiphon's decree included the same language used in two (or three) other honorific decrees (as we consider in §3 of this chapter). The passage that is repeated from one decree to the next must have focused on "saying and doing what is best for the polis." When Aristonikos and Demomeles drafted their honorific decrees, in 340 and 338, Demosthenes had not yet created the board of tribal *teichopoioi* and had not yet made his donation as one among them; so, obviously, the particular service that Ktesiphon featured in his decree was not part of that recurrent praise.

Ktesiphon's focus upon service to the tribe is critical for the next count in the indictment, the charge that it was illegal to crown Demosthenes in the theater at the Dionysia. For the legal hurdle that Aischines raised in 330 may have been no obstacle at all in 336.[32]

In the legal argument proper, Aischines cites a set of laws that allow for crowning in the theater under certain conditions (30–31, 40–44), and among those was a rule that honors granted by tribe, *trittys*, or deme might be proclaimed in the theater if the assembly approved. Aischines expects the defense to cite this law as justifying their decree, and indeed, the original setting may have lent credence to their argument: the decree was proposed in council by Ktesiphon, as a representative of his tribal contingent, and he may have assumed some justification in proposing to honor Demosthenes as benefactor of his tribe.

The prosopography is inconclusive but, all things considered, it seems most probable that Ktesiphon belonged to the same tribe as Demosthenes, Pandionis. The name is not common. Of the few Ktesiphontes attested, the best connected is the son of Ktesippos of the deme Kytheros (*APF* 8889)—that is, of the tribe Pandionis.[33] Among the propertied families, this Ktesiphon Ktesippou Kytherrios is the most likely author of the decree that was targeted in the Crown Case.[34]

If Ktesiphon was a tribesman of Pandionis, it would have been understandable for him, as councilman in 336, to propose that this honorific measure for the tribe be approved in the assembly, to be proclaimed at the Dionysia. After all, the measure seems to be framed around the thank offering for Demosthenes covering the full expense for the tribe. That would be Ktesiphon's answer to both counts of the indictment: the gift to the tribe is not subject to accounting, and the decree does not originate with the demos.

But Ktesiphon went on, of course, to reprise the grand praise of the earlier honorifics, that Demosthenes "carries on saying and doing what is best for the polis." And that refrain would overshadow the tribal honors when the case finally came to trial. In fact, Aischines readily acknowledged that crowning in the theater was legal enough for a benefactor of the tribe or other subgroup (if the people as a body approved) precisely because the crowning in question could no longer be described as such a parochial gesture.

In sum, the original focus on beneficence for the tribe seems in keeping with the laws cited on both sides, but when the decree was revived, the gratitude of the tribe was incidental to the praise of the polis. Aischines now treats the decree as a measure by and for the demos, which should be properly proclaimed in the assembly of the people, not at the Dionysia. He could not make much of that issue in 336, but in 330 it became rather more plausible.

Aischines makes this claim without drawing any distinction to help the jury sort it out (36). Instead, he muddies the waters by insisting that, if there were really two laws on the books so directly in conflict—one allowing the crowning in the theater, the other forbidding it—that conflict would violate the legislation law and trigger a procedure to remove the contradiction (37–40). But, as Aischines himself acknowledges (41, 44), the law allowed a vote of the assembly for any honorific decree of the tribe or local group to be proclaimed in the theater. He discounts that distinction as any sort of defense because, with the renewal of the proposal in 330, the scope of the honor had expanded: the crowning was a decree of the people at large, to honor a benefactor of the polis. And so Aischines insists on the rule that any such crown, granted by the people in their assembly, be presented in that venue.

Falsifying the People's Decrees

On the first two counts of the indictment, in 330, Aischines shifted his strategy because the legal situation had changed. As we turn to the third and crucial charge, we find an even more profound shift in the political implications. For in the original complaint in 336, Aischines could make the argument that Demosthenes was simply ἀνάξιος, unworthy of the honor that Ktesiphon proposed: far from "saying and doing what is best," he had led the city into disaster. But in the argument we have from 330, Aischines has given that description an even more damning character: now he argues that Demosthenes has been systematically building his own *dynasteia* while his backers have promoted this image of him as the archetypal *dēmotikos*.[35] So Aischines embarks upon a caricature of this "man of the people," to show that portraying him in this way is a breach of "all the laws" that expressly bar falsehood in the people's decrees (50).

The basis for this law or laws against falsehood has never been explained with much conviction. Goodwin suggested that Aischines is referring to legislation that actually dealt with documents in the archive; the law was prompted by reasonable concern that promotional publications might make their way into the Metroon.[36] Presumably, there were laws sealing the public record against the sort of false documents that Habicht and others have surveyed.[37] Family and friends would inscribe a monument at their own expense—as evidently the clan of Kallias did for his notorious Peace and Democharès did for Demosthenes—and it was tempting thereafter to recognize that text in a decree or include it in the evidence for trial. But it seems to me more reasonable to suppose that Aischines means something closer to what he says: "all the laws" would be those that he cites in his legal argument, the laws regarding honorific decrees. These would be the *paragegrammenoi nomoi* listed on *sanides.*[38] Each statute would specify the remedies, and among them would be the rule for *graphē paranomōn,* if anyone authors a decree that is unlawful or inexpedient and not what is best for the polis. It would not be surprising to find that these provisions included some specific prohibition against "falsifying the record." Surely honors were barred if the honorand simply had not accomplished what his backers claimed.

In any event, the way Aischines has recast the conventional charge, that the honorand is unworthy, indicates another shift in strategy. In 336 Aischines would have described Demosthenes' career, up to the aftermath of Chaironeia, much as he does in the speech we have. But now, in 330, his profile also includes the developments that followed Philip's death down to 331/0. In regard to that period, most insistently, Aischines ridicules the grand pronouncement of Ktesiphon's decree (and those that preceded it), that Demosthenes "carries on saying and doing what is best for the polis." And that part of his speech may point, again, to what was really at issue in 330.

After the death of Philip, as Aischines claims, Demosthenes had carried on triumphant, as though Philip's successor were a ridiculous pretender, a Margites (160). And then, when Thebes rose in revolt and Alexander came to deal with it, Demosthenes was elected ambassador to negotiate with him, but the vaunted champion of the demos turned back in trepidation—for good reason. Alexander would demand his surrender as one of the instigators of that insurrection (Diod. Sic. 17.15). At that juncture (in 335/4), the Athenians rallied around Demosthenes and refused to surrender him to Alexander or to the synod of Greek states that followed his lead (161). Thereafter, as Aischines tells it, Demosthenes managed to win some indulgence from Alexander through the seductive appeal of a mutual companion (162). And that rapprochement (allegedly) explains why Demosthenes had no proposal to offer when a more plausible match for Macedon emerged, when the Persian king, with all his wealth and power, advanced to meet Alexander in Asia Minor (163–64).

As for the rebellion that arose under Spartan leadership, only to be crushed in 331/0, Aischines demands, "What, after all, did you [actually] do?" (165–66). Evidently Demosthenes put on quite an act: "You whirled around the dais claiming that you were working against Alexander, 'I confess to raising Laconia in revolt, I confess to stirring up the Thessalians [and others] to rebellion.'" (167). Of course Aischines has only contempt for that claim, but there was probably something to it. In any event, however trivial Demosthenes' role in rekindling the rebellion, he was bound to claim credit. Such claims would become known to Alexander and convince him that the time had come at last to hold to account this *dēmotikos* who keeps stirring up insurrection.

It is at this point in the speech (168) that Aischines turns intently upon the consummate "man of the people," matching the true qualifications of such a figure with the failings of Demosthenes (as Aischines sees them). That tag, *dēmotikos,* was probably applied to Demosthenes or assumed by him early on, but it seems to have taken on a special importance at this juncture, when the next-to-last gasp of rebellion was throttled and Demosthenes was likely to be blamed for it. Emissaries from Pella were expected to demand his surrender, but his defenders would protest that Demosthenes was in fact, as his very name proclaims, the bulwark of the people, the one who had steadfastly risked life and liberty to say and do what was best in their cause. And so, to reaffirm their faith in him and preempt the demands of the overlord, his backers had revived Ktesiphon's old decree.

§3. Why Crown Demosthenes (Again) in 330?

Demosthenes tells us that Ktesiphon had honored him in virtually the same language as others had used in two (or three) earlier decrees: by Aristonikos in 340 and thereafter by Demomeles and Hypereides. Why the fetish of coronation? Is it simply that Demosthenes could not satisfy his *philotimia*? Democracy is certainly plagued by politicians, past and present, who have an insatiable appetite for adulation, but if that were all there was to it, we would expect Aischines to say so: here is a self-proclaimed champion of the people who repeatedly calls upon his base to rehearse their adoration. Instead, Aischines himself never mentions the previous crownings. Perhaps that silence is only to avoid lending credibility to the decree at hand, but it may have been more important not to dwell upon the recurrent threat. For, in 330, Alexander was likely to demand the surrender of Demosthenes once again, as he did in 335/4.

As we saw in the last chapter (§1), the second crowning decree was challenged, left for dead, and then resurrected, much as Ktesiphon's would be. In their progress the two measures overlapped. Demomeles' decree was drafted before Chaironeia and indicted thereafter, before the crown could be proclaimed at the Dionysia; it was then three years later that the case came to its conclusion, as

Hypereides successfully defended the decree and it took effect. In the meantime, Ktesiphon seems to have introduced his decree practically as an alternative to Demomeles', before the earlier decree came back to life.

In his speech *Against Diondas,* Hypereides called upon the Athenians to recognize how dysfunctional their remedy against unlawful action might be in the wrong hands. It is a dominant theme in the fragment we have, and the passage that introduces it is worth reading again.

> *I am on trial for what you have already decided.* And yet, gentlemen of the jury, just as you think you must punish those who write decrees, if anyone authors anything against the interest of the demos, so, too, you should hold to account those that bring the indictments [in those cases]. For it is no less a wrong *to obstruct what is in the people's interest* by trumping up charges than it is to draft unlawful acts. (145r. 3–9)

The same passage might easily have found its way into Ktesiphon's defense, as Demosthenes insistently described Aischines as the arch opportunist, biding his time and venturing nothing until a crisis turns to his advantage (Dem. 18.13, 82–83, 216–19, 222–26, 308).

But if the prosecutors' tactics served only obstruction, what standard of constitutional integrity could anyone invoke to dismantle unlawful acts? If it was not enough to show that one statute clashed with another, where could anyone find a fixed standard, to decide between them? The answer, of course, was the very character of the people. But that standard was not a license for self-congratulation; it required self-awareness, for the people to recognize the obligations that came with their decisions.

That principle of implied contract was the dominant theme in Demosthenes' defense: true to his standing as the archetypal *dēmotikos,* he had done what the Athenian *ēthos* demanded. Hypereides alluded to it when he reminded his jurors (or his readers) of the fate of Thebes and the refugees present among them (176r/173v–176v = Carey et al., 5.25–6.1): if the jury rejected Diondas' suit, the Thebans would find proof in their verdict, "that you are standing by the same [commitments you made]. . . . But if you convict, *they would have every right to charge you,* as you condemn yourselves for wrongdoing in the very cause that you called them to join."

In this respect Demosthenes treated the two cases as virtually identical (222–24): to prosecute Ktesiphon for praising Demosthenes' role in the alliance with Thebes was tantamount to retrying what the court had already decided.[39] On a strictly procedural level, of course, the case against Ktesiphon was only a partial parallel: Hypereides' decree (or Demomeles') was ratified in the assembly in 338 and then challenged the next spring, before the honor could be proclaimed at the Dionysia. In Ktesiphon's case, again, it was the council's proposal, the *probouleuma*, that was challenged, before it could be passed in the assembly; and, ordinarily, the viability of any such proposal ended with that council's year (though the author remained liable), as in Aristokrates' case. And yet, Ktesiphon's *probouleuma* was revived in 330; it was probably reintroduced with some irregular maneuvering by factions in the council of 330/29. In Hypereides' defense *Against Diondas*, something similar may have happened: decrees that actually passed in the assembly but were then challenged, left in abeyance and only brought to trial years later, must have been rather rare (Hansen found none in *Sovereignty*, 1974). And at least in the case of Hypereides *Against Diondas*, the mechanism may have been much the same as in Ktesiphon's case: the moribund decree was not likely to be resurrected without some new initiative in council or assembly in defense of the *dēmotikos* who was now in jeopardy.

Two themes in the fragment *Against Diondas* point to this solution. First, considerable weight was put upon the pattern of obstruction: he had regularly taken advantage of the rules to initiate lawsuits without merit—"fifty indictments . . . but have you ever won any?" (175r–174v = Carey et al., 7.27–31). Evidently, his strategy was to coerce payment or compliance, otherwise leaving the accused in limbo without a decision. Such would also be the fate of Ktesiphon's decree if Demosthenes' backers had not taken the initiative to revive it. And second was the claim, which Demosthenes' would revive with his trope on *res judicatae* (224), that Aischines was relitigating settled matters and the people had to reaffirm their conviction, not to overturn what they resolved years before.

Demosthenes' formulation was the more daring, but it was essentially the same as Hypereides' claim, "I am on trial for what you have already decided." To be sure, in the earlier case, Hypereides evidently referred to the fact that the assembly had already passed the decree when it was challenged: so he insisted that the people's decision at last be carried out. Demosthenes' point was rather that, the substantive claim in Ktesiphon's case was the same as was decided in the earlier crowning: the alliance with Thebes had been Athens' saving grace.

Now, as I have argued (§1), the decree for trial in Ktesiphon's case most probably included a provision to balance the penalty assessment, to put the prosecutor in the same jeopardy as the defendant; and that adaptation, departing from the conventional procedure, was probably acceptable because Aischines' handling of the case was seen as the same sort of rank obstruction that Diondas and others had made a career of. Hypereides may have made essentially the same maneuver in 335/4, adding a provision that if Diondas should try to quash this measure again, the case must at last proceed to trial. At least, with such a precedent, the irregular procedure in Ktesiphon's case becomes less remarkable: neither speech explains it very plainly because it was a recurrent issue. In any event, when Demosthenes and his allies resorted to this strategy, to threaten the obstructionist with a more damning penalty, it was not novel. The issues were much the same: this measure to defend the leader who "carries on saying and doing what is best for the polis" must not be thwarted by the same tactics that blocked so many initiatives in the people's interest. Faced with legislative intervention of this sort, Diondas had no better option than to risk the penalties for reckless prosecution. And Aischines would face much the same predicament.

Thus the timing of the Crown Case may be explained by the parallel turn of events. The reckoning was indeed set in motion by the recent rebellion (of Agis) and came to court on the heels of defeat. But the prosecution was not revived by Aischines in triumph. Demosthenes had boasted of his role in fomenting insurrection and, once again, he was likely to face the wrath of Alexander. So Ktesiphon and other backers, with some maneuvering among the members in council, managed to reintroduce the old proposal. The purpose was to achieve precisely what Aischines warned of in crowning before accounting: to prejudice the jury of the people before they had to decide their leader's fate (9–12). For Aischines reveals not only that the crowning is back on the agenda but also that Demosthenes faces serious jeopardy: the Athenians must "send him away, to be rid of this disaster afflicting all Hellas" or "seize him like a thief . . . for retribution."[40] If they crown him, they make common cause with those who violate the peace; only if they do "the opposite," by conviction, can they absolve themselves.

Here at last Aischines seems to acknowledge what many of the jury would expect, that Alexander would demand the surrender of Demosthenes, to make an example of him. The court's verdict would have as much to do with that looming ultimatum as with any contradiction between the proposal and the standing law. As it turned out, the reckoning would be years yet in coming, but Aischines' case in 330 seems perilously close to the turning point, between Hypereides' defense of Demosthenes in 334 and the conviction for corruption a decade later, when Hypereides joined his accusers.[41]

Law's Measure

> The decision is for you to make, among the same sworn jurors who decide the other issues as well.
>
> —Demosthenes, *Against Leptines* (93)

Demosthenes articulated a view of constitutional control that is very different from what many of us take for granted in modern democracies. Thus, in the case against Leptines' law, he described the old template for making new laws and identified the judges at hand with the lawmakers in that process: from one session to another the personnel may change but the sovereign body is the same. By contrast we modern democrats usually (at least in the United States) embrace a principle of separation that owes much to Montesquieu: certain powers are assigned to the legislature and others to the executive, and both are subject to "checks and balances." In that system we have come to respect the court as a separate but equal partner, with the authority to overturn any act by another branch that goes against the fundamental law. And that fundamental law is found in a Constitution that somehow constrains the sovereign people and all their countervailing representatives. Montesquieu's paradigm was inspired by the mechanics of government in Europe (and Britain in particular) in the eighteenth century, where the interests of Crown and Commons must be balanced against the nobility.[1] The court was not a separate estate; its role was to serve as a corrective to actions by the king or the legislature that would prove repugnant or impracticable, not to trump their authority.[2]

Such mechanics had a great appeal to the American Framers, and so Montesquieu's scheme was translated into the new world, however precariously. The executive serves in place of a king (and seems ever more regal),[3] the bodies that were modeled on the commons and the nobility were joined in a bicameral legislature, and the court emerged as the third entity to constrain the others. But the essential principle is much the same: "Let no party be judge in his own case."[4] That maxim guided the Framers here in the United States, as articulated in *The Federalist*: the rationale for empowering a Supreme Court, to prevail in disputes among the states, or between federal authority and the states, is that same incontestable rule, *nemo iudex in sua causa*. Just as a state court could not be impartial in deciding disputes between that state and another, neither could the federal legislature be expected to rule against their own decisions.[5]

At Athens the defining principle was just the opposite. The same men who decided upon legislation in the assembly and other issues in the courts were also called upon to decide under oath when there was an amendment or challenge to the laws. That jury *was* the people: not a superior body with expertise to review what the people's delegates had construed, but a more perfect embodiment of the demos. From their perspective, the constitutional remedies—the lawsuits against unlawful decrees and unfitting laws—were not a curb upon the sovereign people. Rather, that recourse began and continued to be understood as a safeguard against rogue leaders, against councilmen and speakers who ventured beyond their proper role. The standard line of argument in such cases was to show that the wrongful act was contrary to the very character of the people, and the author of that wrongful legislation was leading the demos to betray themselves. Standing against the unlawful actor, the people must uphold the laws that they themselves had laid down as well as the customary roles and rules that they lived by. They had to defend the integrity of the standing laws, not because that set of statutes contained in itself a commandment higher than the will of the people, but because the very character of the community was found in the laws they had made (Dem. 24.210).

This concluding chapter is a profile of that demotic character. We consider first how the Athenians saw the constitutional constraints that they put upon themselves, as a body whose workings were defined in their *nomoi*, and then how their system of legislation and constitutional control developed in that image.

§1. The Search for a Standard

What is the defining trait of the Athenian democracy? We might expect "equal rights under the law" to be fundamental, and there are cases to be sure where the principle of *isonomia* is invoked. But in the suits against unlawful acts and unfitting laws, that catchword is never seized upon as the ultimate test of new legislation. The prevailing emphasis in these arguments is upon the bargain peculiar to the Athenian system: some partners in the *politeia* are, so to speak, more equal than others. After all, the surviving speeches deal with issues of privilege in one way or another. The people's chosen leaders, generals, and administrators have authority over others ex officio, and the people's benefactors earn special treatment, honors, and exemptions beyond the grasp of ordinary Athenians. That code of privilege is consistent with the principle of "equal rights under the law" because everyman (supposedly) has the opportunity to serve the polis and earn similar distinctions. In fact, it is that very bargain, privilege in exchange for singular service, that defines the Athenian *politeia*, as opposed to the regimes at Sparta and elsewhere. "Equality" of a more generic sort is a mainstay of *oligarchies*: there everyone among the ruling class has an equal status with the others, and that egalitarian *ēthos* builds solidarity among the elite. In the democracy, by contrast, there is a vital competition for honors and rewards from the people, and it is their control of that process that safeguards their liberty.[6] On that basis, the checks and balances that sustained the Athenian system were not vested in branches of government but were included in the bargain between a privileged few and the ranks of ordinary citizens who sat in judgment of them.

In these cases of constitutional control, the argument is often about measures that breach the bargain. Androtion's excesses as tax collector, for instance, should disqualify him from the crowning that he claims (for himself and colleagues in council). Here the compelling principle is not *isonomia* so much as common dignity: the rights he violated were not codified in statute but embedded in customary considerations of solidarity and compassion. From this perspective, every Athenian should be outraged by Androtion and his thugs invading their homes to drag them off to jail, driving their neighbors to run and hide like slaves. After all, it is the mark of free men to pay what they owe from their property, not with their persons. By that standard, Androtion's gestapo tactics undermined the city's defining roles and rules, τῆς πολιτείας ἔθη (22.57–59 and 24.169–71). He leads them down the path to "a city of slaves" (22.68).

The system built on asymmetric obligations and lawful disparity called for constant calibration. The special status proposed for Charidemos (in Dem. 23) obviously went too far, however vital he was to Thraceward operations. For the privilege proposed in his honor, a limitless warrant against any (accused) assassin, would undermine a host of rules that preserved the community against bloodshed and reprisal. For each to "have an equal share in the constitution," πολιτείας ἶσον μέτεστιν ἑκάστῳ (86), was not just a matter of procedural integrity; it defined the polis. Against Leptines' law (Dem. 20), Demosthenes had come to that principle from the other direction: assuming every public servant has the opportunity, the heirs of heroes must not be denied the exemptions their fathers earned. Again, the bargain that the demos made with the elite, to grant them such privilege, was precisely what distinguished Athens from the neighboring oligarchies, where no such distinctions were allowed (105–19). Of course, in exchange for that privilege, democratic leaders were fair game for shaming, as opposed to the shield against dishonor that prevailed in oligarchies: so Diodoros would argue against Androtion (Dem. 22.31–32). By a similar reckoning Timokrates' law (in Dem. 24) went too far: it would grant a reprieve to major debtors, to spare them imprisonment; but here Diodoros would argue, if the wealthy can borrow their way out of jail (with sureties), then the court's sentencing is undone and the *politeia* falls apart. Finally, in the crown cases, Diondas and Aischines would argue that whatever singular service Demosthenes had given in office or as benefactor, another coronation was a fraud because his overreach led them into disaster (see chapters 8 and 9).

The *graphē paranomōn* regularly involves a recalculation of that sort: to determine whether the exercise of official power or demagogic clout is within the range of competition or amounts to unlawful action. And that weighing of privilege and liability helps to explain one of the great puzzles in the argumentation: Why is it that, in every case, the controlling principle must be reconstructed from the relevant statutes all over again? The orators of the fourth century never got beyond this process, as Wolff pointed out in *"Normenkontrolle"* (as we noticed in the Introduction). He explained it as a lack of expertise: after all, there was no cadre of jurisprudents, as there would be at Rome, to find and interpret the decisive rule. But it needs no great sophistication to remember basic principles that everyone knows, such as *isonomia* or that "none must be judge in his own case." Why not present that rule at the top of the argument, cite the statutes that codify it, and then conclude that the bill in question is a clear violation (or not)? Instead, invariably, the argument runs in reverse: from a survey of laws in evidence, a general principle is constructed anew in each case. That strategy is dictated by the very nature of the older remedy: it was in origin a recourse against reckless leaders, empowered by their office or by popular support. Their offense cannot be proven without weighing their violations against lawful power and privilege.

There is a glimpse of this calculation even at the turn of the century. In the Arginousai case, in the closing years of the old democracy, it may seem almost perfunctory. So Wolff largely disregarded this dimension of that case, as he focused on the inductive method that prefigured later strategy. But the closing plea of Euryptolemos, as Xenophon recalled it, conveys much the same idea that looms larger than legalities in the later cases as well: "Keep guard over the laws that are properly yours—for it is especially on their account that you are [at your] greatest"

(*Hell.* 1.7.29). The body of laws is not a barrier beyond, against the people's rash initiatives; it represents an intrinsic bond, an implied contract that all have entered into by following the roles and rules of the community. This is the sort of constraint that has been called "associative obligation," not a duty that has to be avowed explicitly, in so many words, but the alliance we all undertake by following in the same path.[7] Such was the sense of belonging felt by men who had often marched along the same mustering routes, from their demes to their *trittys* centers and onward to the agora or the assembly (explored in chapter 2). It is that sense of marching in the same cause—and not in league with our enemies—that Hypereides would invoke against the Macedonian sympathizer, Diondas.[8] And, sixty-some years earlier, it was much the same sense of obligation that weighed upon Socrates in his imaginary plea to the Laws personified (in Plato's *Crito*). It was not that he had made some particular vow or consensual commitment (though he must have sworn allegiance many times); his most compelling loyalty was entangled in the city's way of life.

So it should not be surprising that the Athenian search for some standard or symbol to represent the Laws seems to revolve around their image of themselves, the human face or figure in which they recognized their defining features. That is the likely meaning of the claim attributed to Solon, that the law is the city's coinage—nomos is *nomisma*.[9] Of course, they put their faith and credit in their currency not by weight of precious metal—after all, the silver in it might be worth very little.[10] Laws and coinage together represented the city like an emblem: on the triobol that jurors received in payment, Athena and her owl conveyed a host of loyalties. And much the same symbolism was probably conveyed by the *kanōn* of justice, the measuring device that Lykourgos and Aischines took up in 330.

Lykourgos raised this standard earlier in that year in his case against Leokrates for "treason." The law in question listed several instances of *prodosia* in the functional sense of betraying or abandoning ships, soldiers, or allies. Leokrates had done none of those crimes; he abandoned Athens herself in the crisis after Chaironeia. So Lykourgos calls on the judges to be lawmakers, *nomothetai,* because this more insidious treason was not defined in the law; if it were, they could simply refer to the nomos as they would use a *kanōn*. It's not easy to see what sort of device he had in mind, but whatever it was, the measurement needed was not yet inscribed upon it. Ordinarily, for any betrayal of the sort specified in the statute, the judges could recognize whether the charge fitted the legal description by reading one after the other; but for Leokrates' crime, there was no such caption.

The device that Lykourgos and his jury had in mind might be a kind of yardstick, but he was not using it to measure the length or the breadth of an object.

The Greeks certainly had devices of that sort, derived from an Egyptian model: the standard ruler would show how digits add up to hands, hands to cubits, and so on.[11] If Lykourgos' *kanōn* was something like that Egyptian prototype, his point would be that the law includes various units of measurement for the charge of *prodosia*, like the digits and cubits on the yardstick, but none that fit the case at hand. After all, Leokrates' crime is not equal to any of the examples in the statute; he didn't betray a ship or an ally or any such asset; he abandoned his homeland altogether. And Lykourgos played up that threat so well, he very nearly got a conviction; as Aischines recalled later in the year (3.252), the traitor was acquitted by one vote. So almost half the jury were prepared to be lawmakers, just as Lykourgos asked, and to add some new feature to the canon of treason: not by adding another foot to the measuring stick but by adding another paradigm. The *kanōn* provided a model of proportions, and if the law was to encompass the man who abandoned his city altogether, the jury would have to add a new formulation commensurate with the others.

The matching of one unit of measurement with another, to maintain proportionality, is found on a metrological relief at Salamis and another artifact in Oxford.[12] Both show a footprint framed by the fathom, a human torso with outstretched arms, as though to establish the official length for each and the proportion of one to the other. On the Salamis stone we can see that the various figures serve to coordinate differing units of measurement (figure C.1).

Below the cubit, between the hand of the fathom and the outstretched fingers of the "span," we find a standard measuring rod, a *kanōn* in the strict sense, approximating the Doric foot; beside it, there is a slightly more petite figure representing the Attic or Common foot. As Wilson Jones suggested, the fingertips of the span and fathom probably extend to Attic and Doric yards, respectively (three feet from the axis of symmetry), and an intricate set of proportions is found at the edges of the stone itself.

A device of that sort served as a metrological template: the builder could set his portable yardstick or square (*kanōn* or *gnōmon*) alongside the corresponding figures and mark it accordingly.[13] It would be rather awkward for checking particular artifacts, such as a column drum or a component for the roof structure. So it seems reasonable to suppose, when Lykourgos spoke of the law on treason as a device that lacked the unit of measurement needed, many of his jury would think of some such *kanōn-stēlē* (we might call it) standing at the worksite or in an administrative office. After all, it was probably that sort of template, pioneered by the Egyptians and adapted by the Greeks, that inspired Polykleitos to call his treatise on the human figure "the *Kanōn*," describing proportions illustrated in his Doryphoros.

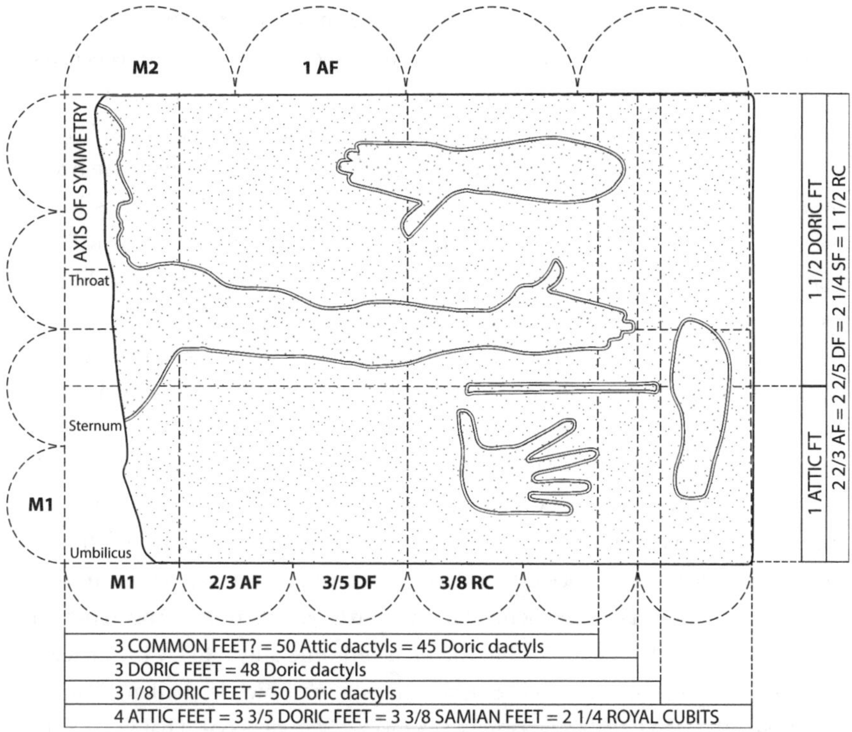

Figure C.1. Analysis of the metrological relief from Salamis by Mark Wilson Jones, "Doric Measure and Architectural Design 1," *AJA* 104 (2000) 82 (with his kind permission).

Later in the year 330 Aischines uses the same trope to condemn Ktesiphon's decree:

> Justice is not indefinite but defined by your laws: Just as in construction, when we want to know what is right (*orthós*) and what is not, we apply a *kanōn* to decide it. So, too, in *graphai paranomōn*, this *sanidion* is presented as a canon of justice [showing] the decree and the laws listed beside it. Show that these are in harmony (συμφωνοῦντα ἀλλήλοις) and then step down—what need to call on Demosthenes? . . . When Ktesiphon recites to you that prologue that was prepared for him, and then carries on with no [proper] defense, remind him, politely, to take the *sanidion* and read the laws alongside his decree. And if he pretends not to hear you, refuse to hear him! (200–201)

Aischines insists that the judges' decision should be dictated by the *sanis;* the board where the targeted degree and the laws that contradict it are posted side by side; the judges are to use it like a *kanōn*. He uses the diminutive, *sanidion*, to suggest how simple the task should be. But surely he speaks with some irony because, if the *sanis* really included all the laws that he cited from it, early in the speech, it must have been an imposing exhibit. For the scope of it, consider table C.1 as a summary, with laws-at-issue paraphrased on the right. There must have been a number of laws regarding the accountability of officers, as well as Demosthenes' own decree for the wall builders accountable to the director of the Theoric Fund, and at least a few statutes to substantiate the other charges. So what kind of ruler was this?

To make sense of the analogy, scholars have turned to modern jurisprudence in the United States. As we noticed in the Introduction (§1), in the 1930s, when Bonner and Smith were completing the second volume of their *Administration of Justice,* they concluded that Athenian *graphē paranomōn* has a parallel in judicial review by our own Supreme Court. Earlier in the decade there had been a landmark opinion that reinforced the parallel. Against the cresting wave of the New Deal, Supreme Court Justice Owen Roberts described his task: "When an act of Congress is appropriately challenged in the courts, as not conforming to the constitutional mandate, the judicial branch has only one duty—to lay the article of the Constitution which is invoked beside the statute which is challenged and to decide whether the latter squares with the former" (297 US 62). That mechanical

TABLE C.1

A glimpse of the sanidion *in the Crown Case*

	(15–16) General law regarding accountability, listing exhaustively offices accountable.
Ktesiphon's decree as quoted and paraphrased passim:	(19) Even trierarchs are accountable, though they receive no public funds . . . (22) Laws indicating that no one is exempt.
Demosthenes is to be crowned in the theatre at the Dionysia	(22–23) Law(s) describing *inter alia* how a man who received no money and spent none shall so report: "nothing in the city is unaccountable."
for exceptional service as wall-builder, paying the contribution for his tribe out of pocket,	(27–28) Demosthenes' decree of 337, for wall builders chosen by tribes.
	(30–31) Laws that prescribe accounting for regular offices *and* those chosen by tribe, *trittys*, or deme to handle public moneys.
	(47–48) Laws regarding tribal, personal, or foreign honors in the theater.
and because "he carries on saying and doing what is best for the polis."	(50) Against "falsehood" in the people's decrees.

method, matching one text with another has been called the "T-square rule," as though Roberts imagines lining them up and using a drafting square to frame the corresponding clauses. His target was the Agricultural Adjustment Act of 1933, which provided subsidies to farmers (who would otherwise lose the farm) and put a tax on the industries that process farm goods, in order to cover those subsidies. Finding no such redistribution among the powers delegated to the federal legislature, Roberts and the majority rejected it.[14]

Roberts identified the critical clause in the Constitution as Article I, Section 8: empowering Congress to provide for "the general welfare." That phrase never appears in the Agriculture Act (though it was invoked by government lawyers defending it) and, in fact, Roberts doesn't offer any serious scrutiny of the corresponding language. Throughout his opinion, he largely relies upon the *Commentaries* of Joseph Story (1891 [1833]), to insist that serving the general welfare, in that critical clause of the Constitution, qualifies the power to tax. And, in Roberts' view, the revenue mechanism in the Agriculture Act was no true tax, as the Framers understood it, but rather encroaches on powers reserved to the states. To introduce that argument, he used the image of squaring one text with another, without emphasis or illustration. It was, after all, a dead metaphor.

On a theoretical level, as Michael Gagarin pointed out, this T-square formulation was a slap at Realism, legal theory that focuses on real life and the good of society.[15] Oliver Wendell Holmes is often seen as a founder or forerunner of that school of thought. A few years before he advanced to the Supreme Court, he famously described the study of law as sorting through Sibylline leaves: in an ever-more-elaborate ritual, parsing the language and the logic, judges read the laws and treatises as "scattered prophecies of the past upon the cases in which the axe will fall." And, for all that conjuring, "[w]hat have we better than a blind guess to show that the criminal law in its present form does more good than harm?"[16]

In the eyes of the Realists, the mechanical approach—binding the judges' decision rigidly to the text—was a Procrustes' bed as old as Aristotle. So it was described by Roscoe Pound in 1922: in contrast to the discretion that rulers and administrators must have, supposedly, the court should have none; for Aristotle, "the judicial office was a Procrustean one of fitting each case to the legal bed," lopping off limbs as needed.[17] Pound follows that principle through a brief history of jurisprudence, to conclude that much legal reasoning was still clutched in that ancient death grip, even in the twentieth century. In that era, Procrustes' bed became a cliché. For instance, in 1915, as a young law professor addressing the American Bar Association, Felix Frankfurter protested against the mechanistic application of the law with the same image, and then again late in his career on the high court he reverted to it.[18]

On the other side of the debate, Roberts' T-square became the default symbol of Positivism: law is in the text that the sovereign people laid down, and any contradiction is resolved in favor of the founding statute, the Constitution.

Now Aischines may be sorting out repugnancy in roughly the same way, reading the laws and the decree side by side. But the modern parallel is not very helpful to those of us struggling to understand the ancient argument on its own terms. After all, Aischines called for Ktesiphon to read the laws *aloud,* to see if his decree resonates with them (συμφωνοῦντα ἀλλήλοις). Most of the jurors would rely on that auditory process, not some visual matching to see if the provisions correspond. And those readings are meant to conjure up a particular model of the man who deserves a crowning, not to match up corresponding clauses.

One could argue that both Lykourgos and Aischines were referring to a "yardstick" on the Egyptian model—showing digits, hands, and cubits—but the point was *not* that the jury should use it like a straightedge ruler, to measure the act or to see if it is "in line" with the relevant law literally. The point of both arguments was that the act in question did not fit the proportions illustrated on the *kanōn*. So, it seems reasonable to suppose, Lykourgos and Aischines and many of their audience probably envisioned a *kanōn* somewhat like the Salamis stone, a standard based on the human figure as a way to harmonize differing units of measurement. After all, any legislation introduces an equivalence that must be commensurate with the slate of standing laws. A new law might formulate another charge by which to convict a traitor. Yet another decree would crown a champion of the people for some particular service. Likewise, in any major project the builders' working ruler, with measurements to scale for foot, cubit, and so on, must be laid alongside the model figures on the official standard and adjusted accordingly. From that familiar practice, what Aischines would mean by using the *sanis* like a *kanōn* is that any decree declaring a leader worthy of a crown must fit the proportional scheme in standing law for officers and their obligations. After all, he poses this metaphor long after he concluded the legal argument where Ktesiphon's decree was matched against the statutes clause by clause. At this point, late in his harangue, Aischines is wrapping up his disquisition on the dubious merits of Demosthenes, against Ktesiphon's claim that "he carries on saying and doing what is best for the polis." Aischines' *kanōn* responds to that portrait of Demosthenes as the true *dēmotikos*.

Of course, Aischines lost the vote badly, but not because his imagery was obscure. Demosthenes understood it all too well. He argued that whatever his failings, his career of service did, indeed, fit the description; but Aischines quibbles over trivial defects, like a customer who has a statue made to order and then faults the sculptor for features that don't quite match.

> [It's] a nuisance suit, . . . shuffling the laws around and snatching bits and pieces, when it's only right to read complete statutes, for those who have sworn to vote according to the laws! And so you say what traits "the man of the people" must have, just like someone who has ordered a statue under contract and then, when he receives it, he finds it does not fit the specifications, [as though] "men of the people" are recognized by some formula and not by deeds and policies. (Dem. 18.121–22)

§2. Scrutiny of the Laws and Second Decision

This image of the slate of laws, standing before the jury like a measuring standard at the building site, emphasizes commensurability. That is one aspect of the governing principle of integrity. The other has to do with the personnel who make the law and apply it. As we saw in chapter 1 (and revisited in the last few chapters), both Aischines and Demosthenes described the legislative protocol—the "confirmation" of the corpus or "correction"—as a way to assure consistency. Demosthenes' description, in particular, seems framed on the same model as the Scrutiny of Laws that Andokides reported from the early restoration era. After all, a vote of confirmation (*epicheirotonia*) for officers on the job and the initial scrutiny (*dokimasia*) to judge their qualifications were standard procedures for assuring the competency of those personnel. Once again, the working model, by which most Athenians understood the constitutionality of their laws, was based on the human figure: the laws and decrees must be judged on the same standard as the officers who enforce them.

And, just as the people have undivided authority over their officers, they also control legislation. The venues may differ but it is the same sovereign body that decides. As Demosthenes put it at the top of this concluding chapter, the final decision falls to "the same sworn jurors who decide the other issues as well" (Dem. 20.93). In this scheme there is no separation of powers: the demos is sovereign and unrivaled, like the personification of Demos, crowned by Democracy, gracing the inscription of Eukrates' law against tyranny (337/6).[19] That statute seems designed to dispel any notion of delegated powers, wielded by one caucus or another independently: even the venerable Areiopagos council of former archons has no authority if democracy is overthrown.

Thus the power of the sovereign people was indivisible. In principle, all those citizens who assembled to debate amendments to the law had sworn the jurors' oath at some point (chapter 2 §§1–2), and that same constituency would make the final decision as *nomothetai*. Conversely, if a new bill was challenged and its fate decided in court by *dikastai*, these were judges drawn from the same cadre. Indeed, the juries of *dikastai* and *nomothetai* were selected, most probably, in much the same way: by lottery from a pool that represented the demos proportionally. Therefore the Athenians looked upon their constitutional control as a "second decision" by the body of the people, not as a check by one arm of the law against another. Whether convened as *nomothetai* or *dikastai*, the jury's vote on a law or decree represents the will of the people reconsidered.

Demosthenes articulated that rationale in *Leptines* and seems to take it for granted elsewhere: the model for making new law was the scrutiny of officers. They must be confirmed first by one body that had sworn allegiance to the laws in council, and then by another in court. By that standard, in *Timokrates*, as well, the most damning illegality is found in the procedural shortcut. Timokrates' law was introduced and passed in a meeting of *nomothetai* convened for fast-track approval of financial adjustments; there was no prior deliberation in council or assembly, so there could be no true second decision.

Demosthenes gives us a tendentious history of the developments that framed that constitutional safeguard and then undermined it. If we adjust for his bias, we can roughly outline the evolving procedures (based on the foregoing chapters) as follows:

1. The Old Legislation Law (as MacDowell called it), which Demosthenes introduced in Leptines' case, originally included no provision for the remedy that he relied upon in that case, the suit against unfitting legislation (γραφὴ νόμον μὴ ἐπιτήδειον θεῖναι). After all, the complex protocol, with a sequence of meetings scheduled in the first prytany and strict requirements for public notice, was designed to expose and counter any repugnant or unfitting bill. If the bill proceeded to the penultimate stage, a decree to convene *nomothetai* to ratify new law, it could be remitted to the court by the old remedy against renegade leaders, the suit against unlawful acts (γραφὴ παρανόμων).
2. That old protocol proved too cumbersome and therefore the fast track prevailed. This alternative was a natural extension of the old way of lawmaking, by decree. It allowed legislation at any time of the year, initiated simply by decree of the assembly, for financial adjustments and other expedients, not to alter the fundamental law of citizen rights and obligations.
3. The remedy against unfitting legislation (γραφὴ νόμον μὴ ἐπιτήδειον θεῖναι) was introduced in close connection with that fast track—either in

response to its abuses or in anticipation of them (no later than 381 BC). Its original aim was to rescind laws newly ratified, not to reverse statutes of long standing.

4. In the 350s, Demosthenes and his associates revived the Old Legislation Law to reinforce their suits against Leptines' law and Timokrates', which had both been enacted on the fast track. It was probably in the sequel to those cases that new penalties were prescribed against presiding officers who failed to observe the old legislation law: they would be fined if they neglected to call for the confirmation of laws in the first prytany or failed to proceed with the protocol for new bills.
5. Perhaps in the same reform, the reach of the lawsuit against unfitting law was extended to legislation-in-progress: when a contested bill was confirmed in the assembly, poised for ratification by *nomothetai*, at that point the lawsuit could block the legislation and take the issue to trial.[20] The tribunal to decide that case would be *dikastai*, of course, drawn from the same cadre as *nomothetai*, citizens who had sworn to uphold the laws. And in their verdict, these jurors would take on the role of *nomothetai*; their vote would enact the new law or reject it.

When Demosthenes praised the principle that legislation be decided by the same body that decided the other crucial issues, he was obeying an old commandment: the protagonists themselves must reconsider. That principle of "sober second thought" was not alien to the American Framers.[21] But in the modern scheme, second decisions are typically reserved for a more venerable body of officers (Senate or Supreme Court). In ancient Athens the people themselves must reconsider. That rule is vital to direct democracy, where there is no "upper house" or higher court. And that unalienable burden was all the more weighty in a community schooled in the annual rite of tragedy on stage, with its constant lessons in "recognition." The vital principle is self-awareness, as even the sovereign people, with its collective wisdom,[22] must sometimes think again. In the modern exercises of direct democracy, we are likely to discount that finding of the ancient experiment;[23] but a second vote, to verify the first, has its advantages. After all, precautionary mechanisms to prevent willful errors often prove perverse, creating their own hazards.[24] Safeguards based on second thinking may prove more reliable, and the American Framers assigned that duty to separate bodies: thus Madison defended the Senate (in *Federalist* 63) against those who saw it as a slippery slope to "tyrannical aristocracy." But the Athenians found it more true to their *politeia* for the people themselves to decide again.

There are, then, two precepts of modern constitutional control that seem most at odds with the ancient model. The ancient democrats constructed no edifice of separate branches with strictly designated powers, serving as "checks and balances" one upon the other: the council prepared the proposals for the demos, not as a check upon its powers but as an agenda; and the *nomothetai* were convened as a quorum of the people, not to trump their decision but to ratify it. These "lawmakers" were not a Roman Senate or British House of Lords. And the Athenians would probably have scoffed at the American construction: it is, after all, founded on a fiction, as all branches represent the same constituency and yield to the same interests.[25] Even the high court, as a check against the legislature or the executive, sooner or later adapts to the will of the people.

The second figment is the "T-square" (or the like). A mechanistic model for judging legislation against the text of the Constitution fits the ancient reckoning no better than "checks and balances." After all, the modern reflex, to set one text beside the other, is natural to us because visual literacy has become second nature. The Athenians needed to hear the rules read aloud to judge whether they were consonant with the *ēthos* they lived by.

In the ancient understanding, there is no truer "ruler" for judging legislation than the character of the people. That figure is difficult to measure with a straight-edged yardstick or a T-square, and it seems clear that the ancient democracy did not really recognize any mechanical standard. Their arguments over what was lawful or unfitting inevitably require them to reconsider: Do we remember who we are? And the better to know themselves, the Athenians turned to their laws—nomos is a *nomisma* coined in their image. In their litany of rules and roles they found a distinctive character, as fitting for them as it would be unfitting at Sparta or Thebes. And even the idea of using laws like a *kanōn,* as Lykourgos and Aischines imagined in 330, probably reflects that conception. Their laws were a framework of proportions by which to judge one man a traitor and another a champion of the people. The statutes formed a model of *symmetria* based upon the demos and their way of life.

The American Framers, by contrast, were fascinated by the mechanism of the world that the Enlightenment had revealed, and they seemed determined to devise a constitution from the "mechanics" of countervailing forces and restraints. Their sense of the inadequacy of the human model for rules and measures is nowhere more striking than in Jefferson's quest for a system of measurement beyond feet and fathoms. He was intent upon finding some constant based on motion amid the revolutions of the cosmos.[26] And that same sense of certainties, to be found in the mechanism of the world, is reflected in the language of our Declaration of Independence: there is a necessity at work in the course of human events.

Now our metaphors are often dead to us. When judges in the highest court claim that they are only virtuous umpires "calling balls and strikes," few of us picture the batter that frames the strike zone crouching at the plate. By contrast, the ancients saw their measuring devices patterned on their own features in vivid proportions: digits to hands, hands to cubits, and feet to fathoms. So, when a litigant raised a standard by which to judge a law or decree, the human figure hovered over it. Man, of course, is "the Measure, of what is . . . and what is not," and one meaning of Protagoras' formulation is simply that we measure the world by our own parameters. The Athenians looked upon the law in that way: there was no higher principle than the roles and rules they lived by. As we noticed (at the top of the Introduction), Hume scoffed at that imperious attitude as "a state of perpetual pupillage, . . . averse to checking themselves by any rule or restriction." Instead, the Athenians were ever ready to "retract and control whatever had been determined," and Hume attributed such reversals to the license of immaturity. But, for better or worse, their recourse to second thinking was meant to enforce the only standard they had: it was a struggle for the people as a body to be true to their character writ large in the laws.

Introduction · The People and the Law—Demos and Nomos

1. Bryce, *American Commonwealth* (1995) vol. 1, ch. 23–25. Three editions appeared by 1894, followed by a fourth in 1910.

2. Goodell, "Athenian Parallel," *Yale Review* 2 (1893) 64. Citing Bryce, Goodell explains, "The same causes that have led the European mind to misunderstand some of the functions of that court have prevented due recognition of the close analogy" between American and Athenian remedies. Neither Bryce nor Goodell give references to show the European misunderstanding, but see Mauro Cappelletti, "Judicial Review in Comparative Perspective," *California Law Review* 58 (1970) 1017–53, and *Judicial Review in the Contemporary World* (1971).

3. Goodwin reported on Goodell's study approvingly in 1895 to the American Philological Association and then followed that approach in his influential commentary on Dem. 18 (1901, 316–32). Cf. Bonner and Smith's *Administration of Justice* vol. 2 (1938) 296–97, but see also Melissa Schwartzberg's essay "Was the *Graphe Paranomon* a Form of Judicial Review?" in *Cardozo Law Review* 34 (2013) 1049–62.

4. As described in Michael Klarman's meticulous study *The Framers' Coup* (2016). Goodell ("Athenian Parallel," 69) seems to see their process for legislative review (examined in the next chapter of this study) as analogous to US constitutional amendment (precarious as it is).

5. In this study "legalism" is used in something close to the sense that Judith Shklar described as constructed by the legal profession; that is, the law is "'there' as a discrete entity, discernibly different from morals and politics" (*Legalism*, 1986, 8–9). In ancient Athens, of course, there was no legal profession, and yet, in the fourth century BC we sometimes find a similar attitude that relies upon mastery of the corpus.

6. "Such determination is to be effected by setting the statute side by side with the Constitution, and considering whether there is any discrepancy between them" (Bryce, *American Commonwealth*, 1889, vol. 1, 241). He went on to describe an old-fashioned standard of repugnancy: "All the court does is to point out that a conflict exists between two laws of different degrees of authority. Then the question is at an end, for the weaker law is extinct" (243).

7. The method is aptly described by Mark Sundahl in his dissertation ("Use of Statutes," 2000), and in "The Rule of Law and the Nature of the Fourth-Century Athenian Democracy," *C&M* 54 (2003) 127–56.

8. To which we can now add a substantial section from Hypereides' defense against Diondas; see chapter 8 §1 and chapter 9 §3 in this study.

9. Benjamin Straumann, *Crisis and Constitutionalism* (2016) 190–237, draws the contrast effectively; see also his discussion of the Roman debate weighing the *Senatus Consultum Ultimum* against *provocatio* (*Crisis and Constitutionalism*, 129–39).

10. This is not to suggest that the Athenian Council (*boulē*) was quite equivalent to the Roman Senate either in powers or qualifications but rather that the *boulē*'s judicial competence was limited by statute decisively, whereas any curb on the senate's power remains doubtful.

11. On impeachment by the people (without court hearing), see Hansen, *Eisangelia* (1975) 51–55.

12. Edward Harris, to the contrary, has supposed that there was some such citizen right enshrined in statute (e.g., *Rule of Law*, 2013, 243, 342), but there is no fragment of it or reference to it; indeed, the arguments that survive would seem beside the point, if there were any particular law that laid down the right to trial by jury (as in Article III, Section 2 of the US Constitution, and in Amendments V–VII). See the discussion in chapter 3 herein.

13. Kahrstedt, "Untersuchungen," *Klio* 31 (1938): 17–25 [1968: 242–52].

14. See James Sickinger, *Public Records and Archives in Classical Athens* (1999) 62–138, esp. 64–90.

15. Triantaphyllopoulos, *Γραφὴ Παρανόμων* (1962) 16–17; adapted from Evangelia Petridou's translation.

16. There are signs of an evolving legislative process in two *nomoi* of the 370s, Nikophon's Coinage Law and Agyrrhios' Grain-Tax Law (RO 25 and 26), published by Ronald Stroud in 1974 and 1998, respectively. Inscriptional evidence on the lawmakers was collected by Marcel Piérart, "Qui étaient les nomothètes" (2000) 229–56, in Levy (ed.) *La codification des lois*. On the palimpsest fragment of the speech against Diondas, in chapter 8 we turn to Carey et al., "Fragments of Hyperides," *ZPE* 165 (2008) 1–19, along with Horváth, "Hyperidea" *BICS* 52 (2009) 187–222, and *Neue Hypereides* (2014).

17. For example, in *"Normenkontrolle"* (1970) 58–60, 65, on Theokrines' case against the father of Epichares ([Dem.] 58), Wolff concludes with a picture of the prosecutor "explaining to the *dikastai* that his adversary's apparently innocent *psēphisma* clashed with the laws enacted for the *security of the oikos-system* and thus with the whole Athenian order of religion and state" (his emphasis).

18. *"Normenkontrolle"* (1970) 67, citing the conclusion of this argument at Dem. 23.43.

19. For example, Dem. 23.207–10, beginning, "If anyone among you knows . . . the house of Themistokles"; discussed here in chapter 4, esp. §5.

20. Nelson, "Eighteenth-Century Background of John Marshall's Constitutional Jurisprudence," *Michigan Law Review* 76 (1978) 893–960, esp. 905–6 and 917. See also Nelson, *"Marbury v. Madison"* (2000) 10–27.

21. Nelson, "Eighteenth-Century Background" (1978) 910–13, and 917 on the Connecticut Supreme Court ruling of 1788.

22. Nelson, "Eighteenth-Century Background," 925, quoting from journal publications of 1782–87.

23. From a letter of Richard Spaith to James Iredell of 1757 (cited by Nelson, "Eighteenth-Century Background," 1978, 927n186).

24. Clinton, *"Marbury v. Madison"* (1989) 18: "[T]he most that may be claimed for judicial review in *Marbury* is that the decision entitles the Court to disregard legislation in resolving particular controversies *only where such legislation bears directly upon the performance of judicial functions*" (emphasis is his).

25. See the review by Dean Alfange calling out "malarkey": "*Marbury v. Madison* and Original Understanding of Judicial Review," *Supreme Court Review* 1993, 333. Bryce seems to agree with Clinton: It is "no mere technicality to point out that the American judges do not, as Europeans are apt to say, 'control the legislature,' but simply interpret the law. The word 'control' is misleading, because it implies that the person or body of whom it is used possesses and exerts discretionary personal will. . . . [T]he American judges have no will in the matter any more than has an English court when it interprets an act of Parliament. The will that prevails is the will of the people, expressed in the Constitution which they have enacted" (*American Commonwealth*, 1889, 247).

26. Cf. Christopher Wolfe, *Rise of Modern Judicial Review* (1994) 17–37, posing the paradox that the framers relied upon a common method (from William Blackstone) but came to such partisan conclusions (e.g., in regard to the National Bank). Blackstone framed the hierarchy of rules as follows: "Where the common law and a statute differ, the common law gives place to the statute; and an old statute gives place to a new one. And this upon the general principle . . . that *'leges posteriores priores contrarias abrogant'*" (*Commentaries*, 1765, vol. 1, §3.7, 89, spelling regularized). He reduced the method of interpretation to four or five signs: the wording, context, subject matter, and consequences, "or the spirit and reason of the law" (*Commentaries*, vol. 1, 59–62).

27. Cf. Jefferson's remarks on the Sedition Act in a letter to Abigail Adams in September 1804: "The judges, believing the law constitutional, had a right to pass a sentence of fine and imprisonment; because the power was placed in their hands by the Constitution. But the Executive, believing the law to be unconstitutional, were bound to remit the execution of it; because that power has been confided to them by the Constitution" (Clinton, *"Marbury v. Madison,"* 1989, 25).

28. Cf. emphasis of Bryce, *American Commonwealth* (1995) 275–76, on Montesquieu and the separation of powers embraced by Blackstone (*Commentaries* 1.2).

29. Alfange, *"Marbury v. Madison"* (1993), argues in effect, that the meaning of *Marbury* is inextricable from the maneuvers of Federalists and Republicans to serve partisan interests.

30. Cf. Straumann, *Crisis and Constitutionalism* (2016) 237, on "Greek vs. Roman Political Thought": in the Athenian speeches, on "even a merely cursory reading," he finds "a deeply *positivist* character," by contrast to the Roman citizen's right of appeal (*provocatio*), which "was ultimately thought to be based, not on its status as statute, but on its being part of higher-order *ius*."

31. See esp. Harvey Yunis, "Politics as Literature" (2007) in Carawan (ed.), *Oxford Readings in the Attic Orators*, 372–90.

Chapter 1 · Making Law and Mending the Constitution

1. *Ath. Pol.* 41.3 and 62.2. It was easy money, with no regular check on qualifications (though concerned citizens could challenge anyone they knew to be disqualified). *Ath. Pol.* 28.3 credits Kleophon with having introduced a two-obol payout (presumably in 405 BC), and the secondary tradition treats that as the origin of assembly pay, followed notably by

Canfora, *Democracy in Europe* (2006) 26 (= *La democrazia*, 2004, 39). But Kleophon's *diobelia* was basic support, not an incentive to pack the assembly but a citizen stipend, "bürgersold," as Wilamowitz concluded in *Aristoteles und Athen* vol. 2 (1893) 212–16. Later assembly pay was almost certainly restricted to the first 6,000 attendees to assure a quorum at dawn.

2. On the career of Agyrrhios, see esp. Stroud, *Athenian Grain-Tax Law* (1998) 16–25.

3. Much like modern "SLOP," self-selected listener opinion polling, described by James Fishkin, *When the People Speak* (2009) 21–26.

4. Mirko Canevaro has provided a thorough review of the documents and the scholarship in *Documents in the Attic Orators* (2013); see also my essay: Carawan, "Documents in the Case: Demosthenes 23–4," *TAPA* 146 (2016) 37–60.

5. This famous case, initiated in 336, finally came to trial in 330. The problematic procedural history is outlined by Yunis, *Demosthenes "On the Crown"* (2001) 7–12; cf. Wankel, *Demosthenes Rede für Ktesiphon* (1976) 18–25. In the present study full discussion of this case is reserved for chapters 8–9.

6. Petit, *Leges Atticae* (1742) 187 [1635: 112–13]: "Aischines makes quite clear in what follows [§40] that these *nomothetai* had the duty of abrogating old laws that were at odds with those they wished to ratify. But were these *nomothetai* any other than those chosen from the ranks of judges for enacting [new] laws? Their task was certainly distinct and . . . quite different. For these [*nomothetai* described by Aischines] repeal standing laws if any is in conflict or invalid among valid, or more than one on each matter. But those [*nomothetai* in Dem. 24.20–23] were allotted to examine and make valid [new] laws. Of course their number is the same." Petit explains that Pollux's count of 1,000 *nomothetai* is a total of court plus council.

7. Petit (1742/1635) continues: "[*N*]*omothetai* who repeal old law were chosen by lot at a different time . . . from *nomothetai* who enact new law. For the latter were always chosen on a scheduled date, the third meeting of the first prytany . . . the former, at no certain or defined time." The repeal process initiated by *thesmothetai* cannot have come so early in their office if they were to discover any laws at odds or superfluous (*quas leges intra tam paucos Magistratus sui dies observasse non poterant*), busy as they were with other duties as well.

8. Wolf, *Demosthenis Oratio adversus Leptinem* (1789) cxxxxvii: "Nimis saepe in istis publicis literis, apud Oratores insertis, serior manus lectorum mihi videtur grassata esse, interpolando, addendo, detrahendo." Wolf concludes (cl, emphasis added): "Contra quum reputo mecum, apud Aeschinem non minus agi de annua emendatione legum, priscis legibus constituta, nihilque ab illo dici, quod cum loco Demosthenis pugnet . . . pronior sum in eam partem, ut Aeschinem, quamvis breviorem, tum de eadem re *vel eius rei preparatione* loqui, tum adeo nonnihil novi ab eo nobis afferri arbitrer."

9. Schömann, *De comitiis Atheniensium* (1819) 260: "[P]ersuadere mihi non possum, tam breve temporis spatium tanto tamque operoso negotio datum esse. Qui enim fieri potuit, ut omne legum corpus intra tam paucos dies accurate pervestigarent, et si quid inesset, quod tollendum videretur, invenirent? cum praesertim non huic uni negotio vacarent, sed alia quoque plurima et difficillima sustinerent. Multo igitur magis consentaneum erat, sub finem anni, cum vel ipso iudiciorum usu accuratiorem legum cognitionem sibi comparassent, censuram earum et emendationem ab iis expectari."

10. Schömann's reversal, siding with Wolf: "Scilicet statuendum est, superioris anni thesmothetas ante quam magistratu abirent illo munere functos, quaeque ab his indicata proposita essent, in prima novi anni ecclesia populo recitata esse" (*Antiquitates*, 1838, 227–28n7). Cf. Höffler, "De nomothesia Attica" (1877) 7–8.

11. Schelling, "De Solonis Legibus" (1842) 47, arguing that the earlier phrasing, νόμους, οὓς ἂν τιθῇ, indicates citizen initiative but the later provisions refer to law produced in the annual review. To which Anton Westermann remarked, "The compositor of the document may have thought so, but whether he is right is another question" (*Untersuchungen*, 1850, 40).

12. Höffler, "De nomothesia Attica" (1877) 7–8. It is not so certain that magistrates could not transfer cases to their successors: cf. Whitehead, "Athenian Laws and Lawsuits," *MH* 59 (2002) 76–79.

13. So concludes Piérart, "Qui étaient les nomothètes" (2000) in *La codification des lois*, ed. Levy, 229–56; followed by Canevaro, "Procedure of Demosthenes' *Against Leptines*," *JHS* (2016) 55–56; cf. Rhodes to the contrary in "Sessions of *Nomothetai*," *CQ* 53 (2003) 124–29.

14. See F. X. Ryan, "Date of the Institution of Proedroi," *JHS* 115 (1995) 167–68.

15. Traditionally, legislative review was seen as a trial before the *nomothetai*, with arguments for the old law and for the new bill. Mirko Canevaro has argued that the first stage of the process *is* properly a lawsuit (γραφὴ νόμον μὴ ἐπιτήδειον θεῖναι) to remove the old law and make way for the new: see Canevaro, "*Nomothesia* in Classical Athens," *CQ* 63 (2013) 139–60, and (developed in detail) Canevaro, *Demostene, "Contro Leptine"* (2016), esp. 12–32.

16. Edward Harris assumes that γράφεσθαι must mean a lawsuit and the bill for replacement comes thereafter, and he translates accordingly: "If someone thinks that any of the existing laws is not good, he can bring a public action against it and substitute in its place another law, whatever he may propose, should the former law be abolished" (*Demosthenes: Speeches 20–22*, 2008, 49). But the mood and aspect (τιθῇ λύων) weigh against that scenario; see chapter 7 §2.

17. Dem. 20.89–90: *ὁ παλαιὸς* . . . *νόμος* . . . οὕτω κελεύει νομοθετεῖν, γράφεσθαι μέν, ἄν τίς τινα τῶν ὑπαρχόντων νόμων μὴ καλῶς ἔχειν ἡγῆται, παρεισφέρειν δ' αὐτὸν ἄλλον, ὃν ἂν *τιθῇ λύων ἐκεῖνον*, ὑμᾶς δ' ἀκούσαντες ἑλέσθαι τὸν κρείττω.

18. Dem. 24.24, 32–34: Οὗτοι πάντες οἱ νόμοι κεῖνται *πολὺν ἤδη χρόνον* . . . διαρρήδην οὐκ ἐᾷ νόμον οὐδέν' ἐναντίον εἰσφέρειν . . . μὴ ἐξεῖναι λῦσαι μηδένα, ἐὰν μὴ ἐν νομοθέταις . . . *ἕτερον τιθέντι ἀνθ' ὅτου ἂν λύῃ* . . . οὐκ ἐᾷ τοῖς ὑπάρχουσι νόμοις ἐναντίον εἰσφέρειν, ἐὰν μὴ λύσῃ τὸν πρότερον κείμενον.

19. On the *merismós* and division of legislative powers between assembly and *nomothetai*, see Hansen, *Athenian Democracy*[2] (1999) 152, 173–75.

20. Timokrates' law was to counteract a decree (not a law) that had been passed in the previous year and was about to disfranchise Androtion and his colleagues (as we see in chapter 6). Backers of the bill might have considered a proper amendment to the relevant laws, but by that route they had to anticipate monthlong deliberation before the bill could actually be brought before *nomothetai*, and that debate would raise the odds against them.

21. On the sense of τὸ κοινόν and the purpose clause, see Stroud, *Athenian Grain-Tax Law* (1998) 25–26, and on the new board of *epimelētai tou sitou*, 68–73.

22. For the role of *pōlētai*, see *Ath. Pol.* 47 and cf. Stroud, *Athenian Grain-Tax Law* (1998) 27–31, esp. 28–29: "It is likely that Agyrrhios omitted explicit mention [where

the sale would take place and who would handle it] because the Athenians had already formulated normal procedures for farming out taxes in existing regulations such as οἱ νόμοι οἱ τελωνικοί, mentioned by Demosthenes (24.96–98, 101, and 122). . . . Agyrrhios may have spelled out in this new law only those provisions that departed from or supplemented current practice."

23. *IG* ii^2 140, a measure moved by one Meid[ias] . . . Eleusinios at the end of the year. It was cast as an addendum to the recent nomos of Chairemonides: the assembly shall retain authority to make adjustments in several areas listed, but council shall particularly attend to whatever the priestly clan Eumolpidai prescribe in regard to the *pelanos* (mixture of oil, honey and grain); once the offerings are collected, council shall dispatch the firstfruits (to Eleusis) and sacrifice as the law requires (at Athens), without need of *adeia* (vote of immunity).

24. As opposed to δεδόχθαι τῶι δήμωι, "be it decided by the people" (e.g., *IG* ii^2 30.4, 105.7, 11.9). In those instances the mover was proposing a measure for the assembly to decide directly. For directive to council, cf. *IG* ii^2 103 (RO 33) 6–9, δεδόχθαι τῆι βουλῆι.

25. *SEG* 12.87, from the ninth prytany of 337/6, introduced with the formula, δεδόχθαι τοῖς νομοθέταις.

26. On the citizenship law, see my studies, "Pericles the Younger," *CJ* 103 (2008) 383–406, and *Athenian Amnesty* (2013), esp. 83–90 (constitutional covenants) and 238–43 (on Nikomachos' duties as law writer).

27. Hansen defends authenticity in "Is Teisamenos' Decree (Andoc. 1.83–84) a Genuine Document?" *GRBS* 56 (2016) 34–48. Canevaro and Harris, "Documents in Andocides' *On the Mysteries*," *CQ* 62 (2012) 110–16, rejected it as a "forgery" and promptly defended their position, "Authenticity of the Documents at Andocides' *On the Mysteries* 77–79 and 83–84," *Dike* 19/20 (2016–17), esp. 33–46.

28. This was Wolf's conclusion on Dem. 24.20–23 (subject of the next section); see also note 8 earlier. On "Teisamenos' decree," see my essay on "Decrees in Andocides' *On the Mysteries*," *CQ* 67 (2017) 407–11.

29. The genitive ὁπόσων is the object of προσδέῃ (MS προσδέοι): the correlative ὅποσοι, plural, should indicate a number of enactments, "as *many* as needed," not what is lacking in any particular law.

30. That is, the *archon basileus* (in charge of homicide trials) would have Drakon's homicide law to consult at the *stoa basileios*; the *archon eponymos* would follow the Solonian laws regarding property rights; and the Eleven, the laws governing arrest and other forcible remedies: all to be found in their traditional text at those offices.

31. The phrase σκοπεῖν τῷ βουλομένῳ should refer to temporary publication, not the permanent inscription: Charles Hedrick, "For Anyone Who Wishes to See," *AncW* 31 (2000) 127–35.

32. This appears to be the procedure in reviving the sacrificial calendar, for which Nikomachos was brought to trial (Lys. 30); see my reconstruction in *Athenian Amnesty* (2013) 233–50.

33. Cf. Schöll, *Über attische Gesetzgebung* (1886) 84–95, concluding that the *koinoi* must be laws common to all jurisdictions. Harris, *Rule of Law* (2013) 140–42, argues that Athenian laws were organized by substance, not by procedure or by officers; cf. Canevaro, *Documents* (2013) 97–99.

34. Stroud, *Athenian Grain-Tax Law* (1998) 9, 25–26, treats ἐν τῶι κοινῶι as "in the public domain," but he acknowledges that the purpose clause may also refer to "a repository for public resources."

35. Dem. 24.23: "Before the assembly (date), of Athenian citizens let anyone willing write up the laws that he is proposing and set them before the eponymous [heroes], so that the assembly may vote with regard to the full body of the laws, concerning the time [scheduled] for *nomothetai*. The one proposing the new law is to write it up on a whitened board and set it before the eponymous [heroes] every day until the assembly is held." That the assembly was to reckon the time by the number of the laws to be enacted (πρὸς τὸ πλῆθος τῶν ἐκτεθέντων νόμων ψηφίσηται ὁ δῆμος περὶ τοῦ χρόνου τοῖς νομοθέταις) suggests that additional days would be scheduled if there were too long a docket for one session.

36. Such is the straightforward meaning of Demosthenes' comment in *Leptines* (20.92–93), supported (or echoed) in secondary tradition. In that regard, Canevaro, "Procedure of Demosthenes' *Against Leptines*," *JHS* (2016), argues that this qualification by oath (ὀμωμοκότες) refers to *dikastai* in court proceedings as the first stage of any repeal-and-replace process; but see chapter 2 §2.

37. Modest penalties for *prytaneis* and *proedroi* seem likely enough, but the disparity is surprising. Schöll, *Über attische Gesetzgebung* (1886) 104–5, favored Westermann's "glückliche Besserung" for the *proedros'* trifling 40 drachmas: the abbreviation μ stood for μυρίας (10,000), corrupted to μ′ for τετταράκοντα (40). But that creates an even worse disparity. Conversely 1,000 drachmas would make sense as total for the whole prytany = 20 drachmas from each of the fifty members.

38. It is tempting to connect this check upon the presiding officers with the law on the *proedria* that Aischines described in *Timarchos* 33.

39. Schöll, *Über attische Gesetzgebung* (1886) 108–9, rejected the date as "ein verkehrter Zusatz, aus §26 der Rede [*Timokrates*] gedankelos übertragen." But see chapter 7 §1 on "The Syndics."

40. Wolff called it sheer trickery, "eine blosse Finte": *Normenkontrolle* (1970) 36.

41. *IG* ii^{2} 29 (RO 19) 18–22, of the year 386, refers to the *merismós* and the *nomoi* that governed it.

42. Cf. Rhodes, "Organization of Athenian Public Finance," *Greece & Rome* 60 (2013) 218–23. Minor adjustments to the *merismós* were described as "add-on" legislation (*pros-nomothetēsai*) in *IG* ii^{2} 222 = ii^{3} 452.41–6, when a stipend was added for benefactor Peisithides of Delos (344/3): τὸν ἐ]π[ισ]τάτην προσνομοθετῆ[σαι τὸ ἀρ]γύριον τ[ο]ῦτο μερίζειν τ[οῦς ἀποδ]έκτας. That is, the chief presider in the next session of *nomothetai* was to add this detail to the agenda. Similarly, *IG* ii^{2} 330 = ii^{3} a327.19–20, funding a crown for Phyleus of Oinoe.

Chapter 2 • Judges and Lawmakers

1. As Mirko Canevaro argues in "Procedure of Demosthenes' *Against Leptines*," *JHS* 136 (2016) 39–58.

2. As I argue in "Trial of the Arginousai Generals," *Dike* 10 (2007) 19–56, and in the next chapter. The following sections of this chapter are adapted from my essay, "Court Reform, *Klērotēria*, and Comic Testimony," *CJ* 111 (2016) 385–416.

3. Scholia suggest that the costume "stingers" in *Wasps* were partly inspired by the jurors' staves; see note 13. In the fourth century the staff was an official token of jury duty, and it seems possible that official staves were introduced in the 420s. But if so, we might expect the conceit to play out differently: some who have the sting (or juror's staff) do not deserve it.

4. Cf. chapter 1, note 3, regarding "SLOP" with Fishkin's study, *When the People Speak* (2009).

5. As described by Victor Bers, "Just Rituals" (2000) in *Polis & Politics*, ed. Flensted-Jensen et al., 553–62; cf. Dow, "Aristotle, the Kleroteria, and the Courts," *HSCP* 50 (1939) 1–34.

6. Illustrations for *klērōtēria* and other artifacts of the courts are conveniently assembled on the Agora website at http://www.agathe.gr/democracy/the_jury.html.

7. Vanderpool, "An Athenian Dikast's Ticket," *AJA* 36 (1932) 293–94. Beside the triobol owl is the imprint of a "double-bodied owl," whose meaning is not so certain. Kroll has suggested that it represents a revalidation of the *pinakion*; but, as the same image is used on two-obol coins, it might also stand for an addition to the stipend, to total five obols (e.g., when serving as *nomothetēs*).

8. Wilamowitz, *Aristoteles und Athen* (1893) 2.201–4; Hansen, "Seven Hundred Archai in Classical Athens," *GRBS* 21 (1980) 151–73; Boegehold, "Many Letters: Aristophanes *Plutus* 1166–67" (1984) in *Studies Presented to Sterling Dow*, ed. Rigsby, 23–29; Paga, "Deme Theaters in Attica and the Trittys System," *Hesperia* 79 (2010) 351–84. Old theories on the ten letter-sections were surveyed (in light of *Ath. Pol.*) by Bruck, "Die 10 Richterabteilungen" (1894) esp. 404–24.

9. The few surviving fragments served for assigning *pōlētai* ("sellers" who auctioned off confiscated goods, etc.). This procedure would also suffice for other boards of ten such as the *apodektai, katalogeis, astynomoi, agoranomoi* (receivers, enlistment officers, and inspectors) mentioned in *Ath. Pol.* 48–51, and, presumably, for the forty deme judges whom Wilamowitz included in the reform of *Ath. Pol.* 62.1 (*Aristoteles und Athen*,1893, 2.201). For illustrations, see "Allotment Tokens" on the Agora website, http://www.agathe.gr/research?q=allotment+tokens.

10. *Ploutos* 1164–67: ὡς ἀγαθόν ἐστ' ἐπωνυμίας πολλὰς ἔχειν . . . / οὐκ ἐτὸς ἅπαντες οἱ δικάζοντες θαμὰ / σπεύδουσιν ἐν πολλοῖς γεγράφθαι γράμμασιν.

11. The explanation in Schömann, *De Sortitione Judicum* (1820), seems most plausible: in a high-profile trial, with a jury of, say, a thousand (or more), the interlopers might go unnoticed. And as Boegehold ("Many Letters," 1984, 27–8) remarked, jurors who recognized the scam might readily collude in it (expecting to do the same).

12. ἐν τῇ σορῷ νυνὶ λαχὸν τὸ γράμμα σου δικάζει, / σὺ δ' οὐ βαδίζεις; ὁ δὲ Χάρων τὸ ξύμβολον δίδωσιν. Translation based on Sommerstein, *Wealth* (2001) 67.

13. Schol. *Plut.* 278 cites *Ath. Pol.* (65.2) on the color-coded spike (σφηκισκόν) at the court entrance and the exchange of staff for *symbolon*. This *sphēkiskon* is glossed as "lintel" by Rhodes, *Commentary* (1993) 711. Schol. *Plut.* 301 suggests a "wasp-prick sticking out behind" (σφὴξὀξὺς ἐκ τῶν ὄπισθεν).

14. See Edmonds, *Fragments of Attic Comedy* (1959) 2.130–3 on Athenaios 10.71/450b–c. In the Renaissance, as Isaac Casaubon, *Animadversiones in Athenaei Dipnosophistas* (1600) 477–78, reported, certain *docti viri* interpreted the riddle as referring to a voting urn and emended accordingly. Dow's solution: "Aristotle, the

Kleroteria, and the Courts," *HSCP* 50 (1939) 11–12; cf. Carawan, "Court Reform," *CJ* 111 (2016) 403–4.

15. For the problem of jury composition and the presumptive entitlement of middle-class farmers, see esp. Todd's essay "*Lady Chatterley's Lover*" (2007) in *Attic Orators*, ed. Carawan, 312–58.

16. The assembly had to specify the arrangements by decree (as Dem. 24 reports). Sufficient funds had to be assigned for a body of a certain size, say two (or three) panels of five hundred each; that quorum would then have to be selected from among the qualified citizens who presented themselves.

17. See esp. Mirhady, "Dikasts' Oath" (2007) in *Horkos*, ed. Sommerstein and Fletcher, 48–59, sorting out the ancient testimony and the history of scholarship.

18. In the cases against Leptines' law and against Timokrates, we might expect Demosthenes or his client to complain that the *nomothetai* had been tricked into violating their pledge against repugnancy, if it were part of the dikastic oath; but see chapters 6–7.

19. It remains doubtful whether the ephebic oath was yet required, but something like it must have been familiar if not standard. Oaths were sworn at times of crisis, such as the oath of solidarity represented in Demophantos' decree (Andokides 1.96–98), and soldiers regularly swore to do their patriotic duty before major engagements (as in the oath of Plataia that was taken as a model for the ephebic oath).

20. Lysias 30.27–28 refers to Nikomachos (lead law writer) as *nomothetēs* (however contemptuously), and ancient scholia to Demosthenes (going back to Ulpian) regularly remarked that the term applied to both the author of the bill and the legislators (e.g., schol. Dem. 3.64–65: νομοθέτης ἐλέγετο παρ' αὐτοῖς καὶ ὁ νόμον καινὸν εἰσφέρων καὶ πάλιν ὁ κρίνων τοὺς νόμους). Cf. chapter 1 §§4–5.

21. Schol. Dem. 20.198: νομοθέται δὲ οἱ αἱρούμενοι δικασταὶ τὸν εἰσαγόμενον νόμον ἢ λύοντες ἢ κυροῦντες.

22. Isokrates, in the year 354/3, says that the swearing was held καθ' ἕκαστον τὸν ἐνιαυτὸν (15.21), but he does not quite say that the oath had to be *re*affirmed by all prospective jurors *every year*.

23. Harpokration (A 229) s.v. Ἀρδηττός· . . . τόπος Ἀθήνησιν ὑπὲρ τὸ στάδιον τὸ Παναθηναϊκόν, πρὸς τῷ δήμῳ τῷ ὑπένερθεν Ἀγρυλέων. ἐν τούτῳ, φασί, δημοσίᾳ πάντες ὤμνυον Ἀθηναῖοι τὸν ὅρκον τὸν ἡλιαστικόν. ὠνομάσθη δὲ ἀπὸ Ἀρδήττου ἥρωος ἀρχαίου, ὃς Ἀθηναίους πρῶτος ἐξώρκισεν. Θεόφραστος δ' ἐν τοῖς Περὶ νόμων δηλοῖ ὡς κατελέλυτο τὸ ἔθος τοῦτο.

24. Pollux 8.122: "Those served as judges who were over thirty years of age and fully competent, not in debt to the treasury. They swore at the court of Ardettos, by ancestral Apollo, Demeter and Zeus the king. Ardettos was near (the river) Ilissos; it was named for a certain hero who swore the people to solidarity when they were divided by faction."

25. Thus *Suda* (A 3807, sv Ἀρδήττης), *Lexica Segueriana* (A 142), and the *Συναγωγὴ λέξεων χρησίμων* (A 2113) all cite Theophrastos for the note that formerly all would swear but the practice had been discontinued.

26. Isokrates *Antidosis* 21 says that in contrast to other states, the Athenians have an annual swearing of the oath, and scholars have taken that to mean that *all* jurors swear *every year*. That may have been true at one time, but Isokrates insists that the oath is

generally disregarded; he is describing the duty in the broadest terms to emphasize the failing.

27. Hesychios (A 7098) reports, "Those who approach their oath (too) easily they called 'Ardettoi'" (τοὺς ῥᾳδίως ἐπὶ τοὺς ὅρκους ἰόντας Ἀρδήττους ἐκάλουν).

28. Hansen, "Graphe Paranomon against Psephismata Not Yet Passed," *C&M* 38 (1987) 63–73.

29. Ida Calabi Limentani argued that the suit was initiated *before nomothetai* ratified Leptines' law ("Demostene XX, 137," *Studi Biscardi*, 1981, 1:357–68). But, if so, Demosthenes and his partners would not have been under such a burden to replace it.

30. In the description of the offense, ἐὰν δὲ τις λύσας τινὰ τῶν νόμων τῶν κειμένων ἕτερον ἀντιθῇ μὴ ἐπιτήδειον, κτλ, the present aspect of the main verb, τιθῇ, should convey ongoing action: there was no need to wait until the law was enacted. In the prior statute, the offense was in the aorist (suggesting a finite act), ἐάν τις μὴ ἐπιτήδειον θῇ νόμον; it constituted a crime when the bill was enacted.

31. Cf. Hansen, *Sovereignty* (1974) no. 25. Lipsius, *ARR* (1905) 1:387–89, proceeded on the assumption that the case against Timokrates was prosecuted by *graphē paranomōn* and likewise the case against Demosthenes' Trierarchic Law, labeled παρανόμων by a scholiast and so described in the later manuscript tradition at Dem. 18.102–3: γραφεὶς τὸν ἀγῶνα τοῦτον παρανόμων.

32. As Lipsius saw it, "Since those who stood to gain by blocking the law from taking effect had achieved their objective [with the *hypōmosia*] but had to fear an unfavorable verdict, if the case went to court . . . this must have come about by a decree that Demosthenes' faction introduced, which the opposition endeavored in vain to block" (*ARR*, 1905, 1:389–90n57). Cf. Wankel, *Demosthenes Rede für Ktesiphon* (1976) 572: "d.h. der Beschluß, mit dem er die Gegner zwang, ihre mit der Hypomosie erklärte Absicht, gegen das Gesetz zu klagen, zu verwirklichen." As early as 1850, Westermann, *Ausgewählte Reden* (1903) 78, supposed that opponents of the bill introduced the decree. Goodwin, *Demosthenes: "On the Crown"* (1901) 75–76, juggled the two theories: "This cannot be the trierarchic law itself . . . but a decree passed after the ὑπωμοσία, which (as West[ermann] explains it) *ordered the suspension of the law*, or (as Blass suggests) provided for the trial of the case."

33. Against the further penalty, barring the same procedure in future, cf. Wallace, "Withdrawing Graphai," in *Symposion 2003* (2006) 57–66.

34. Goodwin, *Demosthenes: "On the Crown"* (1901) ad loc. (following Westermann) explains (ψήφισμα) καθ' ὅ as *secundum quod, ex quo*, not *propter quod*: this is the decree in accordance with or from which the lawsuit proceeded, not a decree targeted by the lawsuit.

35. Talamanca, *Dike ouk eisagogimos* (2017); Carawan, "*Paragraphê*," *GRBS* 51 (2011) 254–95, and *Athenian Amnesty* (2013) 91–113. Cf. Paoli, *Studi sul processo attico* (1933) 77–116, against the older model of separate hearings.

Chapter 3 · "Unlawful Acts" (Paranoma) *and the Case of the Arginousai Generals*

1. For the battle and its background, Debra Hamel gives a very readable account in *Battle of Arginusae* (2015). For the aftermath, see esp. Martin Ostwald's discussion, *From Popular Sovereignty* (1986) 431–45. This chapter is partly adapted from my essay in *Dike* 10 (2007), where further references are given.

2. Edward Harris has concluded to the contrary (e.g., *Rule of Law in Action*, 2013, esp. 243, 342), that the citizen's right to trial was enshrined in statute, but there is no evidence of any such safeguard against a decree of the people.

3. So Schömann concluded in *De Comitiis Atheniensium* (1819) 169; cf. Wilamowitz-Moellendorff, *Aristoteles und Athen* (1893) 2.193–94.

4. Fränkel, *attischen Geschworenengerichte* (1877) 68–69, cited testimony of Philochoros' that officers called *nomophylakes* were introduced in Ephialtes' reforms (*Lex. Cantabrig.* 674). Lipsius, *ARR* (1905) 1:34–37, found Philochoros' testimony conclusive; Jacoby to the contrary, *FGrH* 328 F64b, IIIb Suppl. (1954) pp. 336–39 with n. 10. Cf. Busolt and Swoboda, *Griechische Staatskunde* (1926) 895–96. Jones, *Athenian Democracy* (1957) 103–4 and 109–10, discounted the early *nomophylakes* as mere archivists.

5. Triantaphyllopoulos, *Γραφὴ Παρανόμων* (1962) 6–7; similarly Cloché, "Remarques," *REA* 38 (1936) esp. 412, insisted upon this original intent despite the fact that the remedy was continually misused, to the opposite effect. For review of earlier scholarship, cf. Gerner, "Παρανόμων γραφή," *RE* 18 (1949) 1281–87; Hignett, *History of the Athenian Constitution* (1952) 210–13.

6. *Normenkontrolle* (1970) esp. 11–12: Wolff reproaches scholars, "even the jurists among them," for failing to investigate the *Leitgedanke* that governs the full range of applications.

7. Kahrstedt also objected to the exaggeration, "not before the full body [of six thousand] but before an ordinary court," in "Untersuchungen," *Klio* 31 (1938) 22–23n1 [1968: 248–49n166].

8. *"Normenkontrolle"* (1970) 16–17, citing other studies (esp. Hignett, *History of the Athenian Constitution*, 1952, 212) and the formal phrasing of reports on the early cases. In each instance the suit is identified in the proper technical way, with a genitive of the charge, παρανόμων, and often with γραφή or γράφεσθαι.

9. Even if Andokides' description involves some distortion, it is likely to reflect current assumptions and recent memory ca. 400/399. From his account, Wolff invokes "factual defect" as an element of illegality (*"Normenkontrolle,"* 1970, 48).

10. The case was no later than the departure for Sicily, evidently, as we know of no charges against Demosthenes in the course of his last command. Antiphon frag. 8–14 (Blass), consist of a note in Ps.-Plutarch (833D) and several entries in the lexicographer Harpokration. Hansen, *Sovereignty* (1974) 28, lists it second in his catalog, after Leogoras' case, assuming that the lawsuit targeted an honorary decree and the prosecutor was no longer liable; but see my comment in "Trials of Thucydides," *Historia* 45 (1996) 420–21.

11. Seven citations in Harpokration refer to this speech as Antiphon's. To the same effect, cf. s.vv. Ἀλκιβιάδης· Ἄνδρων [ἀντιγραφήν]· Ἀποτετειχισμένος· Δεκατευτάς· Κελέοντες· Σκαφίον· Συνήγοροι. There is one variant reading in frag. 14 (s.v. Ἄνδρων) referring to Demosthenes' suit as an *antigraphē*, and from this Hansen supposed that we are dealing with suit and countersuit. But it is likely to be this famous speech against Demosthenes to which Harpokration refers repeatedly as πρὸς τὴν Δημοσθένους γραφὴν ἀπολογία. So supposed Blass in his Teubner edition of Antiphon (1892) and Lipsius *ARR* (1905) 1:384.

12. Xenophon *Hell.* 1.7; cf. [Plato] *Axiochos* 368d–e. Hamel, *Battle of Arginusae* (2015) 80, discounts Xenophon's claim that Theramenes stirred up a mob; Peter Krentz

reserves judgment, *Xenophon Hellenica I–II.3.10* (1989) 159. But surely Theramenes would not have missed the opportunity. The Apatouria was a meeting of the phratries, where kinsmen would naturally count their losses. Andrewes, "Arginousai Trial," *Phoenix* 28 (1974) 112–22, concluded from Diodoros (13.100–103) that it was the generals who began the recriminations. Cf. Nemeth, "Arginusen-Prozess," *Klio* 66 (1984) 51–57, for the cast of characters.

13. Plato *Apologia* 32b: στρατηγοὺς τοὺς οὐκ ἀνελομένους τοὺς ἐκ τῆς ναυμαχίας ἐβουλεύσασθε ἁθρόους κρίνειν, παρανόμως, ὡς ἐν τῷ ὑστέρῳ χρόνῳ πᾶσιν ὑμῖν ἔδοξεν. Cf. Xenophon, *Hell.* 1.7.25: τούτους ἀπολλύντες ἀκρίτους παρὰ τὸν νόμον.

14. *Hell.* 1.7.5–10: (hearing in the assembly) οἱ στρατηγοὶ βραχέως ἕκαστος ἀπελογήσατο (οὐ γὰρ προυτέθη σφίσι λόγος κατὰ τὸν νόμον) . . . μάρτυρας παρείχοντο τοὺς κυβερνήτας καὶ ἄλλους . . . πολλούς. τοιαῦτα λέγοντες ἔπειθον τὸν δῆμον· . . . (Kallixeinos' decree) ἡ βουλὴ εἰσήνεγκε τὴν ἑαυτῆς γνώμην Καλλιξένου εἰπόντος τήνδε· Ἐπειδὴ τῶν τε κατηγορούντων κατὰ τῶν στρατηγῶν καὶ ἐκείνων ἀπολογουμένων ἐν τῇ προτέρᾳ ἐκκλησίᾳ ἀκηκόασι, διαψηφίσασθαι Ἀθηναίους ἅπαντας κατὰ φυλάς· θεῖναι δὲ εἰς τὴν φυλὴν ἑκάστην δύο ὑδρίας . . . ἂν δὲ δόξωσιν ἀδικεῖν, θανάτῳ ζημιῶσαι. [Plato] *Axiochos* 368e–69a suggests that the final vote was delayed a day (apparently to install more cooperative *prytaneis*).

15. *Hell.* 1.7.13: εἰπόντος Λυκίσκου καὶ τούτους τῇ αὐτῇ ψήφῳ κρίνεσθαι ᾗπερ καὶ τοὺς στρατηγούς, ἐὰν μὴ ἀφῶσι τὴν κλῆσιν, ἐπεθορύβησε πάλιν ὁ ὄχλος, καὶ ἠναγκάσθησαν ἀφιέναι τὰς κλήσεις. If Lykiskos' amendment had been put to vote, it was likely to pass and effectively short-circuit the challenge. Evidently, Euryptolemos anticipated that outcome and withdrew his challenge before the amendment was put to a vote.

16. The law of impeachment identified particular instances that constituted *prodosia,* and the test case seems to prove that it was not easily expanded: Lykourgos' *Against Leokrates* acknowledges that abandoning Athens in crisis was not listed in the law (9); he lost the case by one vote. For Leokrates' case, see Phillips, *LAA* (2013) 492–95 (no. 387) and for other actions for *prodosia,* nos. 377, 385a. On the broader sense of "treason," cf. Queyrel Bottineau, *Prodosia* (2010), esp. 255–98.

17. Much the same objection was made in defense of an unlawful measure in 349/8: [Dem.] 59.3–8; Hansen, *Sovereignty* (1974) no. 18. Cf. Carey, *Apollodorus against Neaira* (1992) ad loc., with note 40 herein.

18. Notably in Pericles' case (Hansen, *Eisangelia,* 1975, no. 6), Drakontides' decree called for voting on the acropolis with ballots from the altar; Hagnon's rider moved the case to court and recast the charge. For impeachment without a court trial, even in the mid-fourth century, see §5 of this chapter.

19. Vindicated by the court, the proposal was enacted: Hansen, "Graphe Paranomon," *C&M* 38 (1987) 63–73.

20. Lavelle, "Decree of Kannonos," *C&M* 39 (1988) esp. 38–40, concludes that Kannonos' decree (with reference to the water-clock) was most probably an adaptation of the late fifth century.

21. Likewise the "joinder of defendants" in cases involving "the same act or transaction or . . . a common scheme or plan" is standard in the United States; see US Supreme Court, *Federal Rules of Criminal Procedure,* Washington, DC: US Government Publishing Office (2020), rules 8, 13, and 14 (pp. 14 and 25), https://www.uscourts.gov/sites/default/files/federal_rules_of_criminal_procedure_-_dec_1_2019_0.pdf.

22. Hence the joke in *Congresswomen* 1089 (with schol. ad loc.): lusty old women are playing tug of war with the handsome young swain, and he objects that he's being treated like a defendant under Kannonos' decree. There seems to be a pun on διαλελημμένον (cf. Hesychius s.vv. *Kannonou, pandokeion,* διειλημμένους . . . ἑκατερώθεν), as though "restrained on both sides." But in the language of the decree, "taken apart" may originally have meant that each must make his defense separately, without the partisan support they might gain from a joint defense. Cf. Ostwald, *From Popular Sovereignty* (1986) 440–44; Carawan, "Krateros" *BNJ* 342 on frag. 15.

23. ἐάν τις ἢ τὴν πόλιν προδιδῷ ἢ τὰ ἱερὰ κλέπτῃ, κριθέντα ἐν δικαστηρίῳ (22). In the one case he cites (28), against Aristarchos for betraying Oinoe to the Thebans (Hansen, *Eisangelia*, 1975, no. 63), Euryptolemos does not specify whether the case was heard in assembly or court, only that a whole day was given for him "to make his defense as he chose" (ἔδοτε ἡμέραν ἀπολογήσασθαι ᾗ ἐβούλετο καὶ τἆλλα κατὰ τὸν νόμον προύθετε).

24. For further references, see Carawan, "Decrees in Andocides' *On the Mysteries*," *CQ* 67 (2017) 411–17. On citizen oaths in Greece, see Hansen, *Political Obligation* (2015). On the tradition regarding oaths at Plataia and thereafter, see Cartledge, *After Thermopylae* (2013) esp. 12–40.

25. On *provocatio* and its ideological implications, see the perspective on Jean Bodin in Straumann, *Crisis and Constitutionalism* (2016) 279–87. The nature of Solon's *ephesis* has been questioned by Pelloso, esp. "L'ἔφεσις al tribunale popolare," *Index* 45 (2017) 517–56 (disputing the sense of "appeal").

26. See findings for *paranomos* in late fifth-century usage in Ostwald, *From Popular Sovereignty* (1986) 112–29, e.g., 115, commenting on Thoukydides' Plataian debate (3.53–67): "the *nomos* violated does not necessarily involve a treaty or statute and does not necessarily refer to a specific political or religious injunction. . . . [It] constitutes a general code of behavior."

27. For details, see Carawan, "Pericles the Younger and the Citizenship Law," *CJ* 103 (2008) 383–406.

28. As discussed in the next chapter, regarding the singular example of Charidemos, §1 at note 12.

29. For the implications see, for example, Goodwin, *Demosthenes: "On the Crown"* (1901) 316–23, emphasizing the salutary effect: the "vituperative quarrel of rival litigants . . . was to a great extent removed after the expiration of a year, when the process became a sober and dignified trial of a legal question." Goodwin was thinking (rather generously) of the speech *Against Leptines* (a *graphē nomon mē epitēdeion theinai*); Gerner, "Παρανόμων γραφή," *RE* 18 (1949) 1286–87, assumed the same rule.

30. See Hansen, "Athenian *Nomothesia*," *GRBS* 26 (1985) 368–71.

31. Kahrstedt, "Untersuchungen" *Klio* 31 (1938) 25. Heath, *Menander* (2004) esp. 161–65, makes a good case for assigning the manuscript hypotheses for Dem. 18–24 to Menander of Laodicea, the rhetorician of the third century AD. The rhetorician's focus was "issue theory"; he had no interest in distinguishing between laws and decrees. The note that Leptines is no longer liable frames the dispute as a matter of the text and its consequences (§4): στάσις πραγματικὴ ἔγγραφος. Issue theory was often indifferent to distinctions in procedure: see my essay, Carawan, "What the Laws Have Prejudged" (2001) in *Orator in Action*, ed. Wooten, esp. 30–35.

32. *"Normenkontrolle"* 10n8: the evidence of Demosthenes only indicates the rule in *graphē nomon mē epitēdeion theinai*. MacDowell, *Demosthenes* (2009) 155, also cast doubt on the received opinion, saying simply, "[I]t is not known whether there was any time-limit for bringing a *graphe paranomon* against a decree." For a defense of the conventional view, see Giannadaki, "The Time Limit (*Prothesmia*) in the *Graphe Paranomon*," *Dike* 17 (2014) 15–34.

33. Hansen, *Sovereignty* (1974), supposed that the case against Demosthenes the general would be just such a case; cf. Hansen, *Athenian Assembly* (1987) 172n590. But refer back to §1 of this chapter, at notes 10 and 11, and see chapter 5 §1 at note 16.

34. The case against Demades, for proposing divine honors for Alexander (Athenaios 6.58), may involve a suit *paranomōn* prosecuted a year after the honors were enacted. Aelian faults "an excess of impiety" (*VH* 5.12), but he does not say it was a *graphē asebeias*. Presumably the lawsuit came after the death of Alexander, and Hansen, *Sovereignty* (1974) no. 38, dated the decree to autumn 324 to save the assumptions (to precede the lawsuit by less than a year). But the deification decree must have come sometime before the Harpalos affair (Hypereides 1.31)

35. The case involving Autokles and Miltokythes is treated in the next chapter at §1, note 16. Ordinary limitations on rescinding a law are perhaps reflected in the hypothetical cases of issue theory: Hermogenes *Peri Staseon* 8, τὸν ἀντιλέγοντα νόμῳ εἴσω τῶν τριάκοντα τοῦ κυρωθῆναι ἡμερῶν ἀντιλέγειν, μετὰ ταῦτα δὲ μὴ ἐξέστω. Lögdberg, *Animadversiones de actione paranomon* (1898) 35–36, supposed that, indeed, suits against measures enacted were barred after thirty days.

36. Whitehead, *Ideology of the Athenian Metic* (1977) 90–97; followed in the main by Todd, *Shape of Athenian Law* (1993) 194–99. Cf. Wilamowitz-Moellendorff *Aristoteles und Athen* (1893) 2.219–20n4.

37. Stroud, "Theozotides and the Athenian Orphans," *Hesperia* 40 (1971) 280–301. On the case in general, see Carawan "Pericles the Younger," *CJ* 103 (2008) 403–4, and *Athenian Amnesty* (2013) 163–64. Calabi Limentani, "Vittime dell'oligarchia," *Studi Sanfilippo* 6 (1985) 115–28, argued for an earlier date, 410/09; followed by Matthaiou, *Τὰ ἐν τῆι στήληι γεγραμμένα* (2011) 71–81. Whatever the date of the inscription, it is unlikely that Lysias made his argument against Theozotides in 410 or 409.

38. Lysias frag. 6 Gernet = 64 Carey; Hansen, *Sovereignty* (1974) no. 5; cf. Stroud, "Theozotides" (1971) 297–301.

39. Wolff, *"Normenkontrolle"* (1970) 70–72, dismissed this construction as purely rhetorical, by which he seems to mean that such expressions ("laws and customs," "written and unwritten") are often formulaic.

40. See [Dem.] 59.3–8, from the year 349/8 (Hansen, *Sovereignty*, 1974, no. 18), esp. §4, "supposing that the people must be sovereign in their own affairs, to do whatever they will" (κύριον δ' ἡγούμενος δεῖν τὸν δῆμον εἶναι περὶ τῶν αὑτοῦ ὅ τι ἂν βούληται πρᾶξαι); cf. Carey's commentary, *Apollodorus Against Neaira* (1992) 152–57, and notes ad loc. Apollodoros authored an "open" *probouleuma* for the demos to decide whether to divert surplus from the theoric fund to defense (*stratiōtika*); addressing closed matters by an "open proposal" was in itself irregular, and the measure, once passed, was indicted on that basis. It is also alleged that Apollodoros was indebted to the polis and therefore *atimos* when he made the proposal.

41. Thus Pericles and Kleon insisted, "I am the same," when the people were having second thoughts. The most notorious example is Alkibiades' case for the Sicilian expedition (Thuc. 6.18.3–7).

42. *From Popular Sovereignty* (1986) 109. In *Nomos* (1969) esp. 58, Ostwald regards the shift to written law as "absolutely certain . . . by 442" (noting Antigone's appeal to ἄγραπτα νόμιμα).

43. Ostwald, *From Popular Sovereignty* (1986) 115; cf. 119, "contravention of the statutes is not the only—and not even the dominant—idea associated with *paranomia*." The "chronological overlap of legal and nonlegal usages is more extensive in the case of *paranomos* than in the case of any other νόμος-compound." See esp. Thuc. 3.65–67, Plataian debate and comparanda; 4.98.2–6, customary values among the Greeks; 6.15.4 and 28.2, with [Andokides] 4.30, on the "lawlessness" of Alkibiades' lifestyle and ambitions. The persistent sense of nomos as customary practice or traditional role is fully documented in Ostwald, *Nomos* (1969) esp. 24–43. On Antiphon 5.12 and 15, see *From Popular Sovereignty* (1986) 125.

44. See Fisher, *Hybris* (1992) 36–82, esp. 53–56, countering earlier views; cf. Ruschenbusch, "'ΥΒΡΕΩΣ ΓΡΑΦΗ," *ZRG* 82 (1965) esp. 304–9; Gagarin, "Athenian Law against *Hybris*" (1979) in *Arktouros*, ed. Bowersock, Burkert, and Putnam, esp. 233–35.

45. Wees, "The 'Law of Hybris' and Solon's Reform of Justice" (2011) in *Sociable Man*, ed. Lambert, 122. On range of usage, cf. Cairns, "*Hybris*, Dishonour, and Thinking Big," *JHS* 116 (1996) 1–32.

46. Xen. *Hell.* 1.7.23: τούτων *ὁποτέρῳ* βούλεσθε, ὦ ἄνδρες Ἀθηναῖοι, *τῷ νόμῳ* κρινέσθων οἱ ἄνδρες κατὰ ἕνα ἕκαστον διῃρημένων, κτλ. In specifying that defendants be tried separately and with a specific time allotted to their defense, Euryptolemos followed the decree of Kannonos: Ostwald, *From Popular Sovereignty* (1986), 440–44; cf. Carawan, "Krateros" (2007), *BNJ* 342 frag.15 (schol. Ar. *Ekkles.* 1089) with commentary.

47. Xen. *Hell.* 1.7.29: ἀλλ' ἑαυτῶν ὄντας τοὺς νόμους, δι' οὓς μάλιστα μέγιστοί ἐστε, φυλάττοντες, ἄνευ τούτων μηδὲν πράττειν πειρᾶσθε.

48. Hansen, *Eisangelia* (1975) no. 63 (p. 83).

49. This summary is adapted from Hansen's catalog of cases, *Eisangelia* (1975) nos. 82, 85, 86, pp. 92–99, where sources are noted.

50. Hansen concludes that Timomachos' case was sent to court but he failed to appear: *Eisangelia* (1975) no. 91, based on the prologue to Hypereides 3 (*Defense of Euxenippos*). Cases where the venue or the outcome is unknown: Kallippos (no. 92) served as trierarch in Thracian operations in 361/0; Timotheos (no. 93), also general in 360/59, was targeted by the same zealous prosecutor, Apollodoros; and Menon (no. 95), veteran of the Thracian campaign (362/1) with Autokles (no. 90), was also targeted by Apollodoros, who had served as trierarch under him; apparently the case was argued in 360 (presumably in court) and we find that Menon was again general in the crisis of 357.

51. *"Normenkontrolle"* (1970) 20–23, on the positivistic character of this remedy; 49–50, suggesting Euryptolemos would have used a more juristic argument in court.

52. *"Normenkontrolle"* (1970) 66: "The speeches against Aristokrates and Timokrates give eloquent testimony to this. Despite their relatively high level of juristic argument, they indicate a capability for constructing abstract and dogmatic categories as yet undeveloped. They had not yet reached the point where one could extract the

principle that was recurrent in various provisions and recognized to be inherent in them all (cf. Dem. 23.62 . . .) as a super-statutory concept (*überpositiv*), a rationale superior to the particular laws and sufficient in itself to brand as *paranomon* the proposal that clashes with it."

53. *"Normenkontrolle"* (1970) 80: "Zu einem Instrument, das den die Normenkontrolle des heutigen Staatsrechts tragenden Gedanken in einem gewissen Umfang zu verwirklichen vermochte, konnte sich die γραφὴ παρανόμων, nunmehr im Zusammenwirken mit ihrem Schwesterinstitut, der γραφὴ νόμον μὴ ἐπιτήδειον θεῖναι, erst auf Grund der Reform von 403/2 entwickeln."

54. For example, Ostwald, *From Popular Sovereignty* (1986) 125–28, and Hansen, *Athenian Democracy* (1999) 205–12.

55. *"Normenkontrolle"* (1970) 23: "Sie war ein früher . . . Ausfluß der Erkenntnis, daß die attische Demokratie im interesse ihrer eigenen Erhaltung gewisser konstitutioneller Selbstbindungen bedurfte."

Chapter 4 · Privileged Characters: Aristokrates' Shield for Charidemos

1. Parke, "When Was Charidemus Made an Athenian Citizen?" *CR* 42 (1928) 170; followed by Davies *APF* 15380. Kirchner *PA* 15380, had supposed that Charidemos' promotion must go back to the 360s, and Osborne, *Naturalization in Athens* (1981) 1.52–54, defended that chronology; cf. Kelly, "Charidemos's Citizenship: The Problem of *IG* ii^2 207," *ZPE* 83 (1990) 96–109.

2. Dem. 23.16: "ἂν γὰρ ἀποκτείνῃ τις Χαρίδημον" γράψας καὶ παραβὰς τὸ τί πράττοντ' εἰπεῖν, πότερ' ἡμῖν συμφέροντ' ἢ οὔ, γέγραφ' εὐθὺς "ἀγώγιμον ἐκ τῶν συμμάχων εἶναι." Cf. §34, γράψας γὰρ "ἐάν τις ἀποκτείνῃ Χαρίδημον, ἀγώγιμος ἔστω," φησὶν "πανταχόθεν"; 90–91, ἐκ δὲ τοῦ ψηφίσματος αὐτοῦ δείξω σαφῶς οὐδ' αὐτὸν τοῦτον ἡγούμενον εἶναι κρίσιν οὐδεμίαν τῷ τὴν αἰτίαν ἔχοντι. γέγραφεν γὰρ "ἐάν τις ἀποκτείνῃ Χαρίδημον, ἀγώγιμος ἔστω, ἐὰν δέ τις ἀφέληται ἢ πόλις ἢ ἰδιώτης, ἔκσπονδος ἔστω," οὐκ "ἐὰν μὴ παράσχῃ εἰς κρίσιν τὸν ἀφαιρεθέντα."

3. Osborne, *Naturalization* (1981) 2.83, wondered what would be the point. But as Kelly noted, "Charidemos's Citizenship," *ZPE* 83 (1990) 105–6 with note 23, citizenship was regularly granted to others who were not expected to reside at Athens and for those on active duty a measure of enhanced security may have seemed appropriate.

4. *"Normenkontrolle"* (1970) 54 with nn. 148–49, citing Dem. 23.90: τὸ δεινότατον πάντων ἐστί, τὸ μηδεμίαν κρίσιν ἐν παντὶ ποιῆσαι τῷ ψηφίσματι τοιαύτης αἰτίας.

5. The principle that no one be "deprived of life, liberty or property without due process of law" is twice enshrined in the US Constitution, in the Fifth and Fourteenth Amendments. At Athens, as we saw in the previous chapter, there was no such safeguard against the people's decree.

6. *Letter to Ammaios* 4. Dionysios argues against the notion that Demosthenes learned his craft from Aristotle's *Rhetoric*. The *Letter* provides reliable dates for much of the Demosthenic corpus.

7. Kirchner *PA* 15380 dismissed those who postpone the generalship, but he may have misjudged the epigraphic evidence; cf. Kelly, "Charidemos's Citizenship," *ZPE* 83 (1990) 96–109.

8. Charidemos is a common name in this period; at least one other Charidemos (a native Athenian) was active in diplomacy in the same period and the same theater:

cf. Kirchner *PA* 15370 with the conclusion to 15380. The Charidemos at our focus (Philoxenou Acharneus) was made general and crowned (yet again) after Chaironeia, only to be among those whom Alexander demanded from Athens (along with Demosthenes) after the Theban revolt. The end of his career seems suspiciously parallel to Themistokles': he offered his services in Persia and there met his death.

9. Dem. 23.129 tells that Kotys was "in-law to Iphikrates in just the same way as Kersobleptes was to Charidemos" (κηδεστὴς ἦν Ἰφικράτει τὸν αὐτὸν τρόπον ὅνπερ Χαριδήμῳ Κερσοβλέπτης), which is usually taken to mean that each king in turn had married off his sister. But Kotys may have arranged both marriages. The notion that Kersobleptes had married off a *daughter* to Charidemos, just as Kotys had married off a *daughter* to Iphikrates, was dispelled by Ernest Weber, *Demosthenis Oratio in Aristocratem* (1845) lxviii–lxix and ad loc., pp. 390–91.

10. The scholia to Aischines' *Against Ktesiphon* (51–52) tell us that Kephisodotos was deposed and impeached either on account of the agreement with Charidemos or because he was defeated in a sea fight at Lampsakos; cf. Hansen, *Eisangelia* (1975) no. 96.

11. [Dem.] 59.88, Carey's translation, *Apollodorus "Against Neaira,"* ad loc. The passage was cited by Wolff, *"Normenkontrolle"* (1970) 24–25 at nn. 55–56, defending the practical effect of *graphai paranomōn* against Cloché, "Remarques," *REA* 38 (1936) 412, and Mossé, *La fin de la démocratie athénienne* (1962) 268. Cf. Ehrenberg, *Der Staat der Griechen*² (1965) 89; Ruschenbusch, "Δικαστήριον παντῶν κύριον" (1968) in *Zur griechischen Rechtsgeschichte*, ed. Berneker, 364.

12. Thus in §§92–94 Demosthenes acknowledges that the decree is dead but argues that Aristokrates must be punished. Cf. Schaefer's reconstruction in *Demosthenes und seine Zeit* (1885) 1:437–50, esp. 445–46.

13. As in the case against Leptines' law, treated in chapter 7. Against assuming the same rule for decrees: chapter 3 §3.

14. (11–12) ἐσκόπουν οὖν τίν' ἂν τρόπον ἡσυχίαν μὲν ἔχειν ἀναγκασθεῖεν οὗτοι, ἐρήμων δ' ὄντων ἐκείνων ὁ Κερσοβλέπτῃ πράττων τὴν ἀρχὴν Χαρίδημος ἀσφαλῶς πάντα καταστρέψαιτο. εἰ πρῶτον μέν, ἄν τις αὐτὸν ἀποκτείνῃ, ψήφισμ' ὑμέτερον γένοιτο, ἀγώγιμον εἶναι· δεύτερον δέ, εἰ χειροτονηθείη στρατηγὸς ὑφ' ὑμῶν Χαρίδημος. οὔτε γὰρ ὑμετέρῳ στρατηγῷ προχείρως ἐναντία θήσεσθαι τὰ ὅπλ' ἔμελλ' ὁ Σίμων οὐδ' ὁ Βιάνωρ, πολῖται γεγενημένοι καὶ ἄλλως ἐσπουδακότες πρὸς ὑμᾶς.

15. (§12 cont.) ὁ δὲ δὴ γένει πολίτης Ἀθηνόδωρος οὐδὲ βουλεύσεσθαι [sc. ἔμελλεν]· *οὔτε τὴν διὰ τοῦ ψηφίσματος αἰτίαν ὑποδύσεσθαι, ἣ πρόδηλος ἦν ἐπ' ἐκείνους ἥξουσα,* εἴ τι πάθοι Χαρίδημος.

16. The artful chronology, whereby Apollodoros (supposedly) waited more than a year to prosecute Autokles, goes back to Schaefer, *Demosthenes und seine Zeit* (1885) 1:160; followed by Hansen, *Eisangelia* (1975) no. 90. The delay seems accepted by Giannadaki, "Time Limit," *Dike* 17 (2014) 17–20, without delving into the sequence of events. Heskel, *North Aegean Wars* (1997) 70–77, works out a more intricate timeline assuming Autokles was reelected for 361/0 but soon deposed. For the fate of Miltokythes, see note 41 herein.

17. Cf. Jaeger, *Demosthenes* (1963) 104–7, 233–36, on the parties jostling for advantage, as the specter of Philip dwarfed their ambitions.

18. Demosthenes calls for a commitment from every citizen in whatever capacity he can best serve the city, (7, ἕκαστος ὑμῶν, οὗ δεῖ καὶ δύναιτ' ἂν παρασχεῖν αὑτὸν χρήσιμον τῇ πόλει); to send fifty ships, even if citizens themselves must go on board (16); to field a

force drawn from the city itself, not hordes of mercenaries (19); and for a rapid deployment force of two thousand soldiers and two hundred cavalry, of which a quarter must be Athenians (21). In patriotic perspective (24) he recalls how (in the Corinthian War) citizen soldiers and mercenaries, fighting side by side, defeated even the Spartans, but thereafter mercenaries operated alone, often to the detriment of Athens and her allies.

19. Dem. 3.4–5: reminding the assembly of what transpired "three or four years earlier" (counting back from 349/8) "when it was reported that Philip was besieging Heraion Teichos, . . . you voted to launch forty ships and yourselves to serve on board them;" but in Boedromion (Sept./Oct.) of the next year, right after the Mysteries, Charidemos was again sent out to muster an all-mercenary force (ἀπεστείλατ' ἔχοντα κενὰς Χαρίδημον καὶ πέντε τάλαντ' ἀργυρίου).

20. Cf. Wolff's synopsis, *"Normenkontrolle"* (1970) 27:

> "After a brief introduction in which he contrasts the historical background of the bill . . . , the speaker explains that he has three points to make (18): first that 'the decree has been proposed contrary to the laws'; second, that it is 'disadvantageous to the city'; and third, that the beneficiary of the proposed decree is not worthy of the privilege. He will begin with the conflict between the decree and the laws, because . . . his audience has demanded it. To this (19) he adds the admonition (20) that one should now concentrate on the question of the bill's legality, without considering the person; then, of course, (one is to) focus on its usefulness, and in the construction of the speech the political claims occupy the greater part (§§ 100–214). Nonetheless the priority given to the legal questions, as they are handled after all with the utmost care and detail, together with the judges' willingness to hear it . . . and the emphatic essay in the epilogue (215–20) to hammer home once again the multiple contradictions between the law and the indicted proposal, reveal with certainty that the preponderance of argument rests upon the exposition of the legal criteria."

21. Cf. Parke, "When Was Charidemus Made an Athenian Citizen?" *CR* 42 (1928) 170, citing the manuscript hypothesis to confirm that Charidemos was made citizen in 357/6, years before he became general. For the attribution, see Heath, *Menander* (2004) 161–5.

22. They are confirmed by the orator's comments, sometimes verbatim but on other points divergent, plausible, and occasionally confirmed by external evidence; for full discussion see Canevaro, *Documents* (2013) 37–76, and Carawan, "Documents in the Case," *TAPA* 146 (2016) 37–60.

23. Decrees protecting the person of the benefactor, providing "the same retribution as if one kill an Athenian" (88–89); letters of Kersobleptes (115–16); testimony from the trial of Kephisodotos (168–69); letters and agreements involving Thracian kings (174–78) and the general Chares (183–84).

24. Aischines 3.201. This challenge may have been a fairly common tactic.

25. It is, of course, possible that the extant epilogue (215–20) was added by another hand when the corpus was taking shape; the transition from the harangue against Charidemos is surprisingly abrupt. It is nonetheless valuable testimony to documentary practice.

26. The editor probably realized that the list of laws he found attached to the speech would be less marketable in itself, as an appendix, but would appeal to readers' interest

and add a small premium to the copy (priced according to length) if woven into the argument.

27. Dem. 23.22: Δικάζειν δὲ τὴν βουλὴν τὴν ἐν Ἀρείῳ πάγῳ φόνου καὶ τραύματος ἐκ προνοίας καὶ πυρκαϊᾶς καὶ φαρμάκων, ἐάν τις ἀποκτείνῃ δούς.

28. Some of the phrasing may be muddled: Schelling's emendation in *De Solonis Legibus* (1842) 68, εἰσφέρειν δὲ <εἰς> τοὺς ἄρχοντας, is most probably right (accepted by Dilts; δ' ἐ<ς> Butcher); and one wonders whether *καταβλάψῃ* is the right word for doing calculable damage. But, allowing for such defects, Canevaro, *Documents* (2013) 48–54, makes a good case for authenticity.

29. "τοῦτον ἀνδροφόνον λέγει, τὸν ἑαλωκότ' ἤδη τῇ ψήφῳ" (29). "τὸν πεφευγότ' ἐπ' αἰτίᾳ φόνου καὶ ἑαλωκότα" (38).

30. "τῶν ἐπ' ἀκουσίῳ φόνῳ λέγει μεθεστηκότων. τῷ τοῦτο δῆλον; τῷ τ' 'ἐξεληλυθότων' εἰπεῖν, ἀλλὰ μὴ φευγόντων": "He speaks of those who have relocated for unintentional killing. Where is this made clear? In the wording 'of those who have gone abroad' not 'of those exiled'" (45).

31. In §§48–50, he belabors the point that ἐάν τις ἀποκτείνῃ, like other conditions of the law ("if anyone strike another . . . if anyone give bad counsel," ἄν τις τύπτῃ . . . ἄν τις κακῶς ἀγορεύῃ) presumes that there is a question of guilt or innocence for the court to decide. But the subjunctive after (ἐ)άν does not express uncertainty so much as a necessary sequence "more vivid," to be followed by an imperative (or infinitive with the same force) prescribing the penalty: thus in the extant beginning to Drakon's law, "and if a one kill from forethought, he is to flee (into exile)" (καὶ ἐὰν μὴ ἐκ προνοίας κτείνῃ . . . φεύγειν).

32. "By your decree, anyone willing shall bring the killer . . . *forcibly* to the victim's homeland. Aren't you confounding all human decency?!" ἐκ δὲ τοῦ σοῦ ψηφίσματος ὁ βουλόμενος ἄξει τὸν ἄκοντ' ἀπεκτονότα, ἔκδοτον λαβών, εἰς τὴν τοῦ παθόντος *βίᾳ* πατρίδα. ἆρ' οὐ πάντα συγχεῖς τἀνθρώπινα;

33. As Josh Sosin argues persuasively in "Death on a Road (Dem. 23.53)," *Historia* 65 (2016) 155–69.

34. For reconstruction, see Carawan, *Rhetoric and the Law of Draco* (1998), esp. 84–124, on the division of issues among the several homicide courts.

35. *"Normenkontrolle"* (1970) 49–50: "We cannot know whether he would deal directly with specific contradictions between positive law and the wording of the decree in the dikasterion where . . . a 'juristic' argument might count more than a 'political' one. . . . We cannot simply assume that he would have relied on principle, effectively to exploit a juristic argument that the decree, in effect, violated the democratic 'fundamental right' (Grundrecht) to a hearing and verdict in court." But if he did not make the argument on principle, Wolff continues, "this is probably no more than a simple question of the level of technique attained by trial proceedings, which probably still allowed, in narrow archaic fashion, only a direct and literal interpretation of the *paranomia*-concept."

36. Scholars have often fixed on the group verdict as violating the principle καθ' ἕνα ἕκαστον (*Hell.* 1.7.23), but there was plainly no statute prohibiting it, and Euryptolemos emphasized the greater wrong, that there was no proper trial; cf. Ostwald, *From Popular Sovereignty* (1986) 439–41.

37. Wolff, *"Normenkontrolle"* (1970) 51–2, notes the surprising lack of emphasis on such fundamental statutes, as in §86, on the rule against any law that serves particular persons (νόμος ἐπ' ἀνδρί).

38. The principle is developed in the two speeches against unfitting law (see chapters 6–7 of this study); for example, in Dem. 24 (*Timokrates*) 59, regarding the rule against laws ἐπ' ἀνδρί, again, πολιτείας ἴσον μέτεστιν ἑκάστῳ.

39. Dem. 23.85: τῷ μηδεμίαν κρίσιν εἰπεῖν, καὶ τῷ μὴ δίκας αἰτεῖν, καὶ τῷ πανταχόθεν διδόναι λαβεῖν, καὶ τῷ τοὺς ὑποδεξαμένους, ἀλλὰ μὴ *παρ' οἷς ἂν τὸ πάθος γένηται* κολάζειν.

40. Cf. Triantaphyllopoulos, *Γραφὴ Παρανόμων* (1962) 17. For *privilegia ne inroganto* (from Table IX), cf. Cic. *de Legibus* 3.4.11. Jolowicz and Nicholas, *Historical Introduction*[3] (1972) 29, explain, "Laws are to lay down general rules . . . not to penalise a particular individual who has not broken some general rule of the community." Democracy relies on a different sort of privilege, as articulated in Dem. 20 (*Leptines*) 108–24: distinctions of merit set Athens apart from the oligarchies; see also chapter 7 §3.

41. Miltokythes, supposedly a friend of the Athenians (169), was surrendered to their enemy Kardia for an especially cruel execution, and of course Demosthenes puts the blame on Charidemos. Athenodoros was introduced in §10 as acting for the sons of Berisades after his death; at this point (170) Berisades was among the parties that Athenodoros brought to the table.

42. This Chares (*PA/APF* 15292) was active in public life for more than twenty years, from an early generalship in 367/6 to liturgies in the 340s (and perhaps as late as 324, if [Plut.] *Mor.* 848e refers to the same Chares). For the campaign in Euboia, see Diodoros 16.7.2.

43. Charidemos is the subject (173–74): οὕτω γράφει πάλιν συνθήκας πρὸς τὸν Χάρητα, παραγενομένου Ἀθηνοδώρου καὶ τῶν βασιλέων, ταύτας αἵπερ εἰσὶν ἄρισται καὶ δικαιόταται. καὶ ἔργῳ ἑαυτὸν ἐξήλεγξεν ὅτι καιροφυλακεῖ τὴν πόλιν ἡμῶν, καὶ οὐδὲν ἁπλοῦν ἔγνωκε ποιεῖν οὐδ' ἴσον.

44. There follows an obscure section (181–84) regarding Kardia as the key to the Chersonesos. The geographical advantages are clear enough, but Demosthenes speaks of a recent maneuver involving Philip and somehow proving that, if he had gotten his way, Athens would be at war with Kersobleptes and Kardia. A letter from Chares was read in evidence, and it may have had some bearing on the case against Charidemos; for Demosthenes concludes that, of all Athens' so-called benefactors, he "is the only one honored for failing to do [her] the harm he intended."

45. The intervening passage (187–90) anticipates the objection, that Euthykles should have spoken up when citizenship and other honors were proposed and granted. In what follows there is also a sign that Aristokrates' decree was proposed when Charidemos was still serving Kersobleptes, not yet general at Athens.

46. Demosthenes explains the fine as punishment for Kimon's own un-Athenian activities, at odds with Herodotos' tale (6.136.3) that Miltiades incurred the fine and left it to Kimon to pay.

47. Cf. Dem. 3 (*Third Olynthiac*) 26; and Dem. 13 (*On Management*) 28–29, where the commonplace is obviously derivative.

Chapter 5 · Outrage: The Case against Androtion

1. A note on translation: For *hybris* and related words, "outrage" (cf. French *outrager, outrer*) often captures the sense of an act above or beyond one's proper role; cf. Fisher, *Hybris* (1992) 1, "a deliberate activity . . . expressing a sense of superiority."

But in current usage the better match is sometimes "abuse" (as of law officers violating civil rights), so I alternate between the two.

2. Thus Wolff, *"Normenkontrolle"* (1970) 61–2, counts Diodoros against Androtion as well as Androtion's suit against Euktemon (Dem. 24.13–14) as examples where "prosecutors tried to dupe the judges in pursuit of political or purely personal interests" to decide against the legalities.

3. *PA/APF* 915. See Phillip Harding on "Androtion's Political Career," in *Historia* 25 (1976) 186–200; and *Androtion and the "Atthis"* (1994), esp. 13–25; cf. Nicholas Jones' concluding essay for "Androtion of Athens," *BNJ* 324 (online 2015).

4. Dem. 22.33, 56; §68 suggests that Andron was given a day-pass for a religious observance and simply walked away. Dem. 24.125 insists that Andron was imprisoned for successive five-year terms until he "ran off" like a runaway slave.

5. Androtion may have been already active in the early 380s: Demosthenes in the 350s claims that he had been a practicing politician for thirty years (22.36; 24.173), and it is tempting to suppose that this Androtion was the defendant in a case for which Lysias wrote a speech *Against Androtion* (frag. 17–18 Carey); thus Davies, *APF* 913 = 915. But Kirchner gave a separate entry (*PA* 913), and Jacoby was rightly cautious, *FGrH* IIIb Suppl. 1 (1954) 88.

6. Kahrstedt, *Forschungen* (1910) 212–15, concluded that Androtion's tenure as tax collector must belong to the era before the system of three hundred *proeispherontes* (who take responsibility for collecting from the others); followed by Jacoby, *FGrH* IIIb Text (1954) 106–7 (with n. 104), against the older view, esp. Schaefer *Demosthenes* (1885) 1:179 [1856: 158], 350–52 [316–17].

7. *IG* ii^2 216/17 and 261. Lewis, "Notes on Attic Inscriptions," *ABSA* 49 (1954) 40–44, dated the decree to the archonship of Chion (365/4). Cf. Jones, "Philochoros," *BNJ* 328 frag. 181 commentary, casting doubt on the connection between this decree and the melting down of golden crowns.

8. Schaefer, *Demosthenes* (1885) 1:352–53 [1856: 318], saw this measure as a response to financial constraints of the Social War, but how it fits with Androtion's other measures of revenue enhancement remains uncertain. Demosthenes suggests that the liquidation came after the tax gathering, for he says (22.48–9) that Androtion gave the people a choice among three options to make up the shortfall, one of which was to melt down the ceremonial cups; they chose instead to collect from those in arrears.

9. Assuming standard interest of 12 percent; cf. Harding, *Androtion and the "Atthis"* (1994) 20; Jones, "Androtion of Athens," *BNJ* 324 T 7 Commentary.

10. D. M. Lewis argued for an earlier date, 359/8: "Notes," *ABSA* 49 (1954) esp. 40–44; he relied on the record showing only one ship built in that year and moved up the lawsuit to 358/7. But, on balance, the Social War seems a better setting for much that looms large in the argument.

11. See esp. Harding's studies, "Androtion's Political Career," *Historia* 25 (1976) 186–200, and *Androtion and the "Atthis"* (1994) 13–25.

12. The manuscript hypothesis to *Timokrates* claims that the embassy was to protest Mausolos' collusion with Persia against the island allies (presumably restricting trade). In any case, relations seem cordial again in 354/3 when a new *proxenos* from Halikarnassos was favorably received at Athens (*IG* ii^2 136).

13. Plutarch listed Androtion's *Atthis* among works of consolation, *On Exile* 14 (*Moralia* 605C = *BNJ* 324 T 14), but it seems reasonable to suppose that much of it was done at Athens and circulated there before exile. On Androtion as a source for *Ath. Pol.*, see Rhodes' *Commentary* (1993) 15–20; but cf. Pesely, "Did Aristotle use Androtion's *Atthis?*" *Klio* 76 (1994) 155–71.

14. Androtion *BNJ* 324 F 72, from Aristotle *Rhet.* 1406b, shows that Androtion ridiculed Idrieus (successor to Mausolos), but it hardly seems suited to the occasion in F 53, where ambassadors from the Great King were given a hostile reception at Athens (even assuming that Idrieus was among the emissaries). It seems at least as likely that Androtion had special interests in Karia from his tenure as governor in Arkesine, and his opposition to Idrieus had more to do with that business history than any anti-Persian agenda.

15. Aischines 1.165, Dem. 22.21–23. Jacoby supposed that Androtion was discredited because of his opposition to rapprochement with Persia, in an era when any ally against Macedon would be welcome; but cf. Harding, *Androtion and the "Atthis"* (1994) 23–24, and 178–80 on F 53.

16. Schol. Dem. 22.3: ἐζητήθη δὲ "διὰ τί ὁ Ἀνδροτίων μὴ μεταλαβὼν τὸ πέμπτον μέρος τῶν ψήφων οὐκ ἠτιμώθη, ἀλλὰ χρήματα ἔδωκε καὶ ταῦτα Λυσίου λέγοντος;" λέγομεν ὅτι ὁ ἐν τρισὶ δικαστηρίοις ἡττώμενος ἐν διαφόροις πράγμασιν οὕτως ὡς συκοφάντης ἠτιμοῦτο· ὁ δὲ ἐν ἑνί, ὥσπερ Ἀνδροτίων, ἐδίδου χιλίας, ὥς φησιν ὁ Γενέθλιος.

17. Retaining manuscript spelling and accent: in Harris, "Review of MacDowell," *CP* 87 (1992) 79; "Penalty for Frivolous Prosecutions" *Dike* 2 (1999) 126; and "Response to Wallace," *Symposion 2003* (2006) 68–69.

18. Dobree, *Lexicon Rhetoricum Cantabrigiense* (1834) 33. The relevant entry in Harpokration's lexicon is not much help (s.v. ἐάν τις): Ἐάν τις γραψάμενος μὴ μεταλάβῃ τὸ ε′ μέρος τῶν ψήφων, ὀφλισκάνει χιλίας καὶ πρόσεστιν ἀτιμία τις· Λυσίας ἐν τῷ <Ὑπὲρ τοῦ> κατὰ τῶν ῥητόρων νόμου διείλεκται περὶ τούτων καὶ Θεόφραστος ἐν τοῖς Περὶ τῶν νόμων.

19. Followed by comment on Harpokration's entry, ῥητορικὴ γραφή. Harpokration had no corresponding entry for πρόστιμον but only προστιμήματα, referring to statutory penalties of imprisonment or doubling the fine for failing to pay, "as Demosthenes shows in *Against Timokrates*" (esp. 39–41).

20. The sense (or nonsense) would be essentially this: "offenders were fined first with regard to disbarment, so as to be barred from transcribing [any statute?] from the laws, [and barred] from denunciation (*phasis*) and from instructing [or suborning others?]."

21. Thus in [Dem.] 53.1, Apollodoros complains that he is at risk of losing his rights if he loses the case, but as Harris acknowledges ("Penalty for Frivolous Prosecutions," 1999, 127n15), the speaker "exaggerates . . . neglecting to add" the critical detail: "only if he failed to gain one-fifth of the votes." He was not about to diminish the risk by explaining that it only affected some suits and not others.

22. Theophrastos (apparently) attested that "failing to proceed" (entangling a defendant in litigation and then leaving the case unresolved) was also subject to this double penalty (fine and disbarment); but as Wallace has argued, "Withdrawing Graphai" in *Symposion 2003* (2006), that rule was probably written into certain statutes for particular remedies, and (I conclude) was probably not a general rule in all *dikai*

dēmosioi (or not yet). See further, on Aischines' predicament in Ktesiphon's case, chapters 8 §4 and 9 §§1–2 in this study.

23. (21) ὡς ὑβρίζομεν ἡμεῖς καὶ βλασφημίας οὐχὶ προσηκούσας κατ' αὐτοῦ ποιούμεθα.

24. Dem. 22.23–24. Aischines 1.165, without naming Androtion, evidently refers to this case and identifies one Antikles as the keeper of the document (*grammateion*). This would be, most probably, an agreement between the boy's father and the lover (*erastēs*), and not a contract for the court to enforce: see Michael De Brauw and Jess Miner, "Androtion's Alleged Prostitution Contract," *ZRG* 121 (2004) 301–13.

25. See Robin Osborne, "Law in Action," *JHS* 105 (1985) 40–58; "open texture" is taken loosely from Hart, *Concept of Law* (1961) 121–25. Edward Harris rejects the parallel, ad loc., in *Demosthenes: Speeches 20–22* (2008) 179–81 and *Rule of Law* (2013) 175–246, esp. 146n25.

26. Perhaps the most straightforward instance is Dem. 54.1–2, where the plaintiff insists that he could have brought suit for *hybris* but settled for *aikeia* (less aggravated assault).

27. Likewise in Ktesiphon's case, Aischines (3.9–10) explained that the rule against crowning before accounting was meant to prevent prejudice, as jurors would be ashamed to go against their earlier approval.

28. When this point is reprised in *Timokrates* 162, the net return is reduced to five talents.

29. As for the less intrusive tyranny of the Thirty, perhaps the treatment of Eratosthenes and Polemarchos (noncitizens) could be overlooked, but it is surprising that the arrest of Leon (and others) from Salamis seems quite forgotten.

30. Parisini 2934 and 2935. Cf. Dilt's apparatus ad loc. These manuscripts (SY in the sigla) actually omit "μετέχουσιν . . . εἰσπραττομένων" (except for a corrector in S) and then have singular verbs (with Androtion alone as implied subject) "ὑφαιρεῖται . . . καρποῦται." So the original text read simply "ὅ τι τῶν μὲν ὑφαιρεῖται, δι' ἀπληστίαν δὲ τρόπων διχόθεν καρποῦται τὴν πόλιν" (what he steals from some . . . he reaps twofold from the city).

31. The stichometry shows that the last section (69–78) was included in the "first edition" for wide distribution, but the dearth of scholia suggests that ancient commentators were ignorant of it: the last substantial comment deals with the image of Andron "dancing out of his shackles."

32. *Timokrates* 162 adds a note of specificity: the two were attended by *apodektai* and assistants, as well as the Eleven (only the latter mentioned in *Androtion*).

33. The only change is probably a casual lapse, at the end of 22.72 ~ 24.180: among victories that were commemorated on crowns that Androtion melted down, *Timokrates* includes, "Chabrias for the naval battle at Naxos" (from the year 376), which *Androtion* omits.

34. Wayte, in his commentary *Demosthenes Against Androtion* (1893) 229, calls Dem. 24.175 "a weaker substitution for §68 of the Androtion," marked by "platitudes . . . and the obscurity of its allusions."

Chapter 6 • Overthrowing the Court: The Case against Timokrates' Surety Law

1. Galen Rowe, "Two Responses by Isocrates to Demosthenes," *Historia* 51 (2002) 149–62, at 155–6 (e.g., that *Timokrates* §4 replies to *On the Peace* §1); following up his

study of "Anti-Isocratean Sentiment in Demosthenes' *Against Androtion*," *Historia* 49 (2000) 278–302.

2. Based on the manuscript hypothesis attributed to Libanios. The following summary is based on the narrative in the speech (9–15).

3. The *diadikasia* would be handled like property disputes where various parties claimed competing shares, ordinarily with the eponymous archon presiding.

4. The phrasing ἐδόκει δίκαια λέγειν ὑμῖν ἅπασιν (13) with verb in the imperfect, suggests that Euktemon was winning the debate but Androtion et al. lodged their *hypōmosia* before the decree was actually passed; thus the issue came to court without ratification in the assembly. Earlier in the prologue (9) the proceedings are described: πρῶτον μὲν τῆς βουλῆς κατεγνωκυίας, εἶτα τοῦ δήμου μίαν ἡμέραν ὅλην ἐπὶ τούτοις αὐτοῖς ἀναλώσαντος, πρὸς δὲ τούτοις δικαστηρίοιν δυοῖν εἰς ἕνα καὶ χιλίους ἐψηφισμένων. The later claim (196) that Androtion et al. were "condemned by three courts," long before they offered to pay, probably means the same combination of council and a jury of two panels (the latter totaling 1,001 jurors). So concluded Hansen, *Sovereignty* (1974) 32–33, 51–52. The older view was that "three courts" included council and assembly, as well as the trial jury: Schaefer, *Demosthenes und seine Zeit* (1885) 1:332.

5. Dem. 24.33 ad fin.: ἐὰν δέ τις λύσας τινὰ τῶν νόμων τῶν κειμένων ἕτερον ἀντιθῇ μὴ ἐπιτήδειον τῷ δήμῳ τῷ Ἀθηναίων ἢ ἐναντίον τῶν κειμένων τῳ, τὰς γραφὰς εἶναι κατ' αὐτοῦ κατὰ τὸν νόμον ὃς κεῖται ἐάν τις μὴ ἐπιτήδειον θῇ νόμον.

6. Dem. 24.24: Οὗτοι πάντες οἱ νόμοι κεῖνται πολὺν ἤδη χρόνον, ὦ ἄνδρες δικασταί, καὶ πεῖραν αὐτῶν πολλάκις δεδώκασ'.

7. By 340, evidently, the suit against unfitting law could also be invoked against law-in-the-making, as seems to be the case with Demosthenes' Trierarchic Law. Dem. 24.33 reflects that amendment (as argued in chapter 2 §3 of this study).

8. It is usually assumed that this scenario refers to the role of *synēgoroi* at trial, but it probably refers to the debate in the assembly, as the people decide whether to send the bill(s) on to *nomothetai*: if the defenders of standing law do not speak against the bill, its enactment is virtually assured.

9. For this rule in the era of the American framers, see Clinton, "*Marbury v. Madison*" (1989) 18–24.

10. Much of this section is adapted from my essay "Documents in the Case," *TAPA* 146 (2016) 44–56.

11. By contrast, in *Aristokrates* the targeted decree was not repeated in the course of the prosecutor's speech. When proceedings began, the indictment was read out, and then Euthykles plunged into his legal argument so promptly (18) that the text of the targeted decree hardly needed repeating.

12. For Andokides 1.82–89, see my account in *Athenian Amnesty* (2013) 186–93; and on Diokles' law, 266–67.

13. Canevaro, *Documents* (2013) 121, "definitely part of the *Urexemplar*."

14. (71) τῶν προέδρων ἐπεψήφισεν Ἀριστοκλῆς Μυρρινούσιος. His demotic indicates that he belonged to Pandionis, the tribe in prytany (but *proedroi* were chosen from the other nine). Schöll, *Über attische Gesetzgebung* (1886) 132–33, suggested that Aristokles belonged to the deme Mourhinoutta, up the coast from Myrrhinous, from the tribe Aigeis. As Canevaro, *Documents* (2013) 119–20, points out, presiders were chosen for the *nomothetai* in the same way as for council and assembly. Thus in *IG* ii^3 452 (= *IG* ii^2 222)

the *epistatēs* for the *nomothetai* is not the one who presided in the assembly at the enactment of the decree because from one session to the next new *proedroi* were selected.

15. Art. I §9.3 and §10, affecting federal and state law respectively.

16. The editor who adapted this version of Diokles' law may have been misled by Andokides' account (from his trial of 400/399) to suppose that all old laws were limited "from Eukleides," but other evidence shows that old cases from before 403/2, contractual obligations (as in the case against Kallimachos, Isok. 18), and criminal offenses (such as the homicide charged to Euthyphron's father in Plato's dialogue), remained actionable under laws carried over from the old democracy.

17. See Canevaro, *Documents* (2013) 142, and Carawan, "Documents in the Case," *TAPA* 146 (2016) 55.

18. Demosthenes anticipates the defense that Timokrates might claim to have singled out the tax collectors and others because they are the worst offenders (60). That preemptive turn (*prokatalepsis*) probably distorts the argument that one could reasonably expect: those groups are excluded precisely because they have undertaken an obligation voluntarily, for profit, and should be bound by the penalties they have agreed to; those who incur a debt unexpectedly should be given latitude.

19. As dubbed by Rhodes, "ΕΙΣΑΓΓΕΛΙΑ in Athens," *JHS* 99 (1979) 107. Cf. Canevaro, *Documents* (2013) 151–57.

20. Here the text inserted (however credible) is not a close match for the provisions that would actually have been read to the court; the indictment (*graphē*) should begin with the charge that "Timokrates does wrong by enacting a law unfitting" and then present the relevant text of the targeted law.

21. Thus Wayte in his commentary, *Demosthenes* (1893) 153: Timokrates' bill is treated as an affront "calculated to annoy and humiliate the Athenian people by ostentatiously *reversing their decrees*, and to make as much mischief as possible by the ungracious way in which relief is granted" (emphasis added). But the next section (78) is more to the point: the demos in assembly (unsworn) will undo decisions of the sworn jurors, τὰς ὑπὸ τῶν ὀμωμοκότων γνώσεις τοῖς ἀνωμότοις προστάξει λύειν.

22. For *klopē*, the thief is jailed until he pays; for *kakōsis goneōn* and for *astrateia*, a man is barred from public areas (and is liable to arrest if he trespasses).

23. The inserted lawtext at section 105 is (mis)construed from the speaker's comments (esp. 113–15); see Canevaro's analysis in *Documents* (2013) 160–73.

24. (148) ἁπάντων γὰρ κυριώτατον ᾤετο δεῖν εἶναι τὸ δικαστήριον. Sections 149–51 contain the dubious document of the dikastic oath; for summary of scholarship, see David Mirhady, "Dikasts' Oath" (2007) in *Horkos*, ed. Sommerstein and Fletcher, 48–59.

25. Dem. 22.47–78 ~ 24.160–86. On this material see chapter 5 §§2–3 in this study.

26. Wayte, *Demosthenes* (1893) 238, glossed ἀνάδικον as "subject to appeal," but *anadikos* is more offensive: relitigating a closed case.

27. The distinction here seems at odds with the charge in *Androtion*, condemning the defendant in that case for dealing harshly with debtors to the polis. One way to solve the contradiction is to assume a divide between public and private law, but see Liddel, *Civic Obligation* (2007) 211–12. In fact, Demosthenes recalls the earlier charge against Androtion to suggest that Timokrates' *philanthropia* is purely partisan (197–98): as tax collectors they had allowed debtors no leeway but now claim a reprieve for late payment.

28. A famous example of effective visualization, *phantasia*, cited in [Longinos] *On the Sublime* 15.9.

29. Rowe, "Two Responses," *Historia* 51 (2002) 159–60, suggests that Isokrates *Antidosis* 79–81 was added with a glance at Timokrates (and Plato's *Laws*).

30. See chapter 1 §3 on Nikophon's Silver-Coinage Law of 375/4, and chapter 2 §1 on *pinakia*.

Chapter 7 · Breaking the Bargain: The Case against Leptines' Law

1. Dion Chrysostomos 31.128: "When the Athenians had abandoned their hegemony but clung to their liberty, a certain Leptines brought forward a law to take away exemptions . . . and no longer allow such grants to be given. What then—is there any way they could adopt the law? By no means! Instead the suit won conviction." The conclusion might suggest that the law had not passed, but cf. Momigliano, "Contributi alla caratteristica di Demostene" (1975) 248.

2. As Badian argues, "Ghost of Empire" (1996) 102–6.

3. On the sense of "what is fitting" (*epitēdeios*), cf. Canevaro, *Demostene, "Contro Leptine"* (2016) 71–6, "Gli argomenti"; see also his essay on "Athenian Constitutionalism" in *Symposion 2017* (2018) 65–98, with Thür's reply, 99–103. For the old debate over venue, whether this case was to be decided in court or by *nomothetai*, see Schömann, *De causa Leptinea*, in his *Opuscula* (1856 [1848]) 237–46. For modern perspective on constitutional integrity, see Dworkin's discussion, *Law's Empire* (1986) 176–275, and §4 of this chapter.

4. For the range of duties, see Sandys' commentary, *Demosthenes Against the Law of Leptines* (1890) ii-xi; Kremmydas, *Commentary* (2012) 8–23; Liddel, *Civic Obligation* (2007) 264–93. For the present study "civic service" seems the best approximation to λειτουργία (literally, working for the people, λαός); the derivative "liturgy" is sometimes misleading.

5. That lawsuit failed: see Hansen, *Sovereignty* (1974) no. 7, with *Leptines* 75–78, 146–47. The victory at Naxos is also commemorated in Dem. 23.198 and 24.180. But other testimony suggests that Chabrias had fallen from favor and met his death in a desperate bid to recoup it: so concludes Bearzot, "L'orazione demostenica 'Contro Leptine'" (1990) in *Dulce et decorum*, ed. Sordi, esp. 106–10.

6. Sandys' commentary, *Demosthenes Against the Law of Leptines* (1890) xvii-xxvii, is still instructive. Boeckh, *Public Economy* (1857) 119n3, had supposed a wider exemption, but Demosthenes says (25) that the exemptions in question do not affect public revenue, which would not be true if commercial fees were included.

7. Demosthenes seems to have a family connection: for links between the Bosporan dynasty and Athenian elite, cf. Moreno, *Feeding Democracy* (2007) 173–204.

8. Canevaro supposes that the real purpose of the lawsuit was to assure that foreign benefactors such as Leukon not be denied their privilege: "What Was the Law of Leptines Really About?" in *Const Polit Econ* 29 (2018) and in his commentary, *Demostene, "Contro Leptine"* (2016) 77–97.

9. Canevaro, *Demostene, "Contro Leptine"* (2016) 55–63, esp. 61–62: "La sua ammissione per assurdo che 'nessun cittadino sarà esente per via di una trierarchia,' sembra provenire direttamente dagli argomenti di Leptine . . . Demostene cambia immediatamente discorso, per occultare la sua ammissione, e discute il disonore che la

legge di Leptine causerà alla città." Cf. Canevaro, "What Was the Law of Leptines Really About?" in *Const Polit Econ* 29 (2018) 16–17.

10. Here Canevaro finds another sign that Leptines' law would revoke automatic exemptions for the year of trierarchy and the respite years: *Demostene, "Contro Leptine"* (2016) 62, with commentary ad loc.; "What Was the Law of Leptines Really About?" (2018) 17. In the next sections of the speech (27–28) the law governing trierarchies was read to the court, but in that context Demosthenes said nothing to suggest that Leptines' law had altered the terms of that obligation.

11. On the hortatory effect in honorary inscriptions of this period, see Lambert, "What Was the Point," in *Sociable Man* (2011), esp. 205 (on Dem. 20.64).

12. This was the concern in Patrokleides' decree, as represented in Andokides 1.76–79; also in the closing lines of Nikophon's Coinage Law; see chapter 1 §3.

13. Demosthenes describes Leptines' law as enacted (94, 99) but not yet in effect: cf. "οὐδ' ἐστὶν . . . τοῦ ἤθους τοῦ ὑμετέρου κύριον ποιῆσαι τοιοῦτον νόμον" (11) with the status of Timokrates' law, 24.11 (κύριος εἰ γενήσεται). Calabi Limentani, "Demostene XX, 137," in *Studi Biscardi* vol. 1 (1981), argued that Leptines' law was challenged *before* it was ratified by *nomothetai*, but on balance that seems unlikely. Cf. Canevaro, *Demostene, "Contro Leptine"* (2016) 14–16, 180–81: if the law had not yet passed, Leptines would not be immune nor would there be *syndikoi* elected to defend it.

14. As Sandys (1890, xxii-iii) in his commentary pointed out, if the jury "acquitted" the law, it would become enforceable; in the meantime it was in limbo.

15. Kremmydas, *Commentary* (2012) 361, and Canevaro, *Demostene, "Contro Leptine"* (2016) 32, suggest that Apsephion and his colleagues had in fact already begun the nomothetic process in compliance with the old legislation law. But if the bill had been formally initiated in that way, Leptines could hardly suggest that the bill presented to the jury was merely a pretext, never to be legislated.

16. Dem. 22.60. As Davies acknowledged (*APF* 9046), the identification is not certain. Others on the list are not otherwise known, but the point seems to be that they got off easy; see chapter 5 §2, ad loc.

17. Aristophon took the lead in settling affairs on Keos in the 360s (*IG* ii^2 111); for failings in the Social War he was prosecuted by Timotheos; on the trials, see Hansen, *Eisangelia* (1975) 100–101.

18. Arist. *Rhet.* 1411a: at Chares' accounting, Kephisodotos accused him of extorting a favorable decision, "holding the demos in a choke hold" (εἰς πνῖγμα τὸν δῆμον ἔχοντα). Demosthenes evidently refers to them both in *First Philippic* 46: the general's implausible promises point to Chares (*Suda* s.v., X 101), and the scholiasts says that, among politicians who exploit that predicament, Demosthenes "hints at Kephisodotos."

19. [Plut.] *X orat.* 841d reports that Lykourgos called upon Deinias to donate, of his largesse, a plot of land to enhance the Panathenaic stadium.

20. If our Leptines is not the one from Koile, it would be tempting to posit a procedure for choosing among candidates from paired tribes. If he is the one from Alopeke (*APF/PA* 9046, *chorēgos* in 331/0), from the city *trittys* of Antiochis, the *syndikoi* (listed in 146) would all come from different tribes: Leodamas of Acharnai from Oineis, Aristophon of Azenia from Hippothontis, Kephisodotos of Kerameis from Akamantis, and Deinias of Herchia from Aigeis. See note 22.

21. If the rule regarding *syndikoi* were, indeed, aimed at "these men," it could be construed as a violation of the rule against laws ἐπ' ἀνδρί. Kremmydas, *Commentary* (2012) 431, suggests instead "subtle irony or insinuation" that the elected *syndikoi* might be open to the charge of *sykophantia*.

22. Rubinstein, *Litigation and Cooperation* (2000) 42–58, esp. 49, on the law cited by Aischines against Timarchos (1.19). Canevaro, *Demostene, "Contro Leptine"* (2016) 39–40, prefers the theory that the law in question referred to the *syndikoi* who oversaw recovery of property (e.g., Lys. 17), cited in vague (or truncated?) form as though it applies to all *syndikoi*. Nadia Andriolo, "Syndikoi," *DHA* 28 (2002) 11–18, suggests that *syndikoi* for seizing property were probably not elected in the assembly at large but chosen by lot, by tribe; our *syndikoi* may have been chosen to defend the law by some similar arrangement.

23. For instance, Hypereides had been *syndikos* in an earlier case (mentioned in Dem. 18.134) when he joined the *syndikoi* against Demosthenes and others indicted by *apophaseis* from the Areiopagos council in 324/3.

24. Augmented by sections 127–30, 136–38, and 155–59. Kremmydas, *Commentary* (2012) ad loc., esp. 341, describes the whole ensemble as dictated by *ordo Homericus,* putting the weakest units in the middle.

25. In the italicized phrasing, παρεισφέρειν δ' . . . ἄλλον, ὃν ἂν τιθῇ λύων ἐκεῖνον, the present tense should indicate ongoing action, not to finish one and then do the other (illustrated in the next note); rather, the new law supersedes the old. Canevaro has argued to the contrary, that one must first indict the old law and repeal it in court: *Demostene, "Contro Leptine"* (2016) 12–31; "Procedure of Demosthenes' *Against Leptines,*" *JHS* 136 (2016) 39–58.

26. Here, for instance, the combination of aorist and present convey a sequence, one before the other: δὶς δοκιμασθέντας ἄρχειν.

27. (92) "The laws differ not at all from decrees, but the laws *by which decrees must be drafted* are more novel than the decrees!" The clause describing these novel laws, καθ' οὓς τὰ ψηφίσματα δεῖ γράφεσθαι, has been variously interpreted: cf. Hansen, *Athenian Democracy* (1999) 176. But it may be largely inspired by the case at hand: Leptines' law governs decrees (granting exemptions), but it is literally more recent than the decrees that it governs; it is, in this respect, an *ex post facto* law.

28. MacDowell, "Law-Making at Athens," *JHS* 95 (1975) 62–74; corrected by Hansen, "Athenian *Nomothesia*" (1980), and *Athenian Democracy* (1999) 161–77.

29. Neither does the speechwriter anticipate any such defense based on legislation law in Timokrates' case a year or so later (treated in chapter 6 §2), though Diodoros would deal in detail with legislative procedure before he turned to the laws in evidence.

30. The point of Leptines' objection was probably that Apsephion and his colleagues resorted to this maneuver to dodge the lawsuit that would inevitably follow if they tried to enact their measure in (what was then) the ordinary way, simply by introducing a bill that would supersede standing law(s).

31. Wolff, *"Normenkontrolle"* (1970) 36, "eine blosse Finte." Hansen, "Athenian *Nomothesia,*" *C&M* 32 (1980) 88–89, finds the ruse ("repeal of Leptines' law automatically entails ratification of the alternative") repeated in the epilogue (164). But in the latter passage the phrasing allows for a more straightforward interpretation. The first provision, "if you condemn [Leptines' law] . . . the deserving among you will have

their rights" (ἂν μὲν τοίνυν καταψηφίσησθε, . . . , οἱ μὲν ἄξιοι παρ' ὑμῶν τὰ δίκαι' ἕξουσιν), refers to the automatic effect: when the jury vote down Leptines' law, exemptions will be restored under the old law, "grants given by the people shall be valid." The second provision recognizes the contingency: "if anyone is unworthy, in addition to having his grant revoked, he will pay whatever penalty you decide, under the law enacted in its place" (εἰ δέ τις ἔστ' ἀνάξιος, . . . πρὸς τῷ τὴν δωρειὰν ἀφαιρεθῆναι δίκην ἣν ἂν ὑμῖν δοκῇ δώσει κατὰ τὸν παρεισενηνεγμένον νόμον). The participial phrase, "τὸν παρεισενηνεγμένον νόμον," implies a condition, "*when* the law has been enacted in its place." Cf. Canevaro, *Demostene, "Contro Leptine"* (2016) 428.

32. Dem. 20.99: ὑμετέρᾳ ψήφῳ τοῦ τούτου νόμου λυθέντος τὸν παρεισενεχθέντα κύριον εἶναι σαφῶς ὁ παλαιὸς κελεύει νόμος, καθ' ὃν οἱ θεσμοθέται τοῦτον ὑμῖν παρέγραψαν.

33. Canevaro, "Procedure of Demosthenes' *Against Leptines*," *JHS* 136 (2016) 39–58, concludes that the old legislation law required that old statute be repealed by a lawsuit, *before* the replacement bill could be introduced, and Demosthenes claims that is what Leptines should have done (96).

34. As Andokides explains in *Mysteries* 80–82; see chapter 1 §§4–5.

35. Dem. 24.24: οὗτοι πάντες οἱ νόμοι κεῖνται πολὺν ἤδη χρόνον καὶ πεῖραν αὐτῶν πολλάκις δεδώκασιν ὅτι συμφέροντες ὑμῖν εἰσι. See chapter 6 §2.

36. The document at Dem. 24.20–23, however, was not based on the original that Demosthenes invoked in the two speeches but probably followed some account of a later amendment (imposing penalties when the presiders did not put the confirmation vote on the agenda; chapter 1 §§3–5). In *Leptines,* Demosthenes proceeds as though the procedure would be unfamiliar to his jury, but then in *Timokrates* we learn that the confirmation vote had, indeed, been called in the first prytany. That sequence suggests that the former case led to a revival of the practice, not yet an amendment to the law. For *Timokrates* also refers to the law as one of long standing, and if there were some major restatement in the past year, Demosthenes would want to acknowledge it.

37. Chapters 1–2; the two tracks and their remedies are summarized in chapter 6 §2, table 6.1.

38. In Lysias 30.24 there is a bit of wordplay on what was "fitting" for law writers, but the remedy was evidently not available in that case (as I argue in *Athenian Amnesty,* 2013, 270–74).

39. (91) ἐπειδὴ δὲ τῶν πολιτευομένων τινὲς δυνηθέντες, *ὡς ἐγὼ πυνθάνομαι,* κατεσκεύασαν αὑτοῖς ἐξεῖναι νομοθετεῖν, ὅταν τις βούληται καὶ ὃν ἂν τύχῃ τρόπον.

40. Hansen, *Athenian Democracy* (1999) 209–10, describes the principle as "second scrutiny" or "double consideration" and finds a model in *graphai paranomōn,* when a decree already approved by the assembly must be passed again in court.

41. "Each has an enemy: one, Euboulos; another, Diophantos." Canevaro, *Demostene, "Contro Leptine"* (2016) 44–45, rightly reverts to the old interpretation (of Reiske and Schaefer): Leptines et al. should back the replacement law and then each may target his personal enemy with a lawsuit, to revoke his exemption—which they have not dared to do but resort to collective punishment.

42. Demosthenes would use the same phrase against Meidias (21.172), alongside other defects (ἀνανδρίαν καὶ πονηρίαν) that politicians conceal; and we find similar tactics against Aischines (in chapter 9). On the rules regarding *syndikoi,* see §1 of this chapter at notes 21–23.

43. For ἦθος and the "economy of honors," see Canevaro, *Demostene, "Contro Leptine"* (2016) 86–92, esp. 88; cf. Lambert, "What Was the Point?" (2011) in *Sociable Man*, 193–214.

44. This missing decree is sometimes discounted as a false document: cf. Davies, "Documents and 'Documents'" (1996) in *Le IVème siècle*, ed. Carlier, 29–39, with *APF* 1695 (pp. 51–52). But the disposition of land on Euboia was probably part of a decree authorizing *klerouchies*, and the distortion lies in treating it as a posthumous reward given to the hero's son. The scholiast (at 20.115, 273) says that Athenians gave the grant so that their gratitude would not appear inadequate, because their reward to Aristeides was "less than his renown"; they rewarded Lysimachos, who was undeserving (οὐδὲν εὖ ποιήσαντα τὴν πόλιν), only because he was Aristeides' son. But then from an independent account the scholiast adds that the orator "concealed this (καὶ τοῦτο δὲ ἔκρυψεν), that the city had given so much for one who had done such good." He seems to mean that Demosthenes withheld the name of Aristeides, but the decree would have given the patronymic and Demosthenes alludes to inherited privilege after the reading (116, Λυσίμαχον . . . παρὰ τῶν προγόνων).

45. In ancient justice, revolution regularly led to redistribution. In Anglo-American tradition, in contrast, it is "a principle of the common law, . . . that the division of an empire works no forfeiture of previously vested rights of property," as Justice Story observed in *Trustees of Dartmouth College v. Woodward* (1819), 17 U.S. 706.

46. Dem. 20.124: οὐδ' ὁ πλεῖστος ἔμοιγε λόγος περὶ τῆς ἀτελείας ἐστίν, ἀλλ' ὑπὲρ τοῦ πονηρὸν ἔθος τὸν νόμον εἰσάγειν καὶ τοιοῦτον δι' οὗ πάντ' ἄπισθ' ὅσ' ὁ δῆμος δίδωσιν ἔσται.

47. For the text of "De la liberté des Anciens comparée à celle des modernes," see Constant de Rebecque, *Brochures politiques 1819–1821* (2017) 292–311. Cf. Fontana's introduction in Constant de Rebecque, *Political Writings* (1988) 40, and translation, esp. 309–28; Canfora, *Democracy in Europe* (2006) 58–64 (= *La democrazia*, 2004, 85–95). Constant's critique frames the history of scholarship in Liddel, *Civic Obligation* (2007) 4–15.

48. Rousseau, for instance, found a model in the Roman *comitia* in *Social Contract*, book 4, ch. 4. (*"Discourse on Political Economy" and "The Social Contract,"* 1994, 141–50).

49. Dworkin, *Law's Empire* (1986) 184: "Integrity is flouted not only in specific compromises of that character . . . but whenever a community enacts and enforces different laws, each of which is coherent in itself, but which cannot be defended together as expressing a coherent ranking of different principles of justice or fairness or procedural due process." For the texture of "rotten bargains," cf. Sanford Levinson, *Framed* (2012) 43–45, on the Missouri Compromise and its underpinnings in the US Constitution (Article IV, Section 2), with Avishai Margalit, *On Compromise* (2010) esp. 39–67.

Chapter 8 · The Aftermath of Chaironeia

1. For the palimpsest fragment, see Carey et al., "Fragments of Hyperides *Against Diondas* from the Archimedes Palimpsest," *ZPE* 165 (2008) 1–19, with description of the text and credit to earlier research; Lázló Horváth, "Hyperidea," *BICS* 52 (2009) 187–222, and P. J. Rhodes, "Hyperides' *Against Diondas:* Two Problems," *BICS* 52 (2009) 223–28. Horváth provides a text with apparatus at http://hypereidoc.elte.hu.

See also Horváth's detailed commentary in *Der Neue Hypereides* (2014), and now "Postponement of the Trial" (2019) in *Use and Abuse of Law*, ed. Carey et. al., 132–46.

2. The break between p. 2 and p. 3 (136r and 145r) described some injustice affecting "whoever gives the best counsel for our city [but] Diondas denies that this is *paranoma*." From what follows we might suppose that the missing line also involved obstructing measures in the people's interest. On the principle in 136r. 30–31, honors that the demos has given shall be valid, see note 10.

3. Esp. Dem. 18.222–23, and [Plut.] *X orat.* 848F and 846A (mistaking Diondas for "Diodotos"). From these references it was once concluded that there were two decrees, one authored by Demomeles and one by Hypereides, both brought forward and challenged before Chaironeia; and the natural presumption was that both cases were decided in due course, within the year. Spengel, "Demosthenes Vertheidigung," *Abh. K. Akad. Wiss.* 10 (1862) 82n1, supposed that Diondas brought suit after the defeat. Goodwin, *Demosthenes "On the Crown"* (1901) 159, recognized that "the two names probably indicate a decree moved by Demomeles . . . and amended or enlarged by Hyperides."

4. Horváth concluded that "the speech was delivered between January and March 334 BC": "Hyperidea," *BICS* 52 (2009) 196; cf. Horváth, *Neue Hypereides* (2014) 10–17, reinforcing his *terminus post quem* of Dec. 335. Rhodes, "Hyperides' *Against Diondas*," *BICS* 52 (2009) 223–26, suggested that the speech came as late as May/June of 334, when Alexander's gift from the spoils of Granikos (Arr. *Anab.* 1.16.7) perhaps prompted Diondas to take his case to court.

5. Theophrastos frag. 636C Fortenbaugh (cf. *Lex. Cant.* s.v. πρόστιμον); see chapter 9 §1 at note 10. The offender was fined 1,000 drachmas and, evidently, denied the right to prosecute certain cases in future. Wallace, "Withdrawing Graphai in Ancient Athens," *Symposion 2003* (2006) 57–66, argues that in most cases (except "desertion," *lipotaxiou*) the bar to litigation was limited to those instances where the prosecutor took payment to abandon the case; in his response (67–72), Harris insists that the disability applied broadly if the prosecutor failed to appear at *anakrisis* or later at trial.

6. At a minimum Diondas would incur an automatic fine and, unless he paid it, could then be prosecuted (by *endeixis*, etc.) for exercising rights that were forfeit.

7. Perhaps Phokion offended by reading his mythology so cynically: those martyrs gave their lives to win gods' deliverance from the foreign aggressor, not to appease him. Plut. *Phokion* 17 gives a more favorable treatment.

8. Horváth gives detailed commentary, with various parallels, in *Neue Hypereides* (2014) 114–17. Dina Guth, "Rhetoric and Historical Narrative: The Theban-Athenian Alliance of 339 BCE," *Historia* 63 (2014) 151–65, observes that Hypereides' narrative contradicts the scenario that Demosthenes framed in the Crown Case and much of later tradition took for granted. Whereas Demosthenes claims to have secured the alliance before Athenians marched out to support the Thebans, Hypereides suggests that the alliance was still up for grabs when Demosthenes convinced the Athenians to march out. The latter scenario is in line with Philochoros. And this particular passage in *Diondas* (137v. 2–8) must refer to that situation: Demosthenes had promised that Thebes would turn against Philip when it was by no means assured.

9. Horváth, "Hyperidea," *BICS* 52 (2009) 204, linked this passage to the honors targeted in the suit against Philippides. The *proxenoi* that Philip sponsored seem to

have included Euthykrates, whom Hypereides pilloried in the suit against Demades (see §2 of this chapter).

10. More literally, not "to let the honors we have given . . . become valid" (ἃς . . . ἔδομεν τιμὰς κυρίας ἐάσομεν εἶναι). Horváth, *Neue Hypereides* (2014) 134–35, finds here a paraphrase of the law cited in Dem. 20.96. That principle, that "grants given by the demos remain valid," was probably reaffirmed by the verdict against Leptines (as we saw in chapter 7).

11. Δημοσθένη τε πλείους ἢ πέντε καὶ δέκα γραφὰς ἐγράψατο. κατ' ἐμοῦ δὲ τρεῖς τῆι αὐτῆι ἡμέραι ἀπήνεγκεν.

12. εἰς τοῦτο ἀναιδείας ἐλήλυθεν , ὥστε οὐκ ἐᾶι ὑμᾶς χρῆσθαι οὔτε οἷς ὁ δῆμος ὁμογνώμων ἐγένετο, οὓς ἐγὼ προεβούλευσα οὔτε τῆι τοῦ δικαστηρίου γνώσει. From the second relative, masc. οὓς, Carey et al., "Fragments of Hyperides," *ZPE* 165 (2008) 13, 16, reasoned that the antecedent must be persons (nominated for some duty?) rather than decrees (or the like): "he won't allow you to adopt the people on whom the demos agreed, the ones I proposed, nor the decision of the court." But Horváth, *Neue Hypereides* (2014) 2, 141, is probably right to suppose that Hypereides is referring to honorary decrees.

13. Cf. Horváth, *Neue Hypereides* (2014) 140. On Charidemos and his extravagant rewards, see chapter 4 §1.

14. Rhodes, "Hyperides' *Against Diondas*," *BICS* 52 (2009) 224 at n. 7, reads this as referring "probably to decrees on matters of policy rather than to his proposal to honour Demosthenes," and "not . . . a guarantee that Hyperides' decree had passed." The pairing with ἀπαλλαγῆναι here plays on formulae of settlement.

15. In the fourth century, evidently, any citizen was *eligible* to take legal action at twenty years of age (after his *ephēbeia*). The law that bars anyone not yet thirty probably refers to the age limit for those who judge; Horváth, *Neue Hypereides* (2014) 137–39.

16. See the description of the "Archimedes palimpsest" by Carey et al., "Fragments of Hyperides, *ZPE* 165 (2008) 1–2. The pages were patched together for a Byzantine prayer book, without regard to the order of the original text.

17. That is, more than fifty lines (quoted in this section) out of a total of 256.

18. "Fifty lawsuits by the time he's twenty-five" is bound to be an exaggeration but, whatever the total, there must have been another case or two where Diondas either failed to proceed or failed to win even one ballot in five; so this case against Hypereides may have been his third offense, forfeiting his right to prosecute altogether. The theory of a three-strikes rule goes back to Genethlios (3rd century AD). See chapter 5 §1.

19. Cf. Horváth, "Hyperidea," *BICS* 52 (2009) 189, 191–93, on insisting that the demos is complicit.

20. Hansen, *Sovereignty* (1974) no. 28 (p. 37); cf. *Suda*, s.v. Δημάδης: . . . Εὐθυκράτη δὲ τὸν Ὀλύνθιον, ἀτιμωθέντα παρὰ Ἀθηναίοις, ἐψηφίσατο ἐπίτιμον εἶναι καὶ πρόξενον.

21. Hypereides frag. 76 = Apsines 9.547 Walz.

22. *PA* 13912. Philippides and Demosthenes (both of Paiania) may have been hometown rivals for some time: in *IG* ii^2 1613.189–92, they were listed together as trierarchs for 353/2.

23. Philippides' case is Hansen, *Sovereignty* (1974) no. 32. See also Whitehead's thoughtful commentary, *Hypereides* (2000) 27–34. Legislation affecting the presiding officers is indicated in Aischines 1.23, 33–35, and (gaming the system) 3.3–4.

24. *Philippides* 7–8: καὶ ἓν μὲν σῶμα ἀθάνατον ὑπείληφας ἔσεσθαι, πόλεως δὲ τηλικαύτης θάνατον κατέγνως, οὐδ' ἐκεῖνο συνιδών, ὅτι τῶν μὲν τυράννων οὐδεὶς πώποτε τελευτήσας ἀνεβίωσεν, πόλεις δὲ πολλαὶ ἄρδην ἀναιρεθεῖσαι πάλιν ἴσχυσαν. See Whitehead's discussion *Hypereides* (2000) 30 and ad loc.

25. Horváth, "Eine fragwürdige Lesart (Hyp. iv. Kol. V.8)," *Acta Ant. Hung.* 44 (2004) 163–70; *Neue Hypereides* (2014) 177–83. The word ὑπείληφας is extracted from a clumsy erasure. Horváth reconstructs the letter traces as [[ο]]†προσφας†, perhaps deriving from some jibe about Philippides "prophecying" Philip's immortality.

26. Sealey, "Who Was Aristogeiton?" *BICS* 7 (1960) 40, dated the trial of Philippides to 331, supposing that the anti-Macedonian party took the initiative from Agis' last stand. The revival of a long-neglected lawsuit seems unlikely in this instance, but certainly more plausible in light of Diondas' case.

27. See Whitehead's commentary, *Hypereides* (2000) 199–215. As for dating the speech: Molossia and Dodona are claimed by Olympias (25), which seems less likely before the death of her brother Alexandros (who ruled Molossia) in 331/0. But the decree and lawsuit regarding Oropos may go back a few years earlier, perhaps soon after the reprisal against Thebes in 335.

28. The only major town of either tribe that was near enough to profit from the shrine would be Dekeleia (Hippothontis). Euxenippos (son of Ethelokrates) seems devoted to the cult: he made a dedication to Health (*Hygieia*) at the Amphiareion (*SEG* 15.291) shortly before or after this case; Whitehead, *Hypereides* (2000) 154–55.

29. Aischines 3.27: evidently Demosthenes brought forward his decree in the assembly, without *probouleuma*, "on the second and third day of Skirophorion" (the last month of the year).

30. Aischines 3.49: "[Ktesiphon] says in the decree, 'Let the herald proclaim in the theater before the Hellenes, that the Athenian demos crowns [Demosthenes] for merit and manly virtue'; and most of all 'because he carries on saying and doing what is best for the demos'" (Λέγει γὰρ οὕτως ἐν τῷ ψηφίσματι· "καὶ τὸν κήρυκα ἀναγορεύειν ἐν τῷ θεάτρῳ πρὸς τοὺς Ἕλληνας ὅτι στεφανοῖ αὐτὸν ὁ δῆμος ὁ Ἀθηναίων ἀρετῆς ἕνεκα καὶ ἀνδραγαθίας," καὶ τὸ μέγιστον· "ὅτι διατελεῖ καὶ λέγων καὶ πράττων τὰ ἄριστα τῷ δήμῳ"). On the same theme, cf. §§101 and 237.

31. In the 1830s that disparity led Anton Westermann to suppose that Ktesiphon's case went to trial in 335/4: *De Aeschinis oratione* (1833) esp. 10–12 and 23–27. Rudolf Rauchenstein argued to the contrary, that "the Athenians embraced and protected [Demosthenes] . . . as a man most devoted to the *patria*" (when Alexander demanded his surrender), so the situation in 330 was more inviting for Aischines' reprisal: *De tempore quo Aeschinis et Demosthenis orationes Ctesiphonteae habitae sint, Commentatio* (1835) 11–12.

32. Schaefer, *Demosthenes und seine Zeit* (1885) 1:211–14. Cawkwell, "Eubulus," *JHS* 83 (1963) 54, with n. 48, dates Hegemon's law "shortly before 335/4," and that is certainly consistent with Aischines' mention of it as sequel to the dominance of Demosthenes as administrator of the Theoric Fund. A law of Hegemon (probably the same) is cited for maintenance of ships and shipyards in *IG* ii^2 1628.298–301, in Chares' archonship (326/5).

33. Aischines 3.37. The terse phrasing of [Plut.] *X orat.* 846A might suggest that Aischines was assisted by a *synēgoros* (γραφέντος τοῦ ψηφίσματος παρανόμων ὑπὸ

Διοδότου καὶ Αἰσχίνου), but "Diodotos" is almost certainly an error for Diondas, referring to the earlier case.

Chapter 9 · The Crown Case Comes to Trial

1. Esp. Aischines 3.253. Cf. Schaefer, *Demosthenes und seine Zeit* (1887) 3:225–27; Wankel, *Demosthenes Rede für Ktesiphon* (1976) 18–25; Yunis, *Demosthenes "On the Crown"* (2001) 7–12. For earlier scholarship preoccupied with *post eventum* adaptations, see Richardson, *Aeschines "Against Ctesiphon"* (1889) 27–28. For further references on this problem, see also my study, "How the 'Crown Case' Came to Trial and Why," *GRBS* 59 (2019) 109–33.

2. Cawkwell, "Crowning of Demosthenes," CQ^2 19 (1969) 166–67, rightly rejecting limitation on the lawsuit; followed by Worthington, *Demosthenes* (2013) 294–95.

3. Dem. 23.92: ἄκυρόν ἐστι τὸ ψήφισμα· προβούλευμα γάρ ἐστιν, ὁ νόμος δ' ἐπέτεια κελεύει τὰ τῆς βουλῆς εἶναι ψηφίσματα. For the sequence of events in Aristokrates' case, see chapter 4 §1.

4. For example, Blass, *attische Beredsamkeit* 3.2. (1898) 233–34 [= 1880: 205–6]; followed for the most part by Richardson, *Aeschines "Against Ctesiphon"* (1889) 36–37.

5. Aischines 3.191: ὁ δῆμος κατελύθη ἐπειδή τινες τὰς γραφὰς τῶν παρανόμων ἀνεῖλον.

6. Aischines 3.193: Ἤδη δ' ἐκ τῶν τεχνῶν τῶν Δημοσθένους αἰσχρὸν ἔθος ἐν τοῖς δικαστηρίοις παραδέχεσθε. Μετενήνεκται γὰρ ὑμῖν τὰ τῆς πόλεως δίκαια· ὁ μὲν γὰρ κατήγορος ἀπολογεῖται, ὁ δὲ φεύγων τὴν γραφὴν κατηγορεῖ, οἱ δὲ δικασταὶ ἐνίοτε ὧν μέν εἰσι κριταὶ ἐπιλανθάνονται, ὧν δ' οὐκ εἰσὶ δικασταί, περὶ τούτων ἀναγκάζονται τὴν ψῆφον φέρειν·

7. More perfunctory in Aischines 1.175. Cf. Richardson, *Aeschines "Against Ctesiphon"* (1889) 194–95: "the same commonplace is more cleverly applied in Dem. xix. 213."

8. The passage is problematic: see esp. Wankel, *Demosthenes Rede für Ktesiphon* (1976) 171–85. But the turn of thought is concessive: it is wrong (in principle) to deny anyone freedom of speech, but for one who has repeatedly abused the right, there must be consequences.

9. Aischines 3.216–17: καὶ κατὰ τῆσδε τῆς κρίσεως εὐθὺς ἀρχόμενος τοῦ λόγου φέρει τινὰ αἰτίαν, λέγων ὡς ἐγὼ τὴν γραφὴν οὐχ ὑπὲρ τῆς πόλεως ἐγραψάμην, ἀλλ' ἐνδεικνύμενος Ἀλεξάνδρῳ διὰ τὴν πρὸς αὐτὸν ἔχθραν. . . . διὰ τί τὸ μὲν κεφάλαιον αὐτοῦ τῆς πολιτείας ψέγω, τὰ δὲ καθ' ἕκαστον οὐκ ἐκώλυον οὐδ' ἐγραφόμην ἀλλὰ διαλείπων καὶ πρὸς πολιτείαν οὐ πυκνὰ προσιὼν ἀπήνεγκα τὴν γραφήν. Cf. Carey, *Aeschines* (2000) 238, with n. 248, listing passages in response.

10. Theophrastos fr. 636C Fortenbaugh: ἔκειτο τῷ μὴ μεταλαβόντι τὸ πέμπτον μέρος τῶν ψήφων, ὡς Θεόφραστος ἐν πέμπτῳ περὶ νόμων· ἐν δὲ τοῖς δημοσίοις ἀγῶσιν ἐζημιοῦντο χιλίαις καὶ πρόσεστί τις ἀτιμία, ὥστε μὴ ἐξεῖναι μήτε γράψασθαι παρανόμων μήτε φαίνειν μήτε ἐφηγεῖσθαι· ἐὰν δέ τις γραψάμενος μὴ ἐπεξέλθῃ, ὁμοίως· περὶ δὲ τῆς εἰσαγγελίας, ἐάν τις μὴ μεταλάβῃ τὸ πέμπτον μέρος τῶν ψήφων, οἱ δικασταὶ τιμῶσιν. See chapter 5 §1 at notes 16–22.

11. Some of the ancient testimony suggests as much: Plutarch, *Demosthenes* 24.2–3, after confusion over dating the indictment to Chairondas' archonship (338/7), concludes that the judges so emphatically rejected Aischines' case "that he did not receive one-fifth of the ballots; and so he immediately departed from the city."

12. *Vita Aeschinis* 2 (anon.) Blass: μὴ μεταλαβεῖν τὸ πέμπτον μέρος τῶν ψήφων, ἀτιμωθέντα δ' ἀπᾶραι εἰς τὴν Ἀσίαν καὶ ἐλθεῖν εἰς Ἔφεσον οἰηθέντα κατάξειν αὐτὸν εἰς Ἀθήνας Ἀλέξανδρον.

13. *Vita Aeschinis* 3 (Ἀπολλωνίου) Blass: καὶ *ὁρίσαντος τὸ πρόστιμον* ἐὰν μὴ δείξῃ αὐτὸ παράνομον καὶ ἡττηθέντος καὶ *διὰ τὸ μὴ δύνασθαι καταβαλεῖν τὴν καταδίκην, ἣν αὐτὸς ὥρισε*, φυγῇ χρησαμένου. The biographer cites a work "For the Crown" (ὡς καὶ τοῦτο ἔγνωμεν ἐν τῷ ὑπὲρ τοῦ στεφάνου).

14. Photios (cod. 61, p. 20a [Bekker] lines 20–23): καὶ *ὁρίσας τὸ πρόστιμον αὐτὸς ἑαυτῷ*, ἐὰν μὴ δείξῃ παράνομον, μὴ δείξας ὡς ὑπέσχετο ἐξέπεσε τῆς πατρίδος. Photios also reports that Aischines set out to join Alexander and went to Rhodes after the conqueror's death.

15. Leonhard Spengel, "Demosthenes Vertheidigung des Ktesiphon," *Abh. K. Akad. Wiss* 10 (1862), 29–97, at 47–50, 69–70, 90–93.

16. Spengel, "Demosthenes Vertheidigung," 50: "Und Aeschines? Ist er ein Verräther? Unmöglich wäre es nicht, dass er von Philippus bestochen gegen besseres Wissen und Gewissen gesprochen hätte, aber Demosthenes hat es keineswegs bewiesen."

17. The usual protocol is indicated in *IG* ii^2 125 (Tod *GHI* 154) 7–16, of the year 357/6, regarding an attack on Eretria: on the motion of Hegesippos, the council is to prepare a *probouleuma* "for the first assembly, so that the offenders be tried according to treaty." Some of the terms are indicated in the prospective provision: in future if anyone attacks Eretria or other ally, he shall "be condemned to death and his property confiscated, with a tithe to the goddess, and his property be subject to seizure" anywhere in the alliance. It seems clear that there was some change in parameters for *eisangelia* in the late 330s: Hansen, *Eisangelia* (1975) 30; Volonaki, "Abuse of the *Eisangelia*" (2019) in *Use and Abuse of Law*, ed. Carey et al., 293–305.

18. Xen. *Hell.* 1.7.12–16; cf. Carawan, "Trial of the Arginousai Generals," *Dike* 10 (2007) 19–22.

19. Aischines 3.193 (continuing from note 6): οἱ δὲ δικασταὶ ἐνίοτε ὧν μέν εἰσι κριταὶ ἐπιλανθάνονται, ὧν δ' οὐκ εἰσὶ δικασταί, περὶ τούτων ἀναγκάζονται τὴν ψῆφον φέρειν· λέγει δὲ ὁ φεύγων, ἂν ἄρα ποθ' ἅψηται τοῦ πράγματος, οὐχ ὡς ἔννομα γέγραφεν, ἀλλ' ὡς ἤδη ποτὲ καὶ πρότερον ἕτερος τοιαῦτα γράψας ἀπέφυγεν. Ἐφ' ᾧ καὶ νυνὶ μέγα φρονεῖν ἀκούω Κτησιφῶντα.

20. "Was acquitted" would be the regular sense of ἀπέφυγεν, aorist, in §194. In what follows, that Kephalos "was never even prosecuted," the manuscript again has ἀπέφυγε; here Blass, *Aeschinis Orationes* (1896), preferred Franke's reading πέφευγε. Yet, as Horváth "Postponement of the Trial" (2019), 132–46, suggests, Aristophon probably included in his tally many cases where the prosecutor simply did not proceed.

21. Aischines 3.196: ἐξαιτοῦνται τὰς γραφὰς τῶν παρανόμων. Richardson, *Aeschines "Against Ctesiphon"* (1889) 196, finds an example in the support of Phokion and Euboulos for Aischines himself in the Embassy Case (2.184). But those were proceedings of a different sort; here Aischines' point is that *graphai paranomōn* should have a restriction because the constitution itself is at stake.

22. (196 cont.): εἰ γάρ τις ἐν δημοκρατίᾳ τετιμημένος, ἐν τοιαύτῃ πολιτείᾳ ἣν οἱ θεοὶ καὶ οἱ νόμοι σῴζουσι, τολμᾷ βοηθεῖν τοῖς παράνομα γράφουσι, καταλύει τὴν πολιτείαν, ὑφ' ἧς τετίμηται.

23. Conversely, we know from Euxenippos' case against Polyeuktos (Hansen, *Sovereignty*, 1974, no. 35) that the penalty might be negligible; cf. chapter 8 §2. As for the text in Aischines 3.197, Franke (1851) simply deleted the negative (μή) and most editors have followed him.

24. Thus W. E. Gwatkin, Jr., "The Legal Arguments in Aischines' *Against Ktesiphon* and Demosthenes' *On the Crown*," *Hesperia* 26 (1957) 129–41, at 134: "Even if Ktesiphon had made an illegal proposal in 336, by 330 no accounting process would be embarrassed by any crowning of Demosthenes as a magistrate subject to audit in the future. . . . Demosthenes had sensed that the intimation of a single sentence [§117] was more effective than sustained argument, which would have pointed the contrast between the situation in 336 and that in 330, focusing attention upon the earlier year when the legally-minded portion of the jury would be likely to decide that he could not be crowned legally."

25. [Plut.] *X orat.* 846A concludes that 100 minas was the whole of his tribe's contribution: καὶ τῶν τειχῶν ἐπιμελητὴς χειροτονηθεὶς ἀπὸ τῆς ἰδίας οὐσίας εἰσήνεγκε τὸ ἀναλωθὲν ἀργύριον, μνᾶς ἑκατόν.

26. As introduced in chapter 8 §3. Schaefer, *Demosthenes und seine Zeit*[2] (1885) 1:213, explained Hegemon's law as a reaction in 336/5 against the reforms undertaken by Demosthenes and Lykourgos in the previous years; cf. Cawkwell, "Eubulus," *JHS* 83 (1963) 54–57.

27. Aischines 3.25–26: οἱ ἐπὶ τὸ θεωρικὸν κεχειροτονημένοι ἦρχον μέν, πρὶν ἢ τὸν Ἡγήμονος νόμον γενέσθαι, τὴν τοῦ ἀντιγραφέως ἀρχήν, ἦρχον δὲ τὴν τῶν ἀποδεκτῶν καὶ νεωρίων ἀρχήν, καὶ σκευοθήκην ᾠκοδόμουν, ἦσαν δὲ καὶ ὁδοποιοί, καὶ σχεδὸν τὴν ὅλην διοίκησιν εἶχον τῆς πόλεως. . . . ὁ μὲν νομοθέτης, ἐάν τις μιᾶς ἀρχῆς τῆς ἐλαχίστης ὑπεύθυνος ᾖ, τοῦτον οὐκ ἐᾷ, πρὶν ἂν λόγον καὶ εὐθύνας δῷ, στεφανοῦν, ὁ δὲ Κτησιφῶν Δημοσθένην τὸν συλλήβδην ἁπάσας τὰς Ἀθήνησιν ἀρχὰς ἄρχοντα οὐκ ὤκνησε γράψαι στεφανῶσαι.

28. A fragmentary inscription survives from a nomothetic decision in 337/6, *IG* ii[2] 244, regarding the long walls and Peiraieus fortifications. F. G. Maier, *Griechische Mauerbauinschriften* (1959) 1:43, found that such *teichopoioi* were not directly involved with the architects but rather exercised "general oversight" of the project, especially involved with the *tamiai* in "wall funding" (*teichopoiika*).

29. These honorands are all indicated in an inscription of 337/6, *IG* ii[2] 1496.22–51. The only officer in the list who might closely match Demosthenes' situation would be the last, Neoptolemos (πολλῶν ἔργων ἐπιστάτης ὤν), but Demosthenes says nothing to make that parallel more clear.

30. Dem. 18.113, ὀρθῶς ἐπηνούμην, ὅτι τἀνηλωμέν' ἔδωκα καὶ οὐκ ἐλογιζόμην. Yunis, *Demosthenes "On the Crown"* (2001) 177, renders ἐλογιζόμην as "enter [the expenditures] in the [public] account"; Wankel, *Demosthenes Rede für Ktesiphon* (1976) 619, "und nicht berechnete (in Rechnung stellte)."

31. Harris, *Aeschines and Athenian Politics* (1994) 140–50, observes that the law seems to bar crowning before accounting *only if* the crowning was for that particular office; ordinarily, crowning for donations or other extraofficial service would not be barred, as the honorands in Dem. 18.114 would seem to prove.

32. Thus Blass, in the first edition of *attische Beredsamkeit* 3.2 (1880) 186, supposed that the second count, against crowning at the Dionysia (32–48), was added in 330.

33. Ktesiphon Peiraieus (*APF* 8900) was of an earlier generation, as was the Ktesiphon who served on the embassy to Philip in 346, identified by Aischines as "the eldest" (2.42).

34. There is another mention of a Ktesiphon from Demosthenes' deme, Paiania, without patronymic in *IG* ii^2 2409.36–37.

35. Aischines 3.145, hijacking the democracy (to Thebes): αὐτὸς αὐτῷ δυναστείαν κατεσκεύασεν; 220, ὁ δυναστεύων δημηγορεῖ.

36. Goodwin, *Demosthenes: "On the Crown"* (1901) 236–37.

37. Christian Habicht, "Falsche Urkunden zur Geschichte Athens," *Hermes* 89 (1961) 1–35; Noel Robertson, "False Documents at Athens," *Historical Reflections* 3 (1976) 3–24.

38. For example, on the purpose clause in the Dionysiac law, against acquiring *philotimia* with "false decrees" (45).

39. Dem. 18.224, protesting "double jeopardy." Usher, *Demosthenes "De Corona"* (1993) 248 ad loc., found it "sophistical to the point of absurdity," as though "after the first proposer of a crown for Dem. [was acquitted] no subsequent proposer of a crown could be indicted." But the point is that the previous decision was a verdict on Demosthenes' role in the Theban alliance, and the same issue is being retried: thus Spengel, "Demosthenes Vertheidigung" (1862) 82. For detailed comparison of policy arguments in the two speeches (against Diondas and against Aischines), see Horváth, *Neue Hypereides* (2014) 165–76.

40. Aischines 3.253: οὗτος στεφανοῦσθαι ἀξιοῖ καὶ κηρύττεσθαι οἴεται δεῖν. Οὐκ ἀποπέμψεσθε τὸν ἄνθρωπον ὡς κοινὴν τῶν Ἑλλήνων συμφοράν; Ἢ συλλαβόντες ὡς ληστὴν τῶν πραγμάτων, ἐπ' ὀνομάτων διὰ τῆς πολιτείας πλέοντα, τιμωρήσεσθε; . . . (254) δόξετε δ' ἐὰν μὲν τοῦτον στεφανώσητε, ὁμογνώμονες εἶναι τοῖς παραβαίνουσι τὴν κοινὴν εἰρήνην, ἐὰν δὲ τοὐναντίον τούτου πράξητε, ἀπολύσετε τὸν δῆμον τῶν αἰτιῶν.

41. In the Harpalos affair of 324, Deinarchos' client blamed Demosthenes, evidently, for some part in the earlier rebellion: at Athens he went around "prepping speechwriters" and flaunting "a letter he had written on [his] own." Cf. Worthington, *Demosthenes* (2013) 31–25, esp. 317–18, on Dein. 1.34–35. Demosthenes made a brief return after the death of Alexander, but in 322, after the last gasp of rebellion was throttled, Antipater demanded the surrender of Demosthenes and had him hunted down.

Conclusion · Law's Measure

1. Judith Shklar captured this contribution effectively in *Montesquieu* (1987) 112–13: as he "moved from medieval to modern constitutionalism, he also turned the classical notion of the mixed constitution into the more adaptable theory of separation of powers. By comparing the Roman and the English political systems he explained the difference . . . and showed why the latter is more stable. A mixed constitution allowed Roman patricians as well as the people to participate in every function of government . . . Each class and each part of government could veto or check the other . . . There was thus a balance as well as a mixture of powers . . . [with] no specialization of function; each part of the state had judicial powers, which meant a political judiciary, a grave defect in Montesquieu's view. In many ways England, with its two Houses of Parliament and Crown and mutual vetoes, was also a mixed constitution. Its aim, however, unlike Rome's was the liberty of the individual, and so the separation of powers was the cornerstone of its constitution. That meant, first and foremost, an absolutely independent

judiciary." On the American adaptation, see Wills, *Explaining America* (2001) esp. 179–81; and on the lure of mechanical models, Wills, *Inventing America* (1978) 93–131.

2. As Coke explained in *Bonham's Case* and the *Case of Proclamations*: see Clinton, "*Marbury v. Madison*" (1989) 38–42; McIlwain, *Constitutionalism Ancient and Modern*[2] (1947) 78–79 and 142–45; Corwin, *Doctrine of Judicial Review* (1914) 35–54.

3. Posner and Vermeule, *Executive Unbound* (2010), saw the ever-broadening power of that branch as functional and practically inevitable. In recent years, the executive seems to be fulfilling that promise, as though in a bid to replace the high court as "the most dangerous branch."

4. As phrased in Justinian *Codex* 3.5: *Ne quis in sua causa iudicet vel sibi ius dicat*. The rule is invoked explicitly in *Federalist* 10 and 80, and implicit in the argument of nos. 47, 49, 51, and 78.

5. Despite Madison's schemes to the contrary; see Wills, *Explaining America* (2001) 97–125 and 137–54, esp. 149–50.

6. Dem. 20.108: τὰς μὲν διὰ τῶν ὀλίγων πολιτείας τὸ πάντας ἔχειν ἴσον ἀλλήλοις τοὺς τῶν κοινῶν κυρίους ὁμονοεῖν ποιεῖ, τὴν δὲ τῶν δήμων ἐλευθερίαν ἡ τῶν ἀγαθῶν ἀνδρῶν ἅμιλλα, ἣν ἐπὶ ταῖς παρὰ τοῦ δήμου δωρειαῖς πρὸς αὑτοὺς ποιοῦνται, φυλάττει.

7. See Hansen's study, *Political Obligation* (2015), with my review in *Phoenix* 70 (2016) 202–4.

8. Text in Carey et al. (2008) 5.25–26.1 (my translation): "If you reject this lawsuit, [the Thebans present] will rightly conclude that the accuser is out of his mind, raving mad, but that *you* are sticking by the same [commitments you made]. . . . But if you convict, *they would have every right to charge you*, as you condemn yourselves for wrongdoing in the very cause that you called them to join."

9. Cf. Canevaro, "Athenian Constitutionalism" (2018) 79.

10. See esp. Grandjean, "Athens and Bronze Coinage" (2006) in *Agoranomia*, ed. van Alfen, 99–108, with references to Kroll's earlier work.

11. See Lorenzen, *Technological Studies* (1966) 18–30, on Greek and Egyptian *kanones*. Pollitt, "Canon of Polykleitos" (1995) in *Polykleitos*, ed. Moon; Wilson Jones, "Greek and Roman Architectural Theory" (2014) in *Oxford Handbook of Greek and Roman Art and Architecture*, ed. Manconi, 47–53.

12. Dekoulakou-Sideris, "A Metrological Relief from Salamis," *AJA* 94.3 (1990) 445–51. Wilson Jones, "Doric Measure and Architectural Design 1," *AJA* 104 (2000) 73–93, found measurements that more closely correspond to the Doric and other standard units by measuring at the surface of each relief, which must have been the regular practice; critical proportions are also represented in the dimensions of the stone itself. The metrological relief in Oxford was not itself used for measurement but probably indicated an archive; so concluded Fernie, "Metrological Relief," *AntJ* 61 (1981) 255–63.

13. There seem to be adjustments of that type on devices recovered from a shipwreck in 1985: Stieglitz, "Classical Greek Measures," *AJA* 110 (2006) 195–203. This is probably what the Athenians meant where they required the contractor to make his work conform πρὸς τὸν κανόνα τὸν λίθινον, as in *IG* i^3 475.215–22. Here, among work orders for the Erechtheion (409/8), Stevens et al., *Erechtheum* (1927) 339, translated as though the *kanōn lithinos* were a "stone straight-edge" used to assure that surfaces are flush. But there must have been more to it: earlier in this inscription, workers were assigned to

make and maintain *kanones* (*IG* i³ 475.65–71); presumably these were more portable devices that had to be checked daily (καθ' ἐμέραν κανόνα διαρρυ[θμίσαντι]) against the stone standard.

14. The act was defended by Louis Brandeis and Benjamin Cardozo, and a year later Roberts himself took a turn to the left, siding with the majority to uphold a minimum wage law and allowing even the Social Security Act. This change of heart seemed to dissuade Roosevelt from his plan to pack the court; it was called the "switch in time to save nine."

15. "*Eikos* Arguments" (2014) in *Probabilities*, ed. Wohl, 28: "The T-square rule was directed against scholars associated with the legal realism movement, who at the time were arguing that the tenets of legal positivism and judicial objectivism, which had dominated the court's thinking for more than half a century, served primarily to justify the justices' personal views regarding the sanctity of private property and free enterprise."

16. Holmes, "The Path of the Law," *Harvard Law Review* 10 (1897) 457, 470.

17. *Introduction to the Philosophy of Law*² (1954; 1st ed. 1922), 52–53.

18. As Supreme Court Justice in *Brown v. Allen* (1953), Frankfurter wrote, "Judges dealing with the writ of habeas corpus . . . must be left some discretion . . . if law is not to be a Procrustes bed." (344 US 443, 496).

19. "Law against Tyranny," Athenian Agora Excavations, accessed April 5, 2020, http://www.agathe.gr/democracy/marble_stele.html. On the illustration and its symbolism, see Blanshard (2004), "An Exploration of Art and Text in the Law of Eukrates," *JHS* 124: 1–15, esp. 12, on authoritarian implications; cf. Bianchi, "Law of Eukrates," *SHHA* 23 (2005) 313–30; Bearzot, "Political Murder," *AncSoc* 37 (2007) 40–41.

20. This last development seems the most workable explanation for the procedure leading to Demosthenes' Trierarchic Law in 340 and for the composite document in Dem. 24.33, as argued in chapters 1 and 2.

21. Cf. Klarman, *Framers' Coup* (2016) 182–212, at 209 with n. 273.

22. Aristotle *Politics* 3.11.1–15 and 15.7–9.

23. The British referendum to exit the European Union provides a striking example: even after the repeated failure of her most viable plans for an orderly divorce, the prime minister—who initially opposed the exit—insisted that a second referendum, which might overturn the first, would be an insult to the people; see "Theresa May Condemns Tony Blair's New Brexit Vote Call," *BBC News*, December 16, 2018, https://www.bbc.com/news/uk-politics-46582705.

24. As Adrian Vermeule explains in *Constitution of Risk* (2014) and "Second Opinions," *Virginia Law Review* (2011), esp. 1449–51.

25. Cf. Wills, *Explaining America* (2001) 120–23, with Madison in *Federalist* 47 on Montesquieu, "the oracle who is always consulted"; and 179–82 on the ethos of the Athenians as compared to the French (*Esprit* 19.5). The adaptive character of the Supreme Court is the prevailing theme of Friedman, *Will of the People* (2009).

26. See Wills, *Inventing America* (1978), part 2, esp. 106–110: Jefferson grudgingly defended his scheme to find a new standard based on pendulums poised at critical longitudes and elevations, in correspondence with Rittenhouse, 1778.

BIBLIOGRAPHY

Alfange, Dean, Jr. 1993. "*Marbury v. Madison* and Original Understanding of Judicial Review: In Defense of Traditional Wisdom." *Supreme Court Review* 1993:329–446.

Andrewes, A. 1974. "The Arginousai Trial." *Phoenix* 28:112–22.

Andriolo, Nadia. 2002. "Syndikoi." *Dialogues d'histoire ancienne* 28:11–18.

Badian, Ernst. 1995. "The Ghost of Empire: Reflections on Athenian Foreign Policy in the Fourth Century BC." In *Die Athenische Demokratie im 4. Jahrhundert v. Chr.: Vollendung oder Verfall einer Verfassungsform*, edited by W. Eder, 79–106. Stuttgart: Steiner.

Bearzot, Cinzia. 1990. "L'orazione demostenica 'Contro Leptine' e la polemica sulla morte di Cabria." In *Dulce et decorum est pro patria mori*, edited by Marta Sordi, 95–110. Milan: Università Cattolica, Contributi dell' Istituto di storia antica vol. 16.

———. 2007. "Political Murder in Classical Greece." *AncSoc* 37:37–61.

Beck, Hans, ed. 2013. *A Companion to Ancient Greek Government*. Oxford: Wiley-Blackwell.

Berneker, Erich, ed. 1968. *Zur griechischen Rechtsgeschichte*. Wege der Forschung no. 45. Darmstadt: Wissenschaftliche Buchgesellschaft.

Bers, Victor. 2000. "Just Rituals. Why the Rigmarole of Fourth-Century Athenian Lawcourts?" In *Polis & Politics*, edited by P. Flensted-Jensen, T. H. Nielsen, and Lene Rubinstein, 553–62. Copenhagen: Museum Tusculanum, University of Copenhagen.

Bianchi, Erika. 2005. "The Law of Eukrates (336 BC): A 'Democratic Trick'?" *Studia Historica*, Universidad de Salamanca 23:313–30.

Blackstone, William. 1765–69. *Commentaries on the Laws of England*. 4 vols. Oxford: Clarendon Press. Reprint, Chicago: University of Chicago Press, 1979.

Blanshard, A. J. L. 2004. "An Exploration of Art and Text in the Law of Eukrates." *JHS* 124:1–15.

Blass, Friedrich, ed. 1896. *Aeschinis Orationes*. Leipzig: Teubner.

———. 1898. *Die attische Beredsamkeit*. 3.2: *Demosthenes' Genossen und Gegner*[2]. Leipzig: Teubner. First published 1880.

Boeckh, Augustus. 1857. *The Public Economy of the Athenians*. Translated by Anthony Lamb, from *Die Staatshaushaltung der Athener*[2] (Berlin: Reimer, 1851). Boston and London: Little Brown.

Boegehold, Alan. 1984. "Many Letters: Aristophanes *Plutus* 1166–67." In *Studies Presented to Sterling Dow*, Greek, Roman, and Byzantine Monographs no. 10, edited by Kent Rigsby, 23–29. Durham, NC: Duke University.

Böhnecke, Karl Georg. 1843. *Forschungen auf dem Gebiete der Attischen Redner und Geschichte ihrer Zeit*. Berlin: Reimer.

Bonner, R. J., and Gertrude Smith. 1930–38. *The Administration of Justice from Homer to Aristotle*. 2 vols. Chicago: University of Chicago.

Bruck, S. 1894. "Über die Organisation der athenischen Heliastengerichte im 4. Jahrh. v. Chr., II, Die 10 Richterabteilungen." *Philologus* 52:399–424.

Bryce, James. 1995. *The American Commonwealth*. Vol. 1. Indianapolis: Liberty Fund. First American edition, New York: Macmillan, 1889.

Burger, F. 1892. *Stichometrische Untersuchungen zu Demosthenes und Herodot: Ein Beitrag zur Kenntnis des antiken Buchwesens*. Munich: Lindl.

Busolt, Georg, and Heinrich Swoboda. 1920–26. *Griechische Staatskunde*. 2 vols. Munich: Beck.

Cairns, Douglas L. 1996. "*Hybris*, Dishonour, and Thinking Big." *JHS* 116:1–32.

Calabi Limentani, Ida. 1981. "Demostene XX, 137: A Proposito della γραφὴ νόμον μὴ ἐπιτήδειον θεῖναι." In *Studi in onore di Arnaldo Biscardi*, vol. 1, 357–68. Milan: Istituto editoriale Cisalpino, La Goliardica.

———. 1985. "Vittime dell'oligarchia. A proposito del decreto di Teozotide." *Studi in onore di Cesare Sanfilippo* vol. 6. Università di Catania, Pubblicazioni della Facoltà de Giurisprudenza, 96:115–28.

Canevaro, Mirko. 2009. "L'accusa *Contro Leptine*: Crisi economica e *consensus* post-bellico." *Quaderni Rostagni* 8:117–41.

———. 2013. *Documents in the Attic Orators: Laws and Decrees in the Pubic Speeches of the Demosthenic Corpus*. Oxford: Oxford University Press.

———. 2013. "*Nomothesia* in Classical Athens: What Sources Should We Believe?" *CQ* 63:139–60.

———. 2016. *Demostene, "Contro Leptine."* Texte und Kommentare 55. Berlin: De Gruyter.

———. 2016. "The Procedure of Demosthenes' *Against Leptines*: How to Repeal (and Replace) an Existing Law." *JHS* 136:39–58.

———. 2018. "What Was the Law of Leptines Really About? Reflections on Athenian Public Economy and Legislation in the Fourth Century BCE." *Constitutional Political Economy* 29:440–64. https://doi.org/10.1007/s10602-018-9260-7.

———. 2018. "The Authenticity of the Document at Demosth. or. 24.20–3, the Procedures of the *Nomothesia* and the So-Called ἐπιχειροτονία τῶν νόμων." *Klio* 100:71–124.

———. 2018. "Athenian Constitutionalism: *nomothesia* and the *graphe nomon me epitedeion theinai*." In Thür, Yiftach, and Zelnick-Abramovitz, *Symposion 2017*, 65–98.

Canevaro, Mirko, and Edward M. Harris. 2012. "The Documents in Andocides' *On the Mysteries*." *CQ* 62:98–129.

———. 2016–17. "The Authenticity of the Documents at Andocides' *On the Mysteries* 77–79 and 83–84." *Dike* 19/20:9–49.

Canfora, Luciano. 2004. *La democrazia. Storia di un' ideologia*. Rome: Laterza.

———. 2006. *Democracy in Europe: A History of an Ideology*. Translated by Simon Jones. Oxford: Blackwell.

Cappelletti, Mauro. 1970. "Judicial Review in Comparative Perspective." *California Law Review* 58 (5): 1017–53.

———. 1971. *Judicial Review in the Contemporary World*. Indianapolis: Bobbs-Merrill.

Carawan, Edwin. 1996. "The Trials of Thucydides 'the Demagogue' in the Anonymous *Life* of Thucydides the Historian." *Historia* 45:405–22.

———. 1998. *Rhetoric and the Law of Draco*. Oxford: Oxford University Press.

———. 2001. "What the Laws Have Prejudged: Παραγραφή and Early Issue Theory." In *The Orator in Action and Theory in Greece and Rome*, Mnemosyne Supplement 224, edited by Cecil W. Wooten, 17–54. Leiden: Brill.

———, ed. 2007. *Oxford Readings in the Attic Orators*. Oxford: Oxford University Press.

———. 2007. "The Trial of the Arginousai Generals and the Dawn of 'Judicial Review.'" *Dike* 10:19–56.

———. 2007–2017. "Krateros." In *Brill's New Jacoby*, edited by Ian Worthington, no. 342. Leiden: Brill.

———. 2008. "Pericles the Younger and the Citizenship Law." *CJ* 103:383–406.

———. 2011. "*Paragraphê* and the Merits." *GRBS* 51:254–95.

———. 2013. *The Athenian Amnesty and the Reconstruction of the Law*. Oxford: Oxford University Press.

———. 2016. "Court Reform, *Klērotēria*, and Comic Testimony." *CJ* 111:385–416.

———. 2016. "Documents in the Case: Demosthenes 23–4." *TAPA* 146:37–60.

———. 2016. "Review of Hansen, *Political Obligation*." *Phoenix* 70:202–4.

———. 2017. "Decrees in Andocides' *On the Mysteries* and 'Latent Fragments' from Craterus." *CQ* 67:400–21.

———. 2019. "How the 'Crown Case' Came to Trial and Why." *GRBS* 59:109–33.

Carey, Chris. 1992. *Apollodorus "Against Neaira" [Demosthenes] 59*. Warminster: Aris & Phillips.

———, trans. 2000. *Aeschines*. Austin: University of Texas.

Carey, Chris, Mike Edwards, Zoltán Farkas, Judson Herrman, László Horváth, Gyula Mayer, Tamás Mészáros, P. J. Rhodes, and Natalie Tchernetska. 2008. "Fragments of Hyperides *Against Diondas* from the Archimedes Palimpsest." *ZPE* 165:1–19.

Carey, Chris, Ifigeneia Giannadaki, and Brenda Griffith-Williams, eds. 2019. *Use and Abuse of Law in the Athenian Courts*. Mnemosyne Supplement 419. Leiden and Boston: Brill.

Cargill, Jack. 1981. *The Second Athenian League: Empire or Free Alliance?* Berkeley: University of California.

———. 1995. *Athenian Settlements of the Fourth Century* BC. Mnemosyne Supplement 145. Leiden: Brill.

Cartledge, Paul. 2013. *After Thermopylae: The Oath of Plataea and the End of the Graeco-Persian Wars*. Oxford and New York: Oxford University Press.

Casaubon, Isaac. 1600. *Animadversiones in Athenaei Dipnosophistas*. Lyons: Harsy.

Cawkwell, G. L. 1963. "Eubulus." *JHS* 83:47–67.

———. 1969. "The Crowning of Demosthenes." CQ^2 19:163–80.

Clinton, Robert Lowry. 1989. *"Marbury v. Madison" and Judicial Review*. Lawrence: University of Kansas.

Cloché, Paul. 1936. "Remarques sur l'emploi de la *graphe paranomon*." *REA* 38:401–12.

Constant de Rebecque, Benjamin. 1988. *Political Writings*. Translated by Biancamaria Fontana. Cambridge: Cambridge University Press.

———. 2017. *Brochures politiques 1819–1821*. Edited by K. Kloocke and P. Delbouille. Leiden: De Gruyter.

Corwin, Edward S. 1914. *The Docrine of Judicial Review*. Princeton: Princeton University Press. Reprint, Gloucester, MA: P. Smith, 1963.

Davies, J. K. 1971. *Athenian Propertied Families 600–300 BC*. Oxford: Oxford University Press.

———. 1996. "Documents and 'Documents' in Fourth-Century Historiography." In *Le IVème siècle av. J.-C. Approches historiagraphiques*, Etudes anciennes 15, edited by Pierre Carlier, 29–39. Nancy, France: De Boccard.

De Brauw, Michael, and Jess Miner. 2004. "Androtion's Alleged Prostitution Contract: Aes. 1.165 and Dem. 22.23 in light of P. Oxy. VII 1012." *ZRG* 121:301–13.

Dekoulakou-Sideris, Ifigenia. 1990. "A Metrological Relief from Salamis." *AJA* 94:445–51.

Dilts, Mervin R. 1983. *Scholia Demosthenica*. 2 vols. Leipzig: Teubner.

———. 1992. *Scholia in Aeschinem*. Stuttgart and Leipzig: Teubner.

———. 1997. *Aeschinis Orationes*. Stuttgart: Teubner.

———. 2002–2009. *Demosthenis Orationes*. Oxford and New York: Oxford University Press.

Dobree, P. P. 1834. *Lexicon Rhetoricum Cantabrigiense e Margine Ms. Harpocrationis*. Cambridge: Bibl. Publ. Cantab. Dd. 4. 63.

Dover, K. J. 1955. "Anapsephisis in Fifth-Century Athens." *JHS* 75:17–20.

Dow, Sterling. 1937. "The Allotment Machines." In *Prytaneis: A Study of the Inscriptions Honoring the Athenian Councillors. Hesperia* Supplement 1:198–215. Athens: American School of Classical Studies at Athens.

———. 1939. "Aristotle, the Kleroteria, and the Courts." *HSCP* 50:1–34.

Dworkin, Ronald. 1986. *Law's Empire*. Cambridge, MA: Harvard University Press.

Edmonds, John M. 1959. *The Fragments of Attic Comedy*. Vol. 2. Leiden: Brill.

Ehrenberg, Victor. 1965. *Der Staat der Griechen*². Zurich: Artemis. First published 1957–58.

Fernie, Eric. 1981. "The Metrological Relief in Oxford." *The Antiquaries Journal* 61:255–63.

Fisher, N. R. E. 1992. *Hybris: A Study in the Values of Honour and Shame in Ancient Greece*. Warminster: Aris & Phillips.

———. 2001. *Aeschines "Against Timarchos."* Oxford: Oxford University Press.

Fishkin, James S. 2009. *When the People Speak: Deliberative Democracy and Public Consultation*. Oxford: Oxford University Press.

Fränkel, Max. 1877. *Die attischen Geschworenengerichte: Ein Beitrag zum attischen Staatsrecht*. Berlin: Reimer.

Friedman, Barry. 2009. *The Will of the People: How Public Opinion Has Influenced the Supreme Court and Shaped the Meaning of the Constitution*. New York: Farrar, Straus & Giroux.

Gagarin, Michael. 1979. "The Athenian Law against *Hybris*." In *Arktouros: Hellenic Studies Presented to Bernard M. W. Knox*, edited by Glen W. Bowersock, Walter Burkert, and Michael C. J. Putnam, 229–36. Berlin: de Gruyter.

———. 2014. "*Eikos* Arguments in Athenian Forensic Oratory." In *Probabilities, Hypotheticals, and Counterfactuals in Ancient Greek Thought*, edited by V. Wohl, 15–29. Cambridge: Cambridge University Press.

Gerner, F. 1949. "Παρανόμων γραφή." *RE* 18:1281–87.
Giannadaki, Ifigeneia. 2014. "The Time Limit (*Prothesmia*) in the *Graphe Paranomon.*" *Dike* 17:15–34.
Goodell, T. D. 1893. "An Athenian Parallel to a Function of Our Supreme Court." *Yale Review* 2:64–73.
Goodwin, W. W. 1895. "The Athenian γραφὴ παρανόμων and the American Doctrine of Constitutional Law." *TAPA* 26:lx-lxi.
———. 1901. *Demosthenes: "On the Crown."* Cambridge: Cambridge University Press. Reprint, New York: Arno, 1979.
Grandjean, Catherine. 2006. "Athens and Bronze Coinage." In *Agoranomia: Studies in Money and Exchange Presented to John H. Kroll*, edited by Peter G. van Alfen, 99–108. New York: American Numismatic Society.
Guth, Dina. 2014. "Rhetoric and Historical Narrative: The Theban-Athenian Alliance of 339 BCE." *Historia* 63:151–65.
Gwatkin, William E., Jr. 1957. "The Legal Arguments in Aischines' *Against Ktesiphon* and Demosthenes' *On the Crown.*" *Hesperia* 26:129–41.
Habicht, C. 1961. "Falsche Urkunden zur Geschichte Athens." *Hermes* 89:1–35.
Hamel, Debra. 2015. *The Battle of Arginusae: Victory at Sea and Its Tragic Aftermath in the Final Years of the Peloponnesian War.* Baltimore: Johns Hopkins University Press.
Hansen, Mogens Herman. 1974. *The Sovereignty of the People's Court in Athens in the Fourth Century* BC *and the Public Action against Unconstitutional Proposals.* Odense University Classical Studies, book 4. Odense: Odense University Press.
———. 1975. *Eisangelia: The Sovereignty of the People's Court in Athens in the Fourth Century* BC *and the Impeachment of Generals and Politicians.* Odense University Classical Studies, book 6. Odense: Odense University Press.
———. 1980. "Athenian *Nomothesia* in the Fourth Century BC and Demosthenes' Speech against Leptines." *C&M* 32:87–104.
———. 1980. "Seven Hundred Archai in Classical Athens." *GRBS* 21:151–73.
———. 1981. "Initiative and Decision: The Separation of Powers in Fourth-Century Athens." *GRBS* 22:345–70.
———. 1985. "Athenian *Nomothesia.*" *GRBS* 26:345–71.
———. 1987. *The Athenian Assembly in the Age of Demosthenes.* Oxford: Blackwell.
———. 1987. "Graphe Paranomon against Psephismata Not Yet Passed by the Ekklesia." *C&M* 38:63–73.
———. 1999. *Athenian Democracy in the Age of Demosthenes*². Norman: University of Oklahoma Press. First published, Oxford: Blackwell, 1991.
———. 2015. *Political Obligation in Ancient Greece and the Modern World.* Scientia Danica H8, vol. 10. Copenhagen: Royal Danish Academy of Sciences and Letters.
———. 2016. "Is Teisamenos' Decree (Andoc. 1.83–84) a Genuine Document?" *GRBS* 56:34–48.
Harding, Phillip. 1976. "Androtion's Political Career." *Historia* 25:186–200.
———. 1994. *Androtion and the "Atthis."* Oxford: Clarendon Press.
———. 2015. *Athens Transformed, 404–262* BC*: From Popular Sovereignty to the Dominion of the Elite.* New York and London: Routledge.
Harris, Edward M. 1992. "Review of MacDowell, *Demosthenes: Against Meidias (Oration 21).*" *CP* 87:71–80.

———. 1994. *Aeschines and Athenian Politics.* Oxford and New York: Oxford University Press.
———. 1999. "The Penalty for Frivolous Prosecutions in Athenian Law." *Dike* 2:123–42.
———. 2000. "Open Texture in Athenian Law." *Dike* 3:27–79.
———. 2006. "A Response to Robert Wallace." In Rupprecht, *Symposion 2003,* 67–72.
———, trans. 2008. *Demosthenes: Speeches 20–22.* Austin: University of Texas.
———. 2013. *The Rule of Law in Action in Democratic Athens.* Oxford and New York: Oxford University Press.
———. 2013. "The Plaint in Athenian Law and Legal Procedure." In *Archives and Archival Documents in Ancient Societies,* Legal Documents in Ancient Societies no. 4, edited by M. Faraguna, 143–62. Trieste: Università di Trieste.
———, trans. 2018. *Demosthenes, Speeches 23–26.* Austin: University of Texas.
Hart, H. L. A. 1961. *The Concept of Law.* Oxford: Clarendon Press.
Heath, Malcolm. 2004. *Menander: A Rhetor in Context.* Oxford: Oxford University Press.
Hedrick, Charles W., Jr. 2000. "For Anyone Who Wishes to See." *Ancient World* 31:127–35.
Heskel, Julia. 1997. *The North Aegean Wars, 371–360 BC.* Historia Einzelschrift 102. Stuttgart: Steiner.
Hignett, C. 1952. *A History of the Athenian Constitution to the End of the Fifth Century BC.* Oxford: Clarendon Press.
Höffler, R. 1877. *De nomothesia Attica.* Kiel: Haeseler. PhD diss., Academia Regia Christiana Albertina.
Holmes, Oliver Wendell, Jr. 1897. "The Path of the Law." *Harvard Law Review* 10:457–78.
Hommel, H. 1927. *Heliaia: Untersuchungen zur Verfassung und Prozessordnung des Athenischen Volksgerichts, insbesondere zum Schlussteil der Ἀθηναίων Πολιτεία des Aristoteles.* Philologus Supplementband 19.2. Leipzig: Dieterich'sche Verlagsbuchhandlung.
Horváth, László. 2004. "Eine fragwürdige Lesart (Hyp. iv. Kol. V.8)." *Acta Ant. Hung.* 44:163–70.
———. 2009. "Hyperidea." *BICS* 52:187–222.
———. 2014. *Der Neue Hypereides: Textedition, Studien und Erläuterungen.* Texte und Kommentare 50. Berlin: De Gruyter.
———. (2019) "The Postponement of the Trial by Jury in Athens: The Timing of the *Graphē Paranomōn.*" In Carey, Giannadaki, and Griffith-Williams, *Use and Abuse of Law in the Athenian Courts,* 132–46.
Hume, David. 1793. "Of Some Remarkable Customs." In *Essays and Treatises on Several Subjects,* vol. 1, Essays, Moral, Political, and Literary, 361–69. Edinburgh: Bell & Bradfute. First published 1742.
Jaeger, Werner. 1963. *Demosthenes: The Origin and Growth of His Policy.* New York: Octagon.
Jolowicz, H. F., and Barry Nicholas. 1972. *Historical Introduction to the Study of Roman Law*[3]. Cambridge: Cambridge University Press. First published 1952.
Jones, A. H. M. 1957. *Athenian Democracy.* Oxford: Blackwell. Reprinted 1969.
Jones, Nicholas F. 2015. "Androtion of Athens." In *Brill's New Jacoby,* edited by Ian Worthington, no. 324. Leiden: Brill.

———. 2016. "Philochoros" In *Brill's New Jacoby*, edited by Ian Worthington, no. 328. Leiden: Brill.

Kahrstedt, Ulrich. 1910. *Forschungen zur Geschichte des ausgehenden fünften und des vierten Jahrhunderts*. Berlin: Weidmann.

———. 1937–38. "Untersuchungen zu athenischen Behörden." *Klio* 30:10–33 and 31:1–32. Reprint in Berneker, *Zur griechischen Rechtsgeschichte*, 196–262.

Kelly, D. 1990. "Charidemos's Citizenship: The Problem of *IG* ii^2 207." *ZPE* 83:96–109.

Kirchner, Iohannes. 1901–3. *Prosopographia Attica*. Berlin: Reimer. Reprint, Chicago: Ares, 1981.

Klarman, Michael J. 2016. *The Framers' Coup: The Making of the United States Constitution*. New York and Oxford: Oxford University Press.

Kosmetatou, Elizabeth. 2013. "Tyche's Force: Lottery and Chance in Greek Government." In Beck, *A Companion to Ancient Greek Government*, 235–51.

Kremmydas, Christos. 2012. *Commentary on Demosthenes "Against Leptines."* Oxford: Oxford University Press.

Krentz, Peter. 1989. *Xenophon Hellenica I–II.3.10*. Warminster: Aris & Phillips.

Kroll, J. 1972. *Athenian Bronze Allotment Plates*. Cambridge, MA: Harvard University Press.

Lambert, Stephen D. 2011. "What Was the Point of Inscribed Honorific Decrees in Classical Athens?" In *Sociable Man*, 193–214.

———, ed. 2011. *Sociable Man: Essays on Ancient Greek Social Behaviour in Honour of Nick Fisher*. Swansea: Classical Press of Wales.

Lavelle, Brian M. 1988. "*Adikia*, the Decree of Kannonos and the Trial of the Generals." *C&M* 39: 19–41.

Levinson, Sanford. 2012. *Framed: America's 51 Constitutions and the Crisis of Governance*. Oxford and New York: Oxford University Press.

Lewis, D. M. 1954. "Notes on Attic Inscriptions." *ABSA* 49:17–50

Liddel, Peter. 2007. *Civic Obligation and Individual Liberty in Ancient Athens*. Oxford: Oxford University Press.

Lipsius, J. 1905–15. *Das attische Recht und Rechtsverfahren*. 3 vols. Leipzig: O. R. Reisland.

Lögdberg, L. E. 1898. *Animadversiones de actione paranomon*. Upsala: Almquist & Wiksell.

Lorenzen, Eivind. 1966. *Technological Studies in Ancient Metrology*. Copenhagen: Nyt Nordisk.

MacDowell, Douglas M. 1975. "Law-Making at Athens in the Fourth Century BC." *JHS* 95:62–74.

———. 2009. *Demosthenes the Orator*. Oxford: Oxford University Press.

Maier, Franz Georg. 1959–61. *Griechische Mauerbauinschriften*. 2 vols. Vestigia 1–2. Heidelberg: Quelle & Meyeer.

Margalit, Avishai. 2010. *On Compromise and Rotten Compromises*. Princeton: Princeton University Press.

Matthaiou, Angelos P. 2011. *Τὰ ἐν τῆι στήληι γεγραμμένα: Six Greek Historical Inscriptions of the Fifth Century* BC. Athens: Ελληνική Επιγραφική Εταιρεία.

McIlwain, Charles Howard. 1947. *Constitutionalism Ancient and Modern*^{2}. Ithaca, NY: Cornell University Press. First published 1940.

Meier, M. H. E., G. F. Schömann, and J. H. Lipsius. 1883–1887. *Der attische Process*^{2}. 4 books. Berlin: Calvary. First published, Halle, 1824.

Mirhady, David. 2007. "The Dikasts' Oath and the Question of Fact." In Sommerstein and Fletcher, *Horkos: The Oath in Greek Society*, 48–59.

Mitchell, L., and L. Rubinstein, eds. 2009. *Greek History and Epigraphy. Essays in Honour of P. J. Rhodes*. Swansea: Classical Press of Wales.

Momigliano, Arnaldo. 1975. "Contributi alla caratteristica di Demostene." In *Quinto Contributo alla storia degli studi classici e del mondo antico*, vol. 1, 234–66. Rome: Edizioni di storia e letteratura First published in *Civiltà Moderna* 3 (1931): 711–44.

Moreno, Alfonso. 2007. *Feeding the Democracy: The Athenian Grain Supply in the Fifth and Fourth Centuries* BC. Oxford: Oxford University Press.

Mossé, Claude. 1962. *La fin de la démocratie athénienne, aspects sociaux et politiques du déclin de la cité grecque au IVe siècle avant J.-C.* Paris: Presses universitaires de France.

Nelson, William E. 1978. "The Eighteenth-Century Background of John Marshall's Constitutional Jurisprudence." *Michigan Law Review* 76:893–960.

———. 2000. *"Marbury v. Madison": The Origins and Legacy of Judicial Review.* Lawrence: Kansas University Press.

Nemeth, G. 1984. "Der Arginusen-Prozess: Die Geschichte eines politischen Justizmordes." *Klio* 66:51–57.

Ober, Josiah. 2008. *Democracy and Knowledge.* Princeton: Princeton University Press.

Olsen, S. Douglas. 2009. *Athenaeus: The Learned Banqueters.* Vol. 5. Cambridge, MA: Harvard University Press.

Osborne, M. J. 1981–83. *Naturalization in Athens.* 4 vols in 3. Brussels: AWLSK (Verhandelingen van de Koninklijke Academie voor Wetenschappen, Letteren en Schone Kunsten van België, Klasse der Letteren) Jaargang 43, nr. 98; 44, nr. 101; 45, nr. 109.

Osborne, Robin. 1985. "Law in Action in Classical Athens." *JHS* 105:40–58.

Ostwald, Martin. 1969. *Nomos and the Beginnings of the Athenian Democracy.* Oxford: Oxford University Press.

———. 1986. *From Popular Sovereignty to the Sovereignty of Law.* Berkeley: University of California Press.

Paga, Jessica. 2010. "Deme Theaters in Attica and the Trittys System." *Hesperia* 79:351–84.

Paoli, Ugo Enrico. 1933. *Studi sul processo attico.* Padua: Milani. Reprinted 1974.

Parke, H. W. 1928. "When Was Charidemus Made an Athenian Citizen?" *CR* 42:170.

Pelloso, Carlo. 2017. "L'ἔφεσις al tribunale popolare in diritto processuale ateniese: 'impugnazione,' 'rimessione' o 'tertium datur'?" *Index. Quaderni camerti di studi romanistici* 45:517–56.

Pesely, George E. 1994. "Did Aristotle Use Androtion's *Atthis*?" *Klio* 76:155–71.

Petit, Samuel. 1742. *Leges Atticae*[2] with addenda by P. Wesseling, J. Le Paulmier de Grentemesnil, A. M. Salvini, and C. A. Duker. Leiden: Kallewier & Verbeek. First published, Paris: Morel, 1635.

Phillips, David D. 2013. *The Law of Ancient Athens.* Ann Arbor: University of Michigan Press.

Piérart, Marcel. 2000. "Qui étaient les nomothètes à l'époque de Démosthène?" In *La codification des lois dans l'antiquité: actes du Colloque de Strasbourg, 27–29 novembre 1997*, edited by E. Levy, 229–56. Paris: De Boccard.

Pollitt, J. J. 1995. "The Canon of Polykleitos and Other Canons." In *Polykleitos, the Doryphoros, and Tradition*, edited by W. G. Moon, 19–24. Madison: University of Wisconsin Press.

Posner, Eric A., and Adrian Vermeule. 2010. *The Executive Unbound: After the Madisonian Republic*. Oxford: Oxford University Press.

Pound, Roscoe. 1954. *An Introduction to the Philosophy of Law*[2]. New Haven: Yale University Press. First published 1922.

Queyrel Bottineau, Anne. 2010. *Prodosia: La notion et l'acte de trahison dans l'Athènes du v*[e]*siècle. Recherche sur la construction de l'identité athénienne*. Scripta Antiqua 29. Paris: De Boccard.

Rauchenstein, Rudolf. 1835. *De tempore quo Aeschinis et Demosthenis orationes Ctesiphonteae habitae sint, Commentatio*. Aarau: Beccii.

Reich, Heinrich. 1891. "Bemerkungen zum Prozess Ktesiphon." In *Abhandlungen aus dem Gebiet der klassischen Altertums-Wissenschaft [für] Wilhelm von Christ zum sechsigsten Geburtstag, dargebracht von seinen Schülern*, 280–93. Munich: Beck.

Rhodes, P. J. 1979. "ΕΙΣΑΓΓΕΛΙΑ in Athens." *JHS* 99:103–14.

———. 1993. *A Commentary on the Aristotelian "Athenaion Politeia"*[2]. Oxford: Oxford University Press. First published 1981.

———. 2003. "Sessions of *Nomothetai* in Fourth-Century Athens." *CQ* 53:124–29.

———. 2009. "Hyperides' *Against Diondas:* Two Problems." *BICS* 52:223–28.

———. 2013. "The Organization of Athenian Public Finance." *Greece & Rome* 60:203–31.

Rhodes, P. J., and Robin Osborne. 2003. *Greek Historical Inscriptions 404–323 BC*. Oxford: Oxford University Press.

Richardson, Rufus B. 1889. *Aeschines "Against Ctesiphon."* Boston and London: Ginn.

Roberts, Owen J. 1951. *The Court and the Constitution*. Oliver Wendell Holmes Lecture for 1951, Cambridge, MA: Harvard University Press.

Robertson, Noel. 1976. "False Documents at Athens: Fifth-Century History and Fourth-Century Publicists." *Historical Reflections* 3:3–24.

Rousseau, Jean-Jacques. 1994. *"Discourse on Political Economy" and "The Social Contract."* Translated by Christopher Betts. Oxford: Oxford University Press.

Rowe, Galen O. 2000. "Anti-Isocratean Sentiment in Demosthenes' *Against Androtion.*" *Historia* 49:278–302.

———. 2002. "Two Responses by Isocrates to Demosthenes." *Historia* 51:149–62.

Rubinstein, Lene. 2000. *Litigation and Cooperation: Supporting Speaker in the Courts of Classical Athens*. Historia Einzelschrift 147. Stuttgart: Steiner.

Rupprecht, H.-A. 2006. *Symposion 2003*. Akten der Gesellschaft für griechishe und hellenistische Rechtsgeschichte 17. Vienna: Verlag der Österreichischen Akademie der Wissenschaften.

Ruschenbusch, Eberhard. 1965. "ʽΥΒΡΕΩΣ ΓΡΑΦΗ: Ein Fremdkörper im athenischen Recht des 4. Jahrhunderts v. Chr." *ZRG* 82:302–9.

———. 1968. "Δικαστήριον παντῶν κύριον." In Berneker, *Zur griechischen Rechtsgeschichte*, 350–73. First published in *Historia* 6 (1957): 257–74.

Ryan, F. X. 1995. "The Date of the Institution of Proedroi." *JHS* 115:167–68.

Sandys, John Edwin. 1890. *The Speech of Demosthenes Against the Law of Leptines*. Cambridge: Cambridge University Press.

Schaefer, A. 1885–87. *Demosthenes und seine Zeit*[2]. 3 vols. Leipzig: Teubner. First published 1856–58.

Schelling, Hermann. 1842. *De Solonis Legibus apud Oratores Atticos*. Berlin: E. H. Schroeder.

Schöll, Rudolf. 1886. *Über attische Gesetzgebung*. Abhandlungen der Philosophisch-philologischen Classe der K. Bayerischen Akademie der Wissenschaften I. Munich: Straub.

Schömann, G. F. 1819. *De comitiis Atheniensium*. Greifswald: Mauritii.

———. 1820. "De Sortitione Judicum apud Athenienses, ad Sholl. Aristoph. Plut. v. 277." PhD diss., Univeristät Greifswald.

———. 1838. *Antiquitates iuris publici Graecorum*. Greifswald: Koch.

———. 1856. "*De causa Leptinea*." In *Opuscula Academica*, vol. 1, 237–59. Berlin: Weidmann.

Schwartzberg, Melissa. 2013. "Was the *Graphe Paranomon* a Form of Judicial Review?" *Cardozo Law Review* 34:1049–62.

Scigliano, Robert, ed. 2000. *The Federalist: A Commentary on the Constitution of the United States*. New York: Modern Library. First published 1788.

Sealey, Raphael. 1960. "Who Was Aristogeiton?" *BICS* 7:33–43.

Shklar, Judith N. 1986. *Legalism: Law, Morals, and Political Trials*[2]. Cambridge, MA: Harvard University Press.

———. 1987. *Montesquieu*. Oxford and New York: Oxford University Press.

Sickinger, James P. 1999. *Public Records and Archives in Classical Athens*. Chapel Hill: University of North Carolina Press.

Siewert, P. 1982. *Die Trittyen Attikas und die Heeresreform des Kleisthenes*. Munich: Beck.

Snowiss, Sylvia. 1990. *Judicial Review and the Law of the Constitution*. New Haven: Yale University Press.

Sommerstein, Alan H. 2001. *Wealth*. The Comedies of Aristophanes, vol. 11. Warminster: Aris & Phillips.

Sommerstein, Alan, and Judith Fletcher, eds. 2007. *Horkos: The Oath in Greek Society*. Exeter: Bristol Phoenix Press.

Sosin, Josh. 2016. "Death on a Road (Dem. 23.53)." *Historia* 65:155–69.

Spengel, Leonhard. 1862. "Demosthenes Vertheidigung des Ktesiphon: Ein Beitrag zum Verständnis des Redners." *Abhandlungen der Philosophisch-philologischen Classe der K. Bayerischen Akademie der Wissenschaften* 10:29–97.

Stevens, Gorham P., James M. Paton, L. D. Caskey, and Harold N. Fowler. 1927. *The Erechtheum*. Cambridge, MA: Harvard University Press for the American School of Classical Studies at Athens.

Stieglitz, Robert R. 2006. "Classical Greek Measures and the Builder's Instruments from the Ma'agan Mikhael Shipwreck." *AJA* 110:195–203.

Story, Joseph. 1891. *Commentaries on the Constitution of the United States*[5]. Boston: Little Brown First published 1833.

Straumann, Benjamin. 2016. *Crisis and Constitutionalism: Roman Political Thought from the Fall of the Republic to the Age of Revolution*. New York: Oxford University Press.

Stroud, Ronald S. 1971. "Theozotides and the Athenian Orphans." *Hesperia* 40:280–301.

———. 1974. "An Athenian Law on Silver Coinage." *Hesperia* 43:157–88.

———. 1998. *The Athenian Grain-Tax Law of 374/3 BC*. *Hesperia* Supplement 29. Princeton: American School of Classical Studies at Athens.

Sundahl, Mark J. 2000. "The Use of Statutes in the Seven Extant *graphe paranomon* and *graphe nomon me epitedeion theinai* Speeches." PhD diss., Brown University, Providence, RI.

———. 2003. "The Rule of Law and the Nature of the Fourth-Century Athenian Democracy." *C&M* 54:127–56.

Talamanca, Mario. 2017. *Dike ouk eisagogimos: Contributi allo studio del processo attico*. Edited by Alberto Maffi. Akten der Gesellschaft für griechishe und hellenistische Rechtsgeschichte 26. Vienna: Verlag der Österreichischen Akademie der Wissenschaften.

Taylor, C. 2007. "From the Whole Citizen Body? The Sociology of Election and Lot in the Athenian Democracy." *Hesperia* 76:323–45.

Taylor, John. 1774. Δημοσθένους καὶ Αἰσχίνου ἔνιοι λόγοι ἔκλεκτοι. Vol. 2. Cambridge: Woodyer.

Teusch, Theodor. 1894. *De Sortitione Judicum apud Athenienses*. Göttingen: Dieterich.

Thür, Gerhard. 2018. "Gedanken zur Normenkontrolle in Athen: Antwort auf Mirko Canevaro." In Thür, Yiftach, and Zelnick-Abramovitz, *Symposion 2017*, 99–103.

Thür, Gerhard, U. Yiftach, and R. Zelnick-Abramovitz, eds. *Symposion 2017*, Akten der Gesellschaft für griechishe und hellenistische Rechtsgeschichte 27. Vienna: Verlag der Österreichischen Akademie der Wissenschaften

Todd, S. C. 1993. *The Shape of Athenian Law*. Oxford: Oxford University Press.

———. 2007. "*Lady Chatterley's Lover* and the Attic Orators." In Carawan, *Oxford Readings in the Attic Orators*, 312–58. Revised from *JHS* 110 (1990): 146–73.

Traill, John S. 1975. *The Political Organization of Attica: A Study of the Demes, Trittyes, and Phylai, and Their Representation in the Athenian Council*. *Hesperia* Supplement 14. Princeton: American School of Classical Studies at Athens.

Triantaphyllopoulos, Ioannes K. 1962. *Γραφὴ Παρανόμων*. Athens: *Νέον Δίκαιον*. Translation by E. Petridou at http://miun.divaportal.org/smash/record.jsf?pid=diva2%3A613914&dswid=7785.

Usher, Stephen. 1993. *Demosthenes "De Corona."* Greek Orators, vol. 5. Warminster: Aris & Phillips.

US Supreme Court. 2020. *Federal Rules of Criminal Procedure*. Washington, DC: US Government Publishing Office. https://www.uscourts.gov/sites/default/files/federal_rules_of_criminal_procedure_-_dec_1_2019_0.pdf.

Vanderpool, Eugene. 1932. "An Athenian Dikast's Ticket." *AJA* 36:293–94.

Vermeule, Adrian. 2011. "Second Opinions and Institutional Design." *Virginia Law Review* 97:1435–74.

———. 2014. *The Constitution of Risk*. New York: Cambridge University Press.

Volonaki, Eleni. 2019. "Abuse of the *Eisangelia* in the Latter Half of the Fourth Century BC." In Carey, Giannadaki, and Griffith-Williams, *Use and Abuse of Law in the Athenian Courts*, 293–314.

Wallace, Robert W. 2006. "Withdrawing Graphai in Ancient Athens: A Case Study in 'Sycophancy' and Legal Idiosyncrasies." In Rupprecht, *Symposion 2003*, 57–66.

Wankel, Hermann. 1976. *Demosthenes Rede für Ktesiphon über den Kranz*, 2 vols. Heidelberg: Winter. PhD diss., Freie Univeristät, Berlin, 1974.

Wayte, William. 1893. *Demosthenes Against Androtion and Against Timocrates.* Cambridge: Cambridge University Press. Reprint, New York: Arno, 1979.

Weber, E. W. 1845. *Demosthenis Oratio in Aristocratem.* Jena: Croekeriano.

Wees, Hans van. 2011. "The 'Law of Hybris' and Solon's Reform of Justice." In Lambert, *Sociable Man,* 117–44.

Westermann, Anton. 1833. *De Aeschinis oratione advsersus Ctesiphontem Commentatio.* Leipzig: Haack.

———. 1850. *Untersuchungen über die in die attischen Redner eingelegten Urkunden.* Leipzig: Weidmann.

———. 1903. *Ausgewählte Reden des Demosthenes,* vol. 2. Leipzig: Weidmann. First published 1850.

Whitehead, David. 1977. *The Ideology of the Athenian Metic.* Cambridge: Cambridge Philological Society, Supplement 4.

———. 1986. *The Demes of Attica 508/7–ca. 250 BC.* Princeton: Princeton University Press.

———. 2000. *Hypereides: The Forensic Speeches.* Oxford: Oxford University Press.

———. 2002. "Athenian Laws and Lawsuits in the Late Fifth Century BC." *Museum Helveticum* 59:71–96.

Wilamowitz-Moellendorff, U. von. 1893. *Aristoteles und Athen.* 2 vols. Berlin: Weidman.

Wills, Garry. 1978. *Inventing America: Jefferson's Declaration of Independence.* Garden City, NY: Doubleday.

———. 2001. *Explaining America: The Federalist*². New York: Penguin. First published 1981.

Wilson Jones, Mark. 2000. "Doric Measure and Architectural Design 1: The Evidence of the Relief from Salamis." *AJA* 104:73–93.

———. 2014. "Greek and Roman Architectural Theory." In *Oxford Handbook of Greek and Roman Art and Architecture,* edited by Clemente Manconi, 41–69. Oxford: Oxford University Press.

Winiewski, Franz. 1829. *Commentarii historici et chronologici in Demosthenis orationem "De Corona."* Münster: Coppenrath.

Wolf, Friedrich August. 1789. *Demosthenis Oratio adversus Leptinem cum scholiis veteribus et commentario perpetuo.* Halle: Hemmerde.

Wolfe, Christopher. 1994. *The Rise of Modern Judicial Review: From Constitutional Interpretation to Judge-Made Law*². Lanham, MD: Littlefield. First published 1986.

Wolff, Hans Julius. 1968. "Gewohnheitsrecht und Gesetzesrecht in der griechischen Rechtsauffassung." In Berneker, *Zur griechischen Rechtsgeschichte,* 99–120. First published in *Deutsche Landesreferate zum VI. Internationalen Kongreß für Rechtsvergleichung in Hamburg* (1962): 3–18.

———. 1970. *"Normenkontrolle" und Gesetzesbegriff in der attischen Demokratie. Untersuchungen zur graphē paranomōn.* Heidelberg: C. Winter.

Worthington, Ian. 2013. *Demosthenes of Athens and the Fall of Classical Greece.* New York: Oxford University Press.

Yunis, Harvey. 1988. "Law, Politics and the *Graphe Paranomon* in Fourth-Century Athens." *GRBS* 29:361–82.

———. 2001. *Demosthenes "On the Crown."* Cambridge: Cambridge University Press.

———. 2007. "Politics as Literature: Demosthenes and the Burden of the Athenian Past." In Carawan, *Oxford Readings in the Attic Orators,* 372–90. Adapted from *Arion* 8 (2000): 97–118.

INDEX LOCORUM

GENERAL INDEX

The letter "t" following a page number refers to a table; "f" refers to a figure.